CW01020141

Money Code Space

Oxford Studies in Digital Politics

Series Editor: Andrew Chadwick, Professor of Political Communication in the Centre for Research in Communication and Culture and the Department of Social Sciences, Loughborough University

Money Code Space

HIDDEN POWER IN BITCOIN, BLOCKCHAIN, AND DECENTRALISATION

JACK PARKIN

OXFORD
UNIVERSITY PRESS

Oxford University Press is a department of the University of Oxford. It furthers
the University's objective of excellence in research, scholarship, and education
by publishing worldwide. Oxford is a registered trade mark of Oxford University
Press in the UK and certain other countries.

Published in the United States of America by Oxford University Press
198 Madison Avenue, New York, NY 10016, United States of America.

© Oxford University Press 2020

All rights reserved. No part of this publication may be reproduced, stored in
a retrieval system, or transmitted, in any form or by any means, without the
prior permission in writing of Oxford University Press, or as expressly permitted
by law, by license, or under terms agreed with the appropriate reproduction
rights organization. Inquiries concerning reproduction outside the scope of the
above should be sent to the Rights Department, Oxford University Press, at the
address above.

You must not circulate this work in any other form
and you must impose this same condition on any acquirer.

Library of Congress Cataloging-in-Publication Data
Names: Parkin, Jack, author.
Title: Money code space : hidden power in bitcoin, blockchain, and
algorithmic decentralisation / Jack Parkin.
Other titles: Money, code, space
Description: New York, NY : Oxford University Press, [2020] |
Series: Oxford studies in digital politics | Includes bibliographical references and index.
Identifiers: LCCN 2020004730 (print) | LCCN 2020004731 (ebook) |
ISBN 9780197515075 (hardback) | ISBN 9780197515082 (paperback) |
ISBN 9780197515099 | ISBN 9780197515105 (epub) | ISBN 9780197515112
Subjects: LCSH: Bitcoin. | Blockchains (Databases) |
Cryptocurrencies—Social aspects. | Finance—Social aspects.
Classification: LCC HG1710 .P36 2020 (print) |
LCC HG1710 (ebook) | DDC 332.4—dc23
LC record available at https://lccn.loc.gov/2020004730
LC ebook record available at https://lccn.loc.gov/2020004731

9 8 7 6 5 4 3 2 1

Paperback printed by LSC Communications, United States of America
Hardback printed by Bridgeport National Bindery, Inc., United States of America

For Joy and Eric Iliffe

Contents

Preface

Disruptive Dreams

> When I first started taking Bitcoin seriously in 2012, I thought it was just a currency. That was my first exposure to it and I was really excited for what it was going to do to the financial system. It was really going to give it some liberty and freedom. . . . As I've grown in my understanding of what Bitcoin is, and how it is just the first app on the blockchain, I've realised how impactful and exciting the blockchain actually is. I think you will all agree with me: this is the single most exciting, most revolutionary idea that has hit in the past, probably, one hundred years. . . . This is going to change everything. And you being here as part of this program—all the things that each and every one of you are building . . . with the tools that many of the companies here have helped build previously— you're building the future. . . . We're really excited to see what people have built and where the future is going. You being here in these seats tonight means you are some of the earliest adopters in the world in what will change every single industry on this planet. (Developer Evangelist, BitPay)

I was sitting in a crowded room in Mountain View, Silicon Valley. Around me sat a plethora of programmers, lawyers, entrepreneurs, CEOs, start-up employees, consultants, and other business men and women from a range of different professions: some were about to present their projects and others had come to observe the products that had emerged from six weeks of learning and collaboration. The enthusiastic speech just cited was one of a handful of introductions preceding the Blockchain University demo night. I had heard different variations of this rhetoric in the San Francisco Bay Area over the previous months as I attended meet-up groups and conferences, interviewed investors and start-up companies, and immersed myself in the regional technology economy. It was mid-2015 and the buzzword within the cryptocurrency industry—if it could still be given that compartmentalised label anymore—was "blockchain": the (once) unique anatomy of the Bitcoin protocol.

I first heard the word "Bitcoin" in the summer of 2013 during heated Orwellian debates over global security and privacy. This sudden agitation was sparked when Edward Snowden publicly leaked classified information concerning the US National Security Agency (NSA) global surveillance programs (Gellman & Poitras, 2013; Greenwald, 2013). I was speaking to a software engineer at a barbecue in Shropshire, England, discussing the implications of the PRISM data-mining program used to extract public communications from highly reputable household technology companies such as Google and Yahoo (it was a fun party!). He mentioned that WikiLeaks, an (in)famous organisation that publishes before-secret information like the Snowden documents, had been able to bypass a banking blockade by accepting donations of a networked digital currency called Bitcoin (see also Matonis, 2012). Money, it appeared, was being remade from the bottom-up by an ingenious group of cryptographers—computer programmers who use digital cyphers to obscure certain aspects of data.[1] Here, value seemed to be 'changing hands' via a *crypto*currency running on top of a distributed payment mechanism, operating freely in the absence of central authorities.[2] I would later find out, although Bitcoin embodies a rich prehistory (Brunton, 2019), it was built to do just that; released in the fallout of the 2008 global financial crisis, its software was devised to bypass the institutions that had caused the crash. Fast-forward to 2015 and Bitcoin's algorithmic architecture (blockchain) was being re-envisioned in Silicon Valley as a new disruptive spanner ready to be jammed into the traditional cogs of world systems.

Brave New Coin, one of the many emerging press outlets reporting on cryptographic ledgers, portrayed Blockchain University as an institution that offered a developer-focused course taught by leading Silicon Valley blockchain start-up founders. The overarching aim was to "educate seasoned software engineers about cryptocurrency and provide them with the knowledge for developing applications" (Schuhmacher, 2014).[3] This would counter the skills shortage in Silicon Valley for emerging enterprises looking to design business models on top of various blockchains. Through public and private training programs, hackathons, and demo events, Blockchain University equipped its attendees with the proficiency to initiate blockchain innovations across multiple industry sectors. My fellow 'students' included developers, product managers, attorneys, designers, entrepreneurs, and intrepreneurs from Google, AT&T, Infosys, PwC, Oracle, Visa, Raytheon, Saint Gobain, and the Federal Reserve Bank of San Francisco. We were taught by 'lecturers' from renowned ventures in the industry such as Tom Ding (Koinify), Juan Benet (Protocol Labs), Ryan X Charles (BitGo), Ethan Buchman (Monax), Vitalik Buterin (Ethereum), Matthieu Riou (BlockCypher), Greg Slepak (DNSChain), Atif Nazir (Block.io), Srinivasan Sriram (Skuchain), and Ryan Smith (Chain).

My educational journey began with the payment of two bitcoins to Blockchain University, then roughly the value of $500 USD but close to $40,000 by the end of 2017 (Bitcoin is capitalised when referring to the software protocol yet uncapitalised, or abbreviated to BTC, when referring to individual currency units).[4] I have purchased various amounts of bitcoins over the years for research purposes and I retain a small investment in cryptocurrencies as a result. This modest stake has fluctuated violently with the price swings of an emerging market but my commercial interests remain small. For the most part, these quantities of cryptocurrency have been spent on goods and services like the tuition fees for Blockchain University.

Back there, our course was culminating that evening with the presentation of a team project. The "test" was the products we had designed and through them we would 'graduate.' During my weekends I had been going to the China Fortune Land Development TechCode Incubator (affectionately dubbed Consensus HQ for Blockchain University purposes) and other notable venues in Silicon Valley (such as IDEO and Singularity University) to learn from industry specialists about the algorithmic morphology and associated applications of different blockchains: coding, discussing, listening to presentations, solving problems, and designing business models.[5]

Computational algorithms are a sequence of digitally executed mathematical steps that transform a data input into an output (Cormen et al., 1990): they move, manipulate, (re)organise, and (re)present information into different forms. Blockchains are protocols (codified rules for communication) assembled through interacting algorithms that work together like component parts of an engine. As distributed peer-to-peer software, each computer maintaining a blockchain acts as a node in a connected network. Together the nodes use cryptographic techniques to authorise transactions and cement them into a shared ledger; simultaneously, as information periodically updates, a consensus is reached as to what the 'true' network state is. Bitcoin, for example, uses a consensus model in an attempt to transfer and lock value-carrying digital units through space in a 'secure' and 'permissionless' manner. When bitcoins are sent, all parties can see the change of ownership transparently on any node running the Bitcoin protocol (although the identity of the transacting parties is obscured). Such properties offered by the algorithmic patterns of blockchains, where 'trusted' records can apparently be attained without an authorising third party, promotes a techno-decentralist ideology: a mission to democratise societies by eradicating centralised points of control in economic systems. This vision has proven to be extremely compelling for entrepreneurial programmers in Silicon Valley and around the world.

On the 18th May 2015, it was finally time for our Blockchain University cohort to demonstrate its knowledge and showcase newly learnt skills. The 'president' of Blockchain University (an ex-PayPal employee) called a fellow team member and I to the stage to kick off the event. My group's product, Squirrel, utilised blockchain's 'non-repudiation' system of record keeping—which is another way of saying its data is indisputable—by creating an application for streamlining letters of credit in global supply chains. Pete Rizzo (2015b) from *CoinDesk*, the world leader in news and information pertaining to cryptocurrencies and blockchain technology, was in the crowd and would later report:

> To attack this issue, Squirrel developed a system by which parties could enter into a purchasing agreement at a lower risk level. Funds, the team proposed, could be sent to escrow accounts by both manufacturers and vendors. Squirrel, in turn, could act as a source of capital and security so that projects [could] be produced.

Escrow accounts are a contractual arrangement where traditionally 'non-biased third parties,' usually lawyers, handle money for the transacting parties to minimise the risk of a bad actor corrupting the agreement. As a programmable form of money (conditions can be set as to how coins are spent), Bitcoin allows the building of smart contracts to manage funds based on pre-written digital parameters. Smart contracts are self-executing pieces of code that facilitate transaction outputs (payments, deeds, votes) based on pre-defined inputs (date, stock price, signatures). Because blockchains are supposed to resemble 'decentralised,' 'sequential,' and 'permanent' records of 'truth,' the data they contain, and constantly build upon, can be used to lock and unlock these smart contracts. In essence, this can 'remove' the adjudicating middle(wo)man and 'automate' transactions.[6]

Global supply chains are littered with producers, consumers, and regulators separated by space, time, culture, language, and currency. As such, they are deeply connected by networks of trust. With Squirrel we used smart contracts to 'remove' the risk contractors are forced to take on when making purchase orders to vendors (who may or may not fulfil them). By assigning commodities a digital identity, their lives could be tracked via a blockchain and cryptocurrency could be released as they cross certain predetermined checkpoints. The idea was to make money flow (via cryptocurrencies) symbiotic with product movement across a supply chain. In other words, trusted records for multiple and potentially untrustworthy participants (blockchains) were proposed to 'automate' purchase orders as multiple stakeholders reached a consensus on the whereabouts of goods. Because the entire history of items can be recorded in blockchains, they are often regarded as 'secure,' 'transparent,' and 'auditable' systems for realising economic transactions like this.

Other group projects that followed were Chainmail, Kar.yt, Cardify, P2P insurance, In & Out Checkout, Revocable, BlockchainMe, and BlockNotary. Following the presentations, I was approached by a blockchain consultant—an occupation that had not existed a few years prior—who wanted to introduce us to a Chinese commercial bank for potential collaboration. This bank was also examining the capacity of smart contracts and distributed ledger technologies like blockchains for streamlining credit issuance and debt settlement to increase operational efficiency and extend their services (with reduced risk) into broader markets. Squirrel was never established as a commercial enterprise and so we did not take up this offer, yet such a request demonstrates the attention blockchains were starting to garner from traditional financial institutions.

Similarly, these new digital architectures have also caught the attention of central banks: on a trip to the Bank of England that same year, I was told they were examining the capacity of cryptographic distributed ledgers for automating settlements and creating a national digital cash (sovereign cryptocurrency). Due to the spectrum of potential stakeholders, the innovations of small entrepreneurial blockchain enterprises have become the subject of enormous amounts of interest and investment from large established financial institutions and venture capitalist firms looking to profit from their disruptive potential. Some of the Blockchain University projects, for example, went on to become start-ups themselves, like BlockNotary, which received angel investment from Silicon Valley Plug and Play.[7]

The blockchain hype—an innervation of innovation—buzzing around Silicon Valley during 2015 was, and to a large degree remains, palpable (see Gloerich et al., 2018). It was extremely stimulating, and at times intoxicating, to be part of a crowd who saw themselves at the forefront of an imminent technological upheaval. Blockchain University was not only a learning environment but a space where blockchains and their applications were being made—both on a technical level, with code, and on an ideological one, through discourse, debate, and design. The underlying assumption: carefully assembled software can dismantle the centralised powers that have historically ordered economies. *Algorithmic decentralisation* was presented as the crux around which new societies could, or rather should, be built. And Blockchain University was certainly not alone: as Bitcoin companies had done two years before, embryonic blockchain start-ups were popping up all over Silicon Valley and other global technology hubs, taking an early position in a newly forming industry. Today, over $22 billion USD worth of venture capital has been invested in cryptocurrency and blockchain-related initiatives (Glasner, 2019).

The monumental promise of distributed ledgers to transform the organisational 'structure' of everyday socioeconomic life quickly seeped into popular media (The Economist, 2015). With the proliferation of such disruptive dreams, the need to decipher the technological, economic, cultural, political, and geographic nuances of blockchains is increasingly pressing. Drawing from multi-sited research, it is the task of this book to detail the political economy of

Bitcoin and other blockchain technologies as they are produced and practised across a multitude of tessellated spaces. From the empirical evidence gathered, I construct a narrative on the broader factors influencing, negotiating, and revolutionising financial practices through the visions and materialities of decentralised algorithmic architectures. In the process, I help delineate the dislocations and contradictions between blockchain imaginaries and practice (see also Gloerich et al., 2018; DuPont, 2018). Consequently, this account becomes a story of tension between digital visions of emancipation and material realities of restraint. In the process, I uncover the political relationship between money, code, and space as they are realigned via blockchains. The core argument outlined—threading together disparately and seemingly unrelated matters, conditions, and topics—is that algorithmic decentralisation becomes inherently paradoxical as it is practised because it is predicated on, and ordered around, certain degrees of socialised and spatialised cohesion.

Acknowledgements

This book would not have been possible without guidance from Donald McNeill and Ned Rossiter whose generous feedback repeatedly pulled my writing back into focus when the vivid research topic was running off in all directions. I am specifically grateful to Donald for sharpening the ethnographic aspect of my work and to Ned for driving conceptual developments. It has been a great pleasure to navigate their sometimes quite contrasting inputs and this monograph is only stronger for that balance.

Praise must also go to my editors at Oxford University Press whose constant efforts have made this journey an incredibly enjoyable one. The experience and professionalism of Andrew Chadwick and Angela Chnapko has shone through at every turn. Their contributions have not only been invaluable to the book but they have also put me behind the wheel to steer important decisions. Enthusiasm and attentiveness abound; I could not have asked for a more rewarding publishing experience. Alexcee Bechthold, Narayanan Srinivasan, and Timothy DeWerff have also helped bring the last stages of the publication together.

Thank you to the Institute for Culture and Society at Western Sydney University for its financial support during the research phase of this book. Tribute must also be paid to my colleagues who have provided a fantastic support network over the years: Andrea Pollio, Ilia Antenucci, Jasbeer Musthafa Mamalipurath, Isaac Lyne, Tsvetelina Hristova, Cecelia Cmielewski, Luigi Di Martino, Oznur Sahin, Alexandra Coleman, Harriette Richards, Daniel Musil, Alejandro Miranda Nieto, Mithilesh Kumar, Giulia Dal Maso, Sebastián Martín Valdez, Christiane Kühling, Alejandra Villanueva, and Andrea Del Bono.

I would like to thank Liam Magee for broadening my thinking in terms of software infrastructure as well as his consistent interest in other areas of my work. My gratitude is extended to Andrew Leyshon and Nathanial Tkacz whose encouraging comments have proven extremely productive when shaping the overall book narrative. Thanks also to Matthew Zook and Ilan Talmud who helped guide the final brush strokes.

I am grateful to Aaron van Wirdum and Michael Folkson, as well as members of Bitcoin Core for challenging the conceptual framework I outline in Chapter 5. While they may not agree with my conclusions, their insight and critique has been extremely constructive. I only hope this book encourages further debate around the topic of blockchain governance.

For her enduring support I am eternally grateful to my mother, Louise Iliffe. While she may never entirely understand how Bitcoin works she will undoubtedly remain my greatest fan. Other notable patrons, who have played an array of supporting roles, include: Freddie Parkin, Helen Barcham, Charlie Parkin, Jeffery Gregson, Jane Griffin, Carl Griffin, Andrew Weddell-Hall, Greg McElroy, Ross Stinton, William Bradley, Thomas Bradley, Christopher Prentice, Callum Smith, Benjamin Hampton, Yara Hawari, Nick Gill, Christine Jones, Neil Partridge, Anika Berkman, Justin Amos, Kenz Mroue, Eleanor Drage, Hector Kociak, David Ewington, Andy Auld, Simon Blaxall, Alex Warehime, David Wiese, James Please, Rory Horne, Sean Shepherd, Georgia Good, and Jake Byrnes. I am also grateful to Roy Peake for helping bring my vision of the cover artwork to life.

The book is derived in part from a journal article "The senatorial governance of Bitcoin: Making (de)centralized money" published in *Economy and Society* (2019) with copyright belonging to Taylor & Francis (available online: www.tandfonline.com/10.1080/03085147.2019.1678262). Permission granted to reproduce this work is very much appreciated.

It is certain I would not be in this position today if not for Ian Cook who saw something in my work as an undergraduate, inspired me to pursue an intellectual journey, and encouraged me to "follow the thing." So, I thank Ian for his infectious enthusiasm.

Finally, I would like to thank everyone within the cryptocurrency and blockchain communities who animated my research.

Introduction

Algorithmic Decentralisation

Bitcoin is a technical infrastructure embodying a maelstrom of interconnected human stories. Its vast algorithmic architecture, blockchain, works day and night to weave together economic transactions conducted by people widely separated, but curiously connected, through space. I have been researching Bitcoin for so long now that I often forget to take a step back and marvel at how far the 'experiment' has come. Just over ten years ago it was merely a hacker pipe dream; today, around a billion USD worth of value flows through its digital veins daily.[1] It is fascinating, bizarre even, how a grassroots peer-to-peer network not only evolved to carry precious 'currency tokens' but also arose to challenge a financial system occupied by deeply entrenched central and commercial banks. More outstanding is how Bitcoin appears to operate without institutions like these because a host of independent software nodes work together to form its interdependent whole. In other words, decentralisation is allegedly achieved through cumulative, networked, algorithmic mechanisms that allow the protocol to 'take care of itself.'

Distributed ledger technologies like blockchains remain largely misunderstood outside of the boutique industries of micro-finance, technology start-ups, and the cutting edge of digital media research, yet they are fast moving into the mainstream. But if this narrative began as distributed Davids vs centralised Goliaths, then part of the tale has already taken a dramatic turn. In an ironic twist, financial giants and nation-state authorities are reimagining and redeploying blockchains for themselves. Meanwhile, a burgeoning economic sector is developing these tools to transform, reorganise, and (most important) decentralise a plethora of industries from real estate to voting, stock trading to health care, and supply chain management to the Internet of Things (Swan, 2015; Raval, 2016; Mougayar, 2016; Tapscott & Tapscott, 2016; CB Insights, 2018). Bitcoin has stimulated and catalysed these (r)evolutions, hurling them headlong into a complex ecosystem.

Money Code Space. Jack Parkin, Oxford University Press (2020). © Oxford University Press.
DOI: 10.1093/oso/9780197515075.001.0001.

If the vignette in the Preface of this book proved even a little daunting or disorientating then take some solace in the knowledge that this was intentional. Once dropped into the world of cryptocurrencies and blockchains, perplexity is a common feeling: even now banks, governments, and the financial press are scrambling to understand their ramifications. Distributed ledgers are difficult to grasp, not least because their lofty ideals often become compromised through everyday workings that create peculiar paradoxes and contradictions (DuPont, 2018). At its core, this book pays close attention to times when human behaviour meets high-level philosophical ideas (like decentralisation) through these new technologies and the moments when they dislocate. As the pages are turned, the many threads laid bare in the Preface will disentangle to reveal a conceptual framework for understanding distributed architectures like Bitcoin.

It may already be clear that relying on these new code structures to underpin human interaction could significantly perturb the spatial organisation of future global economies. In many ways a substantial shift has already begun. For example, Bitcoin, the first fully functioning blockchain-based cryptocurrency, was presented to the world in 2009 as a 'non-hierarchical' mechanism for transferring money. This perception of a flattened, egalitarian software model is shared by most blockchain proponents, from anarchist programmers to national governments. It forms the basis of a driving political ambition: creating fairer, or at least more efficient, economies. This focus on levelling or redistributing financial wealth and power among publics has become a foundational tenet for decentralist ideologies, and blockchains have been elevated as the vehicle for success (Brekke, 2018). Conversely, this book helps trace the key power structures emerging through 'decentralised' systems by illuminating a geography of Bitcoin and other blockchain architectures like Ethereum. Geographies are particularly useful for unwinding political tensions because they help situate asymmetric technical, social, and economic relationships. They are examined here to unpack the contradictions at play in a world governed by the mathematical constraints of computer code and demonstrate the material limitations of digitally distributed software in terms of technology start-ups, business models, code, humans, and machines.

What is meant by material is not so much the Marxian legacy of materialism that pursues an analytical study of historical change wrought by economic and institutional forces, but rather materiality as a method prominent within science and technology studies, actor-network thinking, and non-representational theory. While this may include a 'loose materiality' of the people and places researched, the term is used more as a following, focusing, and framing device with respect to the socialised tangibilities of blockchains (version control systems, silicon chips, servers, Bitcoin mines, start-up company offices) as technical systems (Kittler, 1995; Packer & Wiley, 2011; Harvey, 2012; Parikka, 2015). In other words, materiality is the collection of physical objects around, or through, which cultural, political, and economic practices are performed.[2] It is this understanding of materiality as an assemblage of things (with affordances and limitations) that informs the method of this investigation: by tracing out the technical capacities and properties of blockchains as digital architecture and tangible infrastructure, their spatial scales and connectivities are better understood.[3]

Many of those who uncritically champion algorithmic decentralisation necessarily present blockchains as dehumanised machine spaces where the mathematics of computer code can suddenly be trusted to organise society (money, identity, voting, trading) in the absence of coercive oversight from people. At a time when there is a certain degree of obsession and fear concerning 'robots taking over the world' with the rise of artificial intelligence (Tett, 2018), it is appropriate to distinguish what the human and non-human parts—or hybridities—of blockchains are (De Filippi & Loveluck, 2016; Musiani et al., 2018).[4] In response to the anxieties of automation, the question is asked whether anyone is in control of these contemporary codified systems or if they truly are autonomous data structures on a never-ending, tamper-proof, mechanical loop?[5] The aim is to grapple with both the technical non-human infrastructure at the same time as injecting the human back into blockchain analysis to understand where the power to influence certain aspects of their architectures resides.

Taking inspiration from works examining the "social life" of things (Appadurai, 1986), information (Brown & Duguid, 2000), money (Dodd, 2014), financial derivatives (LiPuma, 2017), and Bitcoin itself (Dodd, 2018), the algorithmic decentralisation of code and money via blockchains is examined through a social-spatial lens (Lesyhon & Thrift, 1997; Kitchin & Dodge, 2011; Coeckelbergh, 2015). By delving into the social life of Bitcoin and (some other) blockchains, I argue that despite, or rather through, processes of decentralisation, concentrations of power consolidate across their architectures. Precisely, the book highlights the persistence of certain practices (code governance, cryptocurrency mining, and network transactions) to be funnelled through centralised bottlenecks (lead developers, mining pools, and start-up companies). Here, specific actors have varying amounts of control over certain pieces of networks. Practically speaking, the dynamics and shortcomings of algorithmic decentralisation are relevant findings for blockchain programmers, technology start-up companies, global banks, accountancy and legal firms, speculators, policy makers, and the general public. After all, these stakeholders are performing and affecting decentralisation in different ways and so shedding light on their role in (re)constructing economies is an important line of investigation.

Fundamentally, the book interrogates how blockchain architectures take shape spatially, culturally, and politically. An ethnographic research methodology informed by science and technology studies is specifically designed to explore how different actors in blockchain ecosystems employ decentralisation. It describes governance mechanisms that coordinate the builders of blockchains, the material hardware that executes code, and the technology agglomeration economies that build business models on the back of these new architectures, demonstrating how control is not distributed evenly among people in blockchain economies but rather consolidates around a small number of centres from which they are ordered.

Charting a Mode of Enquiry

The book is situated at the intersection of three influential scholarly fields of recent years. First, it contributes to debates about the nature of centralisation and spatiality surrounding the financial system, currency, and banking, which has been discussed by economic geography, sociology, and anthropology scholars, among others (Tsing, 2004; Knorr Cetina & Bruegger, 2002; Hall, 2011, 2012, 2013; Coeckelbergh, 2015). This has become an increasingly important area of research following the 2008 global financial crisis and subsequent developments in financial technology (FinTech). To build a rationale for exploring decentralised digital currencies, the book draws from works on the geography (Leyshon, 1995, 1997, 1998; Leyshon & Thrift, 1997), sociology (Baker & Jimerson, 1992; Dodd, 1994, 1995, 2014; Callon, 1998a, 1998b, 2007; D. Mackenzie, 2004, 2006; Knorr Cetina & Preda, 2005), and anthropology of money (Maurer, 2005, 2006, 2015). More specifically, it navigates the interdisciplinary realm of economic geography to thicken accounts of algorithmic decentralisation by recognising "all economies must take place" (Lee, 2006, 430). Leaving blockchain analysis solely to the abstract models of neoclassical economics would not only risk overlooking their inherent complexity (Dicken & Lloyd, 1990; Hudson, 2005; Pike et al., 2006; Knox & Agnew, 2008), but could also work to externalise them from social relations (Granovetter, 1985; Zelizer, 1997; Becker, 1997; Thrift, 2000a).

Second, the book contributes to a growing body of knowledge that examines the increasing role of software in mediating and conditioning social practice and human experience (Manovich, 2001, 2008; Fuller, 2003, 2008; A. Mackenzie, 2005, 2006; Chun, 2011; Berry, 2011). As blockchains take on a degree of autonomy in the form of algorithmic ledgers, important questions are posed around how they work, both culturally and technically. This research contributes most significantly to works that have developed a material account of digital media (Kittler, 1995; Galloway, 2004; Starosielski, 2015; Rossiter, 2016) as well as the geographies of code (Graham, 2005; Kitchin & Dodge, 2011; Kitchin & Perng, 2016; Ash et al., 2019). However, the arguments also find relevance in the subdiscipline of network culture that has made a significant impact over the last twenty years in terms of understanding the interface between humans and software (Lovink, 2002; Terranova, 2004, Rossiter, 2006, 2016; Golumbia, 2009; Lovink et al., 2015; Tkacz, 2015).

Third and finally, the book commits to the methodological pursuit of detailed ethnographies surrounding the production and nuances of techno-cultures (Miller & Slater, 2000; Zaloom, 2006; Downey & Fisher, 2006; Boellstorff, 2008; Miller, 2011). This body of knowledge has worked hard to reject ontological bifurcations between the cultural and the technological spheres, repeatedly proven an unproductive theoretical chasm: "[l]eaving technology out of analyses of culture has the unintended implication that it is an autonomous realm of human activity" (Downey & Fisher, 2006, 5). In opposition to this, ethnographies have looked to "undermine accounts of change that privilege technology as the sole, driving, causal agent" (Downey & Fisher, 2006, 5). This mindset is useful for investigating blockchain ecosystems because it helps provide a fine-grained narrative concerning their interwoven tapestries of culture, economy, and technology through space. The methods in this book are inspired particularly by participant observation conducted in software companies (Ross, 2003; Indergaard, 2004; O'Rian, 2004; Girard & Stark, 2005; O'Mahony, 2006; Takhteyev, 2012).

This threefold convergence of literature on finance capital, software studies, and infrastructure ethnographies is used to interrogate the nascency of Bitcoin and blockchain technology by focusing on the diverse assemblages of humans and non-humans that constitute them. A 'follow the thing' methodology is used both for data collection and as an analytical tool to trace out these social and spatial connections that form decentralised architectures. The three literatures outlined earlier are brought into conversation with each other through empirical observations where blockchains enigmatically place the concepts of money, code, and space in a novel relationship.

Considering the vast quantity of commentaries pertaining to cryptocurrencies and blockchains, there is a dearth of detailed ethnographic work in the field (DuPont, 2019). This is not altogether surprising given the algorithmic nature of these architectures. "Understood as sets of instructions that direct the computer to perform a specific task, algorithms are essentially used to control the flow of actions and future events" (Bucher, 2018, 28). But they often appear detached from everyday places, operating busily out of view. When it comes to distributed ledger technologies, codified logic buried within computer networks is used to achieve what I call *algorithmic decentralisation*. This process aims to direct social interaction without the need for hierarchal human decision-making and carries with it ideas of openness, equality, non-repudiation, automation, and disintermediation. However, it is important to remember that "algorithms do not work on their own but need to be understood as a much wider network of relations and practices" (Bucher, 2018, 20).

I use the concept *geographies of algorithmic decentralisation* to unpack the spatial and relational distribution of everyday materials, capital, transactions, institutions, labour, ideologies, practices, and regulations that work together to assemble blockchains. This approach avoids slipping into some of the nebulous terminologies reminiscent of media theory in the late 1990s and early 2000s that saturated discourse surrounding "cyberspace" (Benedikt, 1991; Burrows & Featherstone, 1995; Munt, 2001; Buckingham & Willett, 2006). Treating computational environments as bounded entities necessarily reinforces an imaginary of 'the digital' as an ethereal fourth dimension removed from the tangibilities of 'real space.' This imaginary can promote a "hyper-globalist" (Dicken, 2015, 4) vocabulary that reflects a borderless world and begins to eradicate the need for geographical understandings of the digital/economical. Sentiments of radical globalisation—that invariably push 'the virtual' into discursive realms of spacelessness—still echo throughout new media rhetoric (Kinsley, 2013a). Perhaps unsurprisingly, they now reverberate around cryptocurrency and blockchain industry commentaries. This vernacular neglects how globalisation (even via digitally decentralised architectures) necessarily intensifies spatial complexity and unevenness so that specific geographic connectivities become more relevant than ever (Sokol, 2011).

Situating Research

The enquiry of this book is heavily influenced by the work of Ian Cook et al. (2004, 2006, 2008, 2014, 2017) and other cultural geographers, anthropologists, and ethnographers whose research involves following things (Mintz, 1986; Appadurai, 1986; Marcus, 1995; Bestor, 2000; Scheper-Hughes, 2000; Barndt, 2002; Dibbell, 2007). As Phillip Crang (2005) explains:

> Things move around and inhabit multiple cultural contexts during their lives. Cultural Geographers are especially interested in the changes that happen to a thing in this process: material changes; and changes or 'translations' in the thing's meanings. They are also interested in the knowledges that move with the things, especially about their earlier life. How much do people encountering a thing in one context know about its life in other contexts? Who mediates this knowledge? What role do imaginative geographies of where a thing comes from . . . play in our encounters with objects? (178)

The usefulness of thing-following as a methodological tool for uncovering the social relations that permeate money has been recently debated in economic geography (Christophers, 2011a, 2011b; Gilbert, 2011). As Brett Christophers (2011a) notes, although difficult, following money can "reveal and examine the social and economic relations both underpinning and occasioned by money's creation and circulation" (1069–1070). Because Bitcoin has been proposed as an anarchist form of digital money, its peculiar character can be illuminated, and those claims tested, by tracing out its "social and spatial pathways" (Christophers, 2011a, 1068). In the context of urban theory, Donald McNeill (2017) suggests: "[w]e might think about world city-*making* systems rather than world city systems" (150). Borrowing and repurposing this phrase to approach another complex ensemble, I think about blockchain-*making* systems rather than just blockchain systems. In this sense, drawing on some of the tools associated with actor-network thinking for "framing field sites and research objects" (Madden, 2010, 584), I attempt to follow things, people, and ideas as they collide through blockchains.

I carve three exploratory paths to navigate and disentangle the complexity of Bitcoin and copycat blockchains. First, I examine the spatial articulations and contradictions that Bitcoin and other implementations of blockchains enact as certain practices, such as forking software or storing bitcoin, coalesce around them. Second, through this spatial organisation, I develop an understanding of algorithmic decentralisation and demonstrate how its internal contradictions correlate to power harnessed through the network. Third, I assert how different actors control certain channels in the (de)centralised networks of blockchains and (re)shape their digital-material architectures with competing political ideologies.

Ultimately, all work to develop a critical understanding and theorisation of algorithmic decentralisation through money, code, and space. While some technological and economic ideologies preach an impending world of distributed global transactions, the materiality of economies points to something different. Centralisation, on some level, is necessary for economies to function. This pattern is not dissimilar to the evolution of the TCP/IP protocol once dreamed up as the ultimate form of decentralisation (Galloway, 2004). This protocol sets out the rules machines must follow in order to send and receive information to and from each other via the Internet. The Bitcoin protocol, in turn, rests upon this network and uses it to connect separated copies of the same currency ledger together. Like the Internet before it (and, partly, because of it), the *making* of blockchains, shaped by a myriad of evolving actors, is turning them into architectures with some radical differences to how they were first conceptualised (see also De Filippi & Loveluck, 2016; Musiani et al., 2018; DuPont, 2018; Gloerich et al., 2018). While some hackers attempt to stay aligned with ideologies of economic decentralisation, Silicon Valley and global banks have been steering blockchains towards traditional models of capital accumulation. Just as the

Internet was moulded around centralised governments (Clayton et al., 2006; Zhang, 2006), undersea network cables (Starosielski, 2015), software platforms (Srnicek, 2017), and data centres (Rossiter, 2016), so blockchain architectures are again demonstrating the material reality of particular forms of networked communication.

Book Layout

Chapter 1, "Pandora's Blocks," opens the lid on Bitcoin so that all of its attributes, problems, and connotations come spilling out. At the same time, it pulls these disparate strands back into focus by outlining the many discrepancies that will be examined in subsequent chapters. So while in some ways the chapter acts like a primer for cryptocurrencies, blockchains, and their political economies, the material laid out works to set up the book's underlying argument: asymmetric concentrations of power inevitably form through processes of algorithmic decentralisation.

The second chapter, "Money/Code/Space," provides a theoretical discussion of these three concepts, as well as their increasing codependency, to foreground the emergence of Bitcoin as a radical response to existing economic structures. Using the history of central banking and software production, Bitcoin is compared to traditional modes of centralised governance to outline some of the political context of algorithmic decentralisation. In doing so, the binary of centralised-decentralised is rendered impotent and reductive when describing complex digital networks. Instead, building upon the work of Francesca Musiani et al. (2018), Michel Callon's (1986) concept of obligatory passage points is adapted into a framework for understanding (de) centralisation in algorithmic networks. This provides an account of money/ code/space that encapsulates the cultural and economic messiness of Bitcoin and blockchain technology, bringing places of power to the forefront of related discourse.

Chapter 3, "Follow the Digital Thing," presents a methodology accommodating the theoretical positions laid out in Chapter 2. Acknowledging how Bitcoin is geographically contingent and diverse, the follow the thing research design outlined allows for tracing the connections between different aspects of its protocol, practised by a multitude of people in various places. This is done by documenting traditional follow the thing work and explaining how knowledge can be gathered from such a technique before adapting this research process for the task at hand. The breakdown then shifts into sketching a specific yet malleable research method that harnesses the flexibility necessary for understanding the complex political economies of Bitcoin and other blockchains.

The fourth chapter, "Building the Future," describes how technological decentralisation emerged with advancements in cryptography and acted as a political counterweight of resistance to the encroachment of governments across (online) space. The decentralist worldview is shown to be rooted in the specific political geography of the West Coast of the United States that, during the latter half of the 20th century, became a crucible of counterculture and entrepreneurship (Barbrook & Cameron, 1996). Fuelled by this vision, a monetarist desire to create fairer economies through algorithmic decentralisation gave rise to the advent of cryptocurrencies. The intersection and slippage of this technologically deterministic imaginary (preaching a freedom from hierarchy and control) with geographies of material practice is developed throughout following chapters.

Chapter 5, "Programming Politics", outlines the community of developers who have contributed to Bitcoin's source code. Drawing from ethnographic data and existing political economy theorisations of cryptocurrencies (De Filippi & Loveluck, 2016; Musiani et al., 2018; DuPont, 2018), the governance of the Bitcoin codebase is understood through obligatory passage points found among key individuals and groups involved in the creation of Bitcoin. The consensus model for making changes to the Bitcoin software shows how code is inescapably bound up with political tensions that arise through coordinating geographies of production. Pressures between different stakeholders are exposed to show how conflicts in code development and the increased likeliness of the project 'forking' as it scales, demand degrees of centralisation at the architectural level of cryptocurrency design in order for actions to be resolved and implemented. The overall political framework for altering the Bitcoin code is described as senatorial governance: a (de)centralised model where bureaucratic parties compete to change the monetary policy (codified rules) of the protocol.

The sixth chapter, "Grounding Cryptocurrencies," documents a more specific and exploratory follow the thing research technique to uncover the digital-material architecture of Bitcoin. Treating the Bitcoin code as both a text and material, a single bitcoin is followed *through* the decentralised protocol 'from' Australia 'to' the United States. By tracing the spatial relationships between miscellaneous paraphernalia from personal computers to Bitcoin mining rigs facilitating the transaction, the chapter navigates the material culture of the Bitcoin blockchain. This involves opening up software for inspection to uncover the functional performativity of the network. The spatial lens used reveals several material infrastructures such as undersea cables, data centres, pools of Bitcoin mines, active nodes, and third-party wallet software that assemble to form operational modes of centralisation.

Drawing from ethnographic research conducted within the Silicon Valley cryptocurrency and blockchain industry, Chapter 7, "Embedded Centralism," provides an account of the situated frictions among varying stakeholders in high-technology culture. The clashing of libertarian anarchy and entrepreneur-ial profit-seeking are forced into a singular vision reminiscent of the Californian Ideology, contributing to tensions of a splintering community: Bitcoin adher-ents are increasingly fragmenting as it becomes clear the protocol cannot fulfil all of their ambitions. Blockchain technology is symptomatic of this polarising worldview. As 'radical' and 'disruptive' start-up companies are absorbed into the embedded spatial ties of the surrounding economy, they become increas-ingly 'normalised' by their investors at the same time as scaling to enrol more users within their platforms. This has the effect of funnelling financial practices on blockchains through proprietary software controlled by a small number of technocrats, who can be more easily regulated by nation-state jurisdictions. The entrepreneurial geographies of high technology agglomeration industries thereby act as another spatial limitation to algorithmic decentralisation.

The final chapter, "Blueprinting Blockchains," dives deeper into the territory of spin-off blockchains offered as technological modes of organisation for decen-tralising a host of socioeconomic practices. Recent discussions of platform capi-talism are used to critique claims that blockchains are an incorruptible mode of democratic governance. Instead, blockchain capitalism is offered as a more accu-rate transaction model where capital accumulation necessitates certain points of centralisation through dominant distributed ledger technologies. A close exami-nation of blockchain typologies reveals the co-option of these architectures by the very centralised banking firms and governments they were initially designed to bypass. As financial giants and central banks design their own distributed led-ger systems to increase the efficiency of business practices and monetary policy, innovation from the disruptive edges is once again absorbed into 'the centre' by the corporate/state powers that be.

Algorithmic decentralisation itself is shown to be an inherent contradiction as spatial trajectories coalesce at different points around blockchain networks. This provides a starting point for understanding the political economies of distrib-uted blockchain networks that, on one hand, are open for all to see and, on the other, work beneath the surface of cryptographically concealed code. Following Bitcoin into different aspects of its network reveals how money, code, and space are not relegated to an autonomous machine world but emerge as a complex web of humans and non-humans formed through cultural, political, and economic practice. In doing so, the book debunks some of the libertarian and liberatory claims of cryptocurrencies by illuminating modes of uneven power. It is only by understanding these limitations that pathways can be taken to building more equitable, or at least less sensationalist, blockchain forms.

1

Pandora's Blocks

Introduction

Bitcoin has unleashed a myriad of successive ideas, architectures, and debates into the world. The resultant frenzy has already been referred to as "the paradigm of decentralization" (Griziotti, 2018, 195). Indeed, distributed ledger technologies continue to capture diverse imaginations: hooked on the pursuit of transforming societal organisation(s). But the blockchain hype is seductive, and emancipatory visions that accompany it can distort realities of distributed architectures. This chapter speaks to such dislocation by unpacking the principles and processes of Bitcoin while busting some of the myths that surround blockchain architectures (see also de Jong et al., 2015; Dodd, 2017; DuPont, 2018).

Initially, the chapter describes the genesis story of Bitcoin and the political undertows that fuelled its development. The idea of using code to regulate human action is discussed and directed to open up fertile ground for examining some of the contradictions brought about by blockchains. This moves into an account of the community that formed around developing the Bitcoin protocol before outlining a schematic depiction of the technical apparatus they work(ed) to establish. Bitcoin mining and the incentive mechanism of cryptoeconomics are introduced as underlying processes for keeping the network 'safe' from 'attackers' while exposing some of the vulnerabilities that emerge from their application. These sturdy cryptographic processes feed into the value formation of bitcoins. The emergence of entrepreneurial start-up companies like exchanges are then highlighted as having a key role in extending Bitcoin's utilisation to wider markets. Finally, the Bitcoin mining arms race teases out some of the problems and discrepancies that emerge when distributed architectures are fused together with modes of capital accumulation.

Money Code Space. Jack Parkin, Oxford University Press (2020). © Oxford University Press.
DOI: 10.1093/oso/9780197515075.001.0001.

In the Beginning . . .

It started, simply enough, on the 31st October 2008 when someone (or some people) going by the name of Satoshi Nakamoto posted in a "low-noise moderated mailing list devoted to cryptographic technology and its political impact" (metzdowd.com, 2020).[1] The post contained an abstract and link to a white paper hosted on the previously unheard-of website bitcoin.org. This online paper barely ruffled any feathers. Few took notice and those who did entered into sporadic and speculative dialogue surrounding the merits and flaws of the conceptual apparatus it posited. The white paper was titled "Bitcoin: A Peer-to-Peer Electronic Cash System" and it outlined a blueprint for a decentralised form of cryptographic currency for the Internet (Nakamoto, 2008). Cryptography was not only used here to cloak transactions but cryptographic hash functions were used as the very backbone of the protocol, chaining every transaction into a shared chronological ledger (blockchain) to prove validity (see Chapter 5).

The repercussions of the 2008 global financial crisis acted as the political Petri dish in which Bitcoin was cultivated. Although the white paper itself was published as a technical document without any mention of an agenda, in other places it was resoundingly clear that Bitcoin was formed as an anarchical currency created in response to the government-corporate control of money (Jia & Zhang, 2018). In fact, buried in the (raw hex) data of the first block (dubbed the genesis block) of its blockchain is the following text:

The Times 03/Jan/2009 Chancellor on brink of second bailout for banks.

This method for timestamping the Bitcoin software proves it was initiated after the included date, with Nakamoto intentionally referencing the front page headline of an article from a UK newspaper, *The Times*, that described the British government using taxpayers' money for saving banks (Elliott, 2009). It was with purpose that this politically charged "Easter egg" was embedded in the codified structure, which offered a radical alternative to existing monetary systems (Frisby, 2014, 107). It points to manifestations of 'Lemon Socialism' made clear by the 2008 financial crisis: a term coined by Mark Green (1974) to describe governments intervening in the marketplace to prop up failing firms, thus preventing wider systemic collapse. This interposition contradicts the supposedly neoliberal form of world capitalism that preaches a 'free marketplace' because public servants had helped privatise the profits of big business while socialising the costs. The 'too big to fail' mentality governments had proliferated (when they saved the large oligopolistic banks from collapsing) fuelled Nakamoto's political thesis.

A bottom-up 'hacker' resistance was launched as the given solution and computer code was the nominated tool of disruption. Satoshi Nakamoto offered Bitcoin as a means of emancipating people from the conventional means of monetary control, as stated on the networking website for peer-to-peer systems development, P2P Foundation:

> It's completely decentralized, with no central server or trusted parties, because everything is based on crypto proof instead of trust. The root problem with conventional currency is all the trust that's required to make it work. The central bank must be trusted not to debase the currency, but the history of fiat currencies is full of breaches of that trust. Banks must be trusted to hold our money and transfer it electronically, but they lend it out in waves of credit bubbles with barely a fraction in reserve. We have to trust them with our privacy, trust them not to let identity thieves drain our accounts. Their massive overhead costs make micropayments impossible. . . . With e-currency based on cryptographic proof, without the need to trust a third party middleman, money can be secure and transactions effortless. (Nakamoto, 2009)

Bitcoin, then, was a direct monetarist response—a belief that economic performance is dictated by changes in monetary policy/supply—to the compulsory investment (and breaches) of trust systematically installed by centralised controls over money, so heavily influenced by the capitalist market and the liberal state.

This is an admirable mission but there is a gaping hole in its logic. Many programmers—particularly cryptographers who use techniques to secure and obscure data (see Chapter 4)—tend to view the world through a philosophical lens that mirrors the mathematical processes of the software they produce. From this perspective, because code is formulaic it carries a form of repeatable integrity that can be used to represent universal truths—however many times I repeat the sum 1 + 1, for example, it should always equal 2. On the surface this line of thinking seems reasonable and is often extrapolated into Lawrence Lessig's (1999) popular mantra "code is law" which claims software can regulate conduct in a similar way to legislation. However, while code can certainly direct human action in certain ways (Kitchin & Dodge, 2011), the social and spatial networks with(in) which it interacts expose a web of complexity not always reducible to computational axioms. For example, Satoshi Nakamoto's idea that trust can be eradicated and replaced with "crypto proof" is antithetical to the socioeconomic makeup of money (Marx, 1867; Simmel, 1900; Zelizer, 1997; Ingham, 2004; Maurer, 2006; Dodd, 2014). Value is formed through constantly evolving networks of people (and other materials) that establish certain things (i.e., bank notes) as monetary forms (see Chapter 2). Bitcoin is no different: a mutual faith in the operational procedures of its protocol has allowed its embedded currency units (bitcoins) to become precious (Maurer et al., 2013). Crypto proof, then, is its own form of networked trust (Mallard et al., 2014; Coeckelbergh, 2015; Werbach, 2018). Similarly, as this book will show, code cannot always enforce decentralisation as clinically as its calculative rules might suggest.

Cultivating a Community

The geographies of Bitcoin's inception are extremely hazy thanks to the ano-nymity of its creator Satoshi Nakamoto—this glorified incognito adds to the 'anarchist' and 'hacker' mythology surrounding cryptocurrencies. Following the publication of Nakamoto's white paper in 2008, Bitcoin remained a concept circling among a specialist set of cryptographers with discussion concerning its feasibility continuing in dribs and drabs on the cryptography mailing list for a little over two months. Theory was put into practice at 18:15:05 GMT on the 3rd January 2009 when the codebase Nakamoto had been building was initi-ated on a couple of unknown machines somewhere out in the world. In doing so, they became the only nodes on the Bitcoin 'network'; the software was also made available for download on the website sourceforge.com so others could participate.

The early political-economic discourse surrounding Bitcoin heightened when a second-year computer scientist at Helsinki University of Technology called Martti Malmi (screen name serius-m) began cooperating with Nakamoto. Malmi renovated the bitcoin.org website, helped design the Bitcoin symbol, and became the first person given permission to contribute directly to the Bitcoin source code (Popper, 2015a). In the process he intentionally politicised the Bitcoin vocabulary to appeal to groups of various (radical) political persua-sions (such as anti-state.com) in an effort to encourage broader adoption of the software (Popper, 2015a).[2] Perhaps Malmi's most significant contribution to Bitcoin, however, was the advent of the Bitcoin Forum in the autumn of 2009, which provided an online environment for proponents and critics to discuss the protocol. The forum attracted an array of programmers who began analysing the conceptual apparatus of Bitcoin: critiquing, disassembling, shaping, recon-structing, and reaffirming the theoretical (pseudo-code) and practical (source code) architecture. It was also in these online environments that terms like 'cryptocurrency' (Bitcoin Mailing List) and Bitcoin's tagline 'Vires in Numeris' (Bitcoin Forum) —Latin for 'Strength in Numbers'—were first used.[3]

In December 2010, Nakamoto uploaded the Bitcoin source code to the online repository GitHub and a community of programmers, called Core developers, began to help Satoshi Nakamoto, then Lead Developer, advance the protocol. An online community of practice emerged (see Wenger, 1998; Wenger et al., 2002, 2009; Bryant et al., 2005; Dubé et al., 2005; Murillo, 2008). Programmers from all over the world (although the majority from the United States) gathered online to innovate the conceptual, technical, philosophical, and increasingly practical apparatus of Bitcoin through its adolescent stages. The open source software became a technological vehicle for delivering utopian visions: an experimental sandbox created by a "grass-roots collaboration of enthusiasts" (Taylor, 2013, 1). Some contributors (like Gavin Andresen, Wladimir van der Laan, Peter Wuille, Matt Corallo, Gregory Maxwell, and Peter Todd) became key figures in the community through the Bitcoin Forum, GitHub, and social media sites such as Reddit and Twitter.

On the 4th December 2010, WikiLeaks, a "journalistic non-profit organisation dedicated to publishing selected secret and classified information provided by anonymous sources" (Champagne, 2014), fell under a financial blockade from Paypal, Bank of America, Visa, Mastercard, and, later, Western Union. Following the public disclosure of Iraqi and Afghan War documents by the organisation, the US government applied pressure on these financial institutions to cut the economic lifeline on which WikiLeaks survived: monetary donations. For the then largely libertarian Bitcoin community (see Chapter 4), this blockade personified the ultimate form of corruption by state powers and demonstrated the control enjoyed by an oligopoly of financial companies; collusion had isolated WikiLeaks from the entire global economic structure. To the majority of Bitcoin proponents, the US government's reaction seemed to be an act of self-(pre)serving malfeasance, especially considering organisations like the Ku Klux Klan could still accept donations facilitated through MasterCard, Visa, and PayPal (Mross, 2014). Additionally, a significant proportion of Bitcoiners were politically aligned with the idea of WikiLeaks that stands for transparency, the freedom of information, and the accountability of justice—largely against the 'wrongdoings' of the centralised state.

The blockade of WikiLeaks also provided the fledgling Bitcoin community with an opportunity to test their creation's potency as an alternative financial channel for sending donations where no centralised institution could be intimidated to withdraw their services. The Bitcoin Forum was rife with comments supporting this political intervention but not everyone shared such optimism. Satoshi Nakamoto opposed the excitation writing, "No, don't 'bring it on'. The project needs to grow gradually so the software can be strengthened along the way" (Nakamoto, 2010a). But then an article in *PC World Magazine* conjectured the Bitcoin-WikiLeaks solution to a wider audience (Thomas, 2010). Nakamoto responded with a final post on the Bitcoin Forum: "It would have been nice to get this attention in any other context.

WikiLeaks has kicked the hornet's nest, and the swarm is headed towards us" (Nakamoto, 2010b).

Nineteen hours later, Nakamoto put out Version 0.3.19 of Bitcoin and then disappeared from the public eye. Gavin Andresen, a software developer from Massachusetts who had become Nakamoto's closest collaborator, had recently accepted an invitation to talk at the US Central Intelligence Agency (CIA) where he hoped to persuade them Bitcoin posed no threat to government institutions (Mross, 2014). Whether or not this was the reason for Nakamoto's departure from the project, the creator(s) of Bitcoin became a ghost soon after and Andresen took up the role of Lead Developer. Contributors came and went but the Bitcoin code continued to be built.

Bitcoin managed to save WikiLeaks and the organisation continues to operate today. Many use events like this to paint a picture of the Bitcoin protocol as an apolitical structure that 'distributes control' and thus 'removes centralised power' from its currency network (see Kostakis & Giotitsas, 2014). Yet this is a semantic mirage. The very idea of creating decentralised software as an alternative to embedded financial systems is nothing if not a deeply political act (Kostakis & Giotitsas, 2014). Additionally, although there are multiple ideological strands contributing to Bitcoin's production, a heavy vein of libertarianism fuelled its early advancement and continues to haunt its discourse/development today (Golumbia, 2015; 2016b; see Chapter 4 and Chapter 7). To make this (a)political contradiction even more clear-cut, this book sets out a number of instances where control is not equally distributed across the Bitcoin protocol. One of these examples is the (de)centralised governance structure by which various stakeholders coordinate to develop Bitcoin; here, hierarchy invariably creeps back into the picture (see Chapter 5). But if Bitcoin can be used to bypass financial blockades, then something quite special must still be going on here. How, exactly, can this happen?

The Decentral Bank

Centralised institutions have long and often been necessary to guarantee the value of money and create order in its production to generate trust (Thornton, 1802). In the United Kingdom, the role of the central bank evolved over time into an intentionally dislocated arm of government designed to adopt a 'non-biased' administrative role to the production and regulation of money (Goodhart, 1991; Elgie & Thompson, 1998). Different central banks enjoy different levels of independence but the world's oldest, the Bank of England, is positioned today so that it cannot be *directly* influenced by the economic whims of revolving governments in an effort to maintain longitudinal monetary stability (see Appendix 1).[4]

Despite the presence of such an entity in an overwhelming majority of nation-states (Shah, 2008), boom and bust economic cycles have remained a reoccur-ring global phenomenon in the practical application of neoclassical economics played out by capitalism. Some see financial crises as a breach of responsibility and an inherent flaw in the current system governed by central banks. This comes down to central banks acting as a monetary safety net for commercial banks—the lender of last resort (Goodfriend & King, 1988; Fischer, 1999; Goodhart, 2011; Flandreau & Ugolini, 2011). Few would argue against the postulation that the modern deregulated markets commercial banks operate in created an envi-ronment for the 2008 global financial crisis to occur: fostering a moral hazard with little rule or consequence.

In contrast to central banks, the Bitcoin blockchain exists as distributed, peer-to-peer software: every person running the protocol maintains a copy of the dig-ital ledger (or blockchain) that designates currency units to particular accounts (or addresses). The shared maintenance of a ledger is intended to remove the need to trust centralised third parties, like commercial banks, to keep records. It also contributes towards the robustness of the protocol because there is no singular point of failure to attack or hack. The blockchain is designed to be an active database and 'permanent' record of every Bitcoin transaction ever made. Transactions are sent to all nodes in the Bitcoin network at once, and roughly every ten minutes these transactions are bundled into a block and added to the blockchain like new pages in a ledger (see Figure 1.1). Thus, nodes in the global network update the state of the blockchain 'simultaneously' so that a *consensus* is reached as to which addresses hold amounts of bitcoin. While transactions made with bitcoins are transparent, addresses are pseudonymous in the sense that they are not tied to the identity of users.[5] This not only changes the transac-tion structure from traditional systems but also facilitates a new inbuilt privacy model (see Figure 1.2). Here, disclosing one's identity to an authorising body is not a prerequisite for making a transaction and so personal information is no longer required for authorisation as it is with a commercial bank. Instead, each user holds private keys to sign transactions via their addresses where bitcoins are 'stored.' This allows people to act as their own personal bank via the network.

Here lies an important problem with the canon 'code is law.' In Figure 1.1, when Alice sends 10 bitcoins to Bob, "identity is no more and no less than the use of a particular private key. If Alice lets someone else use her private key, that someone will appear completely identical to the 'real' Alice. Indeed, from a cryp-tographic perspective that other person *is* the real Alice" (Day, 2018, 292). So, when the mathematical integrity of cryptography is used to define ownership, the protocol can be 'tricked' to release coins for an attacker who has stolen Alice's private keys (de Jong et al., 2015). But in terms of the protocol's rules it has not been fooled at all. Because such 'fraudulent' activity perfectly obeys coded laws,

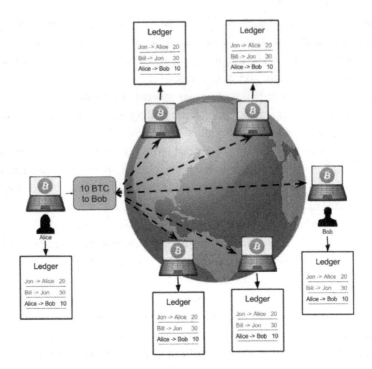

Figure 1.1 A Bitcoin transaction where Alice sends 10 BTC to Bob by broadcasting it to every other node in the network. They all update their ledgers 'simultaneously' (source: Brikman, 2014).

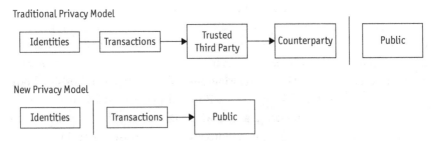

Figure 1.2 Traditional privacy model offered by financial institutions in comparison to the privacy model offered by Bitcoin (source: Nakamoto, 2008).

a great deal of onus is put on individuals to keep their private keys safe. In other words, control and security measures over monetary administration reside with each user instead of a third party. If blockchains are indeed permanent ledgers, then these transactions should be, and the vast majority are, undoable (see Chapter 8 for the revocability of blockchain transactions).

The monetary policy of Bitcoin also follows the dictum 'code is law' as it is defined and governed by the algorithmic structure of the blockchain. In regulation terms, operations can only be made within the codified parameters set by the protocol, reflecting Alexander Galloway's (2004) argument that decentralised computational networks do not eradicate control; rather, power is defined by the rules of systems. For example, monetary production is codified into the protocol so that bitcoins are released slowly over time in an exponentially declining manner until a maximum of 21,000,000 will be produced by 2140.[6] Inflation, then, is steady, predictable, and declining until it stops entirely. At that point, assuming the demand for bitcoins continues to increase, the cryptocurrency becomes deflationary as, under current protocol rules, no more coins can be created. In fact, because coins can disappear permanently from circulation with the loss of private keys, Bitcoin could even be subject to hyperdeflation (DuPont, 2019). The artificial cap makes Bitcoin analogous to a digital super-transferable precious metal that can be transacted through computers. Indeed, the practice of Bitcoin mining extends this metallic analogy (Maurer et al., 2013): chunks of bitcoin are 'randomly' rewarded by the protocol to people called miners who 'donate' their computer power to both administrate and secure the Bitcoin network (see Chapter 6).

Miners are important because they authorise and execute transactions by putting them into blocks and cementing them in the chain. The foundation for this procedure is a cryptographic technique called a hash function, which is simply an algorithmic formula that "takes an input value and produces a very different output value" called a hash (Day, 2018, 324). Any small change to the input data will radically change the output hash. For other nodes to accept a block of transactions, the hash (output data) must fit a predetermined specification. This is like solving a puzzle: one piece of the input data, a 'number' known as a nonce, is arbitrary and adjustable so miners can try adding as many to the block data as possible in an attempt to create the winning hash on the other side. Because there is no way of knowing which nonce will form the desired hash, miners must use brute force, or do 'work,' in order to find it: dedicating computing power to try as many nonces as possible. Only when the resultant hash fits the predetermined specification, which acts as proof-of-work for other participants to check, can they *mine* a block into the blockchain by submitting it to the network for validation (see Chapter 6).

Put simply, proof-of-work exists when a network user provides evidence their computer has undertaken effort to solve a problem (Dwork & Naor, 1993). Once this proof is disclosed, miners are subsequently rewarded for their efforts (and electricity costs for repeatedly running the hash function) with a quantity of bitcoins. "Mining is therefore a lottery, but those with the fastest machines will, on average, win more often (just as those who buy more lottery tickets will, on average, win more often)" (DuPont, 2019, 94). Furthermore, this process is also how the protocol 'mints' new coins and puts them into circulation: rewards for successful miners started at 50 BTC, but have halved every 4 years and will continue to do so until they eventually disappear in 2140. At that point, transaction fees, which can be included by the sending party, will be the only source of income for miners (who usually include transactions with the highest fees in their blocks to maximise their profits)—transaction fees will also begin to exceed mining rewards some time around 2040. In essence, miners profit from Bitcoin *seigniorage* (DuPont, 2019)—a term traditionally referring to the difference between the cost of creating money (like manufacturing and distributing metal specie) and the value of the coins themselves.

The Bitcoin blockchain, then, is "written by the collective, collaborative, and competitive effort of the participants in the system" (Maurer, 2017a, 112). It is like a digital tapestry of transactions woven by miners who together hire out their computational power to maintain the ledger (Scott, 2014b). Because bitcoins are endemic to the protocol, they *theoretically* cannot be created outside of what has already been predetermined by its codified parameters; this is unlike the process of fractional reserve lending practised by commercial banks or the 'printing' of money by central banks. Instead, Bitcoin attempts to redistribute monetary trust into a 'predetermined' codified architecture that 'decentralises' the control of monetary policy. However, its algorithmic architecture does not omit third parties as it indeed claims to do (Nakamoto, 2008), but rather randomises them (miners) across a 'distributed' network. This randomisation is important because it 'ensures' no single miner can omit transactions from the blockchain and therefore restrict an actor from participating in the network: this is why Bitcoin is often referred to as 'permissionless' in terms of access and is why it could be used to bypass the WikiLeaks blockade.

Cryptoeconomics

A programmer at the Silicon Valley Ethereum Meet-up Group once told me: "the blockchain is truth."[7] This, he explained, is the very point of its existence. A cofounder of a blockchain-based company in the same three-way conversation expanded on this point by saying: "blockchains are a thermodynamic commitment to a point of view of history." What he meant by this is the proof-of-work mechanism (mining), utilised by Bitcoin and many other blockchains, expends electrical energy (generating hashes) to create a trusted record that people in a distributed system can reach consensus on.[8] To understand this vision, it is necessary to describe the process of tying blocks together.

The input data of a block must include the transactions (if any) a miner wishes to submit, a nonce, and the (winning) hash of the last block (see Figure 1.3). When a miner broadcasts a winning block hash to the network, all peers can

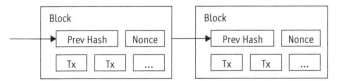

Figure 1.3 The previous block hash forms part of the input data for the next block along with transactions (Tx) and a nonce. The hash ensures all blocks are mathematically linked together into a chain (source: Nakamoto, 2008).

check it fits the predetermined parameters and then include that block in their own copies of the blockchain, thereby coming to a consensus as to what the new network state is. They will then start building on top of this block by bundling its hash together with new transactions and a random nonce—changing the nonce over and over again until they (or someone else) find(s) a winning hash for a new block. And the cycle repeats ad infinitum (previous block hash + transactions + winning nonce = current block hash). Because the last block's hash is mathematically linked (via the formula of the hash function) to all the transactions in that block and, in turn, all the previous blocks going right back to the genesis block, this small piece of information is used to connect the entire history of transactions together in a chain.

Before Bitcoin, reaching consensus in a distributed system like this was an unresolved issue in computer science known as the Byzantine Generals' Problem (Lamport et al., 1982): a dilemma that seeks an algorithm (computational or otherwise) to communicate a common agreement between multiple parties when one or more of them has the potential to be dishonest. The Bitcoin blockchain solved this problem by creating a shared chronological chain of transactions secured by proof-of-work mechanics, which generates a coherent global view of the system state. In this sense, there is "supposed to be a singular version of the blockchain, the idea being that the ledger's sequentially arranged hash-based linkages create an unbroken, monolithic record of all confirmed transactions" (Vigna & Casey, 2015, 149). There are times, however, when two miners can find the correct nonce for a new block within a few seconds of each other and both broadcast their valid block of transactions (nigh on) simultaneously to the network. This causes a split, or fork, where miners go 'rushing off' to mine on top of two competing valid blocks. Because this form of divergence is endemic to the blockchain's mechanics I call this a *systematic* fork; the discrepancy should be quickly resolved by network mechanisms, which happens (on average) two or three times a week (see Chapter 5 for a typology of forks).

Systematic forks are temporary glitches recognised and accounted for by the Bitcoin protocol so their presence is fleeting (Waldman, 2015). Resolution is achieved via the clever incentive scheme mining facilitates, known as cryptoeconomics. This 'ensures' individual miners work in the best interest of the network whole. The idea is miners will begin working on the block that was broadcast to them first while keeping an eye on the other chain when they realise there has been a fork. Once a new block is found, the miners on the shorter chain will switch their power to mining the longest chain, discarding, or 'oprhaning,' the block they were before working on. Any transactions that were in blocks of the shorter chain will go back into the mempool (memory pool)—a list of queued transactions that have not yet been confirmed into a block. This effect occurs because miners will always trust the 'longest chain' as it contains the most proof-of-work and is thus more difficult to undo.[9] To change the state of the network, a miner would have to overtake the longest chain, which is extremely hard because they would be competing against the accumulated power of the rest of the miners: finding a winning hash is mathematically challenging so the more computing power being dedicated to a chain, the greater chance it has to build the next block more quickly than any competing chain. Since the miner should be (selfishly) looking to obtain the block reward (and transaction fees) it would be more economically viable for them to find the nonce on the longest chain rather than expend power (and costs) on an impossible catch-up game while all other miners are ignoring, and thus making irrelevant, the state of the network they are preaching.

This game-theoretical component of the blockchain mining process is also what protects the network from attackers because it should not be in the miner's economic interest to cheat the system:

> If a greedy attacker is able to assemble more CPU power than all the honest nodes, he (*sic*) would have to choose between using it to defraud people by stealing back his payments, or using it to generate new coins. He ought to find it more profitable to play by the rules, such rules that favour him with more new coins than everyone else combined, than to undermine the system and the validity of his own wealth. (Nakamoto, 2008)

Thus, Nakamoto designed a system where self-interest aligns itself with the best interest of the network. In other words, "Bitcoin links economic incentives to a desired system behavior" (Day, 2018, 331). Here, cryptography is used to prove the historical properties of the blockchain while the incentive of obtaining economic value in the form of cryptographic tokens defined by the system encourages those properties (and value) to hold into the future (Buterin, 2017). This is why, when a transaction is made, subsequent blocks built on top of the block containing that transaction are known as confirmations; as the work to undo the chain becomes exponentially harder, that transaction becomes more likely to be cemented (thus confirmed) in the 'historical record' with time. Thereby, consensus is not an end product but is ever-more-closely reached with each subsequent block built on the chain.[10] The mathematics of the system ensures that the probability of an attacker catching up to the rest of the network (without collusion) and changing the ledger state, thus being able to 'double spend' their bitcoins, becomes increasingly infinitesimal through time. Therefore, the Bitcoin consensus model materialises as a codified mathematical process built into the protocol and reached via the longest chain.[11] This 'immutability' of data is often why people refer to blockchains as append-only databases where information can be added but not deleted. However, if multiple miners band together their hashing power they can more easily rewrite the longest chain, thus omitting transactions the protocol had previously confirmed. This kicks up another contradiction: the blockchain is meant to be a permanent record but can be altered if 'attackers' collaborate (see Chapter 5 and Chapter 8).

Making Money

Value is categorically subjective. In fact, the subjectivity of value is the underlying foundation on top of which markets are built; things are never inherently 'precious' on their own accord but are rather culturally defined and calculated/quantified as such. Markets function due to the temporal and spatial subjectivities of worth surrounding particular commodities: people are willing to pay different prices at different times in different places for different goods. This process of price negotiation (say, for Apple shares, gold contracts, oil derivatives, the British pound, Manhattan apartments, or a bitcoin) forms what is known as a market price, which is merely a (moving) consensus of the agreed-upon value for a specific commodity (Callon, 1998b, 1999)—an illusion of objectivity. This mirage is the product of a "classic oxymoron, conflating an empirical quantity with a socially maintained principle" (Brunton, 2019, 9). The globalisation of stock markets along with trading tickers has given the impression of a singular (albeit fluctuating) world price for certain shares and commodities yet, in reality, the vast majority of trades are made at different amounts to the digits running along computer screens. This 'established' market value is actually a moving average of the 'going rate' for goods derived from bundling their entire bid and ask prices together. What seems like an objective value is thus a mathematical accumulation of specific economic transactions: an abstraction of multiple subjectivities personified by individual trades (themselves socialised interactions). To understand markets properly, then, researchers must "trace how the webs of heterogeneous material and social practices produce them. It is these that are performative, that generate realities" (Law, 2007, 12).

Initially, bitcoins held no financial value: they were traded among early users mainly as a means for testing the functionality of the system. But a gathering faith in the cryptographic processes that underlie Bitcoin caused programmers to start parting with fiat currencies in exchange for bitcoins. Value arose slowly over time as more and more people became prepared to give up other valuable assets for the new cryptocurrency. A perceived robustness of the Bitcoin protocol and the stability of its transactions realised by cryptography is ultimately what allows the digital tokens 'running through' its network to act as a form of money.

On the 22nd of May 2009, what is widely regarded as the first Bitcoin transaction for a tangible good took place. Laszlo Hanyecz, a programmer from Florida, offered to pay anyone on the Bitcoin Forum 10,000 BTC for a pizza. A user from London with the screen name jercos placed a long distance phone call to Hanyecz's local Papa John's and paid for two pizzas with a credit card. Once they were delivered, Hanyecz sent 10,000 BTC to jercos's digital wallet (those same bitcoins would have been worth $195 million USD at the time of the 2017 price peak).[12] It is small, incremental practices like this that gradually established and increased the value of cryptocurrencies. Bitcoin's users trusted that these digital tokens could only be unlocked by the person(s) holding the private key to an address; consequently, the value of bitcoins was, quite literally, willed into being through socioeconomic practice (see Chapter 2).

Later that year, on the 5th October, a user of the Bitcoin forum, going by the name of New Liberty Standard, established the first Bitcoin exchange rate by dividing their electricity costs of mining by the amount of bitcoins they generated. The calculation gave the official exchange rate of 1 BTC = $0.0008 USD or 1 USD = 1,309 BTC.[13] New Liberty Standard also established the first online Bitcoin exchange and slowly a market for trading its digital tokens began to grow. Here, people started to speculate over a bitcoin's price, subjecting its value formation to market mechanisms; many were willing to pay more than the costs of electricity for something (a balance in a distributed ledger) they saw as having a greater inherent financial value than the simple equation (electricity costs/ amount of mined bitcoins) allowed for. This not only allowed market value(s) to form, but enabled people not participating in mining to own quantities of bitcoins.

The trade-off for processes of price discovery was (more often than not) the surrendering of private keys to exchanges that would submit transactions to the protocol on their users' behalf. In other words, a third party is (re)introduced, arguably contradicting the original philosophy of Bitcoin laid out by Satoshi Nakamoto and (re)submitting the cryptocurrency to the potentially catastrophic consequences of centralisation. In July 2010 programmer Jed McCaleb created the Bitcoin exchange Mt. Gox, which became extremely popular thanks to a fluid interface that allowed people to hold both bitcoins and dollars with their accounts (an innovation at the time).[14] Underneath the surface, users of the exchange were trusting one person, McCaleb, with their finances: the company was quite literally run from wherever he took his laptop. Nevertheless, Mt. Gox grew into what would become the largest Bitcoin start-up company in the industry. In March 2011, McCaleb sold his exchange to a French programmer living in Tokyo, Mark Karpelès. By July 2011 it was clear Mt. Gox held a monopoly position over global exchange for the cryptocurrency, administrating 80% of all bitcoin trading (Vigna & Casey, 2015). However, at the end of 2013, some early warning signs of internal problems began to appear: withdrawals for customers were delayed for weeks or, in some cases, months.

The company claimed this was a necessary restriction because a bug in the Bitcoin software, which became known as transaction malleability, made it possible for users to double spend coins (see Chapter 5). However, on the 4th February 2014, Mt. Gox announced possible insolvency, having lost 744,448 bitcoins then valued at $473 million USD (Donnelly, 2014).[15] While the software bug did exist, subsequent statistical analysis has disproven its responsibility for such a colossal loss of bitcoins (Decker & Wattenhofer, 2014). Instead, the crisis has widely been put down to company incompetency giving way for theft via the hacking of centrally stored private keys. This collapse reinforced the view of Bitcoin purists who claim any kind of centralisation creates internal vulnerabilities and defies the point of cryptocurrencies. In a similar vein, these centralised points of control reattach public addresses to the identity of customers who must disclose personal information to be serviced and thus places them back within the legislative reach of state governments. There is, however, a benefit to this (re)centralisation: start-up companies increase accessibility to non-technical users and provide new financial tools by offering a variety of services maintained by software layers resting in between users and blockchains (see Chapter 7).

A Growing Start-up Economy

Up until 2012, Bitcoin companies were, for the most part, experimental projects with little to no capital investment run by opportunistic coders who had spotted a gap in an emerging market (Epicenter Bitcoin, 2015). Even as late as 2015, I was often handed business cards with the letters "CEO" printed under the person's name to later find out they were the only one running the enterprise.[16] As more and more companies appeared, they started to settle into particular categories: wallet providers, which manage cryptographic addresses for customers via easy-to-use graphical user interfaces (GUIs); exchanges, which act as a gateway between cryptocurrencies and fiat currencies; payment processors, which provide a point of sale for merchants so that customers can purchase goods with cryptocurrencies; mining companies, which create mining hardware and/or run large-scale mining operations on behalf of their clients; infrastructural developers, which create new distributed ledger technologies or use added layers of software to improve existing architectures; financial services, which build on top of cryptocurrencies and blockchains to create new fiscal instruments and securities, and; investors, who provide capital for the businesses above hoping for future economic returns (see Chapter 7). By 2012, the embryonic industry had begun catching the eye of this last group: venture capitalists.

The lucrative potential of Bitcoin start-up companies entered the world stage when articles such as Bloomberg's "Meet the Bitcoin Millionaires" hit global headlines (Raskin, 2013). Investors first to the table included Roger Ver, Marc Andreessen, David Azar, Cameron and Tyler Winkelvoss, Barry Silbert, Wences Casares, Fred Wilson, Pete Briger, and David Marcus (Popper, 2015a). Many of the early companies, however, have since disappeared due to technical incompetencies, hacks, regulation procedures, a failure to scale, banks refusing to provide business accounts, a lack of demand for their services, or being revealed as scams. For example, BitInstant was shut down from a lack of compliance with US regulation, TradeHill was forced to close when their bank stopped servicing them, and Mt. Gox collapsed spectacularly from a lack of due diligence. The resilient few that survived—like Coinbase, Bitstamp, and BitPay—are now considered by many to be market leaders.[17] In 2013, with growing media attention and more readily available venture capital, they were joined by a second wave of start-ups (Ludwig, 2013). This pattern was explained to me by the Managing Partner of a cryptocurrency and blockchain venture capitalist fund:

> Sometimes being an early mover is overrated. You can add up a lot of errors on your back. A lot of the early guys were passionate about Bitcoin but they weren't good entrepreneurs. It's not good enough to love Bitcoin. You've got to be a good operator, a good entrepreneur, and a good executive. . . . This second wave consists of guys that have built companies before and are frankly more credible.

This trend was personified by the exponential rise in capital investment in the Bitcoin sector: growing from 2.2 million in 2012, to 50.1 million in 2014, 1.15 billion in 2016, and 5.6 billion USD in 2018 (CoinDesk, 2020). The dynamics of this start-up industry and its effect on Bitcoin will be discussed by Chapter 7, while the implications of other pioneering blockchain technologies looking to disrupt a plethora of industries will be picked up in Chapter 8.

For now, it is necessary to highlight these start-up companies as islands of control and vulnerability in the Bitcoin ecosystem. If the Bitcoin protocol defines coin ownership as the ability to use private keys to initiate transactions, then trusting companies to manage these technical procedures begets a new form of intermediary. "These do the work that financial intermediaries have always done: broker settlement and clearance, make equivalence between exchange rates, manage risk and fraud" (Swartz, 2017, 92). It is for this reason that many in the Bitcoin community refer to wallet services as "Bitcoin banks"; the individual using them is no longer directly in control of their funds (i.e., with cryptographic private keys).

Payment processors also act as intermediate gateways for spending cryptocurrencies. Looking back at Laszlo Hanyecz's 10,000-BTC-for-two-pizzas transaction, he did not directly pay Papa John's with bitcoins but used jercos as a third party who accepted bitcoins and used his or her credit card company to pay the pizzeria in US dollars. Typically, the vast majority of merchants who accept bitcoins do not want to hold them (Manusu, 2014; de Jong et al., 2015). Consequently, payment processors play a similar role to jercos by taking bitcoins and paying merchants in the equivalent amount of fiat currency (while taking a fee). This start-up economy creates a new contradiction: Bitcoin is designed to eliminate third parties but many still use them to interact with the Bitcoin protocol, which has the effect of streamlining its use but centralising particular functions.

Despite immense volatility, the value of individual bitcoins has grown considerably over time to provide some of these companies with a unique injection of capital from their appreciating hordes. Similarly, many early adopters have made extortionate amounts of money from early investments, which has serious implications for wealth (re)distribution. Analytics show that 97% of all bitcoins are held by 4% of addresses (Chaparro, 2018), some of which could even belong to the same entity.[18] Similarly, Satoshi Nakamoto owns 980,000 bitcoins but has never touched this trove other than tinkering with the project in its infancy (Wong, 2017a).[19] Like the global distribution of other monies, then, bitcoins tend to be concentrated among a relatively small amount of 'whales' who hold a significant amount of economic power as well as the ability to short exchange markets. Some in the community justify the newfound prosperity of these tech-savvy early adopters given their role as believers in, and pioneers of, a 'liberating' technology. However, in the same stroke, the asymmetry of cryptocurrency affluence reveals the limitations these technologies have for redistributing wealth. Bitcoin "might appear as though it exists outside the financial system, but by promoting scarcity and competition this project aggravates the over-accumulation of capital and exacerbates the social inequalities that it is supposed to combat" (Kostakis & Giotitsas, 2014, 437).

The Mining Arms Race

To accumulate bitcoins, one must mine them, accept them for goods/services, or buy them with other currencies. One of the reasons why exchanges became such lucrative ventures was the increasing difficulty of receiving block rewards for mining. The initial Bitcoin white paper assumed that each computer on the network would have a similar amount of hashing power, making the ability to write the next page in the ledger equal among participants. This dispersion is essential for decentralising control because it means no single entity can 'hijack' the network. For the first generation of miners this mechanism was a success but the landscape would soon mutate.

Towards the end of 2010, miners were beginning to realise they could start using their computers' graphical processing units (GPUs) instead of their computers' central processing units (CPUs) to mine bitcoins more efficiently (Taylor, 2013). GPUs are designed to render thousands upon thousands of polygons and pixels simultaneously for video games, and are thus well-suited for repeating the same mathematical function over and over again on many pieces of data (i.e., darkening every pixel on the screen as a digital sun within a virtual world sets). In other words, they are good multitaskers for simple operations. Miners began scaling their operations by using GPUs that generated more hashes per second than CPUs, and, in turn, increased the likelihood of receiving block rewards, thus maximising their profits. It was not long before miners began daisy-chaining GPUs into custom-built mining rigs; some would even use free electricity from their employer's offices or university dormitory rooms to power their machines (Taylor, 2013).

Silicon chips called field-programmable gate arrays (FPGAs) also started being redeployed as mining machines mid-2011 but they were soon overshadowed by application specific integrated circuits (ASICs), tailor-made to function solely as mining chips (Taylor, 2013). Companies like Butterfly Labs, ASICMINER, and Avalon pioneered this bespoke silicon for the production line and began selling their rigs worldwide (Taylor, 2013). This gave way for huge industrial-sized mining farms that filled warehouses with thousands upon thousands of linked ASICs. The Bitcoin protocol has an inbuilt difficulty curve for finding the winning hash: the more hashing power enters the network the harder it is to generate it. This keeps a steady block creation rate of roughly one every 10 minutes. Gigantic mining farms have pushed the mining difficulty higher and higher, making it nearly impossible for small-scale miners to receive block rewards: as far back as 2013 the collective power of the Bitcoin network was more than 256 times that of the world's top 500 supercomputers combined (Cohen, 2013). Consequently, syndicates called mining pools have emerged that allow individuals to join forces for a share of the profits in proportion to the amount of hashing power they contribute (see Chapter 5 and Chapter 6).

The resultant dominance of mining pools has come under scrutiny in the Bitcoin community due to the possibility of what has been called the 51% attack. This states that if a single party or group gathers over half of the Bitcoin mining power they can hijack the network (Kroll et al., 2013; Eyal & Sirer, 2014).[20] In other words, if a centralised cartel controls mining they can rewrite the historical record to double-spend coins—as well as alter the protocol rules forced by consensus (see Chapter 5)—since they become the network majority. The game-theoretical nature of Bitcoin protects against this outcome because those securing the network in return for financial gain should not act in a way to damage its integrity, as this would result in their own bitcoins becoming less valuable (Nakamoto, 2008). However, this technique could be used by a malicious attacker with enough resources. Thus, another vulnerability is presented: as mining pools grow they endanger the 'distributed' nature of the mining economy by advancing their own power over the network. This was famously personified by the company CEX.IO in 2014 (Gill, 2014). The start-up not only allowed independent miners to join their pool but also offered a cloud mining service called Ghash where customers could essentially buy quantities of hashing power generated by mining rigs it privately ran—acting like shares that paid out cryptocurrency dividends. As the company approached 51%, a backlash from the Bitcoin community convinced CEX.IO to cull their mining power to stay below 40% of the network whole, and urged other mining pools to do the same (Wilhelm, 2014; Bershidsky, 2014). So while cryptoeconomics discourages the 51% attack, the codified rules of the Bitcoin protocol still allow for it.

ASIC mining chips are simple yet powerful pieces of hardware: "you can heat your house with them, you can toast bread with them, and if you don't dissipate the heat from them they will melt" (Antonopoulos, 2015b). Consequently, they consume vast amounts of electricity and contribute to the earth's warming atmosphere (Brunton, 2015). One estimate put the total energy consumption of Bitcoin in 2017 at 30.1 Terawatt Hours, equivalent to the entire nation of Morocco (Kobie, 2017). This has caused many commentators to call Bitcoin environmentally unsustainable (Becker et al., 2013; Malmo, 2015; Appelbaum, 2018; de Vries, 2018). Others, on the Bitcoin Forum for example, have countered this argument by pointing out how the traditional financial system also consumes a vast amount of energy to keep its offices, commuter transport systems, and Internet servers running. However, ancillary services for cryptocurrencies do not disappear and also utilise energy intensive materials like these. The mining arms race, then, is another human-machine process that draws out the many problems and contradictions inherent in Bitcoin, and (proof-of-work) blockchain architectures as a whole.

Conclusion

The crypto-spatial ties of the Bitcoin network allow an unlockable and trans-ferable balance tied to digital addresses to act as a monetary form. This chap-ter has outlined some of the key actors (developers, miners, start-up founders) that assembled to form the Bitcoin ecosystem. In doing so, it has begun to show how the politics of money and code are skewed and reshuffled as a multitude of people interact with the network. These entities are critical for outlining the contours of algorithmic decentralisation as it plays out through new distributed ledger technologies.

So far, I have provided a schematic depiction of Bitcoin and its economy while starting to show how models of power created by human-machine interaction can be flipped upon their head. Some radical differences have clearly emerged as Bitcoin evolved from a theoretical white paper into a practical protocol. While some of its ideals may fall short of the original vision, Bitcoin and other block-chain architectures remain extraordinary technologies currently transforming the socioeconomic makeup of everyday life. And their maturation process is by no means over. The rest of this book will unpack the many entities laid out in this opening chapter to reveal further tensions of Bitcoin's adolescence and the growth of complementary and competing blockchains. It starts by outlining a conceptual framework suitable for understanding how power asymmetries form across cryptocurrency and blockchain economies.

2

Money/Code/Space

Introduction

The title of this chapter is taken from two important works in human geography. The first is *Money/Space: Geographies of Monetary Transformation* by Andrew Leyshon and Nigel Thrift (1997) who exhibited how money is performed and circulates through dense social and spatial networks. As a collection and development of previously published work, the text reflects multiple visions and expressions of money that manifest on different spatial scales. They call the codependent relationship between currency and geography "money/space." Nearly a quarter of a century later, in light of the exponential ubiquity of financial instruments, new payment technologies, the formation of the euro(zone), and the 2008 global financial crisis, this critical text offers a framework for understanding more contemporary financial landscapes. The second key work is *Code/Space: Software and Everyday Life* by Rob Kitchin and Martin Dodge (2011) who examined how software increasingly shapes the modern world. Code, like money, not only *occupies* space but *enacts* it. They call the codependency between software and geography "code/space." The key point made by Kitchin and Dodge is that digital systems are now fundamental to spatial production.

Using *Money/Space* and *Code/Space* as a starting point, in this chapter I examine a threefold relationship between money, code, and space. By building an analytical framework incorporating this three-body system, money/code/space aims to open up the complexity of blockchains as sociotechnical objects brought into being by deeply monetised and codified geographic networks. This is done through an interrogative lens designed to unpack the historical and modern manifestations of decentralisation. The epistemic value of the forward slash is similar to that devised by Michel Foucault (1980) in *Power/Knowledge*, where he demonstrated the inextricability of both terms. Similarly, for Rob Kitchin and Martin Dodge (2011) the slash binds together "code and space into one dyadic concept" (x). The association is "so mutually constituted that if one half of the

Money Code Space. Jack Parkin, Oxford University Press (2020). © Oxford University Press.
DOI: 10.1093/oso/9780197515075.001.0001.

dyad is 'put out of action,' then the entire intended spatial transduction fails" (Kitchin & Dodge, 2005, 173). For example, software is so crucial to the operations of modern airports (booking tickets, check-in, baggage handling, security procedures, air traffic control), if code were to be removed from the equation then their organised spaces would cease to function (Kitchin & Dodge, 2004). So when I use the phrase "money/code/space" I am asserting the assemblage in question (i.e., a blockchain) is in a triadic relationship and is thus dependent on all three elements to exist as it does. As such, the term helps capture dynamics of economic digital geographies.

With this framework in mind, the chapter does five things. First, it places Bitcoin within geographical theorisations of money to better understand how monetary forms are spatially constituted and enacted. Second, it critically deconstructs the term 'decentralisation' amidst its plethoric connotations. Third, a spatial framework is devised for understanding (de)centralisation in relation to digital-material, cultural-economic networks. Fourth, drawing from actor-network thinking, (de)centralisation is redefined using the concept of obligatory passage points to highlight certain connectivities that produce power in apparently distributed architectures (see Callon, 1986; Musiani et al., 2018). Fifth and finally, blockchains are compared to traditional modes of monetary governance administered by central banks. Throughout, money/space is conceptualised via modes of human interaction and, in its contemporary form, is shown to be tied intimately to code/space. This narrative works to present Bitcoin and other blockchain technologies as heterogeneous networks that can be examined—in terms of the digital code, material infrastructure, cultural-economic practices, and discourses of decentralisation held by different groups—to illuminate sites of 'centralisation' across their money/code/spaces.

Cash, Credit, or Crypto?

Money is a peculiar cultural artefact. It is a "socially powerful—and socially *necessary*—illusion" (Dodd, 2014, 6). Often the intrinsic/use value of a thing-as-money is next to nothing: a bank note is almost inherently worthless independent of the value that networks of people ascribe to it.[1] But this simple fact does not make money any less powerful: if I were to climb an urban rooftop and announce via a megaphone that "bank notes are merely pieces of paper" and then drop a million dollars onto the street, people would still surely grab at the notes as they floated down towards the pavement. Peter Pels (1998) draws on literature that follows Karl Marx's (1867) idea of fetishisation to explain this phenomenon; here, a "double attitude" (Freud, 1950), or "double consciousness" (Pietz, 1985), is at play. This form of fetishism is both 'fictional' and 'functional': "a form of misrecognition as well as recognition of reality" (Pels, 1998, 102). The value of money is fictional/false because of its inherent nothingness: the virtuality of value is somewhat detached from the medium itself, so to 'work' it needs institutions, beliefs, and trust. On the other hand, the value of money is functional/true because of what people can(not) do with(out) it. There are, so to speak, two sides of the coin.[2]

The functionality of money is suspended by consensual networks of trust that propel things-as-money into the more-than-material. This is why money has historically been able to adopt many forms: all things-as-money do not hold monetary value outside of the social and temporal settings of human interaction. Consequently, money's peculiar performativity has been historically reified in a bed of materialities such as cowrie shells, beer, salt, glass beads, gold, peppercorns, buckskins, yak excrement, tally sticks, grain, coinage, bank notes, cheques, and credit cards. As Ernesto Laclau (1990) states, a "stone exists independently of any system of social relations but it is, for instance, either a projectile or an object of contemplation only within a specific discursive configuration" (101). Similarly, money objects exist independently of people and do not act as money unless endowed with value through cultural practice. If the materiality of money does indeed embody social relations like this, then the spaces it fills make it culturally specific across disparate geographies. This character of money is described by Andrew Leyshon and Nigel Thrift (1997) as "information circulating in specific, separate but overlapping actor-networks, made up of actors, texts and machines, which think and practise money in separate but overlapping ways" (xiii). These networks culminate to create monetary value, brought into being through independent yet interlinked relationships.

When the Bretton Woods agreement, which tied the value of participating state fiat currencies to gold, dissolved in 1971 the term 'fiduciary' was used to describe trust in money with no backing of precious metal. Yet this application is a misnomer: all money is fiduciary and dependent on trust (Hütten & Thiemann, 2018). Even gold—still widely considered to be the 'holy grail' or 'base' of monetary value—can be seen as an arrangement of atomic particles (an element) that has been ascribed social meaning (a monetary standard) due to its rarity and utility (Graf, 2013). It is only when networks of trust disintegrate that a thing's ability to act as money diminishes. In short, money is what money does; but never externally to its embedded social relations—see Appendix 2 for an account of the West African cowrie shell and Appendix 3 for the Swiss-printed Iraqi dinar.

The networks of practice that create money elevate it as the ultimate commodity (Harvey, 2010). This gives it the ability to flatten other commodities into a relational and relative measurement of value, homogenising them under a quantifiable scale so their independent worth can be compared (Marx, 1867;

Simmel, 1900; Crump, 1978; Roberts, 1994; Maurer, 2006; Dodd, 2014). It is "the great converter of everything into everything else" (Peel, 2000, 32). Georg Simmel (1900) famously explained this phenomenon by calling money a claim upon society: a "socialised debt" between the "individual and a wider payment community" (Dodd, 2014, 125). In other words, money operates *between* people—users have faith it will maintain purchasing power in particular places extending into the future.

Brett Scott (2018) puts an interesting spin on things: "[m]oney is not a store of value. Rather, it is a tokenized claim that enables you to access, control, or mobilize value that resides in goods and services. Burning money does not destroy value. Rather, it burns up your ability to *control* the value embedded in the products of other's labor" (147). This is a thought-provoking statement that neatly demonstrates how money is a placeholder for other things of value. Similarly, when governments print greater quantities of money they are not creating value out of thin air but increasing the amount of claims on existing goods and services in, and outside of, their economies (which has the effect of decreasing the buying power of each individual unit, known as inflation). However, while recognising Brett Scott's point, the networks of trust that suspend money as a substitute, or stand-in, for other desirable things also allow it to become a de facto store of value in and of itself (quite evidently, it can be saved and spent later). In essence, money may only be a claim upon value but this assertion begets its own form of 'independent' value. This is a shared illusion but a powerful one, which makes it very real indeed.

Yet the resultant apparition is by no means infallible. In fact, money is deceptively fickle: being the result of social consensus, it is subject to the cultural constraints of time and space. The effect of money flattening other things is achieved and reinforced by a shared faith in the fungibility of money—that is, each unit of currency carries an identical value to another, making them all interchangeable. However, certain events show how different manifestations of a specific currency can embody some radical differences. For example, in 2008 the foreshocks of the global financial crisis appeared when the British bank Northern Rock sought a liquidity support loan from the Bank of England, which instilled fear in their depositors leading to the first UK bank run in 150 years (Stuckler et al., 2008). For those queuing at Automated Teller Machines (ATMs) ready to swap their digital pounds in Northern Rock accounts for physical banknotes, fungibility between the two manifestations of British currency did not exist. This situation reveals the delicacy of money's networks of performance (see Appendix 4 for greater detail).

The idea of national sovereignty (and identity) is often defined by currency control (Knapp, 1924; Keynes, 1930a). Here currencies are issued by central banks, informed by governments, administered by commercial banks, accepted by businesses, and spent by citizens. All of these actors are essential to the successful performance of sovereign money, which becomes imperative for the articulation of borders (Dodd, 1995; Mezzadra & Neilson, 2013). Chartalism is the name given to the belief that state-backing is *the* crucial factor for defining and enabling money, reinforced by the collection of taxes in specific currencies that necessarily ties them to citizenship (Knapp, 1924; Wray, 2004).[3] Metallism is often presented as the counterview to this claim, stating instead that value is derived from the intrinsic qualities of the thing-as-money itself—like the scarcity, durability, divisibility, and beauty of gold (see Dodd, 2014). Both sides hold a certain gravitas but should not be held in opposition to each other. Traditional coinage, for example, was an attempt to align chartalist and metallist qualities of money into a singular orthodoxy by stamping (precious) metals with state symbology (i.e., the head of the Emperor).[4] In short, while the 'thingness' of money is certainly important, the social networks (like those enforced by a state) performing and constraining it are just as crucial (if not more so) for understanding its elusive qualities.

Cultural-economic networks not only propel fiat currencies into being but also perpetuate regional boundaries so that money is at once a result of predefined parameters and a contributing force to the continued negotiation of national geographic spacing and territorial realities. This creates a monetary perimeter of inclusion and exclusion positioning actors inside or outside of state economies. However, regionalised economies are more complex than the inside/outside of bordered national currencies—for example, many Argentinians hold US dollars as a stable store of value. In this sense, "[m]oney does not map neatly onto territorial space; indeed, it often flows along the internees *between* spaces" (Dodd, 2014, 226). Looking at states as bounded entities with a singular currency, then, is a reductive approach as perimeters are always navigating a tightrope between the somewhat real and somewhat imagined (Terlouw, 2001; Van Houtum & Van Naerssen, 2002; Van Houtum et al., 2005; Walters, 2006). In other words, "[f]lows of commodities, capital, labor, and information always render boundaries porous" (Harvey, 2000, 35). Even more important to the geographic constellation of currencies is the simple fact that nation-states do not have a monopoly over money.

Bitcoin was by no means the first alternative currency in opposition to fiat-based money (Hileman, 2014; Rodima-Taylor & Grimes, 2018; Scott, 2018). Non-state currencies have been used across varying geographies such as the localised Brixton Pound in South London (North & Longhurst, 2013; Taylor, 2014), Ithaca Hours in New York (Jacob et al., 2004; Hermann, 2006), and the more wide-reaching M-Pesa that transcends many African countries. This last one is a mobile telephone airtime credit that evolved into a monetary form after a predecessor started being used for economic transactions in Uganda, Ghana, and Botswana (McKemey et al., 2003). The network providers Safaricom and Vodacom later developed M-Pesa: a 'company-backed' token that largely leapfrogged traditional banking systems in Kenya (Maurer & Swartz, 2015; O'Dwyer, 2015a).[5] To a lesser extent, it later penetrated Tanzania, South Africa, Afghanistan, India, Romania, and Albania (Taylor, 2014, 2015), whereas lobbying by banks stifled its success in Nigeria (Scott, 2016). Mobile phones have saturated these national markets whereas banking facilities remain absent to the majority, thereby providing fertile ground for M-Pesa to thrive. Today it is used by tens of millions of people daily (Rodima-Taylor & Grimes, 2018) and is the "conduit for half of Kenya's GDP" (Lanchester, 2016). M-Pesa was not thrust upon these populations as a currency; nor did it start as money in-and-of-itself; rather, it arose as such through dense cultural-economic networks.

Bitcoin, on the other hand, was conceptualised from the offset as an alternative currency. Unlike its predecessors, its designer(s) aspired to create a substitution for fiat currencies not limited to localised geographic areas: a *global* alternative currency. Existing on distributed ledgers scattered across the infrastructure of the Internet, cryptocurrencies therefore challenge the role of the central bank and claim to overcome existing patterns of financial exclusion (see Castells, 1993; Lash & Urry, 1994; Leyshon & Thrift, 1994, 1995, 1996; Leyshon, 1995). Because banks profit more by catering for the rich, financial services and correlative wealth tend not to trickle down to poorer communities. Algorithmic decentralisation via cryptocurrencies has been championed as a solution to this problem, bypassing financial institutions in developing countries and allowing citizens to become their own banks. The penetration of cellular devices within poor populations has presented an opportunity for entrepreneurial start-up companies to design inclusive 'decentralised' banking models accessed via mobile phones (Rodima-Taylor & Grimes, 2018). The success rate of these 'solutions' will be heavily dependent on how they navigate the complex relationships found in monetary networks.

With all of its promises, Bitcoin, as a form of non-institutionalised code-money, has played a role in challenging contemporary monetary assumptions: questioning concepts of value and offering a currency system allegedly existing outside of networks controlled by centralised institutions. Words like 'decentralised,' 'peer-to-peer,' 'shared,' 'distributed,' 'dispersed,' 'open source,' 'digital,' 'transparent,' 'networked,' and 'global' fill its articulatory toolkit. This vocabulary tends to suggest a border-transcending currency without any locus of control, rhetorically stripping away localities of power from its imaginary. Even the tagline given to Bitcoin by its proponents, "Strength in Numbers," promotes a trust in the reliability of mathematics (the algorithmic architecture of its blockchain) as opposed to the fickleness of people. Sequestering discourse to the realms of autonomous calculation (designed to defuse and diffuse governance) withdraws Bitcoin to the apolitical sidelines by removing it from human agency and hierarchical or geographical control. Indeed, that is its political intent: an "embrace of a libertarian ideology of non-governmental monetary policies and the promise of technology to free us from politics" (Karlstrøm, 2014, 2). It will become clearer throughout the book how this argument is a fallacy: technology is always deeply political and unavoidably harnesses asymmetries.

Geographies of Money

On the surface, Bitcoin might look like a protocol that completely homogenises its users under a set of shared transaction rules. While on some level this is true, inconsistencies in financial practice transcending different places demonstrates how Bitcoin is a tool encompassing varying utilities and visions. For example, thanks to their relative efficiency and low cost, cryptocurrencies are an appealing option for migrant Filipino workers when sending remittances home (Balea, 2014; Hynes, 2017; Rodima-Taylor & Grimes, 2018). Four years ago, Bitcoin was already estimated to "account for 20% of the Asian remittance corridor between South Korea and the Philippines" (Parker, 2016).[6] This emerging market affects the economic sovereignty of different countries, particularly the Philippines, where remittances "are the country's largest source of foreign exchange income, insulating the domestic economy from external shocks by ensuring the steady supply of dollars into the system" (de Vera, 2017). The use of cryptocurrencies, then, is altering the dynamics of global finance.

Elsewhere, in China, the Bitcoin protocol has been used as a means for escaping the country's strict capital controls (Pal, 2013; De Filippi, 2014; Lustig & Nardi, 2015; Böhme et al., 2015; Campbell-Verduyn & Goguen, 2018; Kaiser et al., 2018). Swiss Federal Railways have allowed users to purchase bitcoins with their terminals across the country (SBB, 2016; Higgins, 2016a) and the town of Zug—which is styling itself as "Crypto Valley" with an array of cryptography start-ups—accepts bitcoins as payments for public services (Higgins, 2016b). The Swiss municipality of Chiasso has created a similar system by letting its residents pay taxes with bitcoins (Meyer, 2017). While they all navigate the same protocol, this patchworked pattern of economic practice demands a cultural geography perspective of cryptocurrencies.

A pressing concern, however, is that Bitcoin does not fit neatly into traditional definitions of money. It has consequently been classified as a number of different 'things' (see Table 2.1). In many ways, then, Bitcoin suffers an ongoing identity crisis that feeds and perpetuates wider perceptions of cryptocurrencies as alien and ambiguous apparatuses. Yet a singular definition of money itself is hard to

Table 2.1 **Some existing definitions of Bitcoin**

Definition	Reference
Peer-to-peer electronic cash system	Nakamoto (2008)
Digital gold	Popper (2015)
Internet of money	Antonopoulos (2014, 2016)
Programmable money	Dalal (2014), Noyen et al. (2014), Worner et al. (2016)
Money-like informational commodity	Bergstra & Weijland (2014), Swanson (2014a)
Synthetic commodity money	Selgin (2015)
Technical informational money	Bergstra & de Leeuw (2013)
Censorship-resistant digital currency	Brito (2011)
Speculative commodity	Mittal (2012)
De facto fiat currency	de Jong et al. (2015)
Computer-generated commodity	Cusumano (2014)
Private money	McHugh (2013)
Public ledger currency platform	Evans (2014)
Ponzi scheme	Barok (2011), Grigg (2011), Richards (2014), O'Brien (2015)
Market singularity	Dallyn (2017)
Property	Australian Taxation Office (2014)
Asset	Yermack (2013), Glaser et al. (2014), Baur et al. (2015), Burniske & White (2017), Peetz & Mall (2018)
Commodity	Currie (Goldman Sachs) in Shieber (2014)
Virtual currency	Internal Revenue Service (2014)
Digital currency	HM Treasury (2015)
Payment system	Wikipedia (2018)

come by (Dodd, 2014). After William Stanley Jevons (1875), neoclassical economists maintain money holds three functions: a *medium of exchange,* a *unit of account,* and a *store of value.*[7] While these distinct functions are certainly useful for understanding money, they can often oversimplify what is a complex cultural artefact teaming with social relations (Marx, 1867; Simmel, 1900; Zelizer, 1989,

1997; Ingham, 2004; Maurer, 2005; Dodd, 2014). Consequently, money-in-practice can be more elusive than what this neat conceptualisation allows for; in fact, the neoclassical trinity provides more of an idealised, abstracted, or perhaps 'perfect' model of money. However, no monetary example in history has ever held all of these properties without (sometimes radical) imperfections or trade-offs between them.

The threefold set of monetary functions are not static but move and shift interdependently in complex arrangements:

> The idea that modern money is general-purpose, fulfilling all the possible monetary functions, is simply incorrect. There exists no form of money which serves all such functions simultaneously. Legal-tender notes are rarely used to store value in practice. . . . Cheques, credit cards and bank drafts serve only as means of payment. It is absurd to regard these monetary forms as general-purpose. (Dodd, 1994, xviii)

Viviana Zelizer (1997) adopted a relational view of money to capture this heterogeneity derived from the various ways people use it. She developed the term "earmarking" to demonstrate how otherwise identical currency units are assigned particular roles by their users and thus activated at a microlevel of commerce (i.e., coins and banknotes being stored in a tin to pay for bills at a later date). Put succinctly, earmarking is the "subdivision of funds available to an organization, government, individual, or household into distinct categories, each with its own rules of expenditure" (Zelizer, 1997, 29).

With this cultural patchworking in mind, it is easier to see how different monies might fulfil different functions both spatially and temporally as they are syphoned, pooled, and drained by various entities. As Nigel Dodd (2014) aptly puts it:

> We need to map its different layers and dimensions, its various constituent subspaces, and the myriad interconnections amongst them. . . . [W]hat appear to be singular circuits of money are actually made up of multiple and shifting configurations of meaning that make a crucial difference to how money works in practice. Analytically, what may look from the outside like a single monetary circuit—because it is defined by one monetary form—is organized internally by multifarious networks of meaning and identity. And it is important not to overlook the fact that money flows within localized spaces, too, spaces whose connection with large-scale money might be tenuous at best. This is not the absence of geography, then, but its reconfiguration. (Dodd, 2014, 221)

This understanding must also be extrapolated to more contemporary forms of money like cryptocurrencies. However, there has been a degree of debate as to whether Bitcoin can be classified as money at all.

A convincing argument for this is its extreme volatility (Güring & Grigg, 2011; Forbes, 2013; Courtois et al., 2013; Dowd, 2014; Harvey, 2014; Harvey & Tymoigne, 2015), which has led pundits from a range of fields to call it a speculative asset (Yermack, 2013; Glaser et al., 2014; Baur et al., 2015; Burniske & White, 2017; Peetz & Mall, 2018). This definition stems from the observation that only a small proportion of the entire amount of bitcoins in existence are exchanged on a daily basis whereas the rest remain immobile under the surface like a looming iceberg. Because the transaction data of the Bitcoin blockchain is public, statistical analysis can be used to demonstrate these flows: over different time periods around 70% of coins have been measured to be static (Ron & Shamir, 2013; Ratcliff, 2014; Swanson, 2014b). This has been attributed to hoarding which, some argue, renders Bitcoin an investment vehicle for future returns as opposed to a *medium of exchange* or stable *store of value*. However, one need only look at the globalisation of currency markets and the cross-border flows of capital—here Bitcoin becomes another instrument that threatens to deterritorialise nation-state money—to see how fiat money is also used as an instrument of speculation (Strange, 1998; Gill, 1992, 1993; Walker, 1993). The volatility argument against Bitcoin-as-money finds more traction when used to critique its inability to act as a reliable *unit of account*—that is, measuring the value of different commodities. This effect of money gives almost everything in life a financial price (Marx, 1867; Simmel, 1900). In other words, quantifying the value of things makes them comparable and tradable: in the United Kingdom, if an employee is over 25 years old, the minimum wage for an hour of labour is £8.72 GBP whereas a pint of beer in my local pub costs £3.70.

One example where bitcoins have been used as a *medium of exchange* is the infamous black market website Silk Road, branded the eBay of illegal drugs (Barratt, 2012; Ormsby, 2012). Its creator, Ross Ulbricht, used the platform to facilitate the trading of illicit substances until he was arrested in a San Francisco library in 2013. The FBI shut down the site, seizing 144,000 BTC (Greenberg, 2013; Ball et al., 2013). However, many copycats have since sprung up in its place. The pseudonymity of Bitcoin transactions appealed to this underground market and the cryptocurrency quickly became branded by some as 'drug money' (Broderick, 2011).[8] The worry for governments is: by "[u]sing these systems, the iconic suitcase filled with cash can now be handed metaphorically to someone on the other side of the world as or more easily than it can be handed to someone in a city park in the dark of night" (Bronk et al., 2012, 129). While products on Silk Road were priced with bitcoins, their costs were not static but pegged to the value of fiat currencies and so fluctuated depending on the exchange rate of a bitcoin. This diminishes Bitcoin's ability to act as a consistent *unit of account*—which has been described by some scholars as the core function of money (Ingham, 2001; Maurer, 2017b).[9] However, the process of fixing volatile currencies to more stable examples (like the US dollar) is in no way unique to Bitcoin, but has historically manifested within different monetary networks around the world (see Appendix 5).

Despite the homogenising effects of money, it invariably fills a "constellation of spaces" (Leyshon, 1997, 383). Consequently, there "are cultural nuanced geographies of money that are performed in different sites" (Hubbard et al., 2002, 148). It is within, or rather *through*, these sites that money can be seen as socially, spatially, and temporally constituted. Neoclassical economic theory tends to overlook these subtleties by detaching theories of 'the economy' from space (Dicken & Lloyd, 1990; Hudson, 2005; Pike et al., 2006; Knox & Agnew, 2008). Work in economic geography, especially since the cultural turn (Hubbard et al., 2002), has enlivened the specific social complexity of money instead of treating humans as rational actors represented by highly abstract models (Gibson-Graham, 1996; Zelizer, 1997; Becker, 1997; Thrift, 2000a). The neo-classical reductionist misconception, however, is on some level understandable, particularly when it comes to the peculiarity of money: to quote David Harvey (1989), money is apparently "everywhere but nowhere in particular" (167). To counteract this illusion, work on the geography of money explicitly seeks out the particular to reveal disparate actors who govern a "wide variety of different economic worlds . . . unevenly distributed over space" (Leyshon, 1995, 534).

Conceptualisations of money/space have indicated how the possession and control of different currencies is maintained within specific networked geographies such as (global) cities (Sassen, 1991; Hirst & Thompson, 1992; Hall, 2007), financial institutions (Clark, 2000; Clark & Hebb, 2004; Clark & Wójcik, 2007; Hall & Appleyard, 2009), nation-states (Strange, 1988; Leyshon, 1993, 1995; Wood, 1997), and the "developed world" (Castells, 1989; Corbridge, 1993). Relatively speaking, banking services exist for 'social elites' as opposed to poorer geographic communities who are often underrepresented by the financial sector (Underhill, 1991: Davis, 1992; Lash & Urry, 1994; Leyshon & Tickell, 1994; Philo, 1995; Marshall, 2004; French et al., 2008). This is a capitalistic pattern: banks have divisions that cater for all markets where money can be made. As such, financial services will stretch to poorer communities only when profit seems viable—for example, the aggregation of cheap mortgages that brought about the global financial crisis. On a global scale, contemporary financial services exist mainly for citizens in wealthier countries (Mitchell, 1990; Christopherson, 1993; Leyshon & Thrift, 1995). Consequently, wealth tends to stay concentrated in particular spaces, or, as Gordon Clark (2005) aptly puts it, "money flows like mercury": it "runs together at speed" but pools in a way that is "never ever randomly distributed" (104). Particular actors in monetary networks perpetuate the unequal distribution of financial wealth across different spatial scales.

Bitcoin/Space

Today, only 3% of money in the United Kingdom exists as the 'physical' cash of banknotes and coins; the other 97% is in the form of digital balances controlled by commercial banks who, in turn, have balances on central bank ledgers. Similar figures exist for the global monetary supply (McLeay et al., 2014). The increasing digitisation of money has been described as another evolutionary step in its growing abstraction throughout history (Weatherford, 1997; Coeckelbergh, 2015). This argument is often used to reinforce Karl Marx's (1867) thesis that money is succumbing to dematerialisation: it is "no longer a commodity which is transported hither and thither. It no longer even consists of paper, in the main. Increasingly, money is a set of double entries briefly etched into computer memories" (Leyshon & Thrift, 1997, 22). Similarly: the "movement of money in the global economy is based on code and much of the world's wealth exists as database entries rather than any material form" (Zook, 2012, 1106). While the codependence of money and code is important, its nebulous character should not be overstated lest rhetoric slip into an all-too-easy fetishisation of the digital. By pulling the material out of debates of money/code, arguments step into a dangerous ontological territory because they often lose sight of the material-semiotic connections that bring both money and code into being.[10] This is not the dematerialisation of money but its reconfiguration, or *re*materialisation, via different socio-spatial scales. For example, state-based digital money supported by code is not lost in an ethereal netherworld but is constituted by a host of structured materials including people, servers, computers, offices, mobile phones, ATMs, databases, cables, and wires. Understanding different instantiations of money/code in this way acknowledges distinct geographic assemblages that are constantly brought into being through relational economic practice. This is what I refer to when I say "money/code/space."

Adrian Pel (2015) describes how a resurgence of arguments that claim digital technology conquers space have arisen in relation to Bitcoin. Here, the 'decentralised' architectures of blockchains can supposedly detach money (and other things) from geography (Bergstra & Leeuq, 2013). It has become a cliché in the discipline of human geography to critique past claims that state the digital revolution spelled a borderless world (Ohmae, 1990), the end of geography (O'Brien, 1992), the dismantling of national law (Johnson & Post, 1996), and the death of distance (Caincrross, 1997). While it is certainly true that digital infrastructures have harnessed tremendous globalising effects on the social—contributing to popular concepts such as time-space compression (Harvey, 1989) and a global sense of place (Massey, 1991)—this does not mean space is lost, only that greater care must be taken to examine different geographies as their interconnections become ever more complex and, often, more opaque (Sokol, 2011). Obituaries for space, then, are misleading and it is a core precept of this book to explain how operations of algorithmic decentralisation are fundamentally a spatial process.

Geographical accounts of Bitcoin and blockchain technology, however, remain thin on the ground. For the most part, the word 'geography' only appears in a few technical papers (Bissessar, 2013; Baumann et al., 2014; Gervais et al., 2015; Donet et al., 2014; Lischke & Fabian, 2016; Tschorsch & Scheuermann, 2016). However, a trickle of less well-known work has begun to map more explicitly the spatial ontologies of Bitcoin (Gervais et al., 2014; Pel, 2015; Blankenship, 2017; Pilkington, 2017). Any such attempt demands a conceptualisation of space (Shields, 2013). It is Doreen Massey's (2005) definition that I adopt most strongly here: a relational and processual product of connected and disconnected trajectories that are always in a state of becoming (see Appendix 6). In this sense, space is not simply a container within which things happen (Lefebvre, 1991); rather, "spaces are subtly evolving layers of context and practices that fold together people and things and actively shape social relations" (Kitchin & Dodge, 2011, 13).

From this perspective, bodies are not *in* space but *of* it (Merleau-Ponty, 1963). This means understanding space as a "product of *interrelations*" or a relational flux that is constantly brought into being (Anderson, 2008, 228). Digital code is part of this process: more and more of the world now "emerges through the interplay between people and software in diverse, complex, relational, embodied, and context-specific ways" (Kitchin & Dodge, 2011, 156). From this perspective, software is by no means a separate, inaccessible, or lifeless representation of real space (Massumi, 2002; Rutter & Smith, 2005), but is an assiduous, lively, and forceful constituent of reality. "[E]verything takes-part and in taking part takes-place: everything happens, everything acts" (Anderson & Harrison, 2010, 14).

This ontology postulates an impossibility of holistic and utterly replicable spatiality in place of a more ephemeral and processual understanding of a constantly nuanced "throwntogetherness" (Massey, 2005, 140). Temporality is thus an important component of spatiality. While space-time might be fleeting and constantly changing, 'spatial structures' can hold temporal stability and practices can follow particular patterns. This ontogenetic conceptualisation of space does not deny the salience of structural or institutional expressions of power, variously labeled and analyzed within frameworks such as political economy, corporate capitalism, neoliberalism, or theocratic power, or the processes, practices, or systems of institutionally situated and enacted structures, such as the state and its delegates. (Kitchin & Dodge, 2011, 78)

Rather it recasts structures "as sets of ongoing, relational, contingent, discursive, and material practices, that are citational and transformative, and which coalesce and interact to produce a particular trajectory of interrelated processes" (Kitchin & Dodge, 2011, 78–79). With this spatial ontology in mind, humans possess the agency to (co)produce space, rendering it a distinctly social phenomenon (Lefebvre, 1991).[11] This carries with it opportunities for controlling others by enacting and imposing semi-stable assemblages or 'structures' (i.e., prison walls). To have a hand in creating a specific spatial arrangement like this is to play a part in closing the door to alternative spatial possibilities (Harvey, 2000). Consequently, space is always socially, temporally, and politically constituted; in turn, space helps create and order society, time, and politics (Kitchin, 2019).

Understanding space in this manner has interesting implications for examining how the Bitcoin blockchain is a constant meeting point for a myriad of sociotechnical trajectories that place money and code in a contemporary and dynamic relationship. Such a perspective allows for temporal and geographic complexities, contextualisations, and contingencies to become apparent while softening the binary between centralisation and decentralisation. This book does this by problematising algorithmic (de)centralisation through the coalescence of trajectories that form unique arrangements of money/code/space. In short, I set out with a spatial frame to test if blockchains can obliterate financial centres as they indeed claim to do.

Deconstructing Decentralisation

The etymology of decentralisation is rooted in the French Revolution of the late 18th century and usually promotes secession and separatism from large overruling governments (Schmidt, 1990; Leroux, 2012). It is often used in opposition to centralised forms of control—structures that decentralists see as closed, hierarchal, oppressive, and unequal. Consequently, the term gives off a certain lustre that attracts a varied crowd:

While frequently employed as if it were a technical term, decentralization more reliably appears to operate as a rhetorical strategy that directs attention toward some aspects of a proposed social order and away from others. It is called for far more than it is theorized or consistently defined. This non-specificity has served to draw diverse participants into common political and technological projects (Schneider, 2019, 266).

As both a political vision and tool, the quest for decentralisation has become increasingly popular since the 1970s following a prior post-war trend that saw the increased centralisation of governmental power and resources (Manor, 1999). This pattern led to massive economic gains for certain nation-states but did little to reduce poverty and inequality for their citizens (Manor, 1999).

Slowly, Western scholars and policy makers alike began championing and experimenting with the notion of decentralisation, envisioning it as a tool for bringing about fiscal efficiency and participatory citizenship at a local scale (Rodden et al., 2003). This framework of decentralisation is traditionally used to describe a "mechanism designed to devolve decision-making powers to the lowest levels of government authority and to promote democracy and participation, such that local people are directly involved in decisions and developments which affect them personally" (Nel & Binns, 2003, 108–109). The term 'geography' in relation to decentralisation is only ever really used in this context or its wider practise within nation-states (Burns et al., 1994). Here, decentralisation has become a popular model for "democratising" postcolonial regions—what the West often calls "developing countries" (Bardhan & Mookherjee, 2006; World Bank, 2004, 2009; Cheema & Rondinelli, 2007; Schneider, 2019).

There is a vast literature on decentralisation both as a governmental and financial process. Various typologies are laid out:

> Some are neighborhood-based, some focus on projects and some include the devolution of power to voluntary groups. Some approaches are purely managerial, others seek to widen public involvement in council decision-making. Those on the right even argue that the introduction of market mechanisms into public services is the ultimate form of decentralisation, on the grounds of power, in theory at least, is 'decentralised' to the individual service user who can exercise choice between competing service providers. (Burns et al., 1994, 5–6)

Echoing these tropes, The World Bank (2013) distinguishes four types of decentralisation: political, administrative, fiscal, and market-based. Political decentralisation looks to increase public participation with local electorates to bring decision-making closer to societal interests. Administrative decentralisation redistributes authority from the central state government to more local municipalities. Fiscal decentralisation defers revenue building/spending to lower levels of government. Finally, market (or economic) decentralisation adopts a neoliberal vision of opening up public services to the profit-seeking private sector, transferring government power to the market via deregulation. However, as processes of monopolisation play out, this can merely resemble a "shift of power and resources from one major, centralized power center to another" (Manor, 1999, 5; see also Harvey, 2015).

Bitcoin offers an alternative blueprint for decentralisation. This framework originates from a bottom-up 'hacker' mentality that focuses on individual control and responsibility over transaction management underlined by computer code. In this sense, *algorithmic* decentralisation is supposed to materialise via 'neutral,' pre-programmed, administrative rules set in place by software to unleash the 'self-organising' and 'emancipatory' power of the free market. For this reason, the Bitcoin blockchain is most strongly aligned with market decentralisation that embodies a faith in market mechanisms stemming from laissez-faire economics (Smith, 1776; Hayek, 1944). Consequently, decentralisation has become part of the lexicon for modern-day libertarian ideologues who are skeptical of centralised state power (Loomis, 2005; Kauffman, 2008; Golumbia, 2016b).[12] From this point of view, blockchains are often presented as the algorithmic skeleton to Adam Smith's (1759, 1776) invisible hand of the market.

Algorithmic decentralisation à la Bitcoin does not attempt to shift decision-making down the hierarchal tree but looks to de-centre traditional structures entirely by creating a form of 'self-organising' individualism. To early Bitcoin proponents, political, administrative, and fiscal decentralisation were moribund because their processes still relied on a central, hierarchical core: the governments of nation-states. In other words, the decision to 'decentralise' came from 'upon high' (central governments/the World Bank/the International Monetary Fund) with a greater emphasis on increasing economic efficiency rather than dissolving power. Alternatively, the Bitcoin blockchain model attempted to bypass state governments altogether—a political rift arising from questioning the given order of things and taking direct action (Rancière, 1998; Žižek, 1999; Swyngedouw, 2011). But how can the money/code/space of an algorithmic network that supposedly bypasses centralised institutions be better discerned?

Tracing Networks

Blockchains are infrastructures (the shape of material hardware) as much as they are algorithmic architectures (the shape of semiotic code). Brian Larkin (2013) describes infrastructures as "material forms that allow for the possibility of exchange over space" (327). In doing so, they materialise connective arrangements that generate different modes of organisation. Traditionally, these networked infrastructures have often been categorised into three distinct configurations: centralised, decentralised, and distributed. Such schemas are dependent on the patterns of connectivity between nodes in the network.

Paul Baran (1962) introduced the diagrams in Figure 2.1 to demonstrate the vulnerability and resilience of infrastructural networks under the threat of nuclear attack during the Cold War. Centralised networks consist of "a single central power point (a host), from which are attached radial nodes" (Galloway, 2004, 11). These star-shaped networks are vulnerable because "[d]estruction of the central node destroys intercommunication between the end stations" (Baran, 1962, 3). A "*de*centralised network is a multiplication of the centralized network" (Galloway, 2004, 31) and is called such "because complete reliance upon a single point is not always required" (Baran, 1962, 3). However, destroying a small number of nodes can still sabotage communications. This led Baran to "consider the properties, problems, and hopes for building communication networks that are as 'distributed' as possible" (Baran, 1962). Mesh-shaped distributed networks "have no central hubs and no radial nodes. Instead each entity in the distributed network is an autonomous agent" (Galloway, 2004, 33). These networks are supposed to generate a form of resilience by being "precisely noncentralized, nondominating, and nonhostile" (Galloway, 2004, 29).

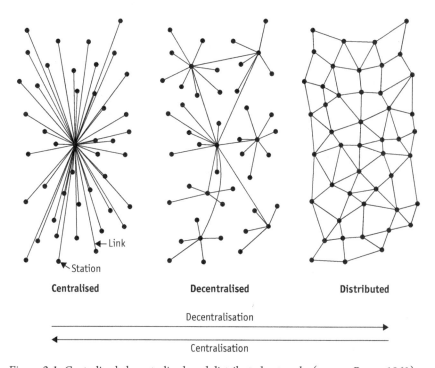

Figure 2.1 Centralised, decentralised, and distributed networks (source: Baran, 1962).

Despite their theoretical differences, the terms 'decentralised' and 'distributed' are often taken to be synonymous—particularly in blockchain discourse where they are almost exclusively used interchangeably (DuPont, 2019). This necessarily confuses what are distinct structural patterns. Usually when blockchain proponents champion decentralised architectures they invariably list all the characteristics of distribution. In response to this, an analytical framework is used here to address such disorientation and articulate an argument that takes the diversity of discourse and material conditions into account. More importantly, it recognises how rhetoric can distract from uneven modes of power.

It is useful to think of the two schemas, centralised and distributed, as two ends of a theoretical scale, or spectrum, for architectural networks. This polarisation is mathematical: on one end of the scale *all* radial nodes must pass through a central node (centralised) and, on the other, all nodes must be able to connect with *any* other (distributed). Yet this should not be treated as a complete binary. The reality is these two end points as network states are rarely (if ever) reached: "[i]n practice, a mixture of star and mesh components is used to make communications networks" (Baran, 1962, 3). Distinguishing between these "stars" and "meshes" can prove to be a wild goose chase (Eggimann et al., 2015). When properly pinned down, however, they often reveal modes of hierarchy.

> discourses of decentralization tend to take on a tragic hue, and justly so; even the most apparently decentralized systems have shown the capacity to produce economically and structurally centralized outcomes. The rhetoric of decentralization thus obscures other aspects of the reordering it claims to describe. It steers attention from where concentrations of power are operating, deferring worthwhile debate about how such power should operate. (Schneider, 2019, 266–267)

When it comes to the algorithmic decentralisation of currency, digital architectures are used to administrate transactions 'neutrally' without need of an overruling entity for authorisation—a quest for moving monetary systems from left to right in Figure 2.1. In other words, Bitcoin is supposed to do with value what early acolytes hoped the Internet would do with information: provide a network that eradicates or flattens power between actors.

The Internet is widely regarded as the world's most distributed network thanks to its extensive connectivity that can relay information between nodes around the world via different communication networks. But, as Alexander Galloway (2004) states, the act of decentralisation is itself an expression of power defined by protocols. Even more pertinent to blockchain studies is how the Internet maintains and embodies centralised and hierarchal modes of organisation (De Filippi & Loveluck, 2016; Benkler, 2016). The Internet's TCP/IP protocol, for example, must engage with hierarchal structures like the Domain Name System to function (Galloway, 2004). This process relies predominantly on centralised gatekeepers like ICANN (Internet Corporation for Assigned Names and Numbers): "a US-based non-profit corporation that is in charge of coordinating all unique identifiers across the world wide web" (De Filippi & Loveluck, 2016, 18). Coordinating decentralised architectures, then, appears to be a role traditionally taken up by centralised institutions. Indeed, "most computer networks are at least partially hierarchal" (DuPont, 2019, 89).

Useful to this understanding is Nicole Starosielski's (2015) ethnography of undersea network cables that helps shatter the popular illusion of a wireless world and instead presents the Internet as a latticework of wires and cables that traverse over land and submerge under oceans. It is at specific loci across this spatial infrastructure that particular actors can situate themselves to enable, but also dominate, network practices. Here, cultures and economies intersect with algorithmic architectures and material infrastructures in different ways, but this relationship is always political.[13] In its entirety, the Internet can be seen as a decentralised network where centralisation creeps back into its distributed anatomy in different places. For example, the "Great Firewall of China" shows how centralised governments can block connectivity to certain nodes in specific geographic areas (Clayton et al., 2006; Zhang, 2006).[14] A similar pattern of restriction is also seen in corporate workplace intranets (Bernard, 1998; Ferraiolo et al., 1999). Additionally, public Internet activity is coordinated and centred through a small number of technology companies, like Google and Facebook, which collect enormous amounts of network data (Langly & Leyshon, 2016; Srnicek, 2017; see Chapter 8). The vast majority of this information exists in massive data centres, predominantly owned by a small number of companies (Rossiter, 2016). Meanwhile, Internet service providers enforce monitoring and control over citizens at the consumer level. These processes have led commentators to claim the Internet is far less distributed than it used to appear (Kopfstein, 2013).

Such case studies suggest there are limitations to using the term 'decentralisation' when describing networked infrastructures:

> Perhaps it is time, then, for activists and political theorists of digital media cultures to take seriously the constitutive work of centralized systems of organization, and stop valorizing decentralized, distributed modes of communication and realize that these decentered modes are predicated on [some form of] centralization. (Rossiter, 2017)

So, by simply calling Bitcoin a decentralised system without any further critical investigation working to pinpoint varying centralities, modes of power in its network are blissfully ignored. Network neutrality is a label often given to architectures that treat all nodes as equals. While this characteristic may make more sense on a technical level, it has repeatedly been proven a fantasy when lifted out of the abstract mathematics of pure code and contextualised within the complex network cultures and economies in which software sits (Lovink, 2002; Rossiter, 2006). In fact, network neutrality is now used more as a term to represent a movement for pushing back against the closure/hierarchy/centralisation of the Internet.[15] The presence of asymmetric power relationships in networked architectures suggest the adjective 'decentralised' should be handled with care and de/reconstructed to encapsulate the complexity of networked systems. As David Golumbia (2016a) aptly puts it, "computerization always promotes centralization even as it promotes decentralization." The same could be said for the 'free' markets that many blockchains try to enhance (see Chapter 7).

Reconstructing Centralisation

The impotence of decentralisation for describing accurately technical, infrastructural, cultural, political, and economic systems demands a rethinking or reframing of its definitional parameters. I therefore pull back from a fetishisation of decentralisation—that goes hand in hand with a sweeping, radical, disruptive potentiality—to open up a more nuanced understanding of its contours. This is done by employing actor-network theory as a toolkit for thinking through coalescence in networks. Echoing tropes of Foucauldian discourse, actor-network thinking became prevalent within the interdisciplinary field of science and technology studies during the 1980s through the seminal work of Bruno Latour (1986), John Law (1986), and Michel Callon (1986). It outlined how a "relational epistemological truth and ontological reality are contingent and depend on the strength of heterogeneously assembled actor-networks of human and non-human entities" (Demeritt, 2002, 775). The term 'actor-network,' then, is simply a name given to assemblages of disparate and interdependent things that work together to form a combined whole (see Appendix 7). It provides a material-semiotic framework for tracing objects, ideas, and systems as they are produced, discussed, maintained, and changed.

John Law (2007) explains how the "actor-network approach thus describes the enactment of materially and discursively heterogeneous relations that produce and reshuffle all kinds of actors including objects, subjects, human beings, machines, animals, 'nature', ideas, organisations, inequalities, scale and sizes, and geographical arrangements" (2). If society is constantly being (re)arranged, then spatial realities do not precede mundane practices but are shaped through them (Mol, 1999; Thrift, 2008; Anderson & Harrison, 2010). From this point of view, it is easy to see how money has embodied a plurality of definitions, as it has manifested contextually in different places. In *The Social Life of Money*—arguably the most comprehensive contemporary synopsis of monetary theory—Nigel Dodd (2014) argues there is "no compelling reason (on empirical or theoretical grounds) to opt for just one. It is not imperative that we settle—finally—upon an overarching definition of money; indeed, doing so would be a mistake. What is needed, rather, is a framework in which money can be understood as a field of variation: not as one entity, but as several" (48).

Employed as a diagnostic tool, actor-network thinking is useful for doing this, as it can reveal important connectivities, hierarchies, and asymmetries in complicated social and technical systems (Latour, 2007; Law, 2009; Mol, 2010). It has previously been used by Nigel Thrift (1994, 1996) to demonstrate how the heterogenous networks that perpetuate money are not abstract but embodied (see also Leyshon, 1997). Consequently, the human and non-human assemblages that support money are "inherently unstable, needing constant effort and attention" (Hubbard et al., 2002, 163). Actors within these networks often strive to "improve their own representations of what money is, how it should be made, distributed and ordered" (Leyshon, 1997, 389). Actor-networks of money are thus essential to its becoming (Dodd, 1994): researching how cigarettes become a commodity money through cultural practice in prisons, for example, one must pay close attention to the material, spatial, and temporal transduction of those things into a particular currency form.[16] In this sense, "[m]oney, primitive or modern, can be understood only in its context" (Baker & Jimerson, 1992, 679).

Actor-network thinking is used in this book to better understand algorithmic decentralisation by unpicking and delineating the bits and pieces that hold blockchains together. Building upon the recent work of Francesca Musiani et al. (2018), this approach is used to develop Michel Callon's (1986) term "obligatory passage points" before applying it to blockchain systems. Callon originally used this term to describe the process of 'coercive' actors (three marine biologists) undertaking strategies to gather other 'disparate' actors (scallops, fishermen, the greater scientific community) into a mutual alignment where they could 'work together' to achieve a 'common goal' (a conservation strategy to preserve scallop stocks in St. Brieuc Bay). The struggles coercive actors took on when making these disparate actors 'co-operate' involved: problematisation, where they attempted to 'convince' other actors they, the coercers, were an indispensable obligatory passage point for solving the problem (depleting scallop stocks); interessement, where they encouraged the disparate actors to "join forces" (208) by defining and proposing interwoven roles to follow (scallops to survive; fisherman to prioritise long-term economic returns and postpone fishing; the scientific community to validate and condone the restocking project); enrolment, where they underwent continuous negotiations and "trials of strength" (211) to ensure the disparate actors 'behaved' and fulfilled the roles given to them (creating supports that help scallops anchor while protecting them from predators, currents, and dredgers; discussions with fishermen; presenting at scientific conferences); and mobilisation, where representatives (scallop larvae samples; fishermen officials; conference attendees) were employed to help coerce the masses involved (scallops; fishermen; scientists) into a "constraining network of relationships" (218). In the case of the conservation strategy of St. Brieuc Bay, the disparate actors eventually dissented and diverted from the conservation strategy being imposed upon them, thus destabilising it (scallops refused to anchor; fishermen betrayed their representatives and continued to fish; scientific colleagues became sceptical).

Infrastructural obligatory passage points tend to be extremely durable because they are often indispensable to network practices, making the costs of replacing them enormous. For example, transoceanic cables are integral for the movement of data packets through the Internet (Starosielski, 2015; Hu, 2015). Dissenting and diverting away from these chokepoints is nigh-on impossible if people wish to stay online. The term 'obligatory passage point' can be refashioned to describe how points of control are afforded to those in networks who create channels through which practices must be funnelled in order to use the system. If this is achieved, coercive actors are raised into positions of power (and profit) as others pass through the obligatory passage points they create.[17] Such bottlenecks, or chokepoints, a suitable framework for understanding the hierarchy of practices in distributed ledgers because they correlate directly with governance mechanisms and illuminate whose voices are admitted or omitted from modes of decision-making. This analytical lens highlights the convergence of particular social relationships in networked structures like cryptocurrencies and reveals (obscured) asymmetries of control—what Primavera De Filippi and Benjamin Loveluck (2016) have elsewhere called the "invisible politics of Bitcoin" (1). Framing coalescence in this way helps diffuse the centralisation-decentralisation binary and allows a plethora of material actors to become accountable in the analysis of algorithmic (de)centralisation. In the process, blockchains are shown to be as much social architectures as they are technical (see also Lustig & Nardi, 2015; Dodd, 2018; DuPont, 2019).

Displacing the Central Bank

Contemporary monetary networks are often branded centralised because central banks control monetary policy and act as the 'banker's bank': commercial banks must hold accounts at a nation-state's central bank, meaning the connections of interaction resemble the centralised network in Figure 2.1. However, these centralised systems are also connected together by other transaction networks such as the Society for Worldwide Interbank Financial Telecommunication (SWIFT) or, more recently, TransferWise. Banking as a whole, then, is not reliant on a singular centralised network but a multitude of connected centralised networks. Global currency markets also integrate monetary systems as different state monies are freely traded against each other. From this perspective, because a vast array of centralised networks interact with each other in an interconnected manner, when zooming out, the overall global banking system appears decentralised despite a reliance on centralised institutions. From the level of the citizen, however, to use a nation's currency is to be a part of a centralised network with potential exposure to central bank corruption or mismanagement (see Appendix 8). In other words, the central bank is an obligatory passage point that commercial banks (and, in turn, citizens) must pass through to manage accounts of money. What I am alluding to here is that patterns of (de)centralisation often mutate depending on the perspective from which they are viewed. The term 'obligatory passage point,' however, works to frame convergence in networks, giving clarity to complex arrangements.

Such widespread collective faith in the global financial system demands trust in the gatekeepers of money including central banks, commercial banks, investment banks, and credit card companies (Vian & Michalski, 2011). The three main roles of a central bank are balancing price fluctuations, maintaining financial stability, and supporting the state's funding in times of crisis (Goodhart, 2011). More specifically, it sets the official interest rate to manage inflation and the currency exchange rate, controls the nation's money supply, regulates the banking industry, acts as the lender of last resort, and manages the country's foreign exchange, gold reserves, and government stock register (see Appendix 9). In contrast, Bitcoin represents an anti-centralised currency move—one that pushes against the nationalism of the financial system embedded in central banks (see Appendix 1). Bitcoin proponents reject the premise of central banks who are afforded control over money and instead adhere to a 'predefined,' algorithmically set monetary policy. It is with a degree of irony, however, that the libertarian strand of early Bitcoin proponents, who align themselves with the political processes of privatisation and deregulation, continue to overlook the role both of these processes played in the spiralling collapse of *deregulated* derivatives issued by *private* banks in the 2008 financial crisis (not to mention the centralising tendencies of free markets towards monopolisation).

Alternatively, the finite supply of bitcoins was designed to mimic gold in the hope of forming a sturdy monetary platform free from manipulation. Gold has often been used as a form of commodity money to establish a 'universal base value' that cannot be tampered with.[18] This attachment is motivated by the desire for having a self-regulating device at the core of political and economic systems—a quest for order, stability, and certainty within a complex, dynamic, and increasingly volatile global economy. Indeed, gold was once located at the heart of the international financial system, stored in the high-security vaults of nation-states whose currencies were pegged to, and backed up by, these deposits. This practice was enforced by the Bretton Woods agreement where the currency values of participating governments were tied to an international gold standard. While the problems with gold-as-money are well known—for example, a limited supply causes value to increase over time, which encourages hoarding and pulls economies into a "deflationary vortex" (Bernanke, 2009, 277)—Bitcoin attempts to simulate its properties (Morris, 2015; Ferry, 2016a, 2016b) and is often referred to as "digital gold" (Popper, 2015a). The Bitcoin code mimics the physical properties of gold, mirroring its finite quantity as a naturally occurring elemental ore—a form of "digital metallism" (Maurer et al., 2013, 262). This is achieved by using supposedly unbreakable cryptographic processes (see Chapter 6).

Ultimately, at the heart of Bitcoin is a motive to redistribute monetary control. As an open source software project built by a community of (voluntary) contributors, Bitcoin was first programmed and championed as a form of anarchist money harnessed by a distributed algorithmic protocol that can be accessed by anyone with an Internet connection from anywhere in the world. Rhetorically, it challenges the monopoly of centralised institutions so blamed for economic catastrophes that echo throughout history. Instead of trusting people inside the brick and mortar organisations of Wall Street or the Federal Reserve, money—as cryptocurrency—can apparently be released from its institutional and geographical constraints, empowering the individual by transferring governance to a 'transparent,' 'decentralised,' peer-to-peer network executed by computer code. However, by beginning to delineate the money/code/space of Bitcoin, this book has already started to reveal many of its contradictions. In the following chapters I work to unwind some of the obscurities and paradoxes presented by algorithmic decentralisation and the asymmetries of power that become apparent when applying obligatory passage points to blockchain architectures.

Conclusion

This chapter has problematised Bitcoin and blockchain technology and provided a framework for understanding their complex networks and geographical constitutions. Money and code can be seen as two things that are more or less centralised or distributed on different levels through space. This becomes an interesting point of interrogation for Bitcoin, as its spatial trajectories stitch together new geographies of exchange. Framing obligatory passage points as loci of coalescence and control in algorithmically decentralised networks is a productive avenue for understanding the sociotechnical relationships that form blockchains (Musiani et al., 2018). Because money is suspended through networks of practice, the Bitcoin blockchain becomes an 'object' that can be studied from an ethnographic perspective to uncover the material-semiotic processes that suspend it into being as a 'value carrier.' Such an approach is appropriate for understanding algorithmic decentralisation as it helps trace certain practices as they coalesce in different spaces. In other words, money/code/space is a useful lens for examining the performativity of blockchains and uncovering the contours of their networked architectures, infrastructures, politics, cultures, and economies. A 'follow the thing' methodology for researching Bitcoin and other blockchain technologies is the ambit of the next chapter.

3

Follow the Digital Thing

Introduction

A common phrase used within the Bitcoin community is "to go down the
Bitcoin rabbit hole" (Moreno, 2013; Antonopoulos, 2015a; Mross, 2015;
Smith, 2015; Lea, 2016; Bitcoin Project, 2017). This expression references the
novel *Alice in Wonderland* and describes the shared experience of losing oneself down a twisting path into a surreal and unknown territory. The journey
is one of self-education composed of devouring every scrap of information
pertaining to Bitcoin one can get hold of: this often involves hours glued to a
computer screen, reading, writing, coding, and learning as much as possible
(Antonopoulos, 2014; Frisby, 2014). Down the rabbit hole is an obsessive
and heterogeneous netherworld of programmers, speculators, entrepreneurs,
and political radicals whose practices contribute to a complex and compelling cultural economy. As it was for Alice in perplexing Wonderland, at times
this intriguing adventure into the unchartered can feel lawless and nonsensical
with scatty and fascinating figures of authority who provide reasons to question previously given or taken-for-granted realities. It is among this composite
crowd I situate my research to illuminate the tensions at play between the disparate actors spearheading a movement to disrupt 'dated' economic systems
with software.

In this chapter I build a 'follow the thing' methodology and discuss the implications when applying it to the Bitcoin algorithmic protocol (blockchain), with
the aim of uncovering some of the human and non-human components bundled
together to create its spatial fabric. This technique involves staying open to the
possibility of pursuing unexpected connections uncovered in the process that
may not have been obvious during the research design. In other words, I seek
to understand Bitcoin's money/code/space not by homing in on a singular
aspect but by letting it run away with me, while viewing it from multiple angles
(Hawkins et al., 2015).

Money Code Space. Jack Parkin, Oxford University Press (2020). © Oxford University Press.
DOI: 10.1093/oso/9780197515075.001.0001.

"Down the Bitcoin Rabbit Hole"

Ethnographies are a form of research method that involves spending prolonged periods of time with specific groups of people so that "grounded social orders, worldviews and ways of life gradually become apparent" (Cloke, 2004, 169). As a multi-sited ethnography, my research process was undertaken in a variety of spaces including venture capitalist firms, FinTech accelerators, start-up companies, and meet-up groups in the San Francisco Bay Area, New York City, London, and Sydney. I gathered qualitative data in the form of participant observation and semi-structured interviews to understand better the roles people play in producing the political economies of Bitcoin and blockchain technology, paying particular attention to any obligatory passage points that were being reinforced across their spatial networks.

Fully aware of my own role in the settings researched, I allowed myself to become part of the cultural milieu as an 'observant participant' (Thrift, 2000b). This provided a rich empirical understanding of the ideological tropes and cultural practices that help weave together the human-machine networks permeating blockchains. At times this was utterly engrossing and it was not until after the six-month research process I realised I had, to some degree, succumbed to ideas of technological solutionism by looking at blockchains through rose-tinted glasses. Post-fieldwork, I was able to dissect my experiences and better understand to what extent I had been caught up in the excitement reverberating so prevalently within the industry (see Chapter 6). Pulling back and detaching myself (as far as an ethnographer can) from this fervour, I managed to regain a critical stance. However, in hindsight, my partial absorption into Bitcoin/blockchain culture was an extremely useful mode of self-reflection and (auto)ethnographic analysis (see Appendix 10).

Today I stand somewhere between a proponent and a sceptic, hoping to stay critical in a sector where many pundits easily absorb sensationalist narratives by straying into the camps of outright partisan or complete naysayer. The inherent contradictions I experienced in my own way of thinking led me to develop the term 'algorithmic decentralisation,' which I use to pull out/apart the centralised and distributed pieces of blockchains. In this sense, to ignore my early partial swaying towards the hype of Silicon Valley (along with troves of speculative online content) would be intellectually dishonest and an analytical limitation. The builders of blockchains are, in some cases, right to be excited about the impact of algorithmic decentralisation, but they should also be wary of slipping into tropes of radical disruption—a utopianism echoing older narratives surrounding the Internet and the New Economy (Ross, 2003; Fisher & Downey, 2006). Blockchains will certainly change the world in their own way (they already have), but not necessarily in the radical manner many early proponents espoused.

The framework/question of algorithmic (de)centralisation solves a number of research quandaries that arise when approaching a global algorithmic architecture facilitating economic transactions concealed by cryptography. Bitcoin appears to be, by its very design, far-reaching, intangible, and untraceable; it exists digitally in a network spanning the globe and uses cryptographic code to hide the identity of its users. How, then, is digital distributed software that grants a significant degree of pseudonymity to be approached/explored? The answer, for me, was made clear by using an ethnographic research method to trace the human and non-human relations (wherever possible) spun across Bitcoin's vast algorithmic fabric. This involved diving into the world of algorithmic code, dwelling in and engaging with online communities, attending Bitcoin and blockchain meet-up, groups, working at Bitcoin and blockchain start-ups, and interviewing different people within its vast community to uncover (some of) the bits and pieces propelling the Bitcoin phenomena into existence.

I initially gained access to the firms I worked for and interviewed via a combination of cold emailing and face-to-face networking at Bitcoin meet-up groups. The second strategy turned out to have a much higher success rate, reflecting the deep social ties within the industry; meet-up groups, for example, were crucibles of interaction between venture capitalists, programmers, CEOs, enthusiasts, and lawyers, to name but a few interwoven identities. I was universally received with a warm reception and enthusiastic interest in my research, leading to many referrals and further introductions. For example, at the San Francisco Bitcoin Devs meet-up, I was invited to attend Blockchain University where I was later asked to join a blockchain company in Mountain View. At the same meet-up, I made friends with a company being incubated at the 'campus' of a venture capital firm, Boost VC, which I visited a number of times, leading to other event attendances like the book launch party for *The Age of Cryptocurrency*. Similarly, at the Sydney Bitcoin Meet-up I met a consultant who worked out of Level39—a technology incubator in Canary Wharf, London—which I was later given open access to after being welcomed by its Head of Development. The key research activity is outlined by Figure 3.1: 14 in-depth interviews were undertaken in addition to well over 100 ethnographic interviews opportunistically conducted in the field. Whenever I worked for a Bitcoin or blockchain company I did so free of charge and I hold no shares nor retain any commercial interest in these ventures.

Face-to-face data collection was complemented with an analysis of online forums, GitHub (where open source code is constructed), social media activity among Bitcoin and blockchain communities, and an experimental exploration of the Bitcoin code and hardware infrastructure (see Chapter 6). This helped

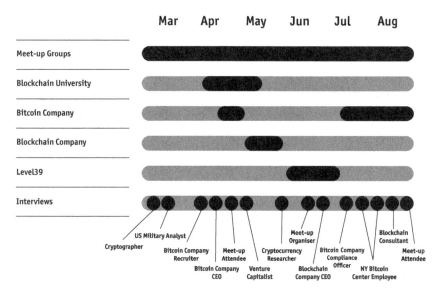

Figure 3.1 Research field activity in 2015.

develop an understanding of blockchain geographies of practice and gather an empirical basis for outlining obligatory passage points in their networked economies. From these datasets I construct a narrative surrounding the visions and materialities of decentralised algorithmic architectures.

Entering the Field

When Bitcoin was conceived in 2008, it largely evaded the pubic radar for the next three years outside of a small but blossoming online community. As such, debate was initially confined to niche online forums and the blogosphere but later found its way into journalism, law, and academia (mostly in that order). When I first started exploring Bitcoin in mid-2013, the nuts and bolts of my learning came largely from a collaborative online community gathering on the Bitcoin Forum, Reddit, and GitHub to further the protocol's development (see Chapter 4). Supporting these resources was content generated by speculative news articles, enthusiast blogs, mailing lists, and other social media networks such as Twitter. As bitcoins began to trade at a higher and higher value, the phenomenon gained greater attention from a host of well-established newspapers and magazines such as *The Wall Street Journal, Bloomberg News, The Economist,* and *The Financial Times.* Bitcoin also featured heavily in more technology-centred mediums such as *TechCrunch, WIRED, Slashdot, TechRadar,* and *Hacker News,* while emerging new media sources within the industry began playing an extensive role in producing and disseminating knowledge, like *CoinDesk, CryptoCoin News, Bitcoin Magazine,* and *News BTC.*

In 2013, Bitcoin mainly appeared as the topic of technical cryptography documents (Reid & Harrigan, 2012; Androulaki et al., 2013; Decker & Wattenhofer, 2013), a handful of working papers (Grinberg, 2011; Barber et al., 2012; Kroll et al., 2013; Moore & Christin, 2013), and a few master's theses (Šurda, 2012; Ortega, 2013; Fletcher, 2013). Brett Scott (2014a) describes the evolving state of Bitcoin scholarship as "almost no academic research" in 2008–2009, "only a trickle" in 2011, "a decent amount emerging" in 2012, the introduction of "big research" in 2013, and "peer-reviewed academic journal articles" in 2014. Bitcoin has since gathered a critical mass of attention in academia: a quick Google Scholar search of "Bitcoin" at the time of writing returns 91,800 results. Because Bitcoin intersects with so many strands of everyday life, disciplinary research has come from a plethora of knowledge bases. Consequently, as a research subject it is inherently multidisciplinary.

The most ethnographic accounts of Bitcoin to date do not come from academics but from journalists who were first to the scene. A number of trade press books have emerged, such as *Bitcoin: The Future of Money?* (Frisby, 2014), *Digital Gold: Bitcoin and the Inside Story of the Misfits and Millionaires Trying to Reinvent Money* (Popper, 2015a), *The Age of Cryptocurrency: How Bitcoin and Digital Money Are Challenging the Global Economic Order* (Vigna & Casey, 2015), and *Bitcoin Billionaires: A True Story of Genius, Betrayal, and Redemption* (Mezrich, 2019). These texts give important early accounts of the peculiarity of Bitcoin and provide compelling popular narratives of the vivid characters and colourful culture of cryptocurrencies. While there is a degree of overlap regarding the places and people that appear in these books and my own work (I also occasionally draw from these rich descriptive anecdotes to support my findings), they rarely engage with theoretical concepts and academic scholarship. In contrast, I maintain a more analytical stance by interrogating Bitcoin through an ethnographic lens to understand how (de)centralisation manifests itself through blockchain architectures. This contributes to critical interventions already made in Bitcoin and blockchain scholarship (Maurer, 2017b; Dodd, 2017; Campbell-Verduyn, 2018; De Filippi & Wright, 2018; Gloerich et al., 2018; DuPont, 2019).

Navigating the Burrow

I speak from experience when I say "going down the Bitcoin rabbit hole" can be a compelling campaign of discovery, having been drawn down it myself in the summer of 2013. Bitcoin is a fascinating research subject that transforms socioeconomic relationships across varied geographies. But its very structuration (allowing for metamorphoses in financial landscapes) makes it troublesome to interrogate. Part of this difficulty involves the cloaking of user identity with cryptography while keeping important information about transactions public. Bitcoin "was designed to be an oxymoron under close observation: regarding its actual technical functioning, it is transparent and public. . . . The social aspects of its use are, however, on a nicely crafted dark side" (Velasco, 2016, 102).

Such opacity can present a problem for researchers. Pablo Velasco (2016) outlines how a number of computer scientists have embarked on different forms of network analysis to unravel some of the hidden characteristics provided by the Bitcoin protocol. Heuristic clustering techniques were used in 2013 to reveal how the majority of transactions flowed through third parties such as Silk Road and Mt. Gox (Meiklejohn et al., 2013). Elsewhere, Alex Biryukov et al. (2014) "unmasked Bitcoin users by linking pseudonyms (or wallet addresses) to the IP addresses of the origin of the transactions" (Velasco, 2016, 102). Velasco also explains how Dániel Kondor et al. (2014)

> measured degree distribution, degree correlations, and clustering over time in the structure of the network . . . to identify two moments in the system, one before business accepted it as a form of payment and one after, and a correlation between accumulated wealth and number of transaction partners. (Velasco, 2016, 103)

Finally, Annika Baumann et al. (2014) used descriptive techniques and network analysis to deanonymise certain entities or "hubs" using the Bitcoin protocol. Here, they demonstrated a "strong relationship of user activity within different time horizons and the exchange rate" (373). Such investigations show that even in cryptographic systems designed to conceal certain data metrics, information is always "from somewhere; about somewhere; it evolves and is transformed somewhere; it is mediated by networks, infrastructures, and technologies: all of which exist in physical, material places" (Graham et al., 2015).

The work done by these researchers not only uncovers aspects of the Bitcoin network but also suggests it experiences centralising tendencies at certain points: even as early as 2013, transactions were predominantly administrated by third parties (Meiklejohn et al., 2013). The research quandary arises: how to draw out different forms of centrality in distributed networks? While there are many ways this could be done, I utilise an ethnographic methodology to tease out the sociotechnical assemblages holding Bitcoin and other blockchains together: tracing aspects of algorithmic architectures "through diverse contexts and phase circulation" (Foster, 2006, 285).

Following Epistemologies

Anthropologist Arjun Appadurai coined the phrase "follow the thing" in 1986 in his book *The Social Life of Things* to explain a methodological strategy for approaching commodities: "exploring the conditions under which economic objects circulate in different *regimes of value* in space and time" (4). The very fact that things move around means

> we have to follow the things themselves, for their meanings are inscribed in their forms, their uses, their trajectories. It is only through the analysis of these trajectories that we can interpret the human transactions and calculations that enliven things. Thus, even though from a theoretical point of view human actors encode things with significance, from a methodological point of view it is the things-in-motion that illuminate their human and social context. (5)

Another anthropologist, George Marcus, extrapolated this methodology in his famous 1995 paper titled "Ethnography in/of the world system: The emergence of multi-sited ethnography" where he outlined a number of techniques of "observation and participation that cross-cut dichotomies such as the 'local' and the 'global', the 'lifeworld' and the 'system'" (95). This "allows the sense of system to emerge ethnographically and speculatively by following paths of circulation" (107). In this sense, follow the thing work is particularly well suited for animating the lives of 'objects' through their multiple social contexts (along with follow the people, follow the metaphor, follow the plot, follow the life, and follow the conflict). I reform and reapply this methodological technique of following to uncover *some* of the cultural economic geographies of Bitcoin and blockchain technology.

Follow the thing work has since been used in a plethora of ways, particularly in material culture literature. In his book *Stuff*, Daniel Miller's (2010) central argument is "the best way to understand, convey and appreciate our humanity is through attention to our fundamental materiality" (4). This focus has led to a great deal of emphasis placed on 'tangible' things: physical objects that can, say, be picked up or broken. Ian Cook and Michelle Harrison (2007), for example, follow a bottle of hot pepper sauce from its consumption point in North London to its production point of rural farmers in Jamaica, presenting the evocative accounts of connected lives through the commodity while kicking up some surprising and diverse connotations of capitalism and its uneven geographies. In doing so, they put the thing and its biography at the centre of the research and attempt to follow the social connections formed through it. Consequently, they stumble upon marketing consultants, bottling plants, container ships, and small-scale farmers all interconnected through the supply chain and all contributing towards bringing a bottle of hot pepper sauce into existence for the consumer.

In this sense, follow the thing work can unveil the politics of consumption by examining the lives of commodities: it has been used elsewhere, for example, to reveal extrapolations of the apparently unassuming papaya fruit whose "body," upon closer examination, is dissected, polyfurcated, and globalised across multiple supply chains to form face-lift treatments, contact lens cleaning materials, indigestion remedies, canned meats, leather goods, shrink-resistant woollen fabrics, and vegetarian cheese (Cook et al., 2004). Other followed things in academic literature include sugar (Mintz, 1986), sushi (Bestor, 2000), tomatoes (Barndt, 2002), cut flowers (Hughes, 2004), broccoli (Fischer & Benson, 2006), human organs (Scheper-Hughes, 2004), natural gas (Forman, 2017), musical practice (Miranda Nieto, 2018), and an unpublished video (Akbari, 2020). Additionally, this methodology has blurred into popular forms of commodity activism that uncover the hidden production processes of everyday objects. Documentaries and non-academic books have followed coffee (Francis & Francis, 2006), corn (Cheney & Ellis, 2007), takeaway food (Christie-Miller, 2009), Mardi Gras beads (Redmon, 2005), hair extensions (Hughes, 2008), jeans (Paled, 2005; Snyder, 2008), second-hand T-shirts (Bloemen, 2001), Primark clothes (Simmonds, 2008), children's toys (Ekelund & Bjurling, 2004), batteries (Mak, 2008), oil (Kashi & Watts, 2008; Marriott & Minio-Paluello, 2012), mobile phones (Balmès, 2005), used electrical goods (Baichwal, 2006), and electronic components (McQueen, 2007).[1]

Much earlier, the literary works of 18th century it-narrative novels *Chrysal, or, Adventures of a Guinea* (Johnstone, 1760) and *The Adventures of a Bank-Note* (Bridges, 1772) beautifully captured the social life of money, as told from the perspective of these two (in)animate objects. In the case of the guinea, as it circulates through the story, it simultaneously narrates, telling "tales from the gold mines of Peru, the streets of London, the canals of Amsterdam, the ports of the Caribbean, and the front lines of the Great War" (Piepenbring, 2016). In doing so, these anthropomorphised tales "offer a non-human autobiography that becomes . . . a bitingly satirical account of a society characterized by greed, ignorance and self-interest" (Lupton, 2006, 403). People move money and are, in turn, moved by it (Maurer, 2017a). Mark Blackwell (2007) refers to this as an account of "human nature" being "overpowered, or banished, by the material world" (151)—a notion that is still prevalent today as people so easily "lose control of themselves through being swayed by the things their society has to offer" (Pels, 2010, 613). But there is something subtler here: a nuanced demonstration of material culture that depicts society dancing with, forming through, and assembling around material things. Both books cleverly and explicitly play with this ontological perspective by self-revealing themselves as material and cultural objects: "speaking formulaically about their own constitution, appearance in print, handling as objects, and the movements of their readers through their pages" (Lupton, 2006, 402). Being "conscious engagements with their own materiality as print and paper" (404), they use this "materiality as an excursion into thought, rather than a stand against it" (417).

Moving away from fictional (re)presentations of the material culture of money to a more methodological stance, follow the thing work has been offered as a means for illuminating its social (justice) life (Christophers, 2011a, 2011b)—producing an empirical form of it-narrative. This kind of research is apt for debunking commodity fetishism, a term first coined by Karl Marx (1867) in *Capital: Critique of Political Economy* to describe the peculiar force that "displaces social relations between people into material relations between things" (Harvey, 2010, 47). In other words, throughout capitalist markets there is an acute focus on the materiality of commodities "rather than the social, political and economic relations that brought them into being" (Crang, 2005, 168; see Appendix 11). In 1990, David Harvey implored radical geographers to "deploy the Marxian concept of fetishism with its full force" and to "get behind the veil, the fetishism of the market and the commodity" (423). Whether money is itself a commodity provokes rigorous academic debate (Gilbert, 2011), yet it is certainly imbued with similar fetishistic qualities. While teaming with social relations (Simmel, 1900; James, 2006), it is often taken at 'face value' (see Chapter 2). Marx (1970) referred to money as the god of commodities: an "estranged essence of man's work and man's existence, and this alien essence dominates him, and he worships it" (Marx, 1975, 172). Money, then, must be "dethroned" to uncover its deep(er) sociality (Nelson, 1999, 46).

Echoing this, Nigel Dodd (2014) argues money is more of a process than a thing. While the character of a thing-as-money still affects how it operates—for example, the physical qualities of gold helps perform and constrain its moneyness in certain ways—this does not happen in isolation. In short, money is a process permeating things. Follow the thing methodologies are often used for uncovering contours of power and are thus suitable for tracing out the dense sociotechnical networks through which money and value are performed.[2] What is often required is a shift in perspective "from things to forms of *interpersonal conduct involving things*" (Agha, 2017, 301). Ethnographic work that actively views something from different angles invariably reveals certain spatial and social connectivities while, unavoidably, masking others.

The form of "geographical detective work" (Hartwick, 2000, 1178) offered by thing-following has already been carried out to track the materiality of money back to its sources—such as non-ferrous metals in coins (Black et al., 2010) and cotton in banknotes (Busk, 2009)—to uncover the "the unseen others that produce the cash in our pockets" (Busk, 2009). Tracing physical cash is relatively straightforward but examining the digital balances controlled by commercial banks, for example, is a harder task. How, then, does one uncover the "fingerprints" left on these fleeting digital etchings never apparently touched by anyone (Harvey, 1990, 422)?[3] The answer lies in the inescapable materiality of the digital and by moving past conceptions that portray cyberspace as some sort of otherly dimension. This is useful because Bitcoin's money/space is directly tied to its code/space (see Chapter 2). To start with, then, such a methodology must 'get behind' something else that has been called "screen essentialism" (Montfort, 2004; Kirschenbaum, 2008). Screen essentialism describes the focus on digital screens as a surface of interaction whose outputs "frame" information for their users (Knorr Cetina & Bruegger, 2002). These pixelated projections delight and distract people (Chun, 1999; Marino, 2006) from the "underlying software, hardware, storage devices, and even non-digital inputs and outputs that make the digital screen event possible in the first place" (Sample, 2011).

Screen essentialism is the preoccupation with data through digital interfaces and thus it shares similarities with commodity fetishism: a concentration on material surfaces and a (blissful) ignorance of the sociotechnical relations that constitute the existence of (digital) things. To better understand the digital, it is important to get behind the screen in the same way that researchers of commodities get behind the fetish (see Appendix 12). Researchers must not only think about the surfaces of engagement (of both screen and commodity) but also understand the deep sociotechnical networks connecting people. This is especially important when insensitivities to the origination of data streams has seeped into digital research ontologies, epistemologies, and methodologies with output-focused approaches (Waldrip-Fruin, 2009). In an alternative push, I attempt to trace Bitcoin *through* its material economies/ecologies and tease out how its *thingness* is established across them. Follow the thing work is one way of doing this, providing a framework for understanding the connection between different entities: the "constant process of folding together people and things in networks of activity means that action is distributed *between* people and things" (Jones & Boivin, 2010, 346, emphasis added).

The anatomy of the Bitcoin blockchain is constantly changed precisely because of the predominance and disparities of people engaging with it in different places. For example, the concentration of Bitcoin mining farms in China bends part of the algorithmic network around a specific economic geography (see Chapter 6). I set out, then, to understand the relationship between culture and technical parameters in order to outline the sites where materials, people, and ideas come together *through* the codified organisations of blockchains. This type of inquiry allows the researcher to "enter into a world that is, so to speak, continually on the boil" (Ingold, 2010, 8). Experiencing different spaces

of interaction helps reveal (partially) the different contextualisations and enactments of a global 'distributed' network.

My adaptation of follow the thing methodologies seeks to enliven the materiality of code by examining its all-important infrastructures. So how does a researcher
examine this greater spatial complexity? And in order to understand societal
organisation, "[s]hould we be following things, people or ideas?" (McNeill, 2017,
150). It is in answer to these two questions that my multi-sited ethnography takes
a bit of a turn away from conventional follow the thing work that meticulously
tracks a specific item through space and, instead, takes a more diverse approach in
uncovering the social relations behind Bitcoin. In fact, this is absolutely necessary
when approaching blockchains: diving into the cryptographic code designed to
cloak user activity, while certainly important, can only take one so far. It is for this
reason I try to follow different "paths of circulation" (Marcus, 1995, 107). This is
attuned to the following used by Bruno Latour (1987) in *Science in Action: How to
Follow Scientists and Engineers through Society*, where the word is used as a heuristic device for tracing connections between humans and things in order to illuminate their interoperability, codependence, and correlative power. As such, while
the chapters are chronological, they do not follow a linear, longitudinal narrative
but rest at different spatial settings and obligatory passage points uncovered along
the way. This is precisely because my path constantly deviated as new avenues and
opportunities were uncovered. Consequently, I approach the Bitcoin protocol as
a 'big thing' (assemblage) made up of 'smaller things' (with their own unique
assemblages) that can be more easily followed.[4] Here, the geographies of actor-
networks are used to make complex systems more understandable by examining
their interacting components.

Mapping Methodology

The spatial arrangements of economic practices are, to a large degree, systematically concealed by blockchains. Luckily, however, not all of the components
are enshrouded with cryptography as the identity of users in transactions are.
These 'gaps' can provide a route into the dense cultural economies of blockchains. The methodology for this research project was originally designed in
2014 yet a subsequent publication by Rob Kitchin (2017), "Thinking critically about and researching algorithms," works well to justify (retrospectively)
some of the research avenues I initially laid out. This section outlines five of the
six approaches for researching algorithms documented by Kitchin: examining
pseudo-code/source code; reflexively producing code; interviewing designers
or conducting an ethnography of a coding team; unpacking the full sociotechnical assemblage of algorithms; and examining how algorithms do work in the

world (I did not need to utilise reverse engineering as the code is already openly available online). These approaches are useful for researching Bitcoin as an algorithmic protocol—essentially a 'big' algorithm (or product of mathematical steps) composed of smaller ones that build out a set of rules for communication.[5]

With this recognition in place, how can blockchains be followed? For me, the starting point was to examine the pseudo-code and source code readily available online: Bitcoin is a collaboration of open source software so a swathe of historical and ongoing documentation and discussion is readily available on sites like GitHub, the Bitcoin Forum, Twitter, and Reddit. This process included "carefully sifting through documentation, code and programmer comments, tracing out how the algorithm works to process data and calculate outcomes, and decoding the translation process undertaken to construct the algorithm" (22). Here, I deconstructed how Bitcoin was "re-scripted in multiple instantiations" by different people over time within the public code library GitHub (Kitchin, 2017, 22). In this sense "the question 'how does it work?' is also the question 'whom does it work for?' In short, the technical specs matter, ontologically and politically" (Thacker, 2004, xii). Because the algorithmic structures of blockchains are where trust in their mechanisms, and thus value, is derived, it is particularly "necessary to have a technical as well as theoretical understanding" (Thacker, 2004, xiii).

Online 'spaces' are extremely important to the ongoing cultural conflicts surrounding blockchains and the governance structures for developing the Bitcoin protocol. This was my first step into the Bitcoin/blockchain ecosystem. Chapter 4 looks at the cultural and political geographies of cryptography that gave rise to the invention of cryptocurrencies, whereas Chapter 5 explicitly deals with key online sites by examining the open source governance of Bitcoin's online community of practice, highlighting where hierarchal obligatory passage points lie in its production. From here, in Chapter 6, I move from studying code builders into an in-depth interrogation of the Bitcoin code itself by following a transaction 'across borders.' The digital-material architecture provides an overview of spatial centralisation around different nodes in the decentralised network. When I began researching Bitcoin in 2013 it had already started shifting from a tight-knit (yet geographically dislocated) online project to an emergent economy that endeavoured to carry blockchain technology off in new directions. By examining online community activity and reading industry literature and news articles, I pinpointed three key locations where the Bitcoin economy was firmly taking root: Silicon Valley, New York City, and London. In these places, which house globally renowned finance and technology economies, the density of Bitcoin and blockchain start-up companies and meet-up groups signalled important loci for understanding the entrepreneurial bonds forming around the algorithmic protocol—Chapter 7 and Chapter 8 account for processes of algorithmic (de)centralisation in these different sites. From these geographic starting points I navigated a path through the Bitcoin and blockchain landscape(s) for a period of six months (see Figure 3.1).

Traditional follow the thing work encompasses a unique form of snowball sampling where the researcher lets connections across a thing's life or supply chain determine the people they come into contact with. While this is not necessarily extensive, nor representative in the quantitative sense, it establishes a manageable and exploratory research technique where subjects recommend subsequent participants (England, 2003; Babbie, 2008). This roadmap adopts the mantra that it is "not the sheer *number*, *'typicality'* or *'representativeness'* of people approached which matters, but the quality and positionality of the information that they can offer" (Cook & Crang, 1995, 12; see also McCracken, 1988; Geiger, 1990). Following the spatial links between things, ideas, people, and practices gave me a platform from which to understand the complex cultural economy of blockchains and allowed me to get an idea of their spatial organisation(s) from the inside out. From this position, geographies of (de)centralisation could be more easily critiqued as I personally observed certain practices materialise and coalesce.

While examining source code gives "some insights into the workings of an algorithm . . . [it] provide[s] little more than conjecture as to the intent of the algorithm designers" (Kitchin, 2017, 24). One method for catechising software further is by interviewing or conducting an ethnography of a coding team to uncover "the story behind the production of an algorithm and to interrogate its purpose and assumptions" (Kitchin, 2017). I met a couple of Bitcoin Core developers along the way and even engaged in lengthy debate with some key contributors. In addition to this, the politics of programmers is often well versed through various mediums of social media like Twitter. However, my journey took me deeper into the realms of proprietary software generated by start-up companies where I interviewed programmers, CEOs, recruiters, lawyers, risk managers, and venture capitalists. Throughout this process I adopted an ethnographic sensitivity by engaging in participant observation with different Bitcoin and blockchain start-ups, organisations, and meet-up groups while attending other important events.[6] Understandings of these spaces developed by "watching, observing and talking to [people] in order to discover their interpretations, social meanings and activities" (Brewer, 2000, 49). Sitting with programmers in their work environments, for example, provided "insight into the contingent, relational and contextual way in which algorithms and software are produced" (Kitchin, 2017, 25). This was not only true for new blockchain structures themselves (some of which were not open source) but also for the software service economy that was beginning to gather around Bitcoin and other distributed ledgers like Ethereum.

To some extent, ethnography is inevitably *auto*ethnographic. The point here is "presence enacts itself as an embodied activity" (Taylor, 2002, 44) and so the body becomes an "instrument of research" (Crang, 2003, 499). It is in this vein that following different spatial connections also took me briefly into the realms of reflexively producing code myself (Kitchin, 2017)—at Blockchain University I attended weekend 'lectures' among entrepreneurial professionals constituting a hands-on learning/creating environment. In these 'classrooms,' I learnt how to engage with different blockchains: using the Bitcoin Testnet (a copycat of the Bitcoin protocol designed for developer experimentation), attendees were taught how to run applications on top of them. The skills learnt in lectures taught by industry specialists helped me build blockchain-based products—providing an intriguing insight into the practices, logics, and ideologies of code builders— and gave me the opportunity to experience (despite not having the background of a software developer) some of the problem solving occurring in blockchain code production. This is a crucial endeavour because the "basic purpose in using these methods is to understand parts of the world as they are experienced and understood in the everyday lives of people who actually live them out" (Cook & Crang, 1995, 4).

Correspondingly, the "ethnographer inhabits a kind of in-between world, simultaneously native and stranger" (Hine, 2000, 5). Creating blockchain projects and working for Bitcoin start-ups was extremely exciting and absorbing to the extent that I sometimes leant more towards a "native" than "stranger" (see Appendix 10). This balancing act can sometimes be hard to navigate in sites of emotion and expression (Davidson & Milligan, 2004). Such tendencies can become a limitation when the researcher encounters the "inherent subjectivities involved in doing auto-ethnography and the difficulties of detaching oneself and gaining critical distance to be able to give clear insight into what is unfolding" (Kitchin, 2017, 23). Personally, I became caught up in a surrounding optimism about blockchains being at the forefront of an impending technological revolution. At the same time, however, as I tried to maintain a critical stance (particularly during post-fieldwork reflection), the 'auto' that inescapably exists in all ethnographic research was invaluable for understanding some of the ideologies (re)emerging with the development of Bitcoin and blockchain technology. I therefore echo, in "most qualitative research methods (such as interviewing and ethnography) embodied moments are crucial to intersubjectivity, interpretation and understanding" (Parr, 2003, 66). Researchers are unavoidably human and strengths come from recognising the impossibility of complete objectivity rather than pretending it can be accomplished.

The fluidity and flexibility of following was well equipped for penetrating the Bitcoin and blockchain cultural economy and, to paraphrase Kitchin (2017), for unpacking the full sociotechnical assemblage of algorithms. This involves sub-scribing to an understanding that

> algorithms do not work in isolation, but form part of a technological
> stack that includes infrastructure/hardware, code platforms, data and
> interfaces, and are framed and condition[ed] by forms of knowledge,
> legalities, governmentalities, institutions, marketplaces, finance and so
> on. (Kitchin, 2017, 25)

Finally, Kitchin offers discursive analysis as a method to "help reveal how algo-rithms are imagined and narrated, illuminate the discourse surrounding and promoting them, and how they are understood by those that create and promote them" (Kitchin, 2017). This form of rationale also played a role in my research as I scanned online forums and noted the language used by different actors within Bitcoin and blockchain ecosystems. Ultimately, following the thing allowed for a plurality of interpretations.

Conclusion

Although I have been implying their interoperability, I am still yet to explicitly reconcile an actor-network analytical lens with a follow the thing methodology, which I will conclude the chapter with. These terms often seem to brush up against one another, yet there is little in academic discussion that considers their cross-pollination. At first glance they may seem antithetical, emanating from dif-ferent strands of discourse. For example, actor-network thinking, with its pre-occupation with hybrid relationships, may seem radically 'post-structuralist,' whereas thing-following methodologies might, more commonly, be associated with exposing the inequalities of different socioeconomic 'structures' like capi-talism. Ian Cook et al. (2004, 2006, 2008, 2014, 2017), for example, conduct empathetic research and storytelling along commodity chains to expose hidden labour (behind the fetish) and bring about circumstantial/deliberate activism and public pedagogy. It is, however, possible to navigate a path through these dif-ferent influences. This is less a rapprochement of terms than it is carefully articu-lating what I take from each. In doing so, actor-network thinking becomes just one way of looking at empirical data retrieved from a follow the thing research technique.

There has been a great deal of debate, or dissatisfaction, in the social sci-ences between micro and macro, local and global, scales of analysis (Latour, 1999a). Put simply, micro levels tend to be associated with (individual) agency and macro levels with (collective) structure. But there always appears to be something lacking in each: with face-to-face interactions in local settings, "many of the elements necessary to make sense of the situation are already in place or are coming from far away" (Latour, 1999a, 16); yet, similarly, the formative "abstraction of terms like culture and structure, norms and values, seems too great, and [one feels the need] to reconnect, through an opposite move, back to the flesh-and-blood local situations from which they had started" (Latour, 1999a, 17). Actor-network thinking does not side with the former or the latter, but is a way of "paying attention to these two dissatisfactions, not again to overcome them or to solve the problem, but to follow them elsewhere and to try to explore the very conditions that make these two opposite disappointments possible" (Latour, 1999a, 17). It is, then, a pertinent analytical lens to apply to, and make sense of, follow the thing work that, by its very design, constantly entangles the researcher within heterogenous networks, circulations, and flows that seem to be all at once localised and globalised (see Appadurai, 1990).

Indeed, George Marcus (1995) documents the influence of Bruno Latour (1987, 1988) and Donna Haraway (1991) in pushing multi-sited ethnographies, and follow the thing work in particular, towards these frames of analysis while "think[ing] unconventionally about the juxtaposed sites that constitute their objects of study" (104).[7] Here, actor-network thinking does not dictate a particular approach but "go[es] about systematically recording the world-building abilities of the sites to be documented and registered" (Latour, 1999a, 21). It is not, then, at least in my interpretation or employment of the term, an all-in-one empirical-theoretical package, or template, used to explain societal processes but, instead, a thinking tool that helps delineate what the researcher observes/interprets (hence my use of actor-network 'thinking' as opposed to actor-network 'theory'). In this sense, the term 'obligatory passage point' is used as a technique to place specific spaces—where a melting pot of actors collide—under a microscope to highlight the hybrid connectivities, hierarchies, and asymmetries that form blockchains.

In science and technology studies, the metaphor 'black box' is often used to describe the obscurities of unseen elements in hybrid systems (Callon & Latour, 1881). Here, technical work achieves a form of stability, making the inner workings invisible so that only inputs and outputs are acknowledged (Winner, 1993; Hinchliffe, 1996; see Chapter 6). For example, if I type a word into Google and press 'search' it returns a host of relevant websites but this tells me little of the process by which they appear on my screen. The operation has become black-boxed, the assemblage veiled by its own success (Latour, 1999b). While the analogy is not limited to digital networks, the rise of online platforms has made algorithmic black boxes a growing concern. For example, Frank Pasquale (2015) worries about the extent of personal information that is being siloed by enormous companies positioned across the Internet (Facebook, Google, Amazon, etc.) and what is happening to that data behind the curtain. In many respects, the Bitcoin blockchain is meant to counter this pattern by making information public while obscuring individual identities.

While certainly useful, it is important not to let the black box metaphor distract from the multiple, processual, and heterogenous nature of algorithms (Bucher, 2018). After all, black boxes are always contextual, a matter of perspective: infrastructures are not opaque to the engineers who fix them on a daily basis (Larkin, 2013). In other words, different aspects of a protocol will be obfuscated for different people. Consequently, what is concealed to (or ignored by) a computer programmer might be clear to (or acknowledged by) a social scientist and vice versa (Bucher, 2018). This, then, is where the strength of actor-network thinking lies: it helps the researcher enter a fray of knowns and unknowns by tracing the sociotechnical links between humans and non-humans. The follow the thing methodology outlined in this chapter is designed to view the Bitcoin blockchain from a multitude of angles: unravelling *some* of the complexities and obscurities that constitute the money/code/space of distributed architectures. This grants greater clarity when discerning how obligatory passage points, and thus degrees of (de)centralisation, operate.

4

Building the Future

Introduction

The globalisation of capitalism, for all its rhetoric of progress, is failing to deliver quality of life for everyone it envelops. As unemployment grows, wealth inequality soars, and the natural/built environment is placed under ever-greater pressure, alternative modes of (world) governance are becoming prominent vehicles for imagining better economies. David Harvey (2000), in *Spaces of Hope*, partially outlines the long and tumultuous history of utopian thinking that comes in many shapes and sizes (Harvey, 2000).[1] A common thread that ties these disparate visions together is allusions to (and illusions of) grandiose solutions realised by "some promised land or other space beyond the horizon" (Harvey, 2000, 27). Harvey argues that escaping the embrace of capitalism is difficult without its eradication because it necessarily creates uneven temporal and geographical developments—and, in turn, these spatial inequalities help sustain it (see also Lefebvre, 1976). Alternatively, the first incarnations of blockchains as cryptocurrencies offered a technical fix to capitalism by restoring balances of power through 'free markets' via cryptography and the algorithmic decentralisation of monetary policy. In other words, blockchains emanate from a contemporary breed of utopianism: crypto/spaces of hope.

"Techno-utopianism tends to be characterized by a language of revolutionary change, and thus carries important political dimensions; it is linked to a (real or imagined) mastery of a given technology for a common good" (Zeilinger, 2018, 79). This chapter dissects algorithmic decentralisation as a political movement steeped in techno-utopianism to uncover its lineages and discrepancies of meaning. In doing so the chapter teases out decentralist ideologies that are, later in the book, compared to decentralisation in practice. All infrastructures have a complex history, and to examine them only as they stand in a moment of time and space is to truncate their existential understandings. Consequently, an analysis of Bitcoin's money/code/space must involve uncovering the ideological roots

Money Code Space. Jack Parkin, Oxford University Press (2020). © Oxford University Press.
DOI: 10.1093/oso/9780197515075.001.0001.

that precede and (in part) sustain the development of cryptocurrencies. I first embarked on following Bitcoin by unearthing the empirical footprints historically documented by books, journals, white papers, source code, policy documents, websites, forums, blogs, and documentaries. It is by following ideas via these mediums that I 'went down the Bitcoin rabbit hole,' so they are a suitable starting point for analysing the idealised and glorified concept of (algorithmic) decentralisation and further unpacking the contradictions that surround it.

The chapter begins by outlining the growing practice of digital cryptography as it has increasingly transformed spatial relationships between people connected by computer networks. Following World War II, modern cryptographic practices became partially decoupled from their tight historical relationship with the state as techniques were further developed by countercultural 'anarchists' through digital means to protect themselves from the 'threat' of centralised 'big brother' government. As privacy, individualism, entrepreneurship, and counterculture grew out of the San Francisco Bay Area (Turner, 2006), and into other burgeoning 'copycat' technology hubs, the axiom of decentralisation was brandished as a form of moral organisation: an unequivocal positive and philanthropic advancement for human societies. Consequently, I discuss Richard Barbrook and Andy Cameron's (1996) concept of the Californian Ideology and use it to develop understandings of ideological decentralisation as a form of technopolitics with deep ties to anti-statist, anarchic, and free-market mantras. I then develop an account of Bitcoin and blockchain technology that encompasses the diversity of their increasingly fragmented communities.

The Rise of Digital Cryptography

Algorithmic configurations have been referred to as both a language and an infrastructure because the syntax written by a programmer self-executes by design. In this sense, code "does what it says" (Galloway, 2004, 193). Software, then, can seem strangely alive or autonomous—Adrian MacKenzie (2006) calls this a "secondary agency" (8). Furthermore, to those not familiar with how it operates, code is relatively difficult to understand: it "often appears to be 'automagical' in nature in that it works in ways that are not clear and visible, and it produces complex outcomes that are not easily accounted for by people's everyday experience" (Kitchin & Dodge, 2011, 5). Yet code's independence is largely a mirage as people are constantly writing and reforming it.[2] Algorithms, then, are fundamentally *social* artefacts and can be infused with any number of political ideologies (Coleman, 2012).

Like utopianism, cryptography has a deep history with "vibrant connections to language, science, and art" (DuPont, 2014). However, this broad lineage has been overshadowed with twentieth-century developments, which concentrated on the concealment of digital information (DuPont, 2014). It is these advancements I focus on here because they have become strongly attached to ideas of algorithmic decentralisation.

Cryptography, in its most dominant form, is the "study of mathematical techniques related to aspects of information security such as confidentiality, data integrity, entity authentication, and data origin authentication" (Menezes et al., 1996, 4). Its etymology derives from the Greek *kryptos* meaning 'hidden' and *graphien* meaning 'to write' (Mollin, 2000). In other words, cryptography utilises "secret codes and ciphers to scramble information so that [it is] worthless to anyone but the intended recipients" (Levy, 2001). History is punctuated with cryptographic codes like this (Singh, 1999): from the ciphering of hieroglyphics on an Ancient Egyptian tomb as far back as 4,000 years ago (Khan, 1967), to the cracking of the German Enigma code during the Second World War by Alan Turing's team at Bletchley Park (Hinsley & Stripp, 1993). The constant historical struggle between codemakers and codebreakers—described by Ralph Simpson (2016) as "crypto wars"—has driven many innovations behind cryptography, now recognised as an independent academic doctrine. I now briefly introduce the modern political history of cryptography and the protagonists who have championed it before explaining the rise of cypherpunks and their dreams of electronic money.

The spaces cryptographic codes transduce and actualise have changed dramatically over time. One common use of cryptography was to protect secrets and strategies practised by militaries, governments, and diplomatic services (Menezes et al., 1996). Cryptography, in short, safeguarded information in transit. Inscriptions moved through space in different forms where only those with the correct cryptographic keys could decipher their meaning. This remains true today but, with revolutions in digital technology, information increasingly travels across nation-state borders in the form of signals through cables and wires:

> We interact and transact by directing flocks of digital packets towards each other through cyberspace, carrying love notes, digital cash, and secret corporate documents. Our personal and economic lives rely more and more on our ability to let such ethereal carrier pigeons mediate at a distance what we used to do with face-to-face meetings, paper documents, and a firm handshake. Unfortunately, the technical wizardry enabling remote collaborations is founded on broadcasting everything as sequences of zeros and ones. (Rivest cited in Menezes et al., 1996, xxi)

Those with the technical skills for eavesdropping can listen to pretty much everything unprotected online: "we think we're whispering, but we're really

broadcasting" (Levy, 2001). The uptake of 'globalised' communication networks is making cryptography an ever more important component of the spatial
make-up of everyday life, what could be called "crypto/space."

The production of cheap digital hardware in the 1950s pulled cryptographic
practices out of the narrow industry of mechanical computing and into people's
homes (Diffie & Hellman, 1976). Ongoing development in computing since the
1960s has lowered the cost of information communication technologies over
time. With the help of personal computers, university research, start-up companies, and stay-at-home enthusiasts, cryptography has been injected into an
increasing array of everyday practices. This includes public-key infrastructures
used in email and Internet banking, transport layer security in web browsers,
and file-sharing software such as BitTorrent. All of the modern cryptographic
innovations of blockchain technology rest upon this previous work.

The growing ubiquity of cryptographic techniques in commercial applications has been catalysed by the NSA hacking scandal in 2013, that involved the
mass surveillance and storage of public online data in collusion with many reputable Internet companies. The security measures taken to preserve anonymity
are now a "useful strategy for contesting the pervasive surveillance apparatus of
the state and large corporations within societies of control" (Taffel, 2015a, 2).
Messaging service WhatsApp, for example, now provides end-to-end encryption by default largely in response to the public backlash sparked by this event.
Elsewhere computer passwords, ATMs, satellite television, mobile phones,
urban transport travel cards (e.g., London Oyster and Sydney Opal), and online
commerce are all actualised by cryptographic protocols that protect the passing of information between clients and servers in digital-material infrastructures. Spaces, then, are increasingly crypto/spaces: a unique form of code/space
allowing disparate people to interact via digital systems that conceal data and/
or makes it incorruptible. The politics of algorithmic decentralisation applied to
crypto/spaces draw predominantly from the 'hacker' side of the cryptography
ecosystem that came to fruition with the rise of the Internet.

The Cypherpunk Movement

Digital money had long been dreamt of by those associated with the libertarian-
leaning cypherpunk movement of the late 1980s. Cypherpunks arose as an
anarchist grassroots community who utilised the Internet for social cohesion
and the proliferation of their ideologies, seeking to harness technology as a
means of liberation from what they saw as a growing technocratic Orwellian
society (Ludlow, 2001; Levy, 2001; Farmer, 2003; Crofton, 2015; Brunton,
2019). Their tool of resistance was cryptography, which they saw as a means of

achieving societal and political change: the ultimate form of non-violent direct action (Assange et al., 2012).

Different methods have been invented for administering cryptographic systems: "[o]ne solution lay in equipping networks with centralized key distribution centers, 'trusted third parties' that could provide each pair of users with the required key pairs without the need for prior interaction" (Blanchette, 2012, 42). However, many cryptographers believed the users of these mechanisms should not have to trust others for securing communication because "any system that relied on centralized authority put the user at risk of having her personal information disclosed, even if that authority was well intentioned" (Blanchette, 2012, 42). This gave rise to the problem of sending secure communications over insecure digital channels without using a mediating centralised institution (Merkle, 1978). To solve this, Whitfield Diffie and Martin Hellman (1976) designed one of the first public-key protocols brandishing a "decentralised view of authority" (Diffie cited in Levy, 2001).[3] Public-key encryption, and similar techniques, became cypherpunk bread and butter: a practice heavily wrapped up in the political belief that centralised power should be avoided at all costs.

Although cryptography is now a respected academic discipline, for some time many state regulators regarded it as a dark art and even sanctioned against non-governmental cryptographic activity. In 1977, the NSA targeted those participating in its development by threatening prospective attendees of a cryptography symposium, issuing them with letters explaining how their rituals could breach an arms regulation law that classified cryptography as a threat to national security equal in severity to handling munitions (Levy, 1993). Academics practising cryptography were therefore forced to do so in relative secrecy and publishing material became a risky venture.

> One particular software package, PGP (for Pretty Good Privacy), became the movement's cause célèbre, and its author, Phil Zimmerman, its first martyr, after becoming in 1993 the target of a three-year criminal investigation over possible breach of export laws. (Blanchette, 2012, 49)

The PGP encryption program was used for concealing/protecting civilian email (Zimmerman, 1995). Utilising a technical loophole in US legislation, PGP Corp started printing their source code into books before exporting them abroad so the text would no longer be considered cryptographic 'software' under legal frameworks (Kantor, 2015). Others embedded code, like the RSA algorithm, into different material artefacts: condensing it down into "a mere three lines of the Perl programming language" and printing it on t-shirts or tattooing it on skin, "instantly turn[ing] the messenger into an international arms trafficker" (Blanchette, 2012, 49).[4] From anarchic actions like these, the yet unnamed cypherpunk movement formed as a bottom-up counterweight to the enclave-like enclosure of intellectual thought. The coders involved rebelled against the warnings they were given by using cryptography to protect themselves, and wider publics, from Internet infrastructures that were beginning to eliminate privacy by architectural default. Here, cypherpunks used the encryption of digital-material networks as a political tool to bypass architectures of power imposed by governments—thus generating their own vehicle for anti-authoritarian practices. Their political ideologies were deeply personified and solidified in the codified compositions they created: protecting free speech with cryptography and defining cryptography as free speech in the process.

Jean-François Blanchette (2012) explains how cryptography "exhibited the firm convictions that technology trumps regulation every time and that encryption as code could not be caged and—once released—would inevitably roam free, spreading security, freedom of speech, and democracy in its wake" (61). Wielding these beliefs, by "the beginning of the 1990s, the cryptography community had seemingly turned on its head a centuries-old relationship with the state, a relationship that had committed the field to obscurity, secrecy, and national security" (54). Blanchette continues:

> Most visibly, in the wake of the public-key revolution, it led to the emergence of an independent academic community, eager to distance itself from the 'Dark Side' of intelligence agencies and state controls over cryptographic research. Yet beyond the media-friendly image of cryptographers as defenders of electronic freedoms, multiple agendas operated simultaneously within the field. (60)

Here, "cryptography's emerging scientific program supported a broad range of positions on the social purposes of cryptographic research, many of a more conservative bent than crypto's well-publicized image suggested" (13). But amongst this plurality, the "explosion of the Internet propelled cryptography to the forefront of the cyberlibertarian movement" (5).

Most cypherpunks remained a rather secretive and tight-knit group hiding from the spotlights of governing bodies who opposed their practice. They were, on the whole, a loose coalition of academics, hobbyists, civil liberties organisations, and hackers (Narayanan, 2013). Many of them exercised ideas of cryptoanarchy to push back against digital infrastructural power (May, 1992; 1994; Crofton, 2015). This is a profoundly political action, offering tools for going unnoticed and bypassing 'the system' altogether. As Julian Assange et al. (2012) once put it:

> The Universe believes in encryption. It is easier to encrypt information than it is to decrypt it. We saw we could use this strange property to

create the laws of a new world. To abstract away our new platonic realm from its base underpinnings of satellites, undersea cables and their controllers. To fortify our space behind a cryptographic veil. To create new lands barred to those who control physical reality, because to follow us into them would require infinite resources.[5]

In other words, cryptographers looked to overcome the spatial limitations of traditional communication by creating their own crypto/spaces that veiled interaction and took power away from centralised authorities.[6]

Due to cryptography's initial legal uncertainty, most cypherpunk communication was originally conducted online through the protected channels they carved out for themselves. However, the community aspect became more organised in 1992 when Eric Hughes, a Berkeley mathematician, invited a group of politically motivated programmers to his home in Oakland of the San Francisco Bay Area where they committed to an online revolution of sorts (Garfinkel, 1995; Manne, 2011). That same year Tim May (1992), who was also present at the gathering, published "The crypto anarchist manifesto": a call to arms outlining the utilisation of personal computers with rapidly growing processing power in achieving privacy from centralised institutions. In doing so it sought to produce alternatives to the constraints of economic transactions controlled by oligarchic banks and governments: "just as the technology of printing altered and reduced the power of medieval guilds and the social power structure, so too will cryptologic methods fundamentally alter the nature of corporations and government interference in economic transactions" (May, 1992). It was under this philosophical banner the group first rallied and it was here, as the story goes, the term 'cypherpunk'—somewhat affectionately and in good humour—was first coined by Jude Milhon from the words "cipher" and "cyberpunk" (Manne, 2011).

In the second ever issue of *WIRED Magazine*, Tim May, Eric Hughes, and Jon Gilmore don white masks for the cover story "Rebels with a Cause (Your Privacy)." Hughes (1993) later released "A cypherpunk's manifesto," championing the protection of privacy and the re-empowerment of citizens envisioned in their brave new world (of crypto/space). The cypherpunks set out to program political realities by infusing ideologies into their code; without their input, and consistent battling with higher powers, the codified geographies of modern computer systems would arguably look very different today.

Technological Decentralism

Post-war computer technology was initially perceived as a dehumanising form of mechanisation that would limit human freedom (Turner, 2006). This impression was later turned on its head when hippie communalism melded with the Cold War technology of "computer networks in such a way that thirty years later, the internet could appear to many as an emblem of youthful revolution reborn" (Turner, 2006, 39). Running parallel to the cypherpunks was a broader cultural-political movement orchestrated by the cyberpunks, who envisioned cyberspace as an anti-materialist digital frontier of the mind, which could emancipate societies from the traditional-material constraints of power (Dyson, et al., 1994). Cyberpunk imaginaries drew heavily from works of science fiction where depictions of futuristic utopias, as well as dystopias, were abundant. The mantra of this (new-)worldview was personified by John Perry Barlow's (1996) essay titled "The declaration of the independence of cyberspace:"

> Governments of the Industrial World, you weary giants of flesh and steel, I come from Cyberspace, the new home of Mind. On behalf of the future, I ask you of the past to leave us alone. You are not welcome among us. You have no sovereignty where we gather. . . . I declare the global social space we are building to be naturally independent of the tyrannies you seek to impose on us.

These tropes became known as cyberlibertarianism: "a collection of ideas that links ecstatic enthusiasm for electronically mediated forms of living with radical, right wing libertarian ideas about the proper definition of freedom, social life, economics, and politics" (Winner, 1997).

From the 1960s the counterculture of San Francisco—rebellious visionaries (Watson, 1995; Charters, 2001), hippies (Braunstein & Doyle, 2002), and gay rights activists (Boyd, 2011)—diffused into the technological entrepreneurialism of Silicon Valley, which was forming forty-five miles south, quickly becoming home to the "densest concentration of electronics and semiconductor companies and highly skilled technological talent in the world" (Saxenian, 1983, 13). The geographic situation in which many of the rallying cypherpunks gathered on the West Coast of the United States is extremely important for understanding the ideological undercurrents that brought about cryptocurrencies and their processes of algorithmic decentralisation. Here, cyberculture grew out of counterculture when computers started to be reimagined as tools for building alternative communities and harnessing communal connection and individual freedom (Turner, 2006). By the late 1980s, cyberlibertarians started regarding the Internet as a new territory that would provide emancipation from traditional authoritative bonds (May, 1994; Borsook, 2000).

Richard Barbrook and Andy Cameron (1996) would later call the product of this cross-fertilisation the "Californian Ideology" to capture the libertarian-entrepreneurial values beginning to saturate the technology industry. The countercultural New Left, promoted by a "loose alliance of writers, hackers, capitalists and artists" (Barbrook & Cameron, 1996, 3), collided with the "entrepreneurial zeal of the New Right" (Barbrook, 2001, 50). What should have been a clash of polarised worldviews reconciled in a tantalising form: a "contradictory blend of conservative economics and hippie radicalism [that] reflects the history of the West Coast" (Barbrook & Cameron, 1996, 15). It preached "an anti-statist gospel of cybernetic libertarianism: a bizarre mish-mash of hippie anarchism and economic liberalism beefed up with lots of technological determinism" (Barbrook & Cameron, 1996, 10). Such a peculiar cultural worldview originally emerged from a geographic anomaly:

> This new faith has emerged from a bizarre fusion of the cultural bohemianism of San Francisco with the hi-tech industries of Silicon Valley. . . . [The] Californian Ideology promiscuously combines the free-wheeling spirit of the hippies and the entrepreneurial zeal of the yuppies. This amalgamation of opposites has been achieved through a profound faith in the emancipatory potential of the new information technologies. (Barbrook & Cameron, 1996, 1)

It is this overarching belief in technological determinism across the hybrid left-right philosophy that fuses the two competing viewpoints together into a singular orthodoxy: "technology, efficiently deployed, will provide 'solutions' to 'problems' generated within the unfortunately messy sphere of human politics" (Hillis et al., 2013, 100). In other words, technological solutionists saw the electronic frontier as a tool for solving socioeconomic problems.

A glorified egocentricism took hold of Silicon Valley taken, in part, from the philosophical writings of Ayn Rand. The Russian-American novelist promoted what she called "objectivism" where, free from authoritative control or restraint, people could become valiant figures by tuning into and following their own selfish desires (Rand et al., 1967; Rand, 1984; Peikoff, 1993). She declared: "man" must empower "his" own rational self-interest because "his highest moral purpose is the achievement of his own happiness" (Rand, 1959). Indeed, "her portraits of heroic individuals struggling to realize their vision and creativity against the opposition of small minded bureaucrats and ignorant masses both foreshadow and inform the cyberlibertarian vision" (Winner, 1997). Individualism free from regulation was the Randian key to a truly free society. Machines, cyberlibertarians believed, could create stability where before there was volatility:

> Ever since the 1970s computer utopians in California believed that if human beings were linked by webs of computers then together they could create their own kind of order. It was a cybernetic dream, which

said that the feedback of information between all the individuals connected as nodes in the network would work to create a self-stabilising
system. The world would be stable yet everyone would be heroic
Randian beings completely free to follow their desires. (Curtis, 2011)

This way of thinking drew heavily from right-wing economics seen as the only
available stand against state control: "[c]rucial to cyberlibertarian ideology are
concepts of supply-side, free market capitalism, the school of thought reformu-
lated by Milton Friedman and the Chicago school of economics" (Winner, 1997).
The economist Alan Greenspan was a regular and early acolyte of Ayn Rand's
weekly meet-up (self-labeled "the collective") at her Manhattan apartment—
here, Rand would read new excerpts of her books, preaching radical individualism and a mistrust in centralised forms of governmental force (Curtis, 2011).

When Bill Clinton was elected president in 1992, Greenspan, by then the
chairman of the US Federal Reserve, encouraged him to cut public expenditure
to decrease interest rates and stimulate economic growth so that free markets
could transform the United States as opposed to political intervention (Curtis,
2011). Meanwhile, advocates of the service-based New Economy anticipated
"a world without business cycles, where technology, ever-increasing productivity, and globalization were to usher in unprecedented prosperity and unre-
lenting expansion" (Fisher & Downey, 2006, 1). Here, integrated circuits were
believed to hold the power for harnessing digital realms of production. Labour
was also primed for transformation led by pioneering software start-up companies: when an "anti-authoritarian work mentality took root . . . it grew its
own rituals of open communication and self-direction, adopting new modes
and myths of independence along the way" (Ross, 2003, 9-10). Even critics of
the New Economy became swayed by its tempting utopian dreams (Gordon,
2000). Confidence surged with the swelling of stock share prices as Clinton and
Greenspan endorsed the arrival of perpetual prosperity (Greenspan & Wilcox,
1998; Blinder, 2000). But then the dotcom bubble burst and Internet companies everywhere collapsed.

Initially "driven by declining borrowing costs and rising corporate profits, the
stock market boom came unmoored from the real economy when it latched onto
the 'new economy' promised by Internet-based companies" (Srnicek, 2017, 21).
In December 2000, the waning productivity of dotcom companies caused their
NASDAQ evaluations on Wall Street to halve (Mann & Luo, 2010). As the dust
settled, a few companies, like Google and Amazon, appeared to have survived
the wreckage and they went on to carve out business models across the infrastructure of the Internet, which became increasingly commercialised and priva-
tised. As Barbrook and Cameron predicted (1996), the Internet evolved into a
mixed economy with the creative and antagonistic hybrid of state intervention,

capitalist-corporate entrepreneurship, and DIY (do it yourself) culture initiatives. But, perhaps counterintuitively, the 2001 'tech wreck' was not the death of the Californian Ideology. Instead, the doctrine has only matured with the "colonisation of the Net by corporate behemoths and the exposure of their collaboration with the USA's spy agencies . . . [so that] its analysis has never been more relevant" (Barbrook, 2015, 8). In the process, cyberlibertarianism has become an unhappy coalescence of fundamentally contradictory tenets. The introduction of blockchain technology (a product of the growing sophistication of cryptography) is, for the most part, an extension of these ideas. The prehistory of Bitcoin, as the first successful cryptocurrency, is therefore littered with motives to redistribute power through the medium of technology (see Brunton, 2019).

A Genealogy of Cryptocurrencies

Unlike the bastions of technology start-ups who operated in the spotlight of the global stock markets, most cypherpunks attempted to fulfil their own strand of cyberlibertarian dreams in the shadows. By the 1990s the cypherpunk community had already made significant contributions to online privacy, yet some turned their attention to something they saw as more socioeconomically pressing and potentially emancipating: the concept of digital money. To them the economic infrastructures being proposed for the Internet looked as though they would systematically reveal an "individual's life-style habits, whereabouts, and associations from data collected in ordinary consumer transactions" (Chaum, 1985). This sent "chills up Cypherpink spines" (Levy, 1993). David Chaum was a strong advocate for privacy and a pioneer in the field of digital money in a time where few took him seriously (Levy, 1994). He first conceptualised ecash in 1983 with a white paper on untreatable payments (Chaum, 1983) and later realised it in 1990 as the corporation DigiCash, which offered a cryptographic form of digital money harnessing public-key cryptography. However, these digital signatures were still signed on servers held by Chaum's company and the platform as a whole was dependent on his firm's success.

By 1996 other forms of digital cash had sprung up—Cybercash, NetBill, First Virtual, and Mondex to name but a few (Kienzle & Perrig, 1996)—challenging Chaum's leading position on what looked like the beginnings of a monetary revolution. He pitched his idea to government officials, central bankers, commercial bankers, technology leaders, and financial policy makers with the idea of selling licenses for the privilege of using his new monetary system that enhanced transaction privacy and reduced intermediary costs (Vigna & Casey, 2015). Many were more than interested: the Dutch government signed a contract to use the system for toll-road payments; Deutsche Bank, Advance Bank of

Australia, Credit Suisse, and Sumitomo obtained licenses; Microsoft and Visa took an interest and began collaborating with Chaum; and Credit Suisse First Boston gave Chaum's team a lucrative space in its Manhattan offices (Vigna & Casey, 2015). Here, the vision of 'hacker money' was already being remoulded to fit the corporate world. Eventually, though, interest subsided and the dreams of a new form of Internet money died away, leaving room for the dated payment infrastructure of credit cards, designed in the 1950s, to be "bolted onto that of the Internet" (Vigna & Casey, 2015, 57).

The rest of the cypherpunk community were not wholly disappointed with the failure of DigiCash, as many disapproved of the risk associated with trusting a central organisation (Chaum's company) to confirm every digital signature needed to authorise transactions. This was the very thing public-key cryptography was designed to eliminate. The criticisms of centralisation proved valid when DigiCash, along with all of its tokens, disappeared after the company filed for bankruptcy in 1998 (Popper, 2015a; De Filippi & Wright, 2018). Elsewhere, others were already designing systems that did not rely on a central point of corruption or failure. Partly inspired by Chaum's work (see Klein, 2019), Stuart Haber and W. Scott Stornetta (1991) devised a method for chaining and time-stamping hashes together to form an immutable record prohibiting the modification of digital documents. This might well be the first example of a 'blockchain,' but the authors admit they overlooked its use for running a monetary protocol (Klein, 2019). Meanwhile, others were beginning to aggregate cryptographic techniques to create more distributed *financial* architectures.

In 1997 Adam Back, a British cryptographer, proposed a digital currency called hashcash based on an early form of proof-of-work (see Chapter 1). This pioneering cryptographic currency was designed to make denial of service (DoS) attacks on Internet resources like email uneconomical by attaching a currency to outgoing emails so that sending them would incur a small cost (Back, 2002).[7] In doing so, Back solved an issue that had always haunted conceived modes of digital decentralised money: the double spend problem. Digital data not protected or authorised by centralised institutions carries the danger of being infinitely copyable: a characteristic that would make currency valueless by disintegrating the networks of trust and practice around it (see Chapter 2). With hashcash, however, users would no longer be able to 'copy and paste' individual digital units of currency (spending them more than once) because there would be a cost to their production (Back, 2002). An adaptation of this cryptographic proof-of-work system, based on expending (electrical) energy on a hash function, is what the game-theoretical structure of Bitcoin mining uses today in order to secure the protocol, administrate transactions, negate double spending, and mint new coins (see Chapter 6).

Although hashcash eliminated the need for a central institution to authorise transactions, its tokens could only be spent once; to spend was to simultaneously destroy. But storing and re-spending currencies has long been a quality of money's long and intricate history (see Simmel, 1900; Davies, 1994; Weatherford, 1997; Graeber, 2011). In 1998 Wei Dai, a computer engineer and cypherpunk, conceptualised b-money to counter this flaw: a digital currency that could be reused and controlled through a shared ledger to publicly broadcast transactions to the rest of the network (Dai, 1998). That same year Nick Szabo (2008), a computer scientist and cryptographer, conceptualised bit gold: a digital currency utilising unforgeable chains, which contained public keys, timestamps, and digital signatures to form a proof-of-work function that could support the transfer of digital tokens. These tokens, unlike hashcash, were also designed to hold value due to their programmed scarcity. Six years later, in 2004, Hal Finney, a cypherpunk who had worked with Phil Zimmermann on PGP Corp and would later become the first collaborator with Satoshi Nakamoto, developed a system called reusable proof-of-work (RPOW). This software administered digital tokens combining many of the cryptographic developments above, allowing them to be owned and traded like money (Finney, 2004). "All of this—the good, the bad and the ugly of the Cypherpunk's idea bank—would go into the intellectual soup from which bitcoin would emerge" (Vigna & Casey, 2015, 51).

Building Decentralised Utopias

Satoshi Nakamoto (2008) created the Bitcoin protocol as a monetarist mechanism for dissolving the financial/monetary power held by both commercial and central banks, instead offering a codified, non-hierarchal architecture bypassing these centralised institutions altogether. In the same move, this process of algorithmic decentralisation could supposedly deterritorialise money by obliterating the financial borders of nation-states with the unrestricted online flow of value (Carmona, 2015; Bashir et al., 2016; Goodman, 2017; Yates, 2017). Algorithmic decentralists, although never using these terms, assert this is precisely achievable because the money/space of blockchain-based cryptocurrencies is enforced by their code/space and vice versa. In other words, the replication and dislocation of connected blockchain nodes (code/space) administer value-carrying units detached from financial firms and governments (money/space). Simultaneously, the economic frameworks and incentives of cryptocurrencies (money/space) encourage users to sustain their peer-to-peer software architectures (code/space). Thus a unique money/code/space is generated.

Harnessing a DIY philosophy, it is no surprise that the advent of cryptocurrencies has become an extension of the bottom-up narrative of re-empowering
citizens. They are an attempt to democratise money (and other things) through
the programming of a fairer political economy: one based on the limited
'untouchable' supply of a digital currency controlled by a network playing by
the rules of an algorithmic protocol. In other words, blockchains are a means for
realising decentralised utopias; their "dreamers are willing a future into being
with their imaginations" (Swartz, 2017, 83).

In *Spaces of Hope*, David Harvey (2000) describes how globalisation (and
its affiliation with neoliberalism) was approached uncritically in the 1980s and
1990s so that it became promoted as a virtue without a thorough examination
of its contradictions. Today, the same is befalling the term 'decentralisation.'
Consequently, and given the gravitas now attached to blockchains for disrupting
and decentralising world economies, greater critical analysis is of the essence.
I have so far demonstrated how cryptographers *envisioned* and *built* new digital spaces to 'retreat into.' I now turn to delineate the dislocations between this
rhetoric and practice.

Harvey explains how traditional architects pursue "utopian ideals" (200) by
mobilising "an intense imaginary of some alternative world (both physical and
social)" (164) in their designs before attempting to make them 'concrete' spatial realities. Yet there is always an inevitable slippage between imagined worlds
and their application. Moreover, subsequent appropriations of the built environment transform it: "[n]o architect can predict the result. No architecture is
free of its context. Architecture is an event par excellence in the sense that it
is a making or a becoming that exceeds the maker's control" (Karatani, 1995,
xxxviii). This effect is well known in studies of infrastructure: systems are not
static but mutate with cultural-economic practice (Bowker & Star, 1999; von
Schnitzler, 2008; Anand, 2011; Larkin, 2013; Fisch, 2013). Digital architects
(programmers) now play a role just as important as their more time-honoured
cousins in creating space (Kitchin & Dodge, 2011).[8] With this in mind, the same
permutations between imagined and built architectural space also apply to the
digital (see Nagy & Neff, 2015).

Although the motives behind algorithmic decentralisation are often admirable, the term tends to embody an underlying fallacy: decentralist imaginaries
assume the eradication of hierarchy and the dissolution of power. Jo Freeman
(2003), on the other hand, explains how utopian ideas of structurelessness are
"organizationally impossible." For cryptocurrencies, such futility materialises on
two levels: its own internal governance mechanisms and its exposure to wider
'free market' forces. In terms of governance, Bitcoin is constructed through an
open source software model that espouses a rhetoric of equal power between its
builders (Tkacz, 2015). Yet, this symmetry is an illusion:

> Contrary to what we would like to believe, there is no such thing as a structureless group. Any group of people of whatever nature that comes together for any length of time for any purpose will inevitably structure itself in some fashion. . . . The very fact that we are individuals, with different talents, predispositions, and backgrounds makes this inevitable. (Freeman, 2003)[9]

Consequently, grand ideas of radical structurelessness, in any form (decentralised or otherwise), are fundamentally unfeasible. This argument finds traction in the Bitcoin development process (see Chapter 5).

The second actualisation of uneven control occurs through the economic processes of capitalism: the "materialization of freemarket utopianism requires that the process come[s] to ground someplace, that it construct[s] some sort of space within which it can function. How it gets framed spatially and how it produces space become critical facets of its tangible realization" (Harvey, 2000, 177). This process is the Achilles heel of decentralist utopias because free market forces of capitalism are geared towards centralising and dominating economic practices through private obligatory passage points (like Google or Amazon) whose controllers pursue the (over)accumulation of wealth. In this sense, ideologies of decentralisation often "preserve highly centralised power . . . behind a veneer of individual liberty and freedom" (Harvey, 2015, 142; see also Herian, 2018). Consequently, blockchain technology does not fix capitalism by putting an end to uneven geographical development (see Chapter 7 and Chapter 8). After all, "'laissez faire' philosophy did not prevent the economically powerful from establishing control over wages, prices, and distribution of goods; it only prevented the government from doing so. Thus structurelessness becomes a way of masking power" (Freeman, 2003). This dislocation between imaginary and practice, Freeman asserts, is the "tyranny of structurelessness" (Freeman, 2003).

The Politics of Bitcoin

Before continuing, it is useful to take a step back and deviate slightly from the narrative of cypherpunk ideologies. Although I have concentrated on the dominant strand of political discourse surrounding developments of digital cryptography and the prehistory of cryptocurrencies, it is pertinent to remember there is always a multiplication of interests and intentions. In doing so, I start to revise David Golumbia's (2015, 2016b) account of Bitcoin as utterly symptomatic and systematic of political-economic right-wing extremism, which, at times, stands as a bitingly eloquent critique but, at others, starts to wander down the path of reductivism. Golumbia's argument is that libertarian ideologies fuelled Bitcoin's development, meaning that the protocol by its very design (a fixed monetary supply, a decentralised consensus system for determining currency ownership, and a pseudonymous transaction ledger) embodies far-right monetarist thinking. In other words, the protocol reflects the assumptions of Milton Friedman (1962, 1993) and the Chicago school of economic theory, which champions gold-backed currency, distrusts inflation, and blames central banks for crises—sometimes to the point of conspiracy theories (Golumbia, 2016b). It is certainly true these tropes helped give rise to Bitcoin but Golumbia also claims all who use it ultimately, and often unwittingly, propagate this politics. This is where I advise caution because there is an increasing pluralism and contention throughout Bitcoin/blockchain communities encapsulating a myriad of stakeholders (see Maurer et al., 2013; Lustig & Nardi, 2015; Dodd, 2018; Dallyn, 2017; Dovey, 2018; DuPont, 2019).

I echo that libertarianism and right-wing monetary policy is (currently) buried into the (original) political architecture of the Bitcoin code and that the protocol will most likely, on some level, continue to reflect this form of politics (in terms of its fixed supply, for example). But early ideological intent should never be extrapolated into permanent, sweeping, or monolithic generalisations of the protocol's future. Creators cannot wholly control their creations. Many early Internet pioneers, for example, adopted fringe politics and saw the TCP/IP protocol as a vehicle for bypassing centralised powers (Abbate, 1999; Galloway, 2004). However, it has since been adopted by a myriad of users and its applications have become incredibly plethoric. The anthropological work of Daniel Miller and Don Slater (2000), examining the Internet in Trinidad, demonstrates how cultural practices across digital networks are contingent and contradictory. If Golumbia's critique is to be acquiesced, then, it must account for how infrastructural politics become wrapped up with a storm of other political intentions over time that can redirect their overall trajectories.

As Nigel Dodd (2018) reflects, Bitcoin "can be many things politically" (6). In making this point, Dodd references Bill Maurer et al. (2013) who explain: "[i]n the world of Bitcoin there are goldbugs, hippies, anarchists, cyberpunks, cryptographers, payment systems experts, currency activists, commodity traders, and the curious" (2). In some cases Bitcoin has even been "presented as a key ingredient in the development of alternative anti-capitalist systems" to create a "currency of the commons" (O'Dwyer, 2014). There is clearly diversity, then, in the politics of Bitcoin.

More prolifically, spinoff blockchains with different codified rules have been imagined for delivering alternative monetary policies to Bitcoin (O'Dwyer, 2015b; Massumi, 2018). While Golumbia does not extend his critique to blockchains as a whole, it is worth noting these architectures can be as much a vision for socialists as they can for right-wing extremists (Huckle & Wright, 2016;

White, 2017). David Bollier (2015) argues, "[b]lockchain technology represents an advance over many of the corruptible institutional systems that we labor under today by providing less-corruptible algorithmic ways to manage interactions within a group." In this sense, the promises of blockchain automation and decentralisation resonate with ideas of commoning that may devolve dominant means of production in capitalist societies.

Algorithmic decentralisation, then, spans the left-right political spectrum (De Filippi & Loveluck, 2016). In reality, however, commons-based projections struggle to escape the grip of capitalism so that blockchains too often fit within Golumbia's rightist framework. After all, they are usually "based on individual sovereignty, private property, rent-seeking and the free market" (O'Dwyer, 2014). Specifically, "Bitcoin is situated in scarcity and property relations that are anathema to the commons" (O'Dwyer, 2014). So while multiplicity certainly exists, the dominant strand of Bitcoin politics is indeed of the right.

The same can be said for the majority of subsequent blockchain projects: "[i]f it is possible . . . to expand cryptocurrencies beyond the conventional, individual, market-fundamentalist, transaction-based functions of money, this is something that is *yet to be invented* and will require a great deal of craftiness" (Massumi, 2018, 90).

> The postblockchain cryptocurrency digital-platform route offers many avenues of response to the capitalist market, but the models now existing or under development so far are stuck in a game of whack-a-mole with it. With every blow against it in one place, the familiar myopic face of one of its constitutive principles *pops up somewhere else*. (Massumi, 2018, 110)

In practice, then, ambitious and experimental projects "often fail to break with the current financial paradigm" (Lotti, 2016, 105). Indeed, many enterprises seek to strengthen the existing system by enhancing economic efficiencies (Swartz, 2017). However, at the same time, as start-up companies become ever more embedded in political-economic space, practices of entrepreneurialism tend to water down the more radical ideas (see Chapter 7 and Chapter 8). In other words, there is more nuance to the politics of Bitcoin and its successors than right-wing *extremism* can account for.

In making this claim, it is important to remember that power is exercised not only by Bitcoin itself but by actors that operate through it. Protocols evolve so they never entirely settle in the forms first envisioned on paper. But the ideologies driving software's conception remain extremely important: while a multiplicity of ideologies surrounding algorithmic decentralisation exists, quite evidently there is a prominent ideological seam of (cyber)libertarianism running through them. So while it is important to keep an eye on Golumbia's warning of entrenched right-wing extremism, the politics of architectures are always open to mutation: while the Internet still holds some of the characteristics it was originally championed to contain (like open flows of information), it has evolved to encapsulate polarising others (like enclosed data silos). Political infrastructures in this light become increasingly multifaceted (and often contradictory) with their maturation and vulnerability to subversion (von Schnitzler, 2008; Anand, 2011; Smith, 2014). This has implications for the often presupposed dualism of centralisation and decentralisation. For instance, in the 1990s, Japanese rail networks largely replaced their Centralised Traffic Control (CTC) with the Autonomous Decentralised Transport Operation Control System (ATOS), combining "advanced information technology and communications with the conventional commuter train apparatus to transform the commuter train network into a type of 'smart' infrastructure" (Fisch, 2013, 322). But this move

> cannot be read simply as the story of a historical shift from a rigid centralized system to a flexible decentralized one. In reality, the complexity and density of traffic on main lines in Tokyo prevented train operators from implementing an absolute centralized control under the CTC, whereas ATOS . . . allows for greater centralization of command than the centralized system ever did. In other words, the centralized system was in some ways very decentralized, while the decentralized system can be extremely centralized. (Fisch, 2013, 332)

Similarly, the developments of cryptocurrency, and blockchain technology as a whole, are expanding the reach of algorithmic decentralisation so that its geographies of practice are becoming many and varied, and its inherent contradictions ever more problematic.

Conclusion

This chapter demonstrated many of the ideological forces that led to the development of cryptocurrencies and blockchains but also left room for the current and future splintering of divergent stakeholders. What is certainly evident is that computer scientists have now stepped up into positions of authority when it comes to building the narratives and architectures of money and finance. I have started to unpack the cultural-political undertones that permeate online spaces of collaboration and their relationship with governance in terms of Bitcoin and wider notions of algorithmic decentralisation via blockchains. But while the concept has strong roots, maintaining a cypherpunk/libertarian bent, algorithmic decentralisation has simultaneously become absorbed into a plethora of less radical political frameworks. At the same time, the process is (almost universally) brandished as an a priori 'social good.' Following the 2008 global financial crisis, on which many blame the recklessness of centralised banking, this is perhaps unsurprising. Yet the ideologies surrounding algorithmic decentralisation are no longer following a singular (cyberlibertarian) path—for example, the same banks and governments that have apparently abused their centralised positions of control are co-opting blockchains for their own benefits (see Chapter 8).

Among the multiplicity, architectures of algorithmic decentralisation now stand to transform the relationship between money, code, and space in intriguing ways. A look back at the maturation of the Internet gives fair warning not to succumb to sensationalist views of 'pure' decentralisation: networked culture of the TCP/IP protocol evolved into something quite different to what its builders first imagined. A similar fate seems to be befalling Bitcoin and blockchain technology. The following chapters expand on the pluralism and paradoxical nature of blockchains, paying close attention to different forms of (de)centralisation.

5

Programming Politics

Introduction

This chapter is reserved for understanding the non-provincial mode of governance offered by Bitcoin in place of the monetary policy of central banks: codified rules created under an open source software model. In doing so, it further
unpacks Bitcoin's money/code/space by examining geographies of production and continues to (re)introduce discussions of centrality and control into
the debate. Bitcoin is upheld as a distributed protocol cultivated and sustained
through open source software practices that supposedly flatten and distribute
power between contributors. Bitcoin's maintenance mechanisms are often said
to be transparent and democratic, as anyone (with programming skills) can contribute to the development of its code (van Wirdum, 2014; Zerlan, 2014; Metz,
2015; Jeftovic, 2017). Some commentators extrapolate this assertion further by
claiming centralised control is systematically eradicated from the production
process (van Valkenburgh, 2017; Gatecoin, 2017). This promotes a techno-
decentralist ideology: espousing an 'egalitarian' and 'non-hierarchal' software
mechanism and technological catalyst for creating fairer economies.

Consequently, blockchains are largely presented as dehumanised machine-
systems where the mathematics of computer code can coordinate people without
oversight from them. The perceived absence of coercion from humans is seen as a
boon by many proponents but also raises questions associated with the threat of
algocracy: "a situation in which algorithm-based systems structure and constrain
the opportunities for human participation in, and comprehension of, public
decision-making" (Danaher, 2016, 246). This raises further questions regarding
human agency. How can the Bitcoin protocol be governed by its users? Where
does power exist between humans and non-humans? Could algorithmic decentralisation spell a post-humanist world?[1] It is the point of this chapter to answer
these questions by tracing empirically the governance structure(s) of Bitcoin.
In response to the hopes and fears surrounding automation, I demonstrate how

Money Code Space. Jack Parkin, Oxford University Press (2020). © Oxford University Press.
DOI: 10.1093/oso/9780197515075.001.0001.

Bitcoin's production actually operates through strict authoritative channels. In fact, discontinuities between different levels of user engagement "have structuring effects on Bitcoin's distributed trust" (Mallard et al., 2014, 4). Such analysis shows how Bitcoin is not a radically autonomous system but is assembled and maintained via human discretion.

Methodologically, the chapter involves tracing connections between the actors of online communities that facilitate Bitcoin's governance. Follow the thing work is often used to uncover the modes of production that bring commodities into being, which can involve a great deal of travelling. Ian Cook and Michelle Harrison (2007), for example, have previously followed hot pepper sauce backwards through its supply chain from table to farm, journeying to a factory in a Trelawny coastal town and the small agricultural village of Gaythorne, Jamaica. Although the research exposed an abundance of political-economic relationships, Cook and Harrison 'got lost' in the logistical webs of global trade and were not able to make a direct, tangible connection between the hot sauce on the table and the peppers on the farm. Unlike traditional follow the thing work, however, I was able to 'teleport' straight to Bitcoin's 'production site' precisely because it is constructed at the online code repository website GitHub.[2] Empirical data is retrieved from a longitudinal study of GitHub practices where the Bitcoin source code is discussed, assembled, and maintained. This is complemented with an examination of protocol dynamics showcased by particular events that both reflect and direct these changes.

As an online collaboration of open source software, a swathe of historical and ongoing documentation is also readily available on sites like the Bitcoin Forum, the bitcoin-dev mailing list, Twitter, and Reddit. Heated debate is exercised in these digital arenas making them important sources for understanding how and why Bitcoin is evolving. They are used here to inform certain events in Bitcoin's code production process. Ultimately, this multi-layered method focuses on how human and machine labour is simultaneously dislocated and connected by processes of algorithmic decentralisation. The overall political framework for altering the Bitcoin code is described as senatorial governance: a (de)centralised model of bureaucratic parties who compete to change the monetary policy (codified rules) of the protocol.

Here, both human and machine agency are essential for suspending the Bitcoin blockchain into being and the relationship between these two entities correlates to power asymmetries across the network. A critical examination of Bitcoin's builders and maintainers reveals how 'centres' of control creep back into the 'distributed' network. These centres are a result of a human struggle to change the protocol rules and are operated by a select few stakeholders who wield considerable power over decision-making. Consequently, control is not distributed equally among its participants but is harnessed by key stakeholders who impose algorithmic rules upon the rest of its user base. Here, the technical parameters of Bitcoin are directly affected by the changing cultures, economies, and politics of its community.

I begin by detailing speculation over Satoshi Nakamoto's identity to unravel an important location of power within the Bitcoin developer community. The chapter then moves into a discussion of the production model in which Bitcoin rests: open source software. Empirical observations and case studies such as the block size debate (De Filippi & Loveluck, 2016) and the 2013 accidental hard fork (Musiani et al., 2018) are used to demonstrate how centralisation manifests in this mode of open source code development and how cultural, political, and economic practices affect the technical parameters of the Bitcoin blockchain. Subsequently, the chapter focuses on the governance model of GitHub and, more specifically, the Bitcoin code repository. Different forms of forking are discussed as political strategies for branching away from certain implementations of Bitcoin to create competing (de)centralised decision-making vehicles.

"The Hunt for Satoshi Nakamoto"

Debates over who and where Satoshi Nakamoto is have circumscribed Bitcoin throughout its short history. Some reports, diving into the forensics of linguistic and coding grammar as well as the political ideologies and skill sets of possible candidates, have pointed to Michael Clear (Davis, 2011), Neal King, Vladimir Oksman, and Charles Bry (Penenberg, 2011), Shinichi Mochizuki (Nelson, 2013; Oates, 2013), Nick Szabo (Frisby, 2014; Hajdarbegovic, 2014), Hal Finney (Greenberg, 2014), Michael Weber (Walker & Wile, 2014), and Donal O'Mahony and Michael Peirce (CoinDesk, 2016a). Such speculation is so embedded in Bitcoin culture that it even forms the basis of a fan fiction comic book narrative: "Bitcoin: The Hunt for Satoshi Nakamoto" (Preukschat et al., 2014). Incidentally, I was once sitting on a table with a renowned Bitcoin Core developer at the Silicon Valley Bitcoin Meet-up Group where this comic was being passed around before a presentation started. Inside, it overtly echoes the political ideologies of the cypherpunk-anarchist subculture that originally formed around cryptocurrencies (see Chapter 4). Mirroring the powerful early rhetoric found on the Bitcoin Forum, the comic glorifies Nakamoto to the point of deity.

The mystification of Satoshi Nakmoto's identity ties into a case study representing a degree of centrality in Bitcoin's mode of software governance. In 2016, Craig Wright, an Australian computer scientist and businessman, publicly 'revealed' himself as Satoshi Nakamoto (Bustillos, 2015) after two proposals, made in *WIRED Magazine* (Greenberg & Branwen, 2015) and Gizmodo (Biddle & Cush, 2015), previously highlighted him as the probable creator of Bitcoin. Wright later 'proved' this to the BBC, *The Economist*, and *GQ Magazine* by cryptographically signing a mined block on the Bitcoin blockchain—something 'only Nakamoto' would have the private key for (BBC, 2016; The Economist, 2016; GQ Magazine, 2016). Cryptographers in the Bitcoin community immediately debunked his claim via channels such as Twitter and Reddit (see Figure 5.1). The block Wright signed was found to have been publicly done so by Nakamoto years earlier and his refusal to sign the genesis block—which many cryptographers attest is the only foolproof way someone can prove themselves Bitcoin's creator—suggested a fraudulent declaration.[3] Andrew O'Hagan (2016), who spent six months with Wright during the ordeal, later concluded in *The London Review of Books* that his assertions were inconclusive and unlikely.[4]

When Wright made his claim, many turned to industry leaders respected by the wider Bitcoin community for confirmation. Among these key figures were Bitcoin Core developers who are responsible for updating and maintaining the Bitcoin code that Satoshi Nakamoto left behind (see Chapter 1). During the incident, Gavin Andresen—who by then had passed on his Lead Developer role to Wladimir van der Laan but remained a contributor to the Bitcoin project—flew

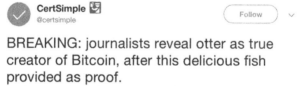

BREAKING: journalists reveal otter as true creator of Bitcoin, after this delicious fish provided as proof.

1:17 PM - 2 May 2016

♡ 4   ↻ 328   ♥ 316   ✉

Figure 5.1 A humorous tweet alluding to Craig Wright's lack of cryptographic proof by which he claimed to be Satoshi Nakamoto.

to London as a 'trusted' and 'revered' certifier of the 'proof' Wright was providing. When Andresen publicly supported Wright's claim on a personal blog post, many Core developers questioned the authenticity of Andresen's declaration. In fear that his online accounts through which he accredited Wright may have been hacked or otherwise compromised, a small group of Core developers chose to revoke Andresen's commit control on GitHub (his ability to make changes to the Bitcoin Core code). This was a precautionary measure, having themselves concluded Wright's 'evidence' was not sufficient to confirm he was Satoshi Nakamoto.

As the project owner, Wladimir van der Laan was the one to pull the plug on Andresen. This clearly demonstrates how a singular authority and centre of power exists within communities of open source GitHub developers. While anyone can voice their opinion through consensual dialogue, it is the Lead Developer who has overruling control both over code changes and over the administrative privileges of other developers. This is somewhat necessary to prevent programmers (miscreants or otherwise) altering the Bitcoin Core source code whenever, and however, they want to—similarly, moderators exist in the open, collaborative model of Wikipedia to prevent people changing content without review, thus maintaining a high standard of contribution (Tkacz, 2015). In the process, however, the imaginary of Bitcoin as a tool for utterly breaking down centralised modes of governance, when regulating money, falls short in practice.

There have been three Lead Developers in the historical advancement of Bitcoin Core's code on GitHub: Satoshi Nakamoto (location unknown), Gavin Andresen (United States), and currently Wladimir van der Laan (Netherlands). Each has had the position passed on to them by the last—Andresen stepping down on the 8th April 2014. Wladimir van der Laan adopts a philosophy 'mirroring' that of blockchain models in that he leads via 'consensus': requiring a certain level of agreement between Bitcoin Core developers before he confirms changes to the source code. If a proposal to change the Bitcoin Core software proves contentious then it is rejected and the status quo is maintained. Before I unpack this further, open source software is problematised as a supposed mechanism for distributed code governance.

Organising Open Source Software

Like all software Bitcoin is a product of labour. The organisation of this work follows an open source model, which means any programmer on a global scale can contribute to the development of the project (Shrestha et al., 2013). The source code is publicly available to copy, modify, and distribute as others see fit (Deek & McHugh, 2008). Consequently, the popular imaginary of open source software is of an "egalitarian network of developers free of hierarchal organization and centralization of control" (Ducheneaut, 2005, 324). It is supposed to promote a bazaar model (Raymond, 2001), purposefully designed to increase the robustness of code through an outsourcing of brains (DiBona et al., 1999).

The success of Bitcoin has led to a cascade of copycat cryptocurrencies called "altcoins" (alternative coins). Because Bitcoin development follows an open source model, its source code is readily available online and can be copy and pasted onto different machines to form new cryptocurrencies. Each new ledger harnesses its own vision of how the parameters of digital currencies should be programmed and so blockchains are being (re)designed to cater for a plethora of worldviews (see Appendix 13). Dissent, then, comes by *forking* away from Bitcoin, allowing disenfranchised members of the community to break away, taking the source code (unowned intellectual property) with them to create competing organisations. This process is the bedrock of open source politics (Tkacz, 2015). It is referred to here as *organisational* forking to highlight the cultivation of projects existing on different networks, often sporting alternative rules (see Table 5.1 for a typology of forks).

Nathanial Tkacz (2015), examining organisational structures in *Wikipedia and the Politics of Openness*, explains how hierarchies of control are usually presented as a rhetorical antithesis to open models. Openness comes across as attractive and ambiguous in equal measure, appearing "seemingly without tension, without need of clarification or qualification" (13). Yet, contradictory to this imaginary, closed and ordered systems stay prevalent in their organisational mechanisms. While Wikipedia champions a benevolent guise of openness— aligned with the buzzwords of collaboration, decentralisation, participation, transparency, and spontaneity—its governance actually operates under precise structures: decisions are closed and voices are excluded through hierarchies that follow predetermined political and philosophical frames set out by policies and guidelines (Tkacz, 2015). In other words, patulous governance demands a degree of hierarchy for organising disparate actors and channelling decision-making.

Open source software development, in general, connects people widely separated by diverse geographies (Johnson, 2001). On a purely user basis, different studies have shown how developers using GitHub are "highly clustered and concentrated primarily in North America and Western and Northern Europe, though a substantial minority is present in other regions" (Takhteyev & Hills, 2010, 1). This pattern of cultural and spatial aggregation is similar for the Bitcoin GitHub repository: the majority of its contributors are (relatively) wealthy males. So although the openness of Bitcoin's source code allows people from all corners of the globe to participate, in practice, the governors of its code are

Table 5.1 **A typology of forks**

Organisational Forks

A product of new (competing) projects. The transparency of open source code allows people to copy it and start new ventures.

Operational Forks

A system of code management endemic to Git version control. Collaborating parties copy the code to their own machines and later push these alterations to the main repository.

Systematic Forks

A temporary split in consensus (competing blockchains) endemic to mining operations: two miners find a nonce at the same time and broadcast their block to the rest of the network simultaneously. This is not a system update and should be temporarily resolved by network mechanics (whichever side of the fork becomes the longest chain with the most proof-of-work wins).

Version Forks

A system update that changes network rules. These come in four types (see below).

User Activated Soft Fork	Miner Activated Soft Fork
Nodes upgrade en masse to start enforcing new rules initially compatible with the old rules. However, this cartel of nodes will begin rejecting blocks mined with old rules after a certain threshold of upgrades is reached.	Miners upgrade to start enforcing new rules initially compatible with the old rules. However, this group of miners will begin rejecting blocks mined with old rules after a certain threshold is reached.
User Activated Hard Fork	**Miner Activated Hard Fork**
Nodes upgrade en masse to start enforcing new rules incompatible with old rules. This group will immediately start rejecting blocks mined with old rules.	A set of miners upgrade and begin creating blocks with new rules incompatible with old rules. This group will immediately start rejecting blocks mined with old rules.

predominantly men situated in Western countries (during my fieldwork in the San Francisco Bay Area I would, from time to time, bump into famous Core developers). This raises questions around whether there is a particular bias surrounding Bitcoin's emancipatory vision (Lustig & Nardi, 2015; Bashir et al., 2016; Hütten & Thiemann, 2018).

Indeed, the ideals of technological utopianism have almost exclusively emanated from masculine voices (Segal, 1985):

> [W]hile notions of empowerment and self-determination are common amongst advocates, Bitcoin was never a project developed by the financially vulnerable or excluded. Instead, Bitcoin has been driven by a tech-savvy predominantly male elite, or, more generally, by groups otherwise understood as privileged, not marginalized (Hütten & Thiemann, 2018, 34).

There are certainly efforts to increase the inclusion of women in cryptocurrency discourse and design, but it seems "the nexus of radical politics, money, and emerging technology (all traditionally male domains) has produced a culture that has both ignored women and systematically excluded them" (DuPont, 2019, 13–14). Additionally, while the Bitcoin white paper has been translated into other languages, the maintenance of the Bitcoin source code is mainly done in English. There are, then, limiting social factors to the eclecticism of Bitcoin's code builders.[5]

The international pool of Bitcoin Core developers is often distracting for commentators who claim the geographical dispersion of contributors makes open source software a distributed model. This is a common misconception. The terms 'dispersed' and 'distributed' are not synonymous. In fact, the title of Lead Developer is an important indicator that modes of organisation in open source software development are fundamentally hierarchal. It was Satoshi Nakamoto who first provided access to Bitcoin for other programmers, created its GitHub repository, and later passed on the role of Lead Developer to Gavin Andresen. If Bitcoin's code/space and money/space are inextricably linked, the maintenance of monetary policy prescribed by the codified rules of the protocol is also subject to hierarchy.

As Nathanial Tkacz (2015) tested the claims of openness among the builders of Wikipedia, I here test the claims of decentralisation among the builders of Bitcoin. While the intentions of open source software are clear (see Appendix 14), its politics does not stop at ideological motivations but extends into, and is manifested by, its practices and governance structures. To repurpose a phrase from Tkacz, I now attempt to capture the organisational politics of Bitcoin and "rub these up against the language of openness[and distribution], revealing [their] tensions, contradictions, subjugations, invisibilities, and lines of force" (13). In other words, I ask: if Bitcoin is supposed to change the plumbing of finance, who are the plumbers and how do they operate? This mode of investigation continues to articulate Bitcoin's money/code/space and shed light on the monetary policy of a 'decentral bank.'

The Block Size Debate

Points of power positioned between the builders of the Bitcoin blockchain are rendered through hierarchal bottlenecks heavily wrapped up in forms of organisational centrality. As such, Bitcoin is caught uncomfortably between a growing and fracturing community who are beginning to tear the algorithmic protocol at its seams. The Lead Developer of Bitcoin Core acts as an obligatory passage point for Bitcoin's code governance by acting as a centre for decision-making. While anyone can voice their opinion through consensual dialogue, it is the Lead Developer who has overruling control over the Bitcoin Core code and the people who are able to contribute towards it. This is personified by the Bitcoin block size debate.

Scalability has been a concern for Bitcoin proponents from very early on in its development. The Bitcoin network was built to (theoretically) handle 7 transactions per second, whereas Visa, for example, processes around 1,677 per second with a maximum capability of 56,000 (Vermeulen, 2017). Many Bitcoiners have made propositions to increase the transaction rate by altering the technical parameters of the blockchain: expand the block size limit so more transactions can be fitted into every block.[6] But this has also came with considerable backlash from other members of the community for a number of reasons: one of these is big blocks discourage network decentralisation because they require more system resources (such as bandwidth) to mine, making it harder for small-scale miners to operate and easier for large-scale miners to achieve network dominance. For some, such disagreement between Core developers caused a degree of stagnation in Bitcoin development (Hearn, 2016a). An employer at the New York Bitcoin Center exemplified this to me in 2016: "Bitcoin has become really boring. It's like a civil war of Core developers, and none of those killer apps we were promised in 2014 are coming out."

For ex–core developer Mike Hearn (2015), the block size deadlock cuts deep: it not only represents a failure of dispute-settling within Bitcoin Core but also personifies the (coercive) centralisation of Bitcoin code maintenance.[7] He once stated: "when you boil away all the noise, there are only 5 people in the world who can make changes to the Bitcoin Core source code" (n.p.). These were, at the time, Gavin Andresen, Jeff Garzick, Wladimir van der Laan, Gregory Maxwell, and Pieter Wuille. Hearn argues that the "illogical" whims of van der Laan ultimately stifled resolution over issues like the block size debate. He notes Gavin Andresen was "a solid and experienced leader who [could] see the big picture" but never, in actual fact, wanted to be Lead Developer:

> So the first thing Gavin did was grant four other developers access to the code as well. These developers were chosen quickly in order to ensure

the project could easily continue if anything happened to him. They were, essentially, whoever was around and making themselves useful at the time. (Hearn, 2016a)

This demonstrates the closed system of governance from within which the code of a global distributed currency ledger is written: commit access is passed around within a tight clique of programmers with one central leader who wields ultimate control. The obligatory passage point of the Lead Developer acts like a knowledge funnel, allowing ideas from programmers to be channelled into discourse and actioned into code by a small circle of Core developers. Such centrality of decision-making later became clear when van der Laan's activity on the bitcoin-dev mailing list showed he favoured smaller blocks. In an interview with *CoinJournal* he stated:

> I mostly have a problem with proposals that bake in expected exponential bandwidth growth. I don't think it's realistic. If we've learned anything from the 2008 subprime bubble crisis it should be that nothing ever keeps growing exponentially, and assuming so can be hazardous. It reduces a complex geographical issue, the distribution of internet connectivity over the planet for a long time to come, to a simple function. (cited in Demartino, 2015)

Mike Hearn (2015) saw this argument as "illogical in the extreme: computer speeds have nothing to do with subprime lending practices. The financial crisis wasn't caused by exponential growth." He continues: "there cannot be any code added to a Core release without Wladimir being satisfied with it. And he believes that *any change to the block size at all* simply can't happen 'any time soon'" (Hearn, 2015). These tensions emanate from a "highly technocratic power structure" (De Filippi & Loveluck, 2016, 1) and start to show how the 'open' model of Bitcoin development cannot harmoniously cater for a multitude of outlooks. This lack of resolution is heavily wrapped up with the (socio)technical parameters of GitHub.

GitHub Version Control

Version control systems "are a category of software tools that help a software team manage changes to source code over time" (Atlassian, 2017; see Appendix 15). Git is now the most widely adopted form of version control for both closed and open source software development. The company GitHub has become a flagship for open source development and the world's largest host of source code (Gousios et al., 2014)—with 36 million users and 100 million repositories (GitHub, 2019a). GitHub was designed to foster a "developer-friendly environment integrating many functionalities, including wiki, issue tracking, and code review" (Thung et al., 2013, 323). It is, essentially, a "platform where [other] platforms are assembled and configured" (Mackenzie, 2018, 37).

Here, not all contributors are equal:

> Actions on code or associated with code include committing, forking and submitting a pull request. Project owners can make *commits*, i.e. changes to the code, by directly modifying the contents of code files. Developers without commit-rights to a project must fork a project, creating a personal copy of the code that they can change freely. They can then submit some or all of the changes to the original project by issuing a pull request. The project owner or another member with commit rights can then merge in their changes. (Dabbish et al., 2012, 1279)

Bitcoin Core exists on GitHub under an "organization" account where "[o]wners and administrators can manage member access to the organization's data and projects" (GitHub, 2019b). As of writing there have been 628 contributors to the Bitcoin project, all of whom can be considered Bitcoin Core developers. However, there are significant levels of contribution: 4,722 of the total 20,861 commits have been proposed by just 5 people. Furthermore, only a few have 'commit access' (the ability to accept changes to the source code proposed by other developers). "[S]ome developers—even among the 'core' team—are clearly 'more core' than others" (Musiani et al., 2018, 151).

Other contributors make changes by downloading copies, or forks, of the Bitcoin source code from GitHub onto their computers, which are said to be 'downstream' from the main, shared repository. These clones are referred to here as *operational* forks because they are a mechanism of open source software development that allow contributors to make their own edits to code independently of other developers who may also be working on the same issue simultaneously. Changes to Bitcoin's codified rules (monetary policy) must be made via Bitcoin Improvement Proposals (BIPs). These proposals can be written by anyone and raised with the Core developer community by posting them to the bitcoin-dev mailing list (bitcoin-dev-request@lists.linuxfoundation.org). If the proposal follows the correct guidelines and is worth further discussion it can be submitted as a pull request into the BIPs repository on GitHub where it is assigned with a number (https://github.com/bitcoin/bips).[8] A contributor may make a bug fix, for example, on their personal operational fork and push their local changes to the rest of the network for review.

New contributors are generally expected to test and review code to gain a reputation before they make pull requests (Song, 2017). Bitcoin Core program-mer Gregory Maxwell, for example, is revered in this community not just for his BIP contributions but for his many years of reviewing and testing (Song, 2017). While proposals are received based on merit as opposed to the identity of their proposers, abiding by standards of etiquette—that is, breaking down "changes into easy-to-review commits of less than 300 lines" and clearly explaining each alteration—help give audibility to particular voices (Song, 2017). The Bitcoin Core community, then, has its own informal hierarchies along with norms and rules of practice. Most important, there is clearly a more formal meritocracy here (Song, 2018): while changes can be constructed by anyone, they are con-stricted by only a few.

The 2013 Accidental Hard Fork

There is a mechanism in the Bitcoin Core governance structure that, on some level, takes power away from developers by making them serve the wider com-munity. As changes are made to the GitHub repository, via the organisational structure outlined earlier, the Bitcoin Core Lead Developer will periodically release a new version of the software, reflecting the decisions made, as an update available for download. It is then up to Bitcoin miners in the network to decide whether they wish to start running the new code: *version* forking onto the lat-est software or not. Consequently, version forks can be much 'stickier' than other types.

On the 12th March 2013, version 0.8 of Bitcoin Core was released. Shortly after, there was a discrepancy between miners over what the latest block number was: some miners were mining on top of block 225,450 and others were min-ing on top of block 225,451. On this occasion the shortest chain was not being eliminated and both sides of the fork continued to grow. In other words, there were two blockchain 'truths' about the state of the network and so consensus was not being reached among all miners. This situation can lead to a disagree-ment over who owns any coins sent after the fork because different transactions will be mined into the competing blockchains. If a fork of this nature were not fixed "there would essentially be two conflicting Bitcoin networks, which would be likely to result in no one trusting either of them, or Bitcoin itself" (Popper, 2015a, 193).[9]

The Core developers got wind of this event and a race to solve the problem began. Bitcoin's Lead Developer at the time, Gavin Andresen, quickly con-sulted Pieter Wullie, Jeff Garzick, and Gregory Maxwell (Vigna & Casey, 2015). It became clear the reconstituted database of version 0.8 was not reconciling with the database records of version 0.7 (Vigna & Casey, 2015). As such, version 0.8 was accepting blocks "not considered legitimate by the old software and the computers still running it" (Popper, 2015, 193). If both versions had been compatible then miners using each could have continued to work somewhat harmoniously: when a miner running version 0.8, for example, mined a block and broadcast it to the network, the version 0.7 nodes would have accepted it as legitimate, whereas the 0.8 nodes would start ignoring any blocks created by the 0.7 miners only once a certain threshold of miners had upgraded. This form of version forking is described as *soft* because, while the upgraded software might provide added features, its new rules are backward-compatible with the rules of the previous version—0.7 miners can come slowly over to the new software without causing a permanent split in the network or the majority of miners can decide to stick with the old rules by staying on 0.7. In other words, the miners can actively vote on soft version forks with their mining power by upgrading to the new software or not.

In this circumstance, however, the 0.7 nodes began rejecting the blocks from the miners who had switched over to the 0.8 version because they were not playing by the original codified rules. This is known as a *hard* fork because two competing blockchains are formed instantaneously (see Figure 5.2).[10] It was decided by the Core developers first to the scene that one of the versions must be accepted as the true blockchain and all miners must be persuaded to move to that chain. Luckily for them, many miners do not operate individually but gather their resources together through mining pools (see Chapter 1).

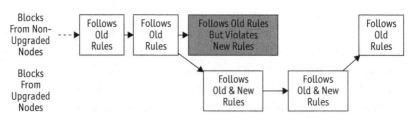

A Soft Fork: Blocks Violating New Rules Are Made Stale By The Upgraded Mining Majority

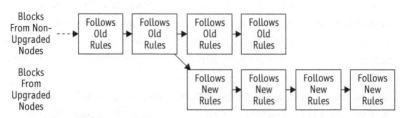

A Hard Fork: Non-Upgraded Nodes Reject The New Rules, Diverging The Chain

Figure 5.2 Soft Fork and Hard Fork (sources: Investopedia, 2018a, 2018b).

One of the reasons Mike Hearn turned his back on Bitcoin Core in 2015 was the sheer power mining pool operators had managed to amass, pointing to a conference called "Scaling Bitcoin" in Hong Kong where a handful of people sitting on a single stage allegedly controlled 95% of the network mining power. Because miners not only secure the network but vote on version forks with their power, Hearn referred to this as centralisation of control—the majority of Bitcoiners have to ride along and accept the decisions made for them by these mining pool giants who act as obligatory passage points for many individual miners.

When version 0.7 and 0.8 fell out of sync in 2013 the Core developers encouraged mining pools to revert back to the 0.7 client in order to fix the problem. The largest mining pools had been the first to switch to the new software and they agreed to follow these orders, giving up any block rewards already mined on the version 0.8 side of the fork. However, because the Bitcoin exchange rate floats on the market, its value is largely derived from trust in the protocol (demand based on buy and sell orders) so the losses could have been "much greater if the entire Bitcoin network lost the confidence of users" (Popper, 2015, 194). This game-theoretical market mechanism is designed to keep all stakeholders interested in perpetuating the blockchain's functional existence to the benefit of everyone else involved. But the 2013 hard fork also shows how the coordination of decision-making, particularly in a time of crisis, is much better orchestrated when channelled through a somewhat centralised group of programmers and mining pool operators (see also Musiani et al., 2018).

Segregated Witness

The obligatory passage point of Vladimir van der Laan as Lead Developer is internal to the Bitcoin Core client built on GitHub. However, other clients can be constructed to connect to the Bitcoin network: as long as they are compatible with other nodes they will not fork and can interact with the same blockchain. Here, different clients "co-exist on the same Bitcoin peer-to-peer network and are therefore part of the same monetary system" (DuPont, 2019, 45–46). Yet new clients can also be introduced to connect to the network for different technical and political reasons.

Alternative clients are usually used for technical purposes: like creating application programming interfaces (bitcoin) or making nodes lightweight in terms of data size (MultiBit).[11] However, new clients can also be used as a political tool by providing a platform for generating an intentional version fork: 'hijacking' part of the network from Bitcoin Core and redirecting it onto a new chain that follows different rules. This subverts the 'singular' obligatory passage point of the Bitcoin Core Lead Developer by creating alternative bottlenecks of code production. Put simply, because Bitcoin is an open network, anyone can create their own clients to interact with it as long as they follow the rules of other nodes. If clients join the network with new rules, they will be dislocated from those following the old ones. They can convince all others to join that chain and thus maintain one singular view of reality or, failing this, partition off to create a separate one. In other words, new clients can offer different obligatory passage points for changing the monetary policy of Bitcoin.

To achieve this soft and hard version forks require activation from miners or users (see Table 5.1). The 2013 split was intended to be a 'miner activated soft fork' where miners running the new software stayed compatible with old versions so they could adopt (and enforce) the new rules incrementally. A common activation method requires miners to signal for readiness by changing metadata in the version field of their mined block (header).[12] This data will have a predetermined meaning so signalling represents support for a certain change. For the new rules to be implemented, the network usually requires a miner signalling threshold of 95% to activate the new software. In March 2013, however, the Core developers accidentally made the new software rules incompatible with previous versions and so the upgrade became a 'miner activated hard fork:' mining power was immediately bifurcated between two chains with incompatible sets of rules (see Figure 5.2).

User activation is another political vehicle in Bitcoin's maintenance that can wrench control away from miners somewhat. A 'user activated soft fork' is a mechanism "that plans to take power of decision away from the miners and into the hands of the market" (Richards, 2017). The goal is to "pressure change through the use of nodes" (Richards, 2017). This works because anyone (not just miners) can download Bitcoin software and start running nodes that reflect certain rules. If enough people do this, they can encourage miners to come over to those rules for financial reasons: user activity on a new chain will attract miners because of the available transaction fees and liquidity on associated exchanges (i.e., there are more people to charge to use the network and sell coin rewards to).

The most famous example of a user activated soft fork to date is the implementation of segregated witness (SegWit) under BIP 141 and its activation via BIP 148 and BIP 91. This alteration to the code was initially proposed by Peter Wiulle in 2015 to eradicate the bug of transaction malleability but later became wrapped up with the block size debate because it also reorganised and reduced transaction data, increasing the carrying capacity of blocks by 70%.[13] In February 2016, "several Bitcoin Core contributors, mining pool operators and other Bitcoin industry members met [in Hong Kong] to discuss the scaling issue" (van Wirdum, 2017a). This event became known as the 'Bitcoin

Roundtable Consensus' or 'Hong Kong Agreement' where a road map was set out for the initiation of SegWit via a *miner* activated soft fork.[14]

Despite this initial alliance, many of the mining pools later refused to signal for SegWit. One reason for this is that miners are not incentivised to upgrade to rules with larger block sizes. Smaller blocks encourage a bidding war between users who will pay greater transaction fees in order for their transactions to be included more quickly in the limited ledger space available (DuPont, 2019)—a case study for the misalignment of cryptoeconomic game theory and the best interest of users.[15] SegWit proponents needed a new activation method. An idea came in the form of a message in the bitcoin-dev mailing list (https://www.mail-archive.com/bitcoin-dev@lists.linuxfoundation.org/msg04703.html) and a post in the Bitcoin Forum (https://bitcointalk.org/index.php?topic=1805060.0) from the developer Shaolinfry who proposed a *user* activated soft fork. This mechanism involves a predetermined 'flag day' where Bitcoin nodes upgrade en masse to start reflecting new backward-compatible rules. If the cartel attracts enough miners to come on board, the soft fork activates and new nodes begin rejecting blocks created by miners not signalling for SegWit. The hope is that all miners and users of the old rules will come across to the new rules to create one monolithic chain. If not, a chain split occurs: two versions of the blockchain with different and thus competing cryptocurrencies.

UASF

BIP 148 was never merged into Bitcoin Core because the developers were worried about a potential hard fork. However, the user activated soft fork mechanism gained a lot of traction in the Bitcoin community: key figures would post photos of themselves wearing baseball caps sporting "UASF" to promote the idea. It snowballed into a popular political movement that stood for the resistance of everyday users against miner control. This is based on the premise that while miners are still needed to join the new chain for a user activated soft fork to work (the blockchain has to be mined into existence), they can be economically coerced into coming across to the version with the most market activity. The rule-changing cartel that encourages this is known as the 'economic majority' because the chain with the most transactions should be most attractive to miners. In this sense, it is not necessarily the greater number of nodes as a percentage that should win but the ones with the bulk of the market interacting with them. In theory, then, not all nodes upgrading to the new rules are equal in terms of their ability to encourage miners to follow suit.

When the Bitcoin blockchain forks, an exchange enforces a greater degree of power than an everyday user running a client node because they can choose whether to list a coin or not for their customers to utilise.[16] If a significant number of people use a particular exchange that has decided to adopt new rules there will be a higher demand for coins on that side of the fork, theoretically increasing their value. Consequently, centralised companies play a role in the survivability of forks, enabling or disabling usability and thereby promoting or demoting their legitimacy.

If enough node operators align, power is transferred to 'the market': "miners have many incentives to follow along. Not following along would make it difficult to sell coins . . . as the blocks would not be accepted by the economic majority. Essentially, miners would be producing an altcoin not recognised by users and exchanges, making them less useful and in lower demand" (UASF Working Group, 2017). The majority of network transactions are submitted by certain institutions, which makes them particularly important for achieving the economic majority. Here, companies achieve considerable market power because they act as obligatory passage points for accessing the Bitcoin protocol and thus carry the weight of their users' transactions while ultimately making decisions on their behalf (i.e., over which version forks to utilise).[17] Additionally, everyday users (people who access Bitcoin via an exchange) and users (people who operate nodes) are different entities. The first group is responsible for the vast majority of Bitcoin transactions, submitted by exchanges who possess the knowledge to run nodes. So user activated soft forks can be a misnomer: they still require miners to create the ledger, benefit from companies upgrading to reflect new rules, and are largely implemented by technology-savvy node operators as opposed to "the people."

Ultimately, achieving consensus around a fork requires a large amount of coordination. The cohesive demand for a node-initiated upgrade of network rules gathers momentum around Bitcoin meet-up groups, forums, blog posts, social networks, conferences, and company offices. Two months after the BIP 148 user activated soft fork proposal, an attempt was made by various stakeholders in the Bitcoin industry to agree on a similar fork before enforcing it. Labelled the 'New York Agreement,' it was designed to put an end to Bitcoin's block size debate. The meeting was orchestrated by venture capitalist Barry Silbert's Digital Currency Group and gathered 58 signatures from prominent exchanges, payment processors, wallet services, and mining pools. They all pledged to activate SegWit and subsequently increase the block size from 1MB to 2MB with a hard fork (the combined proposal was referred to as SegWit2x). The signatories accounted for 20.5 million user Bitcoin wallets, $5.1 billion USD worth of monthly on-chain transaction volume, and 83.28% of mining power running through their companies (Digital Currency Group, 2017).

"As a result, there were two approaches to activate the SegWit update–the BIP 148 Group, which ignored miners, and the second group, which counted on miners" (Buy Bitcoins Worldwide, 2020). The first was a catalyst for the second:

> There was a real threat that the network would split, causing chaos. Fortunately, Bitcoin mining software developer James Hilliard came to the rescue. He initiated BIP 91, which attempted to conciliate the two groups and focus on the key target that they both had in common: the activation of SegWit. (Buy Bitcoins Worldwide, 2020).

Neither approach was orchestrated by Bitcoin Core. Instead, clients were built by alternative groups who led the charge and tried to convince others to run their software thus enforcing SegWit. Thanks to compromise from both groups, SegWit activated on the 24th August 2017. The subsequent hard fork (SegWit2x) was later cancelled due to a lack of consensus. In February 2018, Bitcoin Core released software with full SegWit support and these nodes now account for 97.5% of the network.

While user activated soft forks may present a means for users to alter the economy of Bitcoin, large exchanges and wallet companies (mirroring mining pools) act as secondary obligatory passage points for outlining and invoking change (explained in more detail later). Furthermore, the political strategy of a user activated soft fork still requires developers to create a client that reflects the political will of the market and thus demands the obligatory passage point of a Lead Developer found in version control systems.

Senatorial Governance

The technical functions of the Bitcoin network (and therefore monetary policy) are not set in stone but are constantly evolving. In order for an update to be made, various actors with different roles need to assemble in a particular form. I refer to this assemblage as a senate with reference to how governance once functioned in Ancient Rome—although Bitcoin certainly instils a unique form of senatorial governance. Across its decentralised architecture there is a structured methodology for proposing (programmers), voting on (miners), and lobbying for (companies and node operators) change. At this stage, I will concentrate on Bitcoin Core as an example of a senate.

A version fork is initiated in the following way: Bitcoin Core developers act like advisors by outlining change; the Bitcoin Lead Developer and those whom they give (revocable) commit access act like consuls by initiating change; mining pool operators (and to a lesser degree individual miners) act like senators by voting on change; large companies (and to a lesser degree full node operators) act like the assembly (or lobbyers) by attempting to influence miner voting; and everyday users are reduced to plebeians with little to no say (see Table 5.2). This process is by no means a radical algocracy where automotive, decentralised code is left alone to run economic transactions on behalf of society but is a structured hierarchy of disparate actors jostling for power to change the software design (see Figure 5.3). The channels through which decisions must pass in order to be 'heard by the network' ensure human and machine labour associated with maintaining and changing protocol rules are simultaneously collaborative and competitive. Senatorial governance works to align stakeholders from different camps into a singular orthodoxy or forces them to leave to create other projects. Conflict is ultimately 'resolved' through consensus or ostracisation (although, looking at the stagnation of code development through issues like the block size debate, it could be argued consensus is its own form of conflict). Ultimately, the mechanism of version forking allows different groups of programmers to compete for 'the same' protocol with different clients: a multitude of senates.

Table 5.2 **Power structure for implementing changes to the Bitcoin protocol**

Group	*Senate Equivalent*	*Level of Power*
Idea Forming		
Bitcoin Core developers	Consul advisors	Outline change
Decision-making		
Bitcoin Lead Developer (and those given commit access)	Consuls	Initiate change
Voting		
Mining pools	Senators	Vote on change (large impact)
Bitcoin miners	Senators (minor)	Elect mining pools or vote on change (small impact)
Lobbying		
Transaction companies	The assembly	Lobby for change (large impact)
Node operators	The assembly (minor)	Lobby for change (small impact)
Everyday users	Plebeians	Elect transaction companies or have no say

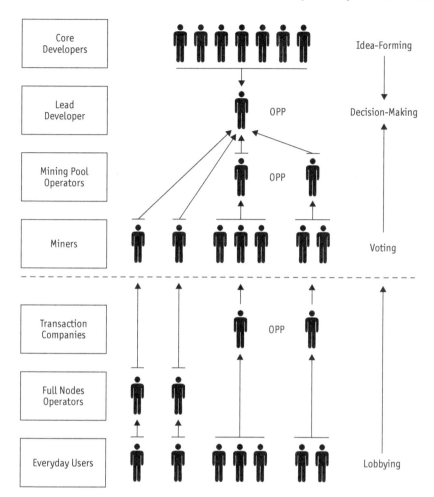

Figure 5.3 The senatorial governance of Bitcoin development. The Lead Developer, mining pool operators, and transaction companies stand out as obligatory passage points (OPP) for changing the rules of a client.

Obligatory passage points are important components to these structures because those who pass through them automatically elect representatives and in the same stroke become "silent actors" (Callon, 1986, 224). Individual developers submit to those with commit access, individual miners submit to mining pool operators, and everyday users submit to Bitcoin companies. All of these coercive actors are raised into positions of power while the decision-making of their subjects is diminished: "[t]o speak for others is to first silence those in whose name we speak" (Callon, 1986, 216). Far from a shift of control from humans to machines, senatorial governance manifests as an asymmetric contestation between different hybrids (developers/version control systems, miners/hardware, and users/company software) with varying degrees of control. This is not human vs. machine but human-machine vs. human-machine.

The analysis offered here should not be taken as an affirmation that actor-network thinking lowers human agency to that of non-humans. Conversely, this lens has shown how humans are very much at the wheel of obligatory passage points in the Bitcoin network (developing, mining, lobbying). But algorithmic agency is present too, arising via consensus: all people using a specific protocol must abide by one set of network rules. The code thus gathers a form of 'independent' agency because its specifications constrain networks of relationships into a singular modus operandi (Bergvall-Kåreborn & Howcroft, 2014). But, while algorithms might structure ways in which humans using particular systems interact with one another (Danaher, 2016), this is not a straightforward post-humanist transition from social to mechanical control. Algorithmic decentralisation via blockchains is predicated on, and ordered around, certain degrees of socialised cohesion.

As it stands, the process of decision-making is not a realisation of radical decentralist ideologies; rather it perpetuates an uneven distribution of power throughout the network. As Vitalik Buterin (2013a) explained after the 2013 accidental hard fork:

> Bitcoin is clearly not at all the direct democracy that many of its early adherents imagined, and, some worry, if a centralized core of the Bitcoin community is powerful enough to successfully undertake these emergency measures to set right the Bitcoin blockchain, what else is it powerful enough to do? Force double spends to reverse million-dollar thefts? Block or even redirect transactions known to originate from Silk Road? Perhaps even modify Bitcoin's sacred 21 million currency supply limit?[18]

The ideology of Bitcoin is somewhat dislocated from its governance practices: it seems a degree of centralisation is imperative for making (important) decisions. This suggests completely distributed governance might be a practical impossibility and would, theoretically, be a liability subject to failure at times of crisis. This is because a truly distributed "ecosystem may fail to respond to unexpected challenges in a timely fashion" (Atzori, 2015, 20).

Bitcoin Cash

The senatorial governance of code production outlined in the previous section is internal to the Bitcoin Core client built on GitHub. However, as the introduction of SegWit shows, multiple clients can be built to connect to the Bitcoin network and divert network rules towards a new paradigm. To do this, they must create their own senates and attempt to enrol as many actors into them as possible. The most successful hard version fork to date was the result of a breaking point between the two camps of the Bitcoin block size debate.

It was clear Bitcoin Core developers envisioned Bitcoin as a settlement protocol, arguing that transaction capability should be increased by added layers of software running on top of its blockchain instead of increasing block sizes (Torpey, 2016). Those who wanted bigger blocks were exasperated further by a wave of new interest in Bitcoin during 2017 that pushed the network past its capabilities, leading to transaction queues in the mempool (sometimes it would take up to 10 hours for these to execute). A bidding war ensued among users, who fought to have their transactions included in a block more quickly. The fee cost rose to around $3 USD per transaction. For 'low blockers,' this was unacceptable because it meant Bitcoin could no longer be used to purchase low-cost items (Popper, 2017; Wong, 2017). Roger Ver, an extremely vocal Bitcoin proponent (leading to the nickname 'Bitcoin Jesus') and early venture capitalist in the space, exclaimed on Twitter: "[s]ince Bitcoin Core is no longer usable as a currency, we should no longer consider it to be a crypto currency." A new client called Bitcoin Cash was offered as a solution by the group Bitcoin ABC.

Bitcoin Cash started development in 2017. Its Lead Developer, Amaury Sechét, was approached by the Chinese mining (pool) company Bitmain, that proposed implementing a 'user activated hard fork' that they would support with their mining power (van Wirdum, 2017c). This meant Bitcoin ABC would set in place new rules for the Bitcoin blockchain, raising the block size from 1 to 8 MB (megabytes). Bitmain would then start mining by this client's new rules, accepting those blocks as valid. The plan was initiated on the 1st August 2017, splitting the blockchain in two—block 478588 being the last common block between the two chains.[19] As miners joined the Bitcoin Cash chain to support the political bifurcation, the chain 'stuck' in place and a 'permanent' schism was made: two separate networks with a shared ancestry.[20]

Political clients that preceded Bitcoin Cash include Bitcoin XT, Bitcoin Classic, and Bitcoin Unlimited. Frustrated by the reluctance of Bitcoin Core to increase block sizes, Gavin Andresen and Mike Hearn created Bitcoin XT in 2015 to include "the latent capacity of accepting and producing an increased block size of eight megabytes" (De Filippi & Loveluck, 2016, 8). This created friction within the community:

> In some cases, the conflict eventually resulted in outright censorship and banning of Bitcoin XT supporters from the most popular Bitcoin websites. Most critically, the conflict also led to a variety of personal attacks towards Bitcoin XT proponents, and several online operators

who expressed support for Bitcoin XT experienced Distributed Denial of Service (DDoS) attacks. (De Filippi & Loveluck, 2016, 9)

The low rate of adoption of Bitcoin XT has been given as one of the reasons Mike Hearn left Bitcoin Core development in 2016 (De Filippi & Loveluck, 2016). Another client software, Bitcoin Classic, looked to "set up a specific governance structure that is intended to promote more democratic decision-making with regard to code changes, by means of a voting process that will account for the opinions of the broader community of miners, users, and developers" (De Filippi & Loveluck, 2016, 9). This client, and its mission to subvert the senatorial governance structure of Bitcoin Core, was initially well-received—its 2,000 nodes once accounted for one-third of the Bitcoin network—but later ceased operations in 2017 with dwindling support (O'Leary, 2017).

Hard version forks following Bitcoin Cash include Bitcoin Gold, Bitcoin Diamond, UnitedBitcoin, BitcoinX, and Super Bitcoin. When these clients establish multiple forks the entire network history resembles more of a block-tree than a singular blockchain (De Filippi & Wright, 2018), where distinct senates (or a multitude of them) govern the software of each branch.[21] Under this model, blockchains are discretionary as opposed to anti-discretionary because version forks, or branches, are not temporary glitches but a vehicle for disagreement and the fragmentation of societies that may never realign (Waldman, 2015). This is akin to the historical partings of communities like the Catholic and Orthodox churches: two religious groups with different beliefs on how Christianity should be practised (Waldman, 2015).[22] In this sense, the politics of Bitcoin is not necessarily set in stone, but certain technical parameters can be changed to fit evolving cultures and economies. There can be multiple governing bodies, and obligatory passage points of code development, as well as different rules (monetary policies), on varying branches of a blockchain/tree.

However, replicating a structure (through organisational or version forking) does not completely address the hierarchy of the structure itself. While it certainly gives others a voice and accounts for fragmentation in the community, power is not flattened among all participants. On the whole, senatorial governance is not a direct democracy but largely materialises as a representative one where certain actors (lead developers, mining pool operators, software companies) are raised into positions of power by grouping individuals (programmers, miners, everyday users) through their obligatory passage points. This is not necessarily a negative revelation for algorithmic decentralisation via open blockchains but it is important not to assume all stakeholders of their protocols are made equal. The cost of collective action is hierarchy.

Human-Machine Labour

Bitcoin mining farms exemplify how human-machine labour is essential to Bitcoin's code production and network maintenance. In 2015, *Motherboard* released a video of life inside a Chinese Bitcoin mine. It showed 3,000 shelved mining chips sitting row upon row, consuming 1,250kw of energy, 24 hours a day, 7 days a week. This creates a torrid environment: buildings encasing these computers are "structured around efficient heat transfer through hot and cold corridors, with machinery neatly labelled in locked cages of perforated sheet metal, alight with flickering LEDs, and rows of Ethernet jacks" (Brunton, 2015, 168). Predominantly male workers, equipped with a deep understanding of computers, conduct menial tasks to optimise the efficiency of the rigs (Mu, 2015). Meanwhile, the machines they tinker with are constantly engaging with the global algorithmic fabric of the Bitcoin protocol (see Chapter 6). Evidentially, there is technical labour involved from both human and machine (Maurer et al., 2013).

However, the mining rigs conduct a very simple task on repeat (generating nonces) and are thus dependent on humans to operate. Not only must they be repaired regularly, but it is their owners who ultimately decide which transactions to include in a block and whether to direct mining power through pools or vote on client updates themselves. Such decisions are largely made to enhance profitability, which highlights how blockchains are set up as a tool for both radical decentralisation *and* capital accumulation. This is somewhat a contradiction: while mechanical work is important, it is human agency that instils centripetal forces into the senatorial governance structure as miners join pools for more consistent profits and software companies attempt to direct as many users as possible through their systems.

In terms of programmers, certain influential Bitcoin Core developers were once sponsored by the Bitcoin Foundation—"a non-profit [organization] that sought to develop standardization and unity in the community" (Hütten & Thiemann, 2018, 3; see Appendix 16). Today, Wladimir van der Laan is sponsored by the MIT Digital Currency Initiative for his work on Bitcoin Core, bringing the voluntary aspect of open source labour into question. Additionally, many other Core programmers co-own and work for various blockchain and cryptocurrency companies, which could foster a vested interest in steering Bitcoin development in certain directions. This is where Mike Hearn's (2015, 2016) critique of Bitcoin Core becomes a little more insidious as he suggests that deep (financial) relationships with external companies create conflicts of interest.

At the time, eight Core developers were working for, and part-owned, a company called Blockstream, which develops protocols like the Lightning Network,

Elements, and Liquid, designed as second-layer protocols resting on top of blockchains to increase their efficiency and interoperability. Hearn's argument is: "developers the Bitcoin community are trusting to shepherd the block chain are *strongly* incentivised to ensure it works poorly and never improves. So it's unsurprising that Blockstream's official position is that the block chain should hardly change, even for simple, obvious upgrades like bigger block sizes" (Hearn, 2015). While this point is by no means evidence for collusion and/or corruption concerning Bitcoin Core developer consensus, there is certainly room for this to occur within its "contours of governance" (Tkacz, 2015, 124). Ultimately, despite a network designed to 'ensure' decisions are made from the bottom-up, the consolidation of obligatory passage points subverts and inverts the imaginary of flattened power among participants. Instead, a new but familiar hierarchy is formed—one where few people are in control of rules that affect many.

What's In A Name?

Unpacking the development of Bitcoin raises some philosophical questions concerning blockchain ontologies. Predominantly: what is Bitcoin and who decides this? Firstly, it should be said this is largely a matter of perspective and there is not necessarily a right or wrong answer. However, approaching quandaries like this is a useful exercise for understanding the Bitcoin protocol.

Quite evidently a vast array of people hold different claims over what Bitcoin is and attempt to move it in different directions. Anyone who operates a node is in effect enforcing their own version of a Bitcoin 'truth.' This is because the conditions of blocks they will accept are embedded in their client software. In other words, blocks are validated by people based on the rules they are themselves running. Each individual node is constantly saying "I agree with you" or "I don't agree with you" depending on its compatibility. Miners also communicate this truth by writing and broadcasting blocks to the rest of the network. In short, node operators entice miners with potential profit and miners entice node operators with a more permanent chain. This negotiation is a two-way street and is how consensus is ultimately reached. At the same time, it keeps developers accountable. For example, if Vladimir van der Laan decided to release a version of Bitcoin Core which altered consensus rules on his own accord, it would undoubtedly be followed by uproar. Both node operators and miners would likely refuse to implement the new software and instead keep running old rules. Additionally, under the situation of a rogue Lead Developer, there is a high probability that other developers would flock around a new client (with a different Lead Developer) to make future changes. They would lose the name Bitcoin Core but Bitcoin as a network would continue to exist.

So what is Bitcoin? Is it the longest chain? The rules outlined in the Bitcoin white paper? Bitcoin Core? The coin with the highest market value? All are certainly legitimate claims. A revered Bitcoin journalist gave me his take on the issue: "Bitcoin is, firstly, whatever people consider to be Bitcoin and, secondly, that will probably always be the coin that is backwards compatible with previous versions of Bitcoin." This is a strong definition for labelling a specific coin "Bitcoin" (as opposed to "Bitcoin Cash," for example). But there is a second option he provided which better encapsulates the Bitcoin ecosystem as a whole with its multitude of forks: every coin that started from the genesis block. When explaining this, the journalist provided me with another keen insight: "under this definition there is no single Bitcoin, there is a family of 'Bitcoin.'" This seems more pertinent when examining the broad political church of Bitcoin governance. The protocol is, after all, many things to many people.

Conclusion

The senatorial governance of Bitcoin shows how blockchains are human-made artefacts: machines are enrolled by people to maintain and direct their networks. Political potentials are generated from struggles to control obligatory passage points, which can create significant rifts in the supposed hegemony of blockchain economies. The senate-like structure for making change is (de)centralised inasmuch as protocol rules are dictated through competing centres crucial for network updates, crisis management, and dispute resolution. Here, power is not exercised purely by the machines and codified rules of the protocol but by human actors operating through them. Various modes of software forking initiated by these actors can take both democratising and de-democratising forms.

While the ideology of decentralisation is to promote systems that cannot be coerced, the necessity for decisions to be coordinated through centralised channels restricts this effect. There are limits to algorithmic decentralisation for the simple reason that software must be made and maintained by people through space, and coordination, therefore, must take place between its builders. This clearly demonstrates that while the geographies of production for Bitcoin may be spatially dispersed, upon closer inspection, connectivities run through specific channels. No matter where stakeholders are situated in terms of Euclidian coordinates, they must abide by the contours of senatorial governance in order to make an impact on the protocol. Often, this involves funnelling practices through centralised bottlenecks and surrendering power to their operators in the process. Such an analysis works to critique a grandiose rhetoric of decentralisation, which, like its terminological cousin openness, can often be "bereft of content" (Tkacz, 2015, 35).

My intent is not to paint open source software models as impotent: they remain incredibly productive environments for solving problems in code development. And with a multiplication of senatorial bodies (clients), Bitcoin governance certainly reflects a decentralised system as shown in Figure 2.1. But centralised obligatory passage points do not disappear; they are, instead, implicit to this pattern. So openness/closure and distribution/centralisation are not repelling binaries that separate like oil and water but rather swirl together through organisational practice in a hybrid and co-dependent capacity. In other words, Bitcoin is decentralised because it has both distributed and centralised pieces. It is in the analytical framing of heterogeneous networks that these complex states can be better illuminated and understood.

If space is the concoction of connected and disconnected trajectories that are constantly in a state of becoming (Massey, 2005), then Bitcoin development can be said to be spatially (de)centralised—where centralisation represents the 'connected' enrolment of trajectories through controlled funnels and distribution represents those that do not have to pass through a singular point (see Figure 2.1). Obligatory passage points act like spatial and political cable ties that gather and coordinate individual loose ends. Senatorial governance is a key driving force behind Bitcoin's money/code/space, as it is the underlying framework for change. Instead of one central bank, the open network allows anyone to build a client with code and plug into it. To influence its technical parameters (monetary policy), however, this new client must reflect updated rules in its code (achieved through centralised version control politics) and then be adopted by network miners, themselves coercible by large companies—time will tell if more ambitious architectures can overcome these 'limitations' (see Chapter 8). The next chapter follows the material infrastructure that operates the Bitcoin code to examine how algorithmic decentralisation is further predicated upon centralised components.

6

Grounding Cryptocurrencies

Introduction

Bitcoin strives to achieve decentralisation via a carefully crafted algorithmic architecture that works to reach a singular network consensus. This agreed state is reached and maintained by multiple ledgers distributed through space. Such a reliance on digital networks can conjure up the semblance that Bitcoin (and other blockchains) exist in an intangible and ethereal dimension (reminiscent of cyberspace imaginaries that circulated during the 1990s). This chapter is dedicated to dismantling that illusion. Here, I ground the Bitcoin code within its materiality—that is, computer hardware and telecommunications infrastructure, as well as the humans/institutions managing them—to understand how its protocological transactions facilitate new geographies of value exchange that 'move' across space in a neoteric fashion. This is done by following a singular unit of bitcoin in a 'cross-border' transaction 'from' Australia 'to' the United States. More than anywhere else in this book it is important to remember here that Bitcoin (as a software protocol) is one thing and *a* bitcoin (as a unit of currency) is another. This is why Bitcoin is often described as both a payment network *and* a form of money: the Bitcoin software is a system that allows the spending of bitcoins within the parameters of its protocol. At the same time, Bitcoin and bitcoins are inextricable; the functionality of one depends on the functionality of the other. Currency units rely on the protocol to administrate them and the protocol relies on the currency units, through the economic incentive of crypto-economics, to keep the payment system running.

Cryptography goes a long way towards obscuring the identity of parties involved in a Bitcoin transaction. Consequently, I decided to follow a bitcoin sent from and to Bitcoin wallets I control so the coin's 'movement' is clearer to see—this is like shining light down two ends of a tunnel to see what lies in the middle. The endeavor involves following information (a bitcoin) through a relatively fluid algorithmic architecture (Bitcoin software) across a relatively

Money Code Space. Jack Parkin, Oxford University Press (2020). © Oxford University Press.
DOI: 10.1093/oso/9780197515075.001.0001.

static infrastructure made up of computers, wires, cables, sockets, Wi-Fi routers, servers, relaying stations, electrical grids, and mining chips scattered across the world (but connected via the Internet).[1] In doing so, the money/code/space of the Bitcoin software architecture and hardware infrastructure is (partially) mapped out, thereby illuminating many of the human and non-human actors enrolled to support the network.

Throughout, the ways in which material hardware connects through centralised points forms a basis for critiquing Bitcoin's algorithmic decentralisation: while the 'abstract' logic of the Bitcoin code certainly emanates distribution, its execution must always operate physically through mediating infrastructures such as circuitry and fibre optic cables that intersect to form unique spatial patterns.[2] This is because information is always formed, first and foremost, through material carriers (Blanchette, 2011), and so points of centralisation necessarily appear where infrastructures concentrate and coalesce. Understanding data in this way demands a recognition that it is both material *and* semiotic; to function, data must rely on both medium *and* message. It is the material component that often ensures data is channeled through centralised infrastructural bottlenecks for efficiency. These points are almost exclusively controlled by private companies that are 'employed' as the gatekeepers to obligatory passage points.

To "study a technological project, one must constantly move from signs to things, and vice versa" (Latour, 1996, 80). This is particularly true for software, which should be read as both material and text (Mackenzie, 2006): it "is a tangle, a knot, which ties together the physical and the ephemeral, the material and the ethereal, into a multi-linear ensemble that can be controlled and directed" (Berry, 2011, 3). To untangle this knot, I delve into the active code of the network to unpack Bitcoin's connectivity. This is to understand code as having a double function: it simultaneously executes a mechanical process and relays the mechanical process in a readable format to the human reader-writer (Mateas & Montfort, 2005). For this reason, software is always mechanical *and* symbolic. Paying closer attention to the material backbone that stitches communication networks together, as well as the code patterns of software, this chapter navigates, deconstructs, and reflects upon underpinning (infra/data)structures: linking immaterial flows back to geographies, jurisdictions, nationhood, and material objects (Herregraven, 2014; Kubrak, 2015). In doing so, the material enactment of code is used to critique spatial limitations of algorithmic decentralisation.[3]

I begin by outlining the conceptual, material, and spatial grounds from which I attempt to trace out the digital cryptographic system of Bitcoin. Pursuing the network geography of a single bitcoin, I first highlight difficulties and tensions that arise when approaching the "socio-spatial materialities" of software (Ash et al., 2016, 14). This leads into a more concrete explanation of Bitcoin—how it exists in digital wallets and how these wallets are, in turn, supported by nodes composed of material components inside computers. The 'distributed' architecture through which these computers communicate is then articulated before the centralised companies that help execute my Bitcoin transaction are explored. From here an understanding is formed with regard to how a Bitcoin node (operating code) initiates and broadcasts a transaction to the rest of the network, releasing my coin from the address to which it is encumbered. Cryptographic hashes are dissected and I demonstrate how they, as mathematical scripts performed by machines, allow my coin to become mined into a block of the Bitcoin blockchain, thus becoming a 'permanent' entry in an algorithmic ledger stored across a network of computers. Modes of centralisation illuminated by following the Bitcoin code through its material network are then elaborated upon to show how the functionality of the protocol is modulated into different segments that can, to a degree, be controlled. Here obligatory passage points demonstrate material limits to algorithmic decentralisation.

Tracing Crypto/Space

Following software is a difficult proposition because it appears to exist 'behind' screens. It is, then, with a degree of experimentation that new methodologies can be fashioned in order to explore the darker spaces of infrastructure. Such innovations are a methodological, analytical, and political necessity (Neilson, 2018). James Ash et al. (2016) encourage researchers to "adopt and embrace an epistemological, ontological, and methodological openness in their engagements with the digital" (14). Indeed, there is ample room to "invent some new methods that can address the distinctive qualities of digital cultural production: its mutability, its multimediality, its massiveness and in particular the uneven spatial dynamics of its interfacial, frictional networking" (Rose 2016, 346).

The rise of the Internet brought with it ideas of a uniform and ubiquitous global network. Work in digital geographies soon shattered this illusion by presenting the multiplicity of political, economic, and social interactions taking place across its architecture (Zook et al., 2004; Zook, 2006). A portion of this work involved a range of methods for spatially mapping the material backbone of the Internet on a number of different scales (Wheeler & O'Kelly, 1999; Townsend, 2001; Gorman et al., 2002; O'Kelly & Grubesic, 2002; Grubesic & Murray, 2004). Similarly, I examine how the Bitcoin and TCP/IP protocol interact together to trace the layers of infrastructure that support them. With this in mind, I embark on following a bitcoin across space (a parallel to this endeavour is drawn up in Appendix 17 where I describe the workings of a more traditional cross-border payment from Sydney to San Francisco). In many ways, then, this chapter most resembles traditional follow the thing work as it involves 'literally' following a specific 'thing' through part of its life—although 'traversing' a digital, decentralised, and cryptographic network makes the effort fairly unique in comparison to existing implementations of this method.

In following a digital thing, I immediately encountered a problem: what is it, exactly, I was attempting to follow? A bitcoin, after all, cannot be picked up, dropped, or broken. How, then, can I observe the trajectory of something that appears to have no real form of matter making it susceptible to touch or visible to the eye? The answer relies on navigating the digital-material architecture of the protocol (Galloway, 2004). In this way, what Bitcoin (software) and a bitcoin (currency unit) actually are, existentially, became clearer the deeper I dove.

The "material architecture which underpins the digital revolution is commonly referred to in terms which postulate only the most tenuous of connections to the hardware layer of contemporary digital ecosystems" (Taffel, 2016, 122). Information communication technology succumbs to a fetishisation of information over the technology, media over the medium (see Chapter 3). As many scholars have pointed out, this, more often than not, creates a fallacious ontological disjuncture reinforcing Cartesian dualisms that allow for the separation of opposing realms, such as body/mind, physical/digital, material/immaterial, hardware/software, medium/media, real/abstract, actual/virtual, and spatial/aspatial (Graham, 1998; Kinsley, 2013a, 2013b; Ash et al., 2016).

The stickiness of binaries should never be completely overlooked, as there is a tendency for humans to define things through opposition and differing (Derrida, 1967)—even scholars dedicated to obliterating dualisms seem to do so in their polarising, yet persistent, terms (for example, centralisation and decentralisation). However, there is much more entanglement and tension at stake with binaries than Cartesian thought allows for: a connection and interplay at the same time as separation and distance.[4] Ontological schisms between alternate spheres neglect to acknowledge how humans are always already caught up in the fabric of the world (Merleau-Ponty, 1963). It is for this reason that Tim Ingold (2000) calls Cartesianism "the single underlying fault upon which the entire edifice of Western thought and science has been built" (1).

Contrastingly, developing a more complex, hybridised, and material account of society has been a key driving force behind academic scholarship over the last forty years (Latour & Woolgar, 1979; Haraway, 1991; Latour, 1987, 1993, 1999; Thrift, 2008; Anderson & Harrison, 2010). This work has revealed how polarising binaries—previously presented as existing in detached environments—are actually "enlaced and intertwined, in a 'being-in-the-world' that precedes and preconditions rationality and objectivity" (Wylie, 2007, 3). It is along similar lines that scholars have battled against vacuous representations of the digital and pushed to generate a more spatial and material lexicon (Graham, 1998; Bontems et al., 2008; Aoyama et al., 2004; Knoespel & Zhu, 2008; Blanchette, 2011).

With this in mind, to study a 'thing' is always to examine "an infinite regress of relationships" (Bateson, 1972, 249). Digital information (whether a news article, video game, tweet, database, or bitcoin) is no different: "computer code creates relationships among multiple symbolic systems, those necessary to move the cogs of the machine, and those necessary for those operations of the machine to be situated within language, and thus, social order" (Blanchette, 2011, 1045). In other words, the order and stability of digital things is achieved heterogeneously. Examining the relationships between the different entities that help constitute them allows for various analytical frames to be applied. For example, the task of this book is to understand centralisation as the enrolment of networked practices through specific spaces/entities, and to trace out the limits of algorithmic decentralisation in multifarious arrangements.

Sy Taffel (2012, 2015b) has already used the idea of digital materiality to *follow* the life cycle of components that make up computers in order to uncover the environmental costs of their production. Differing slightly, I use the material as an analytical technique to explore the functional processes of these components in order to understand how they support the existence of Bitcoin/bitcoins. To use Erving Goffman's (1959) famous phrase, I follow a bitcoin "backstage" into its infrastructural messiness. This helps to describe crypto/space and uncover where certain trajectories congeal. In doing so, "questions are asked around the complexity, and indeterminacy, of matter and about how qualities of liveliness are internal to, rather than in supplement or opposition to, the taking place of matter and materiality" (Anderson & Wiley, 2009, 319).

The enormity of the network geography and material infrastructures that underpin Bitcoin means I cannot form a literal, physical presence among all its pieces; yet the logic of association and connection of *following* defines my ethnographic enquiry (Marcus, 1995). The protocol itself leaves digital breadcrumbs that can be traced via its blockchain (an open database), whereas third-party software can be used to monitor in more detail this network activity. I used these breadcrumbs to follow my transaction as it became solidified in a block and propagated across the network. Downloading the Bitcoin Core software also enabled me to become a fully fledged participant in the algorithmic fabric of Bitcoin—filling up nearly 52 GB (today 267GB) of my hard drive with its very 'substance.' Doing so allowed my version of the blockchain to become a 'research site' ready to be excavated.

Inside Bitcoin Wallets

In order to follow a bitcoin, I needed some to transact. But how does one store a digital unit of cryptocurrency? Firstly, I required a 'wallet' for bitcoin to be assigned to and, in the absence of mining or trading goods or services, I needed to pay someone fiat currency in exchange for it. A Bitcoin wallet is composed of a cryptographically linked public and private key—two unique strings of letters and numbers. The first is used as a receiver for incoming bitcoin transactions and the second acts as a signature for authorising the spending of money from that address. A wallet is the name given to the data structure that contains a private key, public key, and address—the address being the unique identifier for the whole wallet:

> A bitcoin wallet contains a collection of key pairs, each consisting of a private key and a public key. The private key (k) is a number, usually picked at random. From the private key, we use elliptic curve multiplication, a one-way cryptographic function, to generate a public key (K). From the public key (K), we use a one-way cryptographic hash function to generate a bitcoin address (A).... The relationship between private key, public key and bitcoin address is shown [in Figure 6.1]. (Antonopoulos, 2014, 63)

The private key should only be known by the owner(s) of the wallet so only they can sign off on the release, and thereby spending, of funds. Managing cryptographic keys requires specific coding expertise and so third-party wallet providers have created business models based on administrating wallets on their customer's behalf, handling the technical part of the process. In other words, customers trust these companies with their funds to overcome technical barriers associated with using the Bitcoin protocol (possessing and transacting bitcoins).

I began using Bitcoin as a personal means for making global monetary transactions following an international banking fiasco that occurred when I first landed in San Francisco to undertake my ethnographic research (see Appendix 17). As such, Bitcoin wallet services became a trusted channel for sending money 'overseas.' One example of a wallet service provider is the company CoinJar, which accepts Bpay deposits from Australian bank accounts. CoinJar acts as the

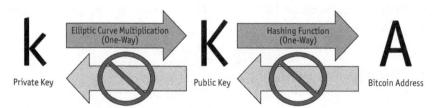

Figure 6.1 The cryptographic relationship between private key, public key, and Bitcoin address in a Bitcoin wallet (source: Antonopoulos, 2014).

gateway between my Australian dollar and bitcoin currencies thanks to its built-in exchange platform that allows me to trade one for the other on demand as opposed to using an 'open market' cryptocurrency exchange such as Bitstamp. Using the Bankwest application on my smartphone, I sent CoinJar $400 AUD via the Australian Bpay system and waited for the transaction to be confirmed.[5] Once CoinJar received the transaction I was attributed a credit of $400 AUD in my Cash Account (see Figure 6.2). I then exchanged $354.66 AUD for 1 bitcoin and the value appeared on my Everyday Bitcoin balance. This means CoinJar had given me access to a certain amount of bitcoins they were in control of in the same way my bank gives me access to an amount of Australian dollars they are in control of, as reflected by my bank account balance—both institutions show me a figure and authorise the movement of funds when I give (or, rather, ask for their) permission to do so.

I also have an account with a Bitcoin wallet service called Coinbase, which is based in the United States. Coinbase allows me to buy and sell bitcoins in exchange for US dollars, which are debited or credited from my Wells Fargo bank account. Money can 'move across' borders in this way because my CoinJar wallet is connected to my Australian bank account, whereas my Coinbase wallet is connected to my American bank account. In short, I can buy bitcoins with Australian dollars and sell them for US dollars. To facilitate this transaction, I logged into my Coinjar account, clicked on the payments tab, selected the account I wanted to send money from (my CoinJar Bitcoin wallet), typed in the address of my Coinbase wallet (13oqZGuUNkGqY6tquFBVghgFcPi3JjPJG), and disclosed the amount of bitcoins I wanted to send. I reviewed this transaction and clicked the 'Pay now' button. The bitcoin was then 'debited' from my CoinJar wallet and 'credited' to my Coinbase wallet (see Figure 6.3).[6]

On the surface this seems like a simple mathematical subtraction from my CoinJar address and an addition to my Coinbase address of 1 BTC: an uncomplicated change of numbers between accounts. However, the simple sum relies on a host of sociotechnical actors swimming beneath the surface. Out of view, but in concert, a multitude of hybrid strings are being pulled together to make the transaction a financial reality. But where does the bitcoin in my CoinJar wallet actually exist? Where is the balance in the wallet 13oqZGuUNkGqY6tquFB-VghgFcPi3JjPJG actually being stored? The short answer is on the Bitcoin blockchain, but this simple fact encompasses a great deal of complexity.

Opening Black Boxes

Every value of bitcoin exists on each copy (or node) of the blockchain, cryptographically locked in place waiting for its 'owner' to spend that amount with

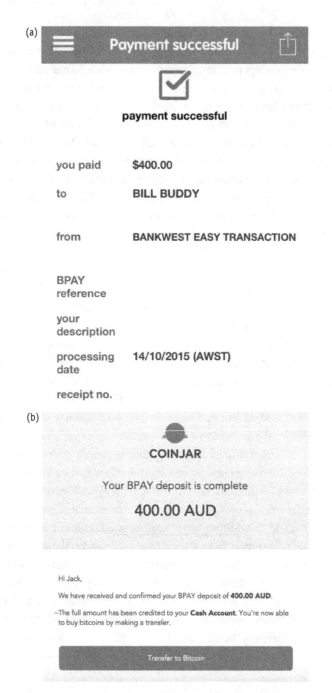

Figure 6.2 My Bpay transaction to CoinJar and authorisation of a $400 AUD deposit credited to my CoinJar account.

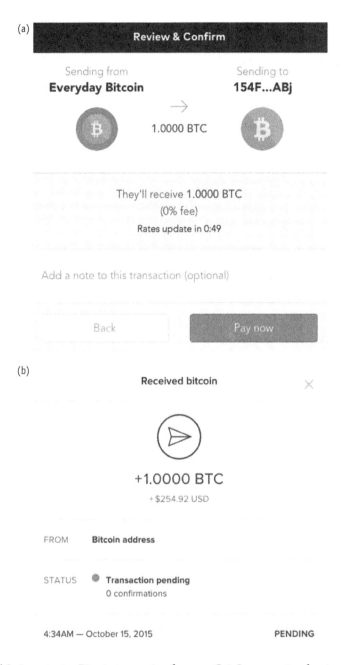

Figure 6.3 An outgoing Bitcoin transaction from my CoinJar account and an incoming transaction from my Coinbase account.

Figure 6.4 The Bitcoin-Qt client software on my Mac dashboard.

their private key. This is done by creating a script: a piece of computer code, or program, that executes a task. The script unlocks bitcoins from a public key and locks them to another public key in the process.[7] Every node will update periodically to reflect any alterations made to balances on a global scale. So, how does the blockchain exist on one of these nodes? My own copy of the Bitcoin blockchain 'lives' on my laptop in the location MacOS: ~/Library/ApplicationSupport/ Bitcoin/blocks (see Figure 6.4). This node is an active participant in the maintenance of the Bitcoin ledger, propagating transactions and updating its state to maintain a publicly distributed consensus.[8]

More specifically, all this activity is being conducted on silicon chips where digital information is stored and manipulated as electrical impulses. So what 'breathes life' into the apparently 'deadened' materials of my computer? The answer is the arrangement of tiny channels etched into integrated circuits. These organise electricity in a manner that can represent (and enact) data. In *The Pattern on the Stone*, a book written by microchip designer W. Daniel Hillis (1998), this phenomenon is poetically described:

> I etch a pattern of geometric shapes onto a stone. To the uninitiated, the shapes look mysterious and complex, but I know that when arranged correctly they will give the stone a special power, enabling it to respond to incantations in a language no human being has ever spoken. I will ask the stone questions in this language, and it will answer by showing me a vision: a world created by my spell, a world imagined by the pattern on the stone. (Hillis, 19998, vii)

Despite intentional allusions to fantasy, this is a strangely accurate description of the performative operations of silicon chips inside computers. My MacBook Air contains four Toshiba 128 GB Solid-State Drive (SSD) chips, which is where my version of the blockchain is stored and enacted (see Figure 6.5). Each chip is composed of thousands upon thousands of tiny silicon 'wires' that interconnect in certain arrangements to create minute logic gates (see Figure 6.6). Each gate acts like an electronic valve, allowing or disallowing electricity to flow depending on the inputs of electricity it receives.

Figure 6.5 Toshiba 128 GB SSD chip found in my MacBook Air (source: iFixit, 2017).

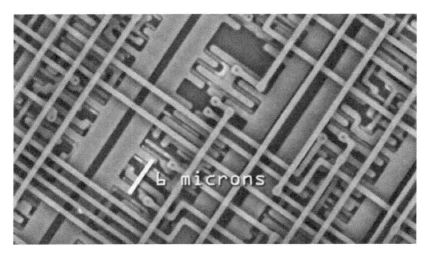

Figure 6.6 The silicon wires of an electronic chip under a microscope (source: Hall, 2012).

Wires are thus either on or off, which are abstracted by computer scientists into a 1 or a 0 respectively and referred to as bits. In other words, the presence or absence of electricity along a wire can be represented as a binary code. Bits are "both logical and material entities" (Blanchette, 2011, 1042). With them, the materiality of electricity in silicon wires can suddenly be quantified mathematically and manipulated through computation. But this binary code only really ever represents existence or non-existence of electrons flowing on a wire (or signals produced by other physical media like pulses of light in fibre optic cables and magnetic polarities on disk drives). The geometric patterns formed by grouping logic gates together can be cumulatively built upon to represent and perform more complex things like colour on a screen or sound through a speaker. With reference to Friedrich Kittler (1995), Alexander Galloway (2006) describes how computer programming languages (code) are formed through layers of the 'software stack' in this way, making them both material and semiotic:

> When basic logic gate functionality is abstracted and strung together into machine commands, translated into assembly op-codes, and then later articulated in a higher-level computer language such as C, the argument from Kittler is that one should never understand this 'higher' symbolic machine as anything empirically different from the 'lower' symbolic interactions of voltages through logic gates. They are complex aggregates yes, but it is foolish to think that writing an 'if/then' control structure in eight lines of assembly code is any more or less machinic than doing it in one line of C, just as the same quadratic equation may swell with any number of multipliers and still remain balanced. The relationship between the two is *technical*. (319)

Put simply, symbolic code and the mechanics by which it runs cannot be pragmatically separated: on circuit boards, signs are directly related to voltage differences as signifiers (Chun, 2006). It is the process of 'functional abstraction' that allows computer scientists to pass, like this, from the world of engineering into the world of mathematics:

> Once we figure out how to accomplish a given function, we can put the mechanism inside a 'black box,' or a 'building block' and stop thinking about it. The function embodied by the building block can be used over and over, without reference to the details of what's inside. (Hillis, 1998, 19)

In science and technology studies the term 'black box' is often used when technical work achieves some form of stability, making the inner workings invisible so that only inputs and outputs are acknowledged (Callon & Latour, 1881; Winner, 1993; Hinchliffe, 1996, Latour, 1999). In other words, an input enters a black box, which spits out an output, while the process by which this happened is ignored. Similarly, in computing, the lids are put on black boxes deliberately so the function of what that box is doing can be concentrated on rather than the complex mechanics, or electrical pathways, that bring that function into being. This has important connotations for how digital architectures are understood: enacted by the whizzing circuitry of computers. Software does not exist *inside* hardware but is *hardware-at-work*. The Bitcoin blockchain, therefore, is not floating around in a fourth dimension somewhere, unmoored from materiality, but rather exists as a relational spatial entity at a micro and macro level: not just embedded *in* but performed *by* the processes of connected silicon chips (and other supporting paraphernalia).

From such a materialist vantage point, hardware and software are by "no means separate or discrete elements of computation" (Marino, 2006).[9] As Friedrich Kittler (1995) explains in his provocatively titled paper "There Is No Software," "code operations, despite their metaphoric faculties . . . come down to absolutely local string manipulations and that is . . . to signifiers of voltage differences" (4). The "material substrate of code, which must always exist as an amalgam of electrical signals and logical operations in silicon, however large or small, demonstrates that code exists first and foremost as commands issued to a machine" (Galloway, 2006, 326). In short, digital culture is always material culture.

While the micro geographies of code are important (i.e., latticeworks of wires in silicon chips), my machine is not running the Bitcoin protocol alone; it is constantly interacting with other nodes at a greater algorithmic macro geography. Because these other nodes are also maintaining the Bitcoin blockchain across the world, my claim on CoinJar's store of bitcoin exists on every machine in the peer-to-peer network. When bitcoins are sent (or spent) no physical movement or tangible exchange of an item takes place. Instead, there is a transfer of ownership via the abstract logging system of a shared ledger that exists as an algorithmic protocol—one, like more traditional ledgers (i.e., stone-and-etching or ink-and-paper), categorically manifested by material and technical means.

Weaving Algorithmic Fabrics

Third-party software can be used to track certain aspects of the Bitcoin blockchain. A monitoring system called BitNodes crawls the Bitcoin network in order to retrieve geographic data based on IP addresses, which indicate where nodes are located worldwide. Figure 6.7 shows the global distribution of these nodes at the time of my transaction. Evidently, with 5,728 full nodes scattered around the world, peer-to-peer protocols are by no means spaceless entities. In fact, in the case of blockchains, their geographic and dynamic complexity characterises and enhances resilience. In other words, Bitcoin does not become formless through digitisation but rather its unique spatial configuration grants it a certain amount of stability. Paradoxically, its design uses (the dislocation of) space to overcome previous spatial limitations (such as transferring value across borders without banks) via separation *and* connection. In doing so, it becomes

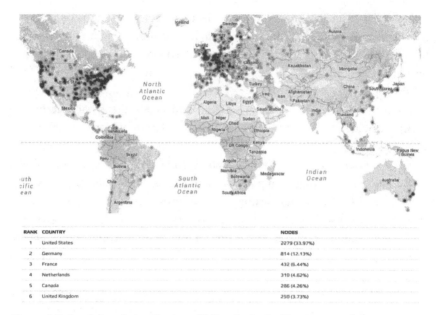

RANK	COUNTRY	NODES
1	United States	2279 (33.97%)
2	Germany	814 (12.13%)
3	France	432 (6.44%)
4	Netherlands	310 (4.62%)
5	Canada	286 (4.26%)
6	United Kingdom	250 (3.73%)

Figure 6.7 A web-based visualisation of full nodes in the Bitcoin network (using BitNodes).

durable: if one node collapses the others continue maintaining the ledger as if it had never existed. In this way, Bitcoin builds sturdiness from spatial elasticity. All of the bits and pieces that interconnect to suspend it carve out new financial linkages and trajectories. It would be ignorant, then, to render Bitcoin a circumventor of space when its neoteric geography (the way various actors align to compose it) is what propels it into existence in the first place, as functioning distributed software. In short, digital peer-to-peer architectures do not nullify geography but emerge as new spatial compositions.

The map in Figure 6.7 tells even more about the nature of the Bitcoin protocol: the nodes are globally distributed but heavily clustered in Western countries (epitomised by the concentration of dots in North America and Europe). While this does not say anything about Bitcoin users, it does demonstrate how 'record keepers' tend to come from affluent countries. To some degree, this is to be expected when considering the 'digital divide' between richer populations, who have a great degree of access to information communication technologies and an abundance of relevant skills, and poorer populations, who often lack these privileges (Norris, 2001; Warschauer, 2004; Selwyn, 2004). While I do not focus on this point, it is worth noting there may be (on some level) geographic, cultural, political, and economic biases to the maintenance of the Bitcoin ledger.

It is also important to remember the map is a snapshot of a dynamic network where nodes are constantly joining and leaving: Bitcoin does not hold a fixed, bounded, algorithmic geography but is a continually evolving spatial connection. Additionally, nodes are not disconnected islands of software but rather interact through signals manifested by a plethora of hardware—running on the rails of the Internet's global, labyrinthine, material infrastructure, where certain components are owned and operated by a multitude of nation-states, private companies, and other institutions. I turn to this later, but first the wallet companies that support my transaction need to be unpacked.

Bitcoin Banks

I now come back to the CoinJar website from where I issued the command to send my bitcoin by clicking the 'Pay now' button. To understand what happens beneath the click I dive through a number of architectural layers. CoinJar controls Bitcoin addresses on the behalf of their account holders and administrate transactions (while managing security) in return for in-built fees. Companies like this are therefore important spaces of control within the Bitcoin ecosystem as they operate layers of software/bureaucracy between users and the Bitcoin blockchain. Although they streamline the Bitcoin experience, allowing more people to participate in its network, these institutions also centralise aspects of the Bitcoin economy through tightly controlled channels. In this way, wallet companies materialise as trusted third parties—the very thing Bitcoin was designed to negate. A point I return to later.

Part of my ethnographic work in 2015 led me to CoinJar's London office situated in Europe's largest financial technology accelerator, known as Level39—named after its floor position within One Canada Square, Canary Wharf.[10] CoinJar was originally founded in Melbourne, Australia, by Asher Tan and Ryan Zhou in February of 2013 but, after the Australian Tax Office defined Bitcoin as an asset thereby subjecting it to Goods and Services Tax (Australian Tax Office, 2014; Han, 2014), the company moved its headquarters to London (Heber, 2014; Swan, 2014; Southurst, 2014). More 'progressive' legislation in the UK meant that registering CoinJar as a British company allowed it to escape the 10% tax on buying and selling bitcoin. This move also gave the company greater access to a global market (Spencer, 2014; Carmody, 2014; CoinJar, 2015). The majority of their team, however, stayed in Melbourne.

Sitting with the UK General Manager of CoinJar in their London office for a couple of weeks, I learnt more about the technical nature of the company's operations. I found that CoinJar manages a series of 'hot wallets'—public keys that have their corresponding private keys stored online so they can be extracted immediately on demand—held on their servers.

When a user signs into the website they are authorising themselves to CoinJar via their password.[11] Once access is granted, the website provides a streamlined and user-friendly experience for managing Bitcoin funds via a graphical user interface (GUI). The website is supported by software designed, maintained, and monitored by CoinJar employees and runs on servers rented from third parties. The information I type in there signals to the software churning away on CoinJar's servers that a value of 1 BTC must be taken from their hot wallets and sent to the address I indicated (154FhxVKSgL1LHqdazwHHQVB9bhoACdABj).

An interview with a CoinJar employee revealed their hot wallet service would have roughly 400 BTC at any one time: "incoming payments land there and outgoing payments come from there." This 400 BTC is not stored in a single address (public key) but a few thousand with a system defined by the CoinJar software for deciding which coins are used for the next transaction (i.e., the 'oldest' coins).[12] To authorise a transaction the software plucks a private key from their servers stored on the cloud and signs the corresponding public key on a CoinJar-operated Bitcoin full node. This is the first point since I started 'following' my bitcoin transaction that the Bitcoin blockchain is actually interacted with (although the value of that bitcoin was stored 'there' the whole time).

There is disagreement in the Bitcoin community over the good and evil of Bitcoin companies that restructure trust around centralised business models associated with traditional banking practices. I was given two contrasting opinions by separate people at a meet-up in San Francisco (coincidentally sponsored by Coinbase): one advised "never trust centralised companies as they are merely Bitcoin banks" and another explained they "always direct first timers to Coinbase because they are certain to have a great experience which encourages Bitcoin use." This personifies a tension between people who have a disdain for centralised institutions as gateways to Bitcoin and others who acknowledge their necessity. "Such walled gardens depend on the gating of entrance and exit points by private intermediaries . . . who often operate in the name of facilitating trust or building community, but who also effectively create closed circuits that place a premium on—and charge a fee for—access" (Nelms et al., 2017, 26). However, there is still a difference here to traditional nation-state monetary models even with the presence of Bitcoin banks: start-ups may control private keys but there is no central bank in charge of the currency's monetary policy. Instead it is subject to the contours of control present in senatorial governance (see Chapter 5). Furthermore, the digital-material infrastructure via which value is transacted operates differently to traditional money/code/spaces, as will become clear throughout the rest of this chapter.

Through the Internet

To add to the geographic complexity of the transaction facilitated by CoinJar, the servers that signed my transaction were not based in the United Kingdom or Australia, but in the United States. Consequently, when I press the 'Pay now' button on the CoinJar webpage I am using a UK registered company, operating (largely) out of Australia, and which utilises servers from North America. What is more, for this to work, the signals prompted by the click are carried through infrastructure owned by a plethora of different actors, like Internet service providers (ISPs) and telephone companies, between Australia and the United States. I initiated this transaction on my laptop from the Institute for Culture and Society at Western Sydney University where it processed the information I punched into its keyboard as electrical signals (resembling bits) that are passed down the software stack and split up into manageable chunks of data by my computer's Transmission Control Protocol (TCP).

These packets are digitally ordered and labelled so the CoinJar server on the other side can make sense of and reassemble them. Because I was using the university Wi-Fi, the information was turned into radio waves by my computer to be transmitted to the wireless router. The router picked up this information and translated it back into digital information (electrical impulses) as the radio waves vibrated electrons in the antenna thus producing electrical current. It was then modulated into bursts of electromagnetic waves by the router to be sent down an Ethernet cable and the copper wires carried by telephone poles to another router owned by an ISP. This router read the packet header containing the destination Internet Protocol (IP). The data then crossed through peered infrastructure owned by various ISPs.

The packets are 'dumb' so do not know where they are heading. However, since their target has been labelled by my laptop's TCP they can be scanned by the router and passed on depending on whether the destination IP address is in its logging table or not. If it is, the router sends the packet towards that IP address and, if it is not, the router relays the packet on to a parent router containing a greater number of logging tables. This process can continue until it reaches 'the top' of an ISP network where, if the router does not contain the destination IP address, it will pass on the packet to the network of another ISP until the IP address is found.

Once located, the packet will be passed 'down' subsequent routers until it reaches the machine with the correct IP address: in this case an Amazon server located in Seattle rented by CoinJar (see Figure 6.8). Different packets will follow alternative paths to their destination because routers will send them down wires with less network congestion to dissipate data 'traffic jams.' Packets will

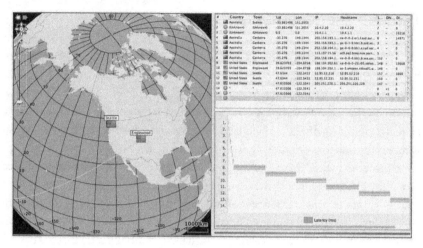

Figure 6.8 A map showing the route a data packet takes from Western Sydney University to CoinJar's servers in Seattle (using Visual Traceroute).

not necessarily take the shortest or quickest route so their mobile geographies are (relatively) randomised inasmuch as data corresponding to the same file can be sent around the world in completely different directions.[13] This 'random' flow of information between different infrastructure is why the Internet is often referred to as distributed (Galloway, 2004).

Throughout this process, the packet will be modulated into various physical mediums to reach the destination IP address. For example, the packet may be in the form of light in order to travel through fibre optic cables but electromagnetic waves when mediated by copper wires. All these translations of information have to occur through space in order for signals to move. Figure 6.8 shows the partial topological geography of a packet moving through space via this infrastructure, relayed by the IP addresses shown. When all of the packets reach the Coinjar server they are reassembled as information. The TCP on the receiving end builds the data back together, using the labels given by the sending TCP/IP, and transfers this data up the server's software stack so that it can be computed.

This seems like a purely mechanical process but it would be a fallacy to neglect the vast quantity of human labour necessary to maintain the infrastructural networks through which data moves (Star, 1999, 2002; Graham & Thrift, 2007; Larkin, 2013; Easterling, 2014; Starosielski, 2015; Hu, 2018). When the packets sent by my computer 'finally' reached the CoinJar servers (taking a matter of seconds), the software housed there recognised my request and executed a transaction on the Bitcoin blockchain via a node. To do this, the CoinJar servers used private keys stored in their hot wallet database to sign one or more of their public keys containing a sufficient amount of bitcoins to make a transaction fulfilling the parameters I provided. From there, the Bitcoin network 'manoeu-vred' to process my transaction.

Unlocking and Locking Scripts

To follow a 'moving' bitcoin via a transaction on the Bitcoin network, it is not only necessary to understand the materiality of data but also how infrastructure ties in with the semiotic aspect of code. In other words, a bitcoin must be understood as an entry in an algorithmic ledger: a number cryptographically locked into the blockchain (or multiple blockchains) by a line of computer code. A value of bitcoin is, quite simply, a yet unspent transaction waiting to be 'unlocked' and thus sent. It is spendable only to those who can 'prove ownership' by composing a script using their private key. Subsequently, the bitcoin value will be 'unlocked' and encumbered to another address with a locking script (where someone can prove ownership in the future with their own private key and therefore spend it again). This is how bitcoins are transferred.[14]

When I clicked the 'Pay now' button, the information I typed in on the CoinJar website reached its servers and a layer of software interacted with CoinJar's copy of the blockchain to issue a transaction to the network. Using the Bitcoin Core client downloaded on my computer, I can make queries to the blockchain to pull up specific information about it. The hash of my transaction acts as a unique identifier (72dee1f9722f2e2b8cf1e0adc2f848960cdb-ba258995c5c538721792627cb4de) and I can find out more about it with the following command:

```
$ bitcoin-cli getrawtransaction 72dee1f9722f2e2b8cf1e0adc2f848960
cdbba258995c5c538721792627cb4de
```

This brings up a raw hex string "exactly as it exists on the bitcoin network" (Antonopoulos, 2015, 45):

```
{
  "result":
"0100000002f9602c9dd2210b9a766cd77af63509c512a5462f0b5d80f95e1f9
32bca3e04a3000000008a4730440220394e84e4482d686f2306f3de319dd6311
97cbcbe19ec124bbc1469e5cdacb4b602206989027dd07584478258c8731a4ef
55999c75d78e9f7966194d441986245c0070141041bf03370fbda6cdff62d00f
981b89974d04d3e65f81afda2f5432ad 46d79a105729d53d53109add7415a4e
6fe678c1b4570b12abb80c6a70b51e201f7866f098ffffffff15bc0ed0c9dae2
afac8e8be5f51f92b73118814fd2af7947c5001b8ded37eb13000000008b4830
4502210087ff990beeca5da432cfb9fc8cd43fa9bcd5964c19f46037a690802f
8bb5cdcc02202f4ee9ac4a252e4982c3a3d3ab1cb2346b363152f6c9fbdf3eb0
```

aefc596a386e014104b2751828d69e39f5f441e935cc0068aa1feff5c6124e22
c61e6fd1c39c39a12f948be04986bc729ba35b8e42d4271a2bd7b6b3fccbd00d
b4f78ac25f9043e7b5ffffffff0200e1f505000000001976a9142c7e06efc6a3
70c453d72b633b50d88b54410eb988ac4d2efc97000000001976a9144e57959a
52cc56e930bd9dd2005c06c9b4380f3288ac00000000",
    "error": null,
    "id": null
}

It can be decoded into a human-readable JSON data structure with the following command:

```
$ bitcoin-cli decoderawtransaction 100000002f9602c9dd2210b9a76
6cd77af63509c512a5462f0b5d80f95e1f932bca3e04a300000
0008a4730440220394e84e4482d686f2306f3de319dd631197c
bcbe19ec124bbc1469e5cdacb4b602206989027dd07584478258c8731a4e
f55999c75d78e9f7966194d441986245c0070141041bf03370fbda6cdff6
2d00f981b89974d04d3e65f81afda2f5432ad46d79a105729d53d53109ad
d7415a4e6fe678c1b4570b12abb80c6a70b51e201f7866f098ffffffff15
bc0ed0c9dae2afac8e8be5f51f92b73118814fd2af7947c5001b8ded37eb
13000000008b48304502210087ff990beeca5da432cfb9fc8cd43fa9bcd
5964c19f46037a690802f8bb5cdcc02202f4ee9ac4a252e4982c3a3d
3ab1cb2346b363152f6c9fbdf3eb0aefc596a386e014104b2751828d69e39
f5f441e935cc0068aa1feff5c6124e22c61e6fd1c39c39a12f948be04986bc729b
a35b8e42d4271a2bd7b6b3fccbd00db4f78ac25f9043e7b5ffffffff0200e
1f505000000001976a9142c7e06efc6a370c453d72b633b50d88b54410e
b988ac4d2efc97000000001976a9144e57959a52cc56e930bd9dd2005c
06c9b4380f3288ac00000000
```

This gives back the following result:

```
{
    "result": {
            "txid":"72dee1f9722f2e2b8cf1e0adc2f848960cdbba25899
            5c5c538721792627cb4de",
            "hash":"72dee1f9722f2e2b8cf1e0adc2f848960cdbba25899
            5c5c538721792627cb4de",
            "version": 1,
            "size": 437,
            "vsize": 437,
            "locktime": 0,
            "vin": [
                {
                    "txid":
"a3043eca2b931f5ef9805d0b2f46a512c50935f67ad76c769a0b21d29d2c6
0f9",
                        "vout": 0,
                        "scriptSig": {
                                "asm":

"30440220394e84e4482d686f2306f3de319dd631197cbcbe19ec124bbc1469
e5cdacb4b602206989027dd07584478258c8731a4ef55999c75d78e9f79661
94d441986245c007[ALL]
```

041bf03370fbda6cdff62d00f981b89974d04d3e65f81afda2f5432ad46d79a
105729d53d53109add7415a4e6fe678c1b4570b12abb80c6a70b51e201f7
866f098",
                                    "hex":
"4730440220394e84e4482d686f2306f3de319dd631197cbcbe19ec124bbc14
69e5cda cb4b602206989027dd07584478258c8731a4ef55999c75d78e9f796
6194d441986245 c0070141041bf03370fbda6cdff62d00f981b89974d04d3e
65f81afda2f5432ad46d79a105729d53d53109add7415a4e6fe678c1b4570b1
2abb80c6a70b51e201f7866f098"
                            },
                            "sequence": 4294967295
                    },
                    {
                            "txid":
"13eb37ed8d1b00c54779afd24f811831b7921ff5e58b8eacafe2dac9d0
0ebc15",
                            "vout": 0,
                            "scriptSig": {
                                    "asm":
"304502210087ff990beeca5da432cfb9fc8cd43fa9bcd5964c19f46037a69080
2f8bb5cdcc02202f4ee9ac4a252e4982c3a3d3ab1cb2346b363152f6c9fbdf3e
b0aefc596a386e[ALL]04b2751828d69e39f5f441e935cc0068aa1feff5c612
4e22c61e6fd1c39c39a12f948be04986bc729ba35b8e42d4271a2bd7b6b3fc
cbd00db4f78ac25f9043e7b5",
                                    "hex":
"48304502210087ff990beeca5da432cfb9fc8cd43fa9bcd5964c19f46037a6
90802f8bb5cdcc02202f4ee9ac4a252e4982c3a3d3ab1cb2346b363152f6c9f
bdf3eb0aefc596a386e014104b2751828d69e39f5f441e935cc0068aa1feff5
c6124e22c61e6fd1c39c39a12f948be04986bc729ba35b8e42d4271a2bd7b6b
3fccbd00db4f78ac25f9043e7b5"
                            },
                            "sequence": 4294967295
                    }
            ],
            "vout": [
                    {
                    "value": 1.00000000,
                    "n": 0,
                    "scriptPubKey": {
                            "asm": "OP_DUP OP_HASH160
2c7e06efc6a370c453d72b633b50d88b54410eb9 OP_EQUALVERIFY OP_
CHECKSIG",
                            "hex":
"76a9142c7e06efc6a370c453d72b633b50d88b54410eb988ac",
                            "reqSigs": 1,
                            "type": "pubkeyhash",
                            "addresses": [
                                "154FhxVKSgL1LHqdazwHHQVB9bho
                                ACdABj"
                            ]
                    }
            },
            {
                    "value": 25.49886541,
                    "n": 1,
                    "scriptPubKey": {
                            "asm": "OP_DUP OP_HASH160

4e57959a52cc56e930bd9dd2005c06c9b4380f32 OP_EQUALVERIFY OP_
CHECKSIG",
                                "hex" :
"76a9144e57959a52cc56e930bd9dd2005c06c9b4380f3288ac",
                                "reqSigs": 1,
                                "type": "pubkeyhash",
                                "addresses": [
                                    "189EdS6GUt2xBYNuUwAkuaun4hVeU
                                    HNGLb"
                                ]
                        }
                }
    ],
    "hex" :
"0100000002f9602c9dd2210b9a766cd77af63509c512a5462f0b5d80f95e1f
932bca3e04a3000000008a4730440220394e84e4482d686f2306f3de319dd63
1197cbcbe19ec124bbc1469e5cdacb4b602206989027dd07584478258c8731a
4ef55999c75d78e9f7966194d441986245c0070141041bf03370fbda6cdff62
d0 0f981b89974d04d3e65f81afda2f5432ad46d79a105729d53d53109add74
15a4e6fe678c1b4570b12abb80c6a70b51e201f7866f098ffffffff15bc0ed0
c9dae2afac8e8be5f51f92b73118814fd2af7947c5001b8ded37eb130000000
08b48304502210087ff990beeca5da432cfb9fc8cd43fa9bcd5964c19f46037
a690802f8bb5cdcc02202f4ee9ac4a252e4982c3a3d3ab1cb2346b363152f6c
9fbdf3eb0aefc596a386e014104b2751828d69e39f5f441e935cc0068aa1fef
f5c6124e22c61e6fd1c39c39a12f948be04986bc729ba35b8e42d4271a2bd7b
6b3fccbd00db4f78ac25f9043e7b5ff ffffff0200e1f505000000001976a91
42c7e06efc6a370c453d72b633b50d88b54410eb988ac4d2efc970000000019
76a9144e57959a52cc56e930bd9dd2005c06c9b4380f3288ac00000000",
    "blockhash" : "00000000000000000cfb1ac5f1ff134d2af6fb28a480b18
    03f826660d6a3eb65",
    "confirmations" : 132538,
    "time" : 1444905414,
    "blocktime" : 1444905414
},
"error": null,
"id": null
}

Here, the "value" of my 1 BTC can be seen in the output data of the transaction as it is sent to the public key of the address 154FhxVKSgL1LHqdazw-HHQVB9bhoACdABj. This can be visualised differently by using third-party block explorer software from blockchain.info (see Figure 6.9). In this instance, the private keys stored in CoinJar's hot wallets executed a transaction using two inputs from two different public keys under its control: 0.03766541 BTC from 16gS8FzUN8rbno5Jgr6G1psBtzqiMbLyiN and 26.4614 BTC from 19c7a88Y-qDWfst6WeQK3sBAxQktsTzhWvQ. This works in the following way:

The fundamental building block of a bitcoin transaction is an *unspent transaction output* or UTXO. UTXO are indivisible chunks of bit-coin currency locked to a specific owner, recorded on the blockchain, and recognized as currency units by the entire network. The bitcoin network tracks all available (unspent) UTXO, currently numbering in the millions. Whenever a user receives bitcoin, that amount is recorded within the blockchain as a UTXO. Thus, a user's bitcoin may be scattered as UTXO amongst hundreds of transactions and hundreds of blocks. In effect, there is no such thing as a stored balance of a bitcoin address or account; there are only scattered UTXO, locked to specific owners. (Antonopoulos, 2014, 114)

Elaborating further:

The UTXO consumed by a transaction are called transaction inputs, while the UTXO created by a transaction are called transaction outputs. This way, chunks of bitcoin value move forward from owner to owner in a chain of transactions consuming and creating UTXO. Transactions consume UTXO unlocking it with the signature of the current owner and create UTXO locking it to the bitcoin address of the new owner. (Antonopoulos, 2014, 115)

So, the bitcoin attributed to both input addresses in Figure 6.9 are actually just bundles of unspent transactions locked to a public key, the value of which is stored in multiple blocks in the blockchain. What the blockchain actually records is the 'location' of these unspent transactions and so "bitcoin[s] can be thought of as a chain of *transactions* from one owner to the next, where owners are identified by a *public key* . . . that serves as a pseudonym [for that person/ machine]" (Meiklejohn et al., 2013, 128).[15] Bitcoin wallets created by third parties, then, do not store balances per se but "count transaction inputs and outputs to display a virtual balance . . . [s]o it is best to think of wallets as an important and *active* part of Bitcoin *infrastructure* rather than passive repositories for money" (DuPont, 2019, 60). Figure 6.10 shows a partial transaction history of

Figure 6.9 A summary of my Bitcoin transaction (using blockchain.info).

these bitcoin values that can be traced back to when they were first brought into existence via a mining block reward—this bundle of new bitcoins is called the 'coinbase' (from which the capitalised company takes its name). Essentially, a transaction allows bitcoins to 'change hands' algorithmically.

The CoinJar node executes this transaction by creating an unlocking script ("scriptSig") that fulfils the conditions of the previous locking script ("scriptPub-Key"), which originally 'stored' it at the public key where it currently resides (see the JSON data structure earlier in this section). CoinJar "produces unlocking scripts containing signatures for each of the UTXO, thereby making them spend-able by satisfying their locking script conditions. The wallet adds these UTXO references and unlocking scripts as inputs to the transaction" (Antonopoulos, 2014, 119). It then creates a locking script to my Coinbase public key (1 BTC to the address 154FhxVKSgL1LHqdazwHHQVB9bhoACdABj), defining the parameters of how the coins can be spent in the future: anyone who can provide an unlocking script with the corresponding private key to its public key (i.e., Coinbase).[16] The transaction has two outputs because the Bitcoin code insists all bitcoins from a wallet in a transaction must be spent. The rest (25.49886541 sent to 189EdS6GUt2xBYNuUwAkuaun4hVeUHNGLb) acts as the 'change' of the transaction and goes into another address owned by CoinJar. There is also a difference between the total inputs (26.4990654 BTC) and total outputs (26.49886541 BTC) of 0.0068 BTC, which acts as a fee for the miner who puts the transactions into a block.

The use of cryptography in a peer-to-peer network does something interest-ing here: it allows for the dispersion, or rather individualisation, of control over spending bitcoins. The logic of locking and unlocking coins—despite being per-formed materially by cryptographic code running on machines in the boundar-ies of nation-states—is what works to defy territoriality because a public key can be used to sign a transaction to a Bitcoin node from anywhere in the world, henceforth submitting it to the network. This allows those with coding skills to spend bitcoins 'autonomously' without permission from third parties. But most people do not have this expertise and so the vast majority of network transac-tions move (the control of) coins (UTXO) from one island of company pro-prietary software to another (like I do here). Since submitting private keys to the network *is* the mechanism for storing and spending bitcoins, whatever the geographic dispersion of the Bitcoin nodes, spatial centralisation can occur via private key management. In other words, because of technical barriers to entry, there exist multiple obligatory passage points (in the form of company software) that the vast majority of the market must pass through in order to access the protocol.

It could be said, then, there are two strata to the Bitcoin network based on private key control: 1) a proprietary layer where transactions are controlled by

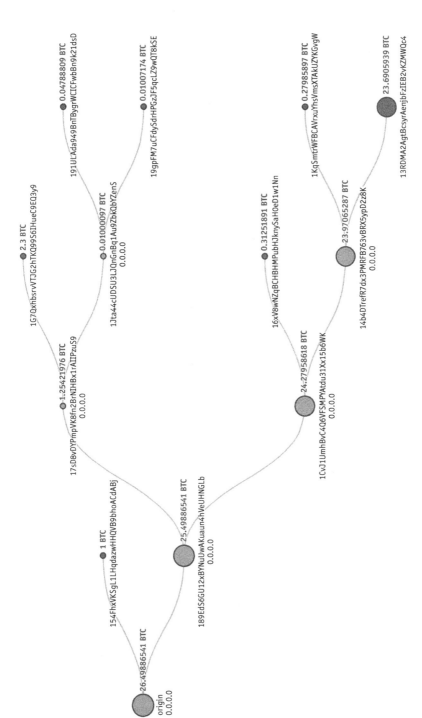

Figure 6.10 A partial history of the chain of transactions across the blockchain that constitute the bitcoin I am following (using blockchain. info).

institutions, and 2) a discrete layer where transactions are controlled by individuals. This can be likened to the surface web where the majority of Internet activity takes place supported by regulated companies and the dark web where content can slide under the surface out of view if one has the knowledge and skills to access it. In terms of this book's overarching critique, the centralisation of private keys occurs via the proprietary layer, which reattaches the control of spending coins to Bitcoin banks and acts as a limitation to algorithmic decentralisation.[17]

Broadcasting Transactions

At this stage the transaction has only been executed on a single Bitcoin Core client located on Amazon's Seattle-based servers rented by CoinJar. To move the value between addresses the transaction must become part of the networked consensus by being mined into a block existing on (multiple copies of) the blockchain. Before this can be done the transaction needs to be broadcast to other nodes in the network:

> Bitcoin is structured as a peer-to-peer network architecture on top of the Internet. The term peer-to-peer or P2P means that the computers that participate in the network are peers to each other, that they are all equal, that there are no 'special' nodes and that all nodes share the burden of providing network services. The network nodes interconnect in a mesh network with a 'flat' topology. There is no server, no centralized service, and no hierarchy within the network. Nodes in a peer-to-peer network both provide and consume services at the same time with reciprocity acting as the incentive for participation. (Antonopoulos, 2014, 139)

This "flat" topology is important to the spatial configuration of Bitcoin because *full* nodes (shown in Figure 6.7) are structurally equal, creating a systematic protocol greater than the sum of its parts. Each Bitcoin node

> is connected to a few other bitcoin nodes that it discovers during startup through the peer-to-peer protocol. The entire network forms a loosely connected mesh without a fixed topology or any structure making all nodes equal peers. Messages, including transactions and blocks, are propagated from each node to the peers to which it is connected. A new validated transaction injected into any node on the network will

be sent to 3 to 4 of the neighboring nodes, each of which will send it to 3 to 4 more nodes and so on. In this way, within a few seconds a valid transaction will propagate in an exponentially expanding ripple across the network until all connected nodes have received it. (Antonopoulos, 2014, 113)

Therefore, the CoinJar node is only connected to a small number of "neighbouring" nodes that it discovers in order to participate.

The term "neighbouring" is topologically, as opposed to topographically, defined: nodes are selected at random across the network as opposed to being chosen due to their geographical proximity (Antonopoulos, 2014). But just because the protocological logic of discovering other nodes is not defined by spatial scales, it does not mean space itself is moribund. It is through the very process of forming random connections, as identified earlier, that the network becomes resilient and allows Bitcoin to maintain spatial stability as a protocol. By connecting to random peers, a node establishes diverse paths into the Bitcoin network:

Paths are not reliable, nodes come and go, and so the node must continue to discover new nodes as it loses old connections as well as assist other nodes when they bootstrap. Only one connection is needed to bootstrap, as the first node can offer introductions to its peer nodes and those peers can offer further introductions. (Antonopoulos, 2014, 146)

It is across this randomised, fluid, mutating, algorithmic, and spatial fabric—running almost parasitically on top of the *relatively* fixed, anchored, and rigid infrastructural host of the Internet—that transactions flow. At the level of protocological logic, this seems to fulfil the ideal of stigmergy: a collective and collaborative self-organising system where distributed agency eradicates hierarchal interaction (see Bonabeau et al., 1997; Tkacz, 2015). The term 'stigmergy' derives from the social makeup of insect colonies composed of many individuals acting autonomously to create a functioning whole. This idea is often extrapolated to the design of particular digital networks, which are valorised for organising humans without centralised control.

Back to the transaction, the server-based CoinJar client executed and broadcast the information to a couple of nodes it was connected to (these could have been located anywhere in the world). It does this using the same TCP/IP protocol and material infrastructure of the Internet that delivered data packets from my computer to the CoinJar server (because the transaction contains no sensitive information about the transactor it can be broadcast across insecure networks). The receiving nodes refer to their own copy of the blockchain and the rules laid out in the locking scripts from where the UTXOs are coming from. If the transaction is invalid (i.e., does not follow the rules already laid out via a senatorial governance model—see Chapter 5), these nodes will not send it any further and will send an error message back to the CoinJar node instead. In this instance, however, the nodes validated the transaction and sent it on to their neighbouring nodes. After a couple of seconds, the transaction was propagated across the whole of the Bitcoin network. Despite the stigmergic logic of the nodes, asymmetrical power can still form in different ways. The spatial distribution of Bitcoin mining is one example of this.

Making a Hash of Things

The geography of bitcoin mining is complex and relatively opaque, although certain characteristics can be discerned. I have so far followed my bitcoin to a point where the transaction has saturated the network. As of yet, however, the transaction has not been recorded in the blockchain but rather is sitting in the mempool of each network node. At a technical level this means each computer running a Bitcoin client is storing the transaction in its memory temporarily; the network knows the transaction is there but it has not yet become solidified in the ledger. Using a web-based blockchain monitoring software created by TradeBlock, my transaction can be seen among other transactions submitted to the network along with a visualisation of the entire mempool at this time: the transaction was one of 8,135 waiting to be mined into a block with a total transaction value of 95,373.15 BTC (1.007 BTC accounting for mining fees) and a total size of 4.29 MB (see Figure 6.11). At the time, the Bitcoin network was experiencing a swell in the amount of transactions due to one or more 'attackers' flooding the network with low-value transactions as a form of protest designed to convince other users that block sizes needed to be raised (Appendix 18).

Some of the network nodes are miners who are looking to add these transactions to the distributed ledger in return for a block reward and transaction fees. To understand these actors, it is crucial to make sense of hashing in context to Bitcoin. Hash functions are the cryptographic backbone to the Bitcoin protocol.[18] They are "algorithms that compress messages into fixed-length strings of bits (usually called hashes, message digests, or fingerprints). That is, given as input a digital object of arbitrary length (e.g., a document, an image, a software program), the hash function will output a fixed-length (e.g., 128- or 160-bit) fingerprint" (Blanchette, 2012, 68). In other words:

A hash function is an easy-to-compute compression function that takes a variable-length input and converts it to a fixed-length output. The hashes in which we are interested, called cryptographic hash functions, are 'one-way', which is to say, they should be easy to compute and 'hard', or computationally expensive, to invert. Hash functions are used as a compact representation of a longer piece of data—a *digital fingerprint*—and to provide message integrity. (Landau, 2006, 330)

These characteristics have led to hash functions becoming integral to digital security systems (Perrig & Song; 1999; Stinson, 2006). Bitcoin utilises hash functions in many parts of the protocol: transactions in a block are hashed together to form a Merkle root, a fingerprint that references all transactions in that block; each block contains the hash of the previous block to ensure it mathematically links to all other blocks (and therefore transactions) in the entire chain (for a schematic diagram of these processes see Figure 6.12); individual transactions are identified with their hash (see Figure 6.9); the process of creating wallets and signing transactions using public key cryptography is based on hash functions (see Figure 6.1); and mining uses hash functions to prove work has gone into

(a)

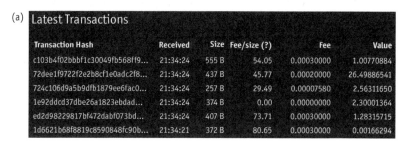

Transaction Hash	Received	Size	Fee/size (?)	Fee	Value
c103b4f02bbbf1c30049fb568ff9...	21:34:24	555 B	54.05	0.00030000	1.00770884
72dee1f9722f2e2b8cf1e0adc2f8...	21:34:24	437 B	45.77	0.00020000	26.49886541
724c106d9a5b9dfb1879ee6fac0...	21:34:24	257 B	29.49	0.00007580	2.56311650
1e92ddcd37dbe26a1823ebdad...	21:34:24	374 B	0.00	0.00000000	2.30001364
ed2d98229817bf472dabf073bd...	21:34:24	407 B	73.71	0.00030000	1.28315715
1d6621b68f8819c8590848fc90b...	21:34:21	372 B	80.65	0.00030000	0.00166294

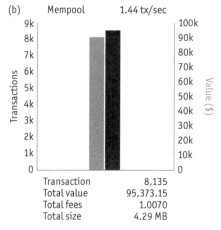

(b)   Mempool   1.44 tx/sec

Transaction	8,135
Total value	95,373.15
Total fees	1.0070
Total size	4.29 MB

Figure 6.11 My transaction sitting among others and a visualisation of the entire mempool (using TradeBlock).

Longest Proof-of-Work Chain

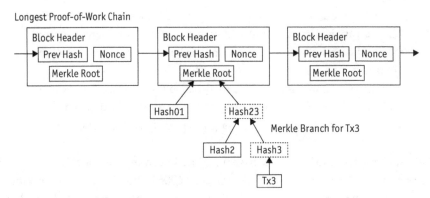

Figure 6.12 Transactions hashed together into a Merkle root and then hashed with a nonce and the overall hash of the previous block to form a chronological chain (source: Nakamoto, 2008).

forming blocks, personifying network security. In fact, cryptographic hashes are what give bitcoins stability as digital 'things': "[t]hrough the use of the hash algorithm, the digital object is, in a sense, ontologically reified" (DuPont, 2019, 150).

It is the last process, mining, that solidifies my transaction from the mempool into the blockchain. Bitcoin mining accomplishes four things: it 1) administrates transactions; 2) negates double spending; 3) mints new coins; and 4) secures the protocol. To do so, it utilises the mechanism proof-of-work, which is a vehicle for effectively proving someone (a machine) has engaged in a significant amount of computational effort to solve a problem—while challenging to solve, the *proof* of said work is easy to verify. The protocol enforces this process by demanding a block hash must fit a certain format in order to be validated (i.e., it has to start with a certain number of zeroes). A random piece of data called a nonce is added to transaction data in order to alter the appearance of the block's hash (see Chapter 1). It is the job of miners to find a nonce that produces an acceptable hash. If the hash does not fit the required format (by having the requisite amount of preceding zeroes) it will be rejected and a new nonce can be tried. Since there is no way of knowing what the resultant hash will look like there is no way of shortcutting the system and so the only way of finding a desired hash is with brute force (trying as many nonces as possible). These attempts are made at incredible speed: during the time of my transaction, the cumulative hashing power of the entire Bitcoin network was 465,548,432 Giga hashes per second (GH/s). Mining machines around the world hash together all the transactions they wish to include in the next block (normally the ones with the highest transaction fees) and rapidly fire nonces at this value to create a resultant block hash that fits the parameters of the protocol (correct number of preceding zeroes). The energy intensiveness of this process is a crucial factor for mining geographies.

Into the Mines

Cryptocurrency mining has its own economic geography dependent on the costs of electricity (to reduce expenditure), atmospheric temperature (to reduce overheating), and access to hardware (to mine in the first place). For example, some mining farms have been established in Iceland where cheap geothermal energy is in abundance and cold temperatures keep chips from overheating (Cuthbertson, 2014; Brunton, 2015; Price, 2016). The State of Washington in the United States also houses a number of mining farms due to its cheap electricity in comparison to other states (Banse, 2014; Higgins, 2016c; CryptoNinjas, 2017). More commonly, however, miners are found in China. Here, coal power stations (and local deals made with them) make the economics of mining considerably cheaper than the rest of the world, leading to an overwhelming geographical concentration (Swanson, 2014b; Vincent, 2016). In fact, over 70% of mining power is based in China (Swanson, 2014b; Vincent, 2016; Tuwiner, 2017).

So while the 'record keepers' of Bitcoin (people running full nodes) are heavily coalesced in Western countries, 'ledger writers' (miners) are predominantly located in China. This makes for a system, supposedly immune to geographical factors (especially the control of nation-states), surprisingly vulnerable to any legislation made by the Chinese government—although the spatial flexibility of the Bitcoin network means it should easily survive any imposition by relocating the mining element of its dispersed algorithmic 'body' to other jurisdictions. More important, however, this pattern currently means the release of new coins is mainly flowing to Chinese miners. In 2017, cryptocurrency exchanges were made illegal in China so these "miners have had to turn to nearby exchanges in Japan, South Korea, and Vietnam in order to exchange mining rewards for local state-issued currency" (DuPont, 2019, 17). This transfers a considerable amount of lobbying power in Bitcoin's senatorial governance structure to exchanges within these countries (see Chapter 5).

There is another way aspects of the Bitcoin network have been affected by its mining geography. In 2015, it became apparent Chinese miners were producing empty blocks at a higher rate than non-Chinese miners. The reason for this was found to be the "bandwidth bottleneck" imparted by the Great Firewall of China (Kaiser et al., 2018, 7; see Chapter 2). As described earlier, it takes time for winning blocks to propagate across the network, which can be slowed down by up to four-and-a-half times due to packet inspection imposed by the Chinese government (Kaiser et al., 2018). Because empty blocks contain less data they are less disadvantaged by this latency. Consequently, a disproportionate amount of Chinese miners began submitting empty blocks to the network (forgoing transaction fees) in order to increase the likelihood of winning block rewards,

Figure 6.13 Bitcoin mining hardware (source: Mu, 2015).

where the most value currently lies (Kaiser et al., 2018). This aspect of Bitcoin's money/code/space caused a dislocation between cryptoeconomic incentives and the best interest of the network because empty blocks are useless for people trying to spend bitcoins. Protocol upgrades later addressed this problem in June 2016 but, for a time, this case study demonstrated how geographic relationships can stifle certain features of digital architectures. Evidently, "space impacts data transfer across locations due to latency and bandwidth" and so "the location of hardware matters" (DuPont & Takhteyev, 2016).

Mining farms come in many shapes and sizes: from home operations in people's garages to industrial-sized warehouses (see Figure 6.13). The Chinese giants exist predominantly in rural areas where connections with power stations, that burn cheap coal or run hydroelectric dams in the mountainous West, provide the most cost-effective enterprises (Mu, 2015; Vincent, 2016; Xingzhe, 2017). Journalists visiting Chinese Bitcoin mines have revealed some interesting insights into their operations: one example used roughly $80,000 USD per month to generate the necessary electricity to function (Motherboard, 2015). Thousands of mining chips filled the warehouse with a constant heat while the perpetual drone of ventilation systems turned it into a giant wind tunnel (Motherboard, 2015). The workload for employees who maintain these warehouses is particularly dull so they fill their time with poker, computer games, mobile phones, and sleep (Motherboard, 2015). These spaces are crucial for understanding software as hardware-at-work:

All of this human and nonhuman labor reminds us . . . [there are] mate-
rialisms, infrastructures that support the Bitcoin code and the network
of Bitcoin users. . . . But first and foremost among such infrastructures
is the electrical grid, on which miners draw, often heavily, to power their
rigs and sustain the P2P network. The electricity 'expended' in the service of Bitcoin energizes not only the miners' race to generate the next
block in the chain but also their interactions with one another, their
own chatter in online forums and elsewhere. (Maurer et al., 2013, 272)

In fact, electricity is a crucial factor for all digital geographies because it is crucial
for activating silicon chips (just see how inert a computer becomes when it is
unplugged). While screen essentialism often hides infrastructural qualities like
this from the users of software (see Chapter 3 and Appendix 12), Bitcoin creates
more of a paradox:

Bitcoin's practical materialism allows the chatter in the code, the proof of
work, the materiality of the machines humming and whirring in mining
rigs to be simultaneously backgrounded and foregrounded. This is not
simply commodity fetishism [or screen essentialism]. The code and the
labor are backgrounded when Bitcoin adherents become latter-day goldbugs. But the code and the labor are foregrounded because they are practically all that Bitcoin enthusiasts ever talk about. (Maurer et al., 2013, 274)

This is an interesting contradiction: while the money/code/space of Bitcoin is
often championed as escaping the bounds of materiality and spatiality, adher-
ents simultaneously reference material and spatial components to demonstrate
how Bitcoin can exist as a decentralised network in the first place.

Building Blocks

At 21:37 on the 15th October 2015, an unknown miner forged the
block containing my transaction into 'existence' with the block hash
00000000000000000cfb1ac5f1ff134d2af6fb28a480b1803f826660d6a3eb65.
More information can be seen by running a command on my Bitcoin client:

```
$ bitcoin-cli getblock 00000000000000000cfb1ac5f1ff134d2af6fb28
a480b1803f826660d6a3eb65
```

This returns an enormous hex string, which I have truncated here:

{
    "result" :
"03000000d8f7bc53da6945767141668b72a51888a206df827db5420e000000
0000000000a442579809f75064f2dbfffc15d85577700a6d7763c600d32fa3f
f00dc70ff08c6811f5672141218449d97cffdc70701000000010000000000000
00000000000000000000000000000000000000000000000ffffffff2e03
73c8050004bb811f5604c97b940c0c67a525809b4b0100000000000a2020202
020200a2f72657365727665642bffffffffff0105da1497000000001976a91489
62b0e97f434b91304e542940782b2db487a8cf88ac00000000010000001354a
96799764a77fa77a935975419220f06759dff7a1a9aa74780e71b6968a11b01
0000006c493046022100ccdef778e1f8e829591473a2ca31e88420d4a673656
45bdc016074e5e2f5cdb902210089f6a
...[many, many characters later]...
e36f7583f99b1c21b9739edb44e15c13caccb6ff96521105aac0b20fa8d6050
12103ac781768f01c110bf69db28f90f68465ce480a4114352b10f2f7278a9b
ebf5b1fefffffffc2d15ad0239147b19582fa65b3c118413a28ddd491fda0c1e
4b14dc2a82ebacd010000006b483045022100e76203c3cbb79cfb85a7ba6cca
c22d4aa5ccaa151f2b2adf7f0f13e4e2aa48030220752ea8d2611404e2429e7
61afaa74b3c41c3d10fdd841c913e2b9f5cb6704a7401210266e6c8a73c142e
6fdfc8a1d5bbc14e2a74c66e87dbccefad7771a8b98679b6cffeffffff02981
e1e00000000001976a91495c57675d843edc7f0bf1cde402665c98ac187e688
ac04005c00000000001976a914022f8e86831b2fa9ef129987a62c266f6a6
4befe88ac68c80500",
    "error": null,
    "id": null
}

Decoding this into a JSON data structure, the block appears as such:

{
"result" : {
        "hash" : "0000000000000000000cfb1ac5f1ff134d2af6fb28a48
        0b1803f826660d6a3eb65", "
        confirmations": 132541,
        "strippedsize": 749184,
        "size": 749184,
        "weight": 2996736,
        "height": 378995,
        "version": 3,
        "versionHex": "00000003",
        "merkleroot":"08ff70dc00ffa32fd300c663776d0a707755d8
        15fcffdbf26450f709985742a4",
        "tx": [
            "569acc2a4c56bc601f99e1cef8574fdf356ab771231b84
            c71fc30655ec8a8dbf",
            "711c305fd880f43923088e11a090d1bbaf7ab9cfd99abe
            84bd0e961cbe933b6a",
            "9f1e00a24e9f0bb821da316f3c371b60a2a55b455f214b
            a81a63bbc4 18d65376",
            "e8a9628b62e01b3c1236811e91ada0756d20619a14b771
            957e3ea146159828a2",
            "6a8822212445776eacc105920fa4e6329b13a676747296
            a3b8e635ee2f9ffc6c",
            "7ffb94b9127c146e2e778f32489a5fcbcb1aa2d8a88560
            91d1bbd6697b44a83a",

```
        ...[many transactions later]...
        "72dee1f9722f2e2b8cf1e0adc2f848960cdbba258995c5
        c538721792627cb4de",
        ...[many transactions later]...
        "9ff74257f73ae805b77d4969dc48e1fda71fbea728b7e6
        17a9ae00d344bd21fe",
        "a951edcb8c9ce00b408a2c3a2e9d42e331cc8c7ae1799b
        f8c9d63966d448dc44",
        "d6e1402845ac1db4b18983639cce533b01b2ab97b411ca
        993e32d92090ec5c82",
        "2ec7bf22343e323eaef34b06e8491b63e4a94c476e4ac0
        41dd2c71e86f806c8a",
        "c67d0da73fc1fd965961a1f459da1c1af6f2a742ca0fc0
        653a46a57034c70920",
        "35d552247630e952081da94673a64561f1f9d18103c693
        536cf82e75ebb4fec5"
      ],
      "time": 1444905414,
      "mediantime": 1444900044,
      "nonce": 3482819908,
      "bits":
      "18121472",
      "difficulty": 60813224039.44035,
      "chainwork":
  "0000000000000000000000000000000000000000000b1eb7bd1b599ea52996
  b8",
      "previousblockhash":
  "00000000000000000e42b57d82df06a28818a5728b664171764569da53bc
  f7d8",
      "nextblockhash":
  "000000000000000003f48e42bb6ad8f85826009a129f1e5f65a747fbee47
  c989"
    },
    "error": null,
    "id": null
}
```

Here, my transaction can be seen among hundreds of others in a block numbered 378,995. These transactions are hashed together to form the Merkle root which is then hashed with the nonce 3482819908 (found by the winning miner at a difficulty value of 60813224039.44035). These lines and lines of code are supported by thousands upon thousands of electrical signals in a multitude of computers that tie together (mathematically) to form a functioning blockchain. TradeBlock software measures the information of the shared blockchain in real time to construct a form of blueprint (see Figure 6.14). The block contained 1,990 other transactions and had a size of 731.63 KB (added to every machine maintaining the blockchain). When the winning miner finds a correct nonce they broadcast their newly formed block to the network, which is checked by the node's peers in the same way a transaction is, with the block hash acting as proof of the work done to form it

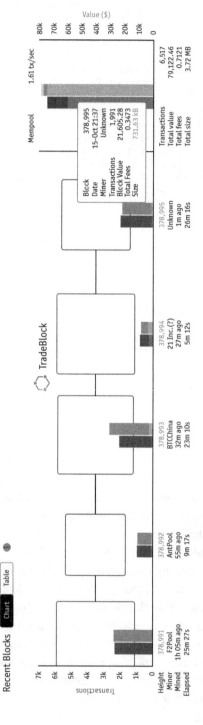

Figure 6.14 A visualisation of the blockchain (using TradeBlock).

(0000000000000000cfb1ac5f1ff134d2af6fb28a480b1803f826660d6a3eb65).[19]
The reason some miners can be identified is blocks have a space that can contain a certain amount of arbitrary metadata and miners now tend to use this
space for 'tagging' the block as a promotional measure.[20] Figure 6.14 shows
how, for my own block, this was not the case but the previous blocks were
mined by mining pools 21 Inc. (US), BTCChina (China), AntPool (China),
and F2Pool (China). The concentration of these pools in 2015 demonstrates
how mining is not just somewhat geographically centralised but institutionally
so (see Figure 6.15).

When the winning miner locked my transaction into a block and broadcast
it to the rest of the network, other miners (and nodes) were able to check
the proof-of-work and start mining on top of that block. As more blocks
'pile' on top of the block containing my transaction it becomes 'buried' in the
ledger's transactional history, making it harder for miners to build a forked
blockchain that could omit it. My transaction therefore becomes more stable
over time as the likelihood this singular version of history can be changed
decreases exponentially—however, rewriting the chain can certainly still
occur (see Chapter 8). This can be seen in the JSON data structure as "confirmations": the "getblock" command repeated earlier was run over two years
after the time of the transaction, accounting for 132,541 confirmations. Once
the block was formed my transaction was locked in place and under control of
Coinbase instead of CoinJar.

From there, I logged onto my Coinbase account, typed in the value of 1
BTC (at an exchange rate of $253 USD) and clicked the 'Sell bitcoin' but-
ton. The Bitcoin value disappeared from my account and the company sent a
bank transfer to my Wells Fargo account (see Figure 6.16). Value had finally
'travelled' across borders via the Bitcoin network supported by a plethora of
paraphernalia. Yet the value of one bitcoin had not really *moved* anywhere: it
was merely an update in an algorithmic ledger where claims upon it from different parties had changed. For this to be achieved, many moving parts across
different world spaces had to cooperate. In the process, they helped form
Bitcoin's vast algorithmic fabric. So, although mining farms are often station-
ary operations, the Bitcoin protocol is always busy: the network constantly
(re)assembles as individual miners leave and join different pools. Borrowing
vocabulary from Arjun Appadurai (1990), certain actors might seem fixed in
space but they cater for "global flows." In this case, the movement of information across Bitcoin's polyfurcated nodes allows value to shift across its restless
algorithmic body.

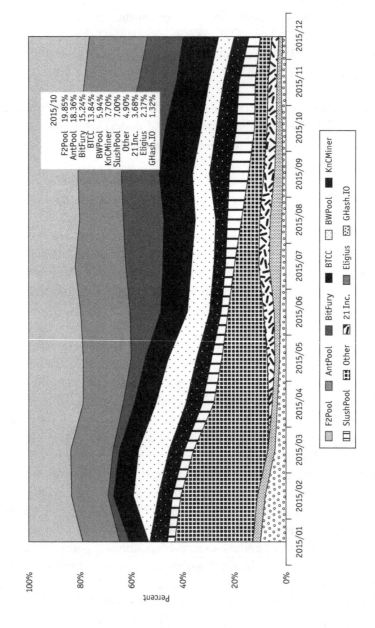

Figure 6.15 Mining pool distribution in October 2015 (using BTC.com).

	2015/10
F2Pool	19.85%
AntPool	18.36%
BitFury	15.24%
BTCC	13.84%
BWPool	5.94%
KnCMiner	7.70%
SlushPool	7.00%
Other	4.90%
21Inc.	3.68%
Eligius	2.17%
GHash.IO	1.32%

F2Pool   AntPool   BitFury   BTCC   KnCMiner

SlushPool   Other   21Inc.   BWPool   Eligius   GHash.IO

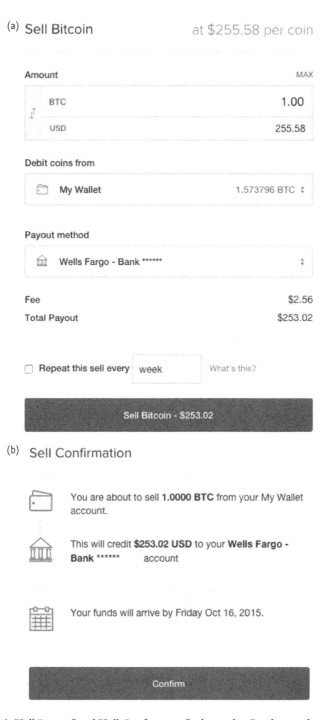

Figure 6.16 "Sell Bitcoin" and "Sell Confirmation" tabs on the Coinbase website.

New Financial Space-Times

Although bitcoins derive value from being part of a network, where "decentralization, as well as the public-key encryption of users' identities, is hardwired into the system" (Maurer et al., 2013, 268), the spatial coalescence of certain practices and trajectories outlined in this chapter illuminate geographies of centralisation. While the software logic is radically distributed, fulfilling cypherpunk dreams, material constraints limit the effects of the process of algorithmic decentralisation. Sy Taffel (2015c) helps explain this phenomenon:

> Although software does play a crucial role in contemporary societies, this role is a relational one that is entirely dependent on a series of other equally crucial areas, such as human attention and reliable sources of electrical energy, silicon and other essential materials for constructing digital architectures. Digital materiality includes the materiality of software but must also go beyond code to explore the broader technocultural assemblages that software is dependent upon. (332)

So, while exploring the technical apparatus of software is important for Bitcoin's money/code/space, other materialities must be considered to understand how power forms across the network. For example, "significant economic forces push towards de facto centralization and concentration among a small number of intermediaries at various levels of the Bitcoin ecosystem" (Böhme et al., 2015, 219–220). Capital accumulation demands degrees of centralisation to enhance profits, which Bitcoin is not immune from (see Chapter 7). As with algorithmic trading (Beverungen & Lange, 2018), humans are not omitted from the picture but compete for different aspects of its architecture (Bitcoin banks for private key control; mining farms and pools for block rewards). The geographies of algorithmic decentralisation are quite evidentially uneven.

Blockchain architectures, however, relate to time as much as space. This is in one sense obvious, as Bitcoin has a brief but rich history (see Chapter 4). In another, this claim is more poignant: software mediates and shapes the spatial *and* temporal flows of society (Kitchin, 2019). For example, codified traffic light signals allow cars to pulse through cities at regular intervals (Kitchin, 2019). In other words, algorithms create algo-rhythms (Miyazaki, 2012). In the case of Bitcoin, individual transactions are grouped and executed in blocks synchronised through the network at the predetermined average rate of 1 block every 10 minutes.[21] This is the heartbeat of the crypto-financial system, regularised and conditioned by the entire downstream series of activities, contingent upon the transfer of currency units. Here, then, are the beginnings of a new sense of temporality—neither the slow cycles of conventional money transfers, nor the millisecond response times of high-frequency trading, but rather a constant metronomic pulse, a block of transactions pushed to every blockchain on a global network in (roughly) 600-second intervals. It could be imagined, blockchains offering a geographic and an algorithmic genealogy—an 'indelible,' persistent sequence of interlinked events that, paraphrasing Rob Kitchin and Martin Dodge (2011), shape the world.

Conclusion

For Stephen Graham (1998), "there is not one single, unified cyberspace; rather, there are multiple, heterogeneous networks, within which telecommunications and information technologies become closely enrolled with human actors, and with other technologies, into systems of sociotechnical relations across space" (178). This chapter supports Graham's conceptualisation by demonstrating how Bitcoin forms part of a fragmented, but connected, multiplicity. Infrastructural research is, then, always partial: it "is a moment of tearing into those heterogeneous networks to define which aspect of which network is to be discussed and which parts will be ignored" (Larkin, 2013, 330). By tracing the material-semiotic networks of Bitcoin's code (with different methods), 'segments' of its money/code/space can be better discerned.

If the recent turn to the materiality of the digital is acquiesced, there comes a resistance of what remains resolutely symbolic—signs, symbols, data, algorithms, information, and informatic structures. Certainly these do not sit on, but are enacted by, hardware (Kitller, 1995). Digital things, therefore, should not escape the scrutiny of material culture scholarship. But at the intersection between the cryptographic and the geographic is a methodological query. Precisely, the desire to reveal, unveil, or lay bare—all elaborations of the Greek word 'graphein,' to write or draw—lie in the background of efforts to map the material (to make geographic) the apparently disembodied and immaterial operations of the digital. Yet it is worth noting, in the limits of method, the difficulties of tracing (at the level of IP packets or Bitcoin transactions) that which is written in such a way as to be hidden. Indeed, earth writing (geography) and code writing (cryptography) can be polarising doctrines. An obvious point here is to draw the lines at where method may begin to delineate the contours, boundaries, and perimeters of what it can survey and, conversely, what remains in these novel digital spaces intentional 'terra incognita.'

Indeed, following the (digital) thing as method may prompt more questions than it answers. It inevitably asks what difficulties the digital ethnographer is likely to encounter when they attempt to reveal what is designed to be obscured even from federal agencies like the NSA. How much of these new algo-geographies remain crypto-geographies, moving beneath the surface, a subterranean set of operations that only leave behind hints of their passage? This can only be answered by engaging more closely with these networks. For Bitcoin, the material geography of cultural-economic flows is, on one hand, fluid and global but, on the other, immobile and local (Appadurai, 1990). At the same time, parts of the network appear distributed and others centralised. Quite clearly, Bitcoin embodies some reiterations of the inequalities geographically produced in other existing currencies to date.

While I have presented a Bitcoin transaction as a linear system, different aspects of the codified architecture maintain their own boundaries. The meta-geographies of deeply localised material infrastructures support an entire network of social relations from Sydney to San Francisco, Iceland to China. But the cryptographic processes that bind the Bitcoin protocol together mean geographies of ownership (where bitcoins are moving to and from) are deliberately opaque despite the fact ledger transparency displays which addresses are spending and receiving coins. There is, then, only a partial severance of coins in the economy from inspection. Crypto/spaces are in a continuous tension between the known and the unknown.

7

Embedded Centralism

Introduction

This chapter takes a step back from the maintenance and operation of Bitcoin code and moves into the entrepreneurial activity that has grown up around it. I extend my critique of algorithmic decentralisation by following Bitcoin into Silicon Valley where a blossoming cryptocurrency and blockchain start-up ecology has taken root. This ecosystem has emerged as an integral site of production, performance, contention, regulation, and normalisation for the development of distributed ledger technologies. Indeed, "[e]ven when proponents of cryptocurrencies and sharing economies push self-consciously against a vision of the money-based economy, such projects are also inextricably intertwined with mobile technologies and digital infrastructures, start-up culture and venture capital" (Nelms et al., 2017, 24).

The term 'obligatory passage point' is initially backgrounded in favour of 'economic embeddedness,' which describes proximate networks of interdependent firms existing in specific industrial spaces. This concept better captures the murky entrepreneurial networks underpinning proprietary software that can act like gateways to blockchains. To do so, I draw from participant observation conducted in start-up companies and meet-up groups to tease out nuances of cryptocurrency enterprise. This works to reconnect globalised blockchain architectures with the milieus of humans who both dream them up and plug into their networks with application software. In the process, I continue to delineate Bitcoin's money/code/space by interrogating the geographic relationships of cryptocurrency businesses currently spearheading (r)evolutions in finance and technology, while further highlighting contradictions of algorithmic decentralisation.

In the past, the hypermobility of information through digital networks has been championed for lifting economic transactions out from their social and spatial settings to create a world market operating without borders (Martin, 1978;

Toffler, 1981; Giddens, 1990; Negroponte, 1995). More recently, this dominating view of the economy has been rendered inaccurate by ethnographers of cultural and economic embeddedness (Ross, 2003; Amin & Thrift, 2002; Tsing, 2005; Zaloom, 2006). Instead, as modern economies have become saturated by digital practices, the role of financial centres, like London or New York City, has not lessened but increased (Graham & Marvin, 1996; Sassen, 1991; Clark & Thrift, 2005; Florida, 2008). The concept of embeddedness is used here to represent the concentration of connections maintained between actors on a number of different spatial scales (Hess, 2004). Far from an imaginary of free-flowing transactions, this understanding highlights urban spaces as "centres of calculation" (Latour, 1987, 215) that can act like financial or monetary valves within broader financial networks (McNeill, 2017).

I set the scene by describing the rise of FinTech: a rapidly expanding industrial sector that has quickly absorbed cryptocurrencies and blockchain technology into its rubric. From here, Silicon Valley is shown to be a key economic site for Bitcoin entrepreneurial activity thanks to its dense historical and geographic networks. This cultural specifity is expanded upon to introduce the tensions at play in the San Francisco Bay Area's urban environment and how these intersect with the growing Bitcoin industry. The Californian Ideology is reintroduced to understand how it becomes enacted in new ways through contemporary settings. The chapter then demonstrates how 'disruptive' technology transitions into the economic status quo (Herian, 2018): as start-ups begin to replace traditional financial services they also become increasingly embedded in situated industrial networks (see also Ferrary & Granovetter, 2009). As this happens, various actors start redirecting cryptocurrency companies down a familiar path of normalisation and capital accumulation where radical politics are diluted. Ultimately, embedded centralism transforms processes of algorithmic decentralisation.

The Rise of FinTech

The conjunction 'FinTech' was first coined in 1993 by Citigroup to refer to their Financial Services Technology Consortium (Kutler, 2015; Hochstein, 2015). It wasn't until the mid-2000s, however, that it became a popular idiom within the financial sector more generally. Since then, it has been used as an umbrella term to encompass time-tested technologies used by financial institutions as well as more 'cutting edge' solutions designed by agile start-up companies that are forcing their traditional counterparts to keep up with the pace of innovation.

On one level, then, FinTech start-up companies represent a paradigm shift of banking services from Wall Street to Silicon Valley.[1] Historically, the global financial sector has been one of the largest markets for technology producers with its vast hunger for hardware, software systems, and databases (Lodge et al., 2015; Holley, 2015). Currently, however, segments of the high-technology sector are stepping away from their contractual role and are attempting to displace existing financial providers through increasingly commonplace services like PayPal, Google Wallet, Apple Pay, Square, Stripe, Dwolla, TransferWise, Venmo, and Monzo. In terms of capitalisation, from 2013 to 2018, $357.4 billion USD was invested in FinTech companies worldwide (KPMG, 2019). By 2019, 41 FinTech unicorns—private companies with a valuation of over $1 billion USD, initially named to symbolise their rarity—existed globally, 15 of which were based in Silicon Valley (CB Insights, 2019).

Cryptocurrencies and blockchain technology have not only been caught up in this wave but have catalysed FinTech's momentum by helping imagine alternative frameworks for facilitating value and governing transactions (Coinbase and Circle stand out as two cryptocurrency unicorns). For example, many new start-ups plug into blockchains like Ethereum to utilise them as a form of external "trust machine" (The Economist, 2015). Here, they provide added services or create their own cryptocurrencies and/or smart contracts to conduct state of the art financial transactions. The boundaries of the financial sector are thus shifting to encapsulate global technology hubs, which very much includes cryptocurrency enterprise. As such, traditional modes of banking are being challenged by the innovations of digital architects.

Post-2008, Wall Street and the City of London were subject to a significant amount of demonisation, personified by the Occupy Wall Street protests. Contrastingly, positive images associated with technology start-ups largely survived the 2001 'tech wreck.' These organisations have maintained 'cool' company cultures, boasting supposedly flattened hierarchies: employees are liberated to make a palpable internal impact and 'change the world,' while being rewarded with appealing stock options (Ross, 2003).[2] This positive depiction of technology firms is helped by consumer attachment to products like iPhones and Google Search. Similarly, popular culture movies like *The Social Network* (2010) celebrate the innovation of Silicon Valley whereas films like *The Big Short* (2015) vilify the testosterone-fuelled recklessness of Wall Street.[3] As Mathew Bishop, US business editor of *The Economist*, once put it: "Google [is] the company that can do no evil and [Goldman Sachs is] the giant vampire squid" (The Economist, 2013).[4]

Layoffs on Wall Street and the enormous accumulation of capital gathered by successful technology entrepreneurs, in an industry barely touched by the financial crisis, have contributed to a growing trend of graduates and careerists moving to Silicon Valley, generating a talent war between banks and technology companies (The Wall Street Journal, 2013). For some in the banking sector, the FinTech movement may thus carry a dual meaning: 1) a series of actions and events fostering a new trend of financial services taken up by the technology industry (akin to a political movement), and; 2) the literal migration of talent and services from financial to technological hubs.[5] This curious cultural osmosis at the intersection of finance and technology has allowed digital pioneers, particularly in the blockchain industry, to preach a form of start-up moral economy. This image is based on creating fairer infrastructures free from the hierarchal control, giant overheads, and massive fees maintained by large banks, notorious for their lack of innovation and their role in creating boom and bust cycles.

This is not a straightforward transition from old to new ways of conducting finance but a contention over competing systems and an ensuing power struggle for future profits. Bitcoin is sitting uncomfortably between conflicting ideologies as it becomes entangled and incongruent amidst a growing number of stakeholders. The rest of this chapter goes on to address the growing fragmentation of Bitcoin proponents to better understand Silicon Valley's role as a guarantor of finance in blockchain economies. In doing so, it delineates the ringed fences built around 'sections' of decentralised protocols. To begin with, I briefly turn to the conceptual development of economic embeddedness.

Embedding Economies

The regional economy of industrialised technology development in Silicon Valley—which now includes San Francisco (see McNeill, 2016)—nurtures an extraordinary start-up creation rate (Zhang, 2003). Reasons behind the Valley's high-technology agglomeration, as a geographical anomaly, have been the subject of many academic papers and corporate white papers since the 1980s (Saxenian, 1983, 1990, 1996; Hall & Markusen, 1985; Angel, 2000; Zook, 2002; Farlie & Chatterji, 2009). Arguments include positive feedback effects (Arthur, 1994), venture capital presence (Lee et al., 2000; Ferrary & Granovetter, 2009), knowledge spillovers (Jaffe et al., 1993; Audretsch & Feldman, 2003), highly skilled mobile labour (Saxenian, 1989a; Angel, 1991; Benner, 2003; Huber, 2011), exceptionally high employment turnover rates (Parden, 1981; Rogers & Larsen, 1984; Kenney, 2000; Koepp, 2002; Zhang, 2003), and niche culture (Delbecq & Weiss, 1990; Harris & Junglas, 2013). The term 'embeddedness' is useful because it can be used to capture many of these processes by encompassing a wide variety of factors. At the same time, it allows nuances to emerge from ethnographic research methodologies. I use it here as a theoretical tool for understanding how algorithmic decentralisation is reshaped through entrepreneurial activity.

The concept of embeddedness helps ground economic theory back to places of material action and cultural practice. However, it is a relatively fuzzy term with a plethora of applications (Hess, 2004). It was first used by Karl Polanyi (1944) to describe economies that function via personal relationships in local space as opposed to more modern, *abstract* markets that seem to be both disembodied and disembedded from material action. In other words, Polanyi saw transactions operating at a global level (across borders) as being detached from everyday human interaction (for a detailed critique see Hess, 2004). Subsequent scholars have worked hard to dismantle this vision of a dislocated global market by emphasising the social and spatial relationships implicit to *all* economies (Granovetter, 1985; Hess, 2004). The idea of embeddedness, then, ensures markets are understood as a plethora of actors (traders, economists, tickers, computer screens, paper, texts) that work together to enact financial transactions (Callon, 1998a, 1998b, 2007; Callon & Muniesa, 2005). Similar to Stephen Graham's (1998) theorisation of the Internet as a multiplicity of different networks, the 'global market' is composed of many tessellated spaces. These are heterogeneously layered so there are, in fact, a multitude of interlocking markets operating simultaneously at different scales.

It is these markets that bleed into each other to form the 'world economy,' yet they continue to maintain (in part) their own distinct boundaries.[6] When talking about the role of specific spaces for enacting economic activity, as this chapter does, it is important to understand that linkages are maintained at many geographic levels (not just the simplified local-global dualism). This is a "shift in the analytical focus, away from fairly abstract economies and societies towards the analytical scales of actors and networks of interpersonal relationships" (Hess, 2004, 170). In short, embeddedness is used here to describe context-specific social, spatial, and political interaction. This focus on nested synergy helps prevent the term from turning into something slippery (see Pike et al., 2000). I thus define embeddedness as the concentration of spatially relevant (dis)connections between an assemblage of humans and non-humans working together to form economies. Before demonstrating how these networks affect processes of decentralisation, I detail the historical economic geography of the San Francisco Bay Area to unpack its role as a key site for the production of blockchains.

The Silicon Valley Model

Despite many endeavours to do so, the success of Silicon Valley is incredibly hard to replicate thanks to a genealogy both geographically and historically specific (Sturgeon, 2000). The economy has evolved contextually and contingently over time: a plethora of individual (but interlinked) actors resonated together to amplify the economic productivity of the regional whole (see Appendix 19). The Valley first rose to fame in the 1950s for its silicon chip production. While the technology sector has experienced its fair share of turbulence in terms of yield, a time-tested (overall) flexibility has allowed it to mutate within a rapidly changing industrial landscape. It did this predominantly by diversifying into

> new industrial sectors such as personal computers (Apple) and soft-ware (Oracle, Sun Microsystems, Symantec, Electronic Arts, Intuit). Later, Silicon Valley gave rise to telecommunication equipment start-ups (Cisco System, Juniper Networks, 3Com) and finally to the internet industry (Netscape, Excite, eBay, Yahoo!, Google). Each new industry was supported by the previous industries. (Ferrary & Granovetter, 2009, 338)

Throughout, Silicon Valley has persistently been the envy of every declining industrial region (Markusen cited in Saxenian, 1981). Today, it is still seen as the standard-setter for technological production (Gordon, 2001). With vary-ing degrees of success, countless municipalities worldwide have attempted to imitate its cultural-industrial milieu and, in turn, its economic output (Malecki, 1981; Taylor, 1983; Miller & Côté, 1985; Saxenian, 1989b; Leslie 1993; 2000; McNeill, 2017).[7]

The key difficulty for industrial impersonators lies in 'synthetically inject-ing' deeply embedded relationships between firms that have been 'organically cultivated' over a long period of time. This history of entrepreneurship has har-nessed many industrial connections, which are often called upon to support pioneers of technological enterprise. While this culture is difficult to export, it can be ethnographically examined to understand distinct subtleties. I argue the "institutional thickness" of Silicon Valley, as a technological-financial centre, has a poignant effect on the trajectory of Bitcoin start-ups and their application of algorithmic decentralisation (Amin & Thrift, 1994). Embedded connectivities of space, that (dis)allow companies to grow, cater for radical technological ideas but also tend to tame ventures as they expand, rendering them manageable and profitable under the Silicon Valley model. Centralisation is very much part of this domestication: the absorption of start-ups within larger entrepreneurial networks dilutes 'disruption' by pulling companies in on themselves as a centre of bureaucratic control. From here, aspects of blockchains (like private keys) are more easily ordered and controlled.

The strong presence of Bitcoin firms in the San Francisco Bay Area is largely down to a continuation of the "historical process of embedding" (Dicken & Thrift, 1992, 287). The rich entrepreneurial networks provide a fertile environment for businesses to thrive. Consequently, pioneers not only originate in the Valley but are attracted to the region from wide and far due to the support their fledgling companies can receive from an economy fine-tuned to cultivate start-ups. When there came a sudden landslide of cryptocurrency and blockchain venture capital between 2014 and 2016, it is no surprise it fell predominantly in this one place (Young, 2015a; Popper, 2015b). By 2016, the area accounted for 53% of global financing in the sector (CoinDesk, 2016b). However, this is by no means unique to the cryptocurrency and blockchain industry as Silicon Valley dominates all US venture capital investment (Harris & Junglas, 2013). Such a pattern has been integral for supporting the local technology industry since the 1950s (Saxenian, 1989a): territoriality of investment has been pinpointed as a key reason for the regional economy's success (Saxenian, 1983; Florida & Kenney, 1988; DiBona et al., 1999; Lee et al., 2000; Ferrary & Granovetter, 2009). Here, free-flowing capital fuels the development of new technology like no other place on the planet (Gershon, 2014).

The connections of economic embeddedness are an increasingly important aspect of money/code/space because software created in industrial regions interacts with, reshapes, and, in some instances, are themselves blockchains. Here, David Golumbia's (2015, 2016b) critique of Bitcoin, as encompassing contradictory tenets of right-wing extremism, becomes particularly compelling (see Chapter 4). However, my ethnographic research demonstrates this is by no means a monoculture: not all individuals in distributed ledger technology industries uphold cyberlibertarian beliefs and values. However, different actors collide and come together in specific ways to form an overall vector reminiscent of the Californian Ideology. Put differently: the sum of individual parts creates a greater whole due to how they interact. In this sense, the Californian Ideology is not necessarily an all-encompassing worldview held by everyone in Silicon Valley (although some certainly adopt this vision) but is more an overall trajectory of varying practices conducted by disparate groups. This gives the impression of a singular philosophy, but the Californian Ideology usually functions like a Californian Assemblage. With regard to this, as I cater for diversity in my ethnographic analysis, I try to understand how cyberlibertarianism is maintained through difference. The concept of embeddedness allows these subtleties to be teased out while observing the role of various stakeholders in regurgitating and maintaining dominant economic practices as a collective whole.

A Crucible of Tension

Walk into most cafes in the San Francisco Mission District today and they will be filled row upon row with people tapping away on laptops. A small but growing group now sitting among them are cryptocurrency and blockchain proponents.

In the financial world, hacking is usually relegated to credit card fraud and identity theft but this new crowd are complicating that relationship somewhat: many see themselves as fighting an evangelistic battle to wrench monetary control away from banks and place it into the hands of publics, like modern-day Robin Hoods. However, certain tensions have arisen as Bitcoin becomes caught uncomfortably between hacker and high technology culture.

A documentary titled *The Rise and Rise of Bitcoin*—once described to me by a strategic advisor at a cryptocurrency wallet company as "Bitcoin porn"—outlines the conception and growth of Bitcoin through its adolescent stages (Mross, 2014). Halfway through, the filmmaker visits a hacker hotel called 20Mission situated in the Mission District of San Francisco.[8] There, he interviews Jered Kenner, founder, and then CEO, of the US based Bitcoin exchange TradeHill. Not only did Kenner operate TradeHill from inside 20Mission, but he was also the subletting 'landlord' of the 41-bedroom co-living/co-working space, where he has housed many other cryptocurrency start-ups (Khoshaba, 2014; Gilbertson, 2015). The wider Mission District, however, is not always so accommodating to technology companies—this became particularly palpable during the dotcom boom when the city arose as one of the densest locational nodes for companies in the global Internet industry (Zook, 2005).

Away from the technology crowds I mixed with for my research, my social life led me to another parallel world. The gentrification-fuelled inflation of rental rates, perpetuated by an influx of "techies" into the area, had pushed my housemates deep into Outer Mission and they had taken with them a disdain for workers in the technology industry.[9] On one occasion, I was invited to an after-party in a fully functioning industrial warehouse of the Mission District that had been simultaneously compartmentalised into an illegal hostel (secretly holding thirteen residents from all over the world in disguised rooms). Sitting on a mismatch of chairs encircling a makeshift table, I was initially met with a degree of hostility when I mentioned my research involved "Silicon Valley." However, after explaining I was examining the cryptocurrency community the tone immediately changed; here, the struggle for bottom-up disruption by 'hackers' was endorsed but the top-down power of giant technology companies vilified. Yet, rightly or wrongly, Bitcoiners often find themselves tarred with the same 'techie brush' as the latter.

In April 2015, I attended a book signing party for *The Age of Cryptocurrency* (Vigna & Casey 2015) held at 20Mission where I met Jared Kenner and many of the hacker hotel residents (see Figure 7.1). The building had already become a landmark for cryptocurrency enthusiasts in the Bay Area. It had once hosted the San Francisco Bitcoin Developers Meet-up but, as I was told by its organiser, "the locals didn't like the idea of white techies hanging around." Members of the Mission District community had notified their district authorities, explaining

Figure 7.1 20Mission book signing party for *The Age of Cryptocurrency.*

how the lower floor of 20Mission was operating as office space when it was legally zoned for retail.[10] While many of the Bitcoiners I met at these meet-ups saw themselves as altruistic philanthropists, looking to flatten power structures for everyday people, local residents could not distinguish them from their technological cousins at Google or Facebook. Perhaps, though, there is no irony to this story: many 'countercultural hackers' and their ambitious start-ups are becoming caught in the jet stream of capitalism, thus losing their radical edge (see Herian, 2018). Before this is explored, it is worth noting how these situated events evoke political tensions and contradictory perceptions among different groups occupying the same urban space. I now describe the cryptocurrency community in more detail and explain how the Californian Ideology plays out in practice.

Cyberlibertarian Hangovers

On the 23rd March 2015, I attended the Blockchain Global Impact conference at Stanford University in Palo Alto (see Figure 7.2). The room was littered with key Bitcoin figures from Core developer Peter Todd to Erik Voorhees, founder of Satoshi Dice, Coinapult, and ShapeShift. The keynote speaker, John Perry Barlow, was a founding member of the Electronic Frontier Foundation (EFF), formed in 1990 to campaign for the preservation of personal freedoms and online civil liberties, and was a key figure for the cyberpunks, having written the Declaration of the Independence of Cyberspace in 1996 (see Chapter 4). This

Figure 7.2 Blockchain Global Impact conference at the Arrillaga Alumni Center, Stanford University.

manifesto mimicked Thomas Jefferson's allegorical tone of discovery and free-dom, which accompanied colonial expansion into the West of North America (Barbrook & Cameron, 1996). By "insisting on decentralization, multiplicity, plurality, and identity fragmentation, these movements rejected traditional forms of institutional authority (parental, educational, state) that were consid-ered to be constraints on individual emancipation" (Ouellet, 2010, 182).

With the widespread utilisation of encryption, many cyberlibertarians believed "free-spirited individuals [would] be able to live within a virtual world free from censorship, taxes, and all the other evils of big government" (Barbrook, 2001, 52). In the process, the EFF became a "leading cheerleader for the indi-vidualist fantasies of the Californian ideology" (Barbrook, 2001, 51). Somewhat surprisingly, however, the chimerical tones of this vision survived the 2001 dotcom crash. Discourse reminiscent of early countercultural digital politics still reverberates around global technology hubs today: exemplified by Barlow maintaining relevance as the headline for a cryptocurrency and blockchain con-ference at Stanford University—an academic institute that itself nurtured the empowering free-to-use DIY culture of the early Internet (Auletta, 2009; Hillis et al., 2013). In fact, there has been a certain revival of this discourse: many cyberlibertarians, who sat down after the Internet failed to fulfil their radical dreams, have dusted off their hymn sheets and stood back up for Bitcoin.

Barlow's speech held a nostalgic romanticism for the Internet's adolescence, which he referred to as a "nervous system." Redolent of anti-statist defiance from old cyberpunks, alloyed with more modern twangs of resistance to government surveillance in light of Edward Snowden's revelations, his rhetoric carried the underlying message: "the Internet was always going to be on some level about freedom from authority." At the same time, however, it was certainly a more sobering account of cyberlibertarianism than its many historical incantations. Barlow even claimed, upon writing his declaration, that he actually "knew better" than to expect the Internet to grow into an ungoverned, global, digital space but thought it would be good to encourage others to fight back against control by trying to subvert "the greatest surveillance tool ever devised as a liberty granting utopia."

Whether this is true or not matters less than what actually happened: the Internet became swamped by enterprise. Yet many Californian Ideologues do not see this as a problem, instead championing the dominance of corporations as expressions of the market (a necessary and unadulterated power). This aligns the 'free' market with personal 'freedom' so that positions of control, as long as they are voted for by dollars, are seen as legitimate. Such capitalisation of cyberspace echoes sentiments of Walter Wriston's (1992) *The Twilight of Sovereignty* that saw technology and unregulated markets as a mechanism able to "take over the responsibility of running much of society from the politicians" (Curtis, 2011). Echoing Hayekian tropes, government-imposed democracy is seen as tyrannical whereas market-imposed democracy embodies 'true freedom' representative of 'the people.'

This cyberlibertarian vision of economic freedom has translated into aspects of cryptocurrency and blockchain discourse with substantial potency. Erik Voorhees, for example, who later that day talked on alternative economies, sees the enrolment of citizens into the banking industry via state-enforced currencies as a form of coercive centralisation (Voorhees, 2015). However, from his point of view, financial services offered by different Bitcoin companies instil a just, market-based centralisation. This distinction, he claims, is crucial: in a world of centralised Bitcoin companies, freedom of choice keeps them from acting with impropriety and thus "Bitcoin enables users to withdraw into the neutral pasture of decentralized finance at any time, which means that any centralized service within the sphere exists only at the pleasure of its customers" (Voorhees, 2015). Here, the "key to judging the legitimacy of centralization is always the ability of users to opt out" (Voorhees, 2015). Under this definition, it is the availability of other services that makes an industry decentralised, whereas a lack of public choice (like the state imposition of central banks) is seen as an intrusive and corrupt form of centralisation. Yet it is important to recognise this vision of decentralisation is akin to 'island hopping' from one centralised service to another. Overlooking or legitimising the power of centralised private companies is a common cultural trait within the cryptocurrency community: a cyberlibertarian hangover that persists.

Incongruities like this are promoted by successful Silicon Valley entrepreneurs who continue to see the digital as a new frontier separate from material space. For example, Peter Thiel, the founder of PayPal and early investor of Facebook, endorses this disconnect, seeing technology as a means for moving beyond the political into "some undiscovered country," which can become "a new space for freedom" (Thiel, 2009). He states:

> In our time, the great task for libertarians is to find an escape from politics in all its forms—from the totalitarian and fundamentalist catastrophes to the unthinking demos that guides so-called 'social democracy'... In the late 1990s, the founding vision of PayPal centered on the creation of a new world currency, free from all government control and dilution— the end of monetary sovereignty, as it were. In the 2000s, companies like Facebook create[d] the space for new modes of dissent and new ways to form communities not bounded by historical nation-states. By starting a new Internet business, an entrepreneur may create a new world. The hope of the Internet is that these new worlds will impact and force change on the existing social and political order.... We are in a deadly race between politics and technology.... The fate of our world may depend on the effort of a single person who builds or propagates the machinery of freedom that makes the world safe for capitalism. (Thiel, 2009)

Thiel's claim that PayPal releases citizens from the monetary control of nation-states is also a lasting spectre and delusion of the Californian Ideology (see Appendix 20). Despite its initial cyberlibertarian goals, the company's politics were increasingly watered down as it matured. This was even recognised by Barlow at the Blockchain Global Impact Conference:

> Then PayPal came along and it was a pretty good shot at it but they really, at the last critical moment, did decide that it was better, whatever their philosophical beliefs, to have an incredibly successful company and become ridiculously rich than to fight over the principle that had been the downfall of many people, like David Chaum, up to that point.

If stubbornness concerning political principles killed Chaum's DigiCash (see Chapter 4), then the malleability of Thiel's PayPal allowed it to succeed. In short, the shedding of radical ideas is useful for achieving economic success. In the process, technological liberation is often held up like a beacon of power-opposition while the industry overlooks its own role in promoting new technologies of control that often perpetuate the capitalist system. It was with an insightful conclusory remark reflecting this notion that Barlow ended his speech, announcing to the room: "you are designing the architecture of liberty and enslavement both in these tools that are being derived around the blockchain and other things like it."

Hackers vs. Suits

The writing of Rebecca Solnit (2014a, 2014b, 2016a) has painted Silicon Valley technologists as a monocultural intrusion sweeping into the urban landscape of San Francisco (see Appendix 21). While from the outside technology crowds may seem like a homogenous incursion, from the inside they operate via a multitude of separate but overlapping ecosystems—from sectors in the regional economy (venture capital firms, law firms, etc.) to coding practices (Angular JS, Python, etc.). This bricolage was also evident in the burgeoning cryptocurrency community, described to me by the COO of a Bitcoin start-up based in Sunnyvale:

> It's really interesting to see how many different lines there are. Because there are efficiency nuts, to 'I just want my payments better,' to 'fuck the government, don't pay taxes,' to 'I want my drugs,' or 'I love cryptography'. . . Right now everyone's together and we're united by a desire to create a Bitcoin economy. Once the Bitcoin economy is created there's less . . . holding all these people together.

The sheer quantity of cryptocurrency and blockchain meet-ups in the San Francisco Bay Area during my research also reflected this bounded diversity.[11] A co-presence of different strata in the community is emblematic of two opposite forces: splintering and cohesion. This contradiction is an important cultural attribute with connotations for algorithmic decentralisation, developed throughout the second half of the chapter. For now, however, I focus upon a more specific oxymoronic co-presence: hackers and suits.

Meet-up groups emerged in 2011 when Bitcoin proponents, who had previously only gathered online, began seeking each other out face-to-face. They quickly became important venues for community building and acted as a springboard for the creation of some early start-up companies (Fletcher, 2013). Starting as a loose handful of enthusiasts talking over a few beers, many have now evolved into more formalised, focused, and goal-orientated events with specific weekly agendas (particularly in technology hubs). In Silicon Valley, they exemplify how the localisation of (in)formal links and the flow of knowledge thrive within the technology economy (Brown & Duguid, 2000). The first meet-up group I attended in the Bay Area was the same San Francisco Bitcoin Developers Meet-up (or SF Bitcoin Devs) that had once been ostracised from 20Mission. On an overcast Sunday morning, I made my way to StartupHouse in SoMa, a building that rents out work space to small companies and hosts group events such as this one. At the door I met a developer who had designed a Bitcoin client using the coding language Python as opposed to Bitcoin Core's C++. We entered the building, which sported a rustic décor, and made our way to a small room at the back (see Figure 7.3 and Appendix 22).

I took a seat around a long table where a small group of programmers sat coding on their laptops before the workshop began. Having arrived from Sydney, I was impressed by the number of meet-ups in the Bay Area and mentioned this to the developer next to me during some small talk. He laughed and said: "I used to go to all those social meet-ups before they were infiltrated by suits." It would become clear throughout my time attending these events that many of them had become a direct meeting point for both the more disruptive 'hacker' and the more capitalistic 'suit.' The San Francisco Bitcoin Developers Meet-up, however, was a realm belonging to the coding crowd (I was the only one in the room not a software developer). They attended for the intellectual challenge of building cryptocurrencies and the upheaval they promised to bring.

Industry leaders were invited to these events to discuss their projects. The meet-up that day was titled "SF Bitcoin Devs Hack Day: Proof-of-Stake and its Improvements." A developer for the cryptocurrency NXT went on to explain the

Figure 7.3 SF Bitcoin Devs Hack Day at StartupHouse, SoMa.

dynamics of the consensus algorithm he had been working on while everyone else chimed in collaboratively. In that small room, I was struck by the focus of the developer-centric betterment of concepts at the very frontier of this new technological arena.[12] This was not a top-down impartment of wisdom but, instead, knowledge was advanced among all the specialist and non-specialist programmers present.[13] Five hours of poking holes in models, critiquing and praising theories, proposing new ideas, and solving complex problems—intermitted with chatter concerning topical developments in the Bitcoin world—meant the attendees, many of whom worked at other cryptocurrency-related start-ups, left with a greater understanding of the topic at hand and with new concepts to utilise. Often, these meetings were recorded and posted online in an effort to promote open source software development on a global scale and thus benefit the Bitcoin ecosystem as a whole.

I continued attending the SF Bitcoin Devs meet-up over the following months. One such event was "Advanced Stellar Development for Bitcoin Developers" at Galvanize in SoMa (see Figure 7.4). Attendees sipped on bottles of IPA and ate slices of pizza (paid for by the company BitPay that sponsored the meet-up) while they waited for the talk to begin. The organiser started by announcing there was a "rockstar in the room." Someone jokingly asked if it was Satoshi Nakamoto, to which he replied: "No, it's his cousin Jed McCaleb!" Behind me sat McCaleb and his partner, Joyce Kim, both of who had recently left the company Ripple to set up Stellar (the enterprise presenting that evening). A former Google Wallet employee, and then developer at Stellar, gave a talk before the room was opened up for questions. Kim then addressed everyone who had attended, explaining how the developing world is where cryptocurrencies would

Figure 7.4 SF Bitcoin Devs Meet-up at Galvanize, SoMa (source: Lewis, 2015).

have the greatest impact due to their fragmented monetary systems that under-serve citizens.[14] This is part of a wider shift in narrative once described to me by a blockchain consultant as the industry moving from "fuck the banks and destroy fiat currency in 2012 to more bubbly things like banking the unbanked and facilitating remittances." At that point in time, (crypto)anarchy was already being repackaged for the sanitised corporate environment.

The meet-up came weeks after a lengthy article in *The Observer* (Craig, 2015) describing Stellar's teething problems.[15] There, McCaleb is described as being part of a coding crowd "market[ing] themselves as libertarian idealists who will pry the grubby fingers of the capitalists from their pristine idea of a frictionless currency" (Craig, 2015).[16] But the article also questions whether the oxymoron of 'corporate hacker' can ever truly achieve this. For one, start-ups constructed by these 'technology rebels' need to be banked, from simply holding accounts to attracting investment. It is common for banks to refuse services for start-ups in the cryptocurrency world. The saviour for many of these ventures has been Silicon Valley Bank (SVB), which has provided both investment and accounts for big names in the industry (like Coinbase and Xapo), taking risks in a field of regulatory uncertainty where others have refused. In a chance encoun-ter on the CalTrain—a railway carrying commuters up and down the spine of Silicon Valley between San Francisco and San Jose—I met a Vice President of SVB who worked on their pre-seed and seed-funded start-ups in San Francisco. She clearly outlined the bank's role in funding sapling companies as well as har-nessing connections with other firms for them to succeed (and thus generate profit for SVB).

Clearly, even the most libertarian 'hacker' needs banking contacts if they are to succeed in making their company dreams a reality. The article in *The Observer* highlighted this contradiction by quoting a San Francisco FinTech executive: "when these guys get together they have to talk disruption, disrup-tion, disruption, blowing everything up, and they are just full of themselves. But then they've got to get on a plane and go to New York looking for capital because it ain't coming from anywhere else" (cited in Craig, 2015). This fric-tion between coders and bankers is emblematic of the Bitcoin cultural economy where both worlds enigmatically collide. I encountered this many times at meet-ups, conferences, and FinTech Expos: watching 'collars' and 'no-collars' (suits and t-shirts) mingling in the same room as they looked to benefit from their alien counterparts.[17] This

> dichotomy affects all of Silicon Valley to some degree—blasphemous "Jobs Couldn't Code" T-shirts have even been spotted. Coders and purist disruptors are automatically cool; dealmakers and executives are tolerated but lame. This dynamic affects financial tech more than any

other sector. The need to present a pinstriped and responsible visage to the most highly regulated industry in the world faces off against the need to appear revolutionary when recruiting talent to actually build the systems. (Craig, 2015)[18]

The financer and the innovator depend on each other for success. It is a productive friction: they collide in a collaborative storm pushing the concepts reified in start-ups forward into the economy to chase profit. Yet, as software is (re)directed down paths conducive for capital accumulation, radical politics are often diluted as the companies prescribe to ideals and practices reminiscent of the Californian Ideology.

Before I move on, it is important to highlight Bitcoin meet-up groups as essential spaces for binding the community together and creating important links for the successful growth of the cryptocurrency start-up economy. If only for a few hours, they bring the multifaceted community together under one banner. I was told by various meet-up organisers their value lies in being a productive platform for networking.[19] A CEO at a company building smart contracts on top of the Ethereum blockchain explained the benefit of this embedded ecology to me:

So basically you need some sort of ecosystem, right? So you need somebody who can plug you in. Somebody who can introduce you to investors, introduce you to potential customers. In order to get those things there has to be some sort of active ecosystem. You mentioned meet-ups. So there has to be some sort of culture of people who are interested in these things who get together. So here there's a FinTech movement, sort of, if you will. Like last night we went to BNY Mellon innovation labs. So they had a meet-up there and I met some interesting people, made some good connections. And so BNY Mellon has a blockchain, kind of, program and would get in contact with those kinds of people. I would not have been able to do this anywhere else.

Such an ingrained industrial ecosystem, with spaces of overlap between different layers, is a crucial feature of Silicon Valley. The term 'knowledge spillover' has often been used to capture cross-firm learning networks (Audretsch & Feldman, 2003; Benner, 2003; Woodward et al., 2006; Huber, 2011). If knowledge indeed spills over between different institutions, then meet-up groups act like receptacles for catching it. Or, to use another metaphor, they are melting pots for mixing disparate actors who exist in an embedded economy. This is particularly useful for smaller, more unstable start-up companies without venture capital funding because meet-ups provide a support network in a volatile industry as well as an avenue for attracting investment (see also Jansson, 2011). Ultimately, however, those who fail to receive funding usually fade away. Consequently, the venture capital-backed start-up remains the key model for 'disruption' in Silicon Valley, which works to embed blockchain practices in more specific geographical space.

Tying It All Together

Bitcoin companies are relatively unique in the FinTech world in that they rest upon an open protocol. Bitcoin—with its mechanisms of algorithmic fiscal policy, public cryptographic ledger, dispersed mode of transaction clearing, pseudonymous privacy model, and open source code maintenance—is supposed to provide a monetary medium for everyone. With this in mind, it can be viewed through a particular lens: a form of global currency commons. In other words, the network could be exhibited as a publicly owned and regulated shared pool of currency accessible to populations across the world. It is, however, a commons with a catch: participants must be relatively well versed in programming languages and cryptographic key management to organise their own finances securely (using a personal copy of the Bitcoin protocol). What is more, potential users must buy-in or mine-in to the currency, creating significant technical barriers to entry. These impediments have presented opportunities for companies to enclose this currency commons by building centralised software gateways for accessing blockchains.

Companies streamline access for non-programmers by providing user-friendly on and off ramps while accumulating capital from fees in the process (see Figure 7.5). As Chapter 6 has shown, these layers of software make blockchains more calculable (i.e., TradeBlock) and operational (i.e., CoinJar). Yet transactional companies can also act like faucets for allowing or disallowing the flow of cryptocurrency through the network. Ultimately, a small number of experts are in control of this percolation. In terms of calculation, such intermediaries are common in traditional finance: offering services "akin to interpretation/evaluation/judgement" (Sassen, 2005, 27). These analytical processes are surprisingly reliant on embedded economies, requiring a "complicated mixture of elements—the social infrastructure for global connectivity—which gives major financial centers a leading edge" (Sassen, 2005, 27). Similarly, when it comes to blockchains, more complex, stratified, and meaningful data visualisations are compiled by software companies working out of urban environments. In terms of operation, intermediaries create more compound, sophisticated, and efficient services. These centres of calculation and operation create silos of more stratified, private information (about users or the overall economy) not available on public blockchains, giving those institutions a greater degree of clarity when interpreting the market. Clusters of these companies in Silicon Valley make the region a consolidated centre for such activity: a localised network of experts.

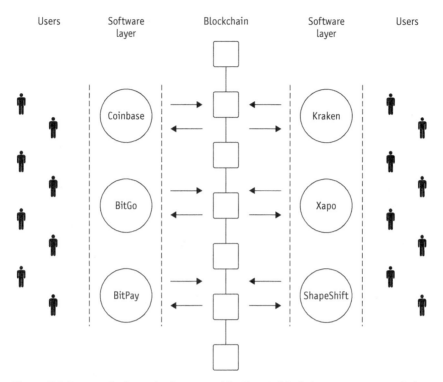

Figure 7.5 Layers of software built on top of the Bitcoin blockchain interacting with the protocol on the behalf of customers. This creates channels of user activity.

Combining the concept of obligatory passage points with empirical observations of entrepreneurial embeddedness has some important connotations because it opens up the cultural-economic processes that enforce certain centralising bottlenecks of network information/transactions. By examining how embedded activity is funnelled through these institutions, and how certain actors transform and control network practices, theories of decentralisation can account for the asymmetric power relations that form in markets. In other words, embedded obligatory passage points are a key component of any money/code/space. The ingrained (inter)actions of start-up companies and their links with other firms, like venture capitalists, ultimately transform algorithmic decentralisation.

Global Signallers

Networks of knowledge and capital are as much historical as they are geographical. Adam Draper, for example, is a third-generation venture capitalist based at "Draper University of Heroes" in San Mateo—an institute for teaching and facilitating entrepreneurship. His father, Tim Draper, is the managing director of venture capital firm Draper Fisher Jurvetson and is famous for coining the term 'viral marketing' (Sparkes, 2015). Going back further, his grandfather, William Draper, author of *The Startup Game* (Draper, 2011), created the first West Coast venture firm in Silicon Valley with Horace Gaither and Frederick Anderson in 1958 (Florida & Kenney, 2000; Zhang, 2003; Ferrary & Granovetter, 2009). The family has since moved into the cryptocurrency space: in 2012, Adam Draper positioned himself as one of the first investors in Coinbase (Money & Tech, 2014).

The Drapers later became owners of a vast quantity of bitcoins. When the FBI arrested the founder of Silk Road, Ross Ulbricht, in October 2013, they seized roughly 150,000 bitcoins and, in June 2014, the US government sold 30,000 of them (when their value was around $19 million USD) in a blind auction to a group of pre-registered bidders (Keneally, 2014; Rizzo, 2014; Rizzo, 2015a; Sparkes, 2015). Tim Draper was the winning bidder and his son, Adam, has since financed many cryptocurrency start-ups with those bitcoins at his community-driven accelerator, Boost VC, housed at Hero City, Draper University (see Figure 7.6). During my time in Silicon Valley I became friends with a few of the many start-ups working out of Boost VC who had come from all over the world to be incubated there. They arrived in "tribes" of over twenty companies periodically living and working together for three months in the same shared living and office space designed to help grow their business.[20] At the time, each

Figure 7.6 Hero City at Draper University, San Mateo.

company received $15,000–25,000 USD worth of bitcoins in return for a 6% share (Epicenter Bitcoin, 2015).

Silicon Valley is a hotbed for investors like the Drapers who retain an enormous amount of entrepreneurial knowledge and draw upon a vast industrial network. As such, their investments act as signals to the rest of the world, indicating the next big start-ups and innovative new technologies to take note of (Ferrary & Granovetter, 2009). This creates a global gaze from smaller investors: all eyes rest upon Silicon Valley. For this reason, the words and actions of prominent venture capitalists in the Bay Area also have normalising effects on what can first appear to be quite radical projects. Signalling technologies like Bitcoin as revolutionary reduces many anxieties surrounding them. For example, Marc Andreessen, cofounder and general partner of Silicon Valley–based Andreessen Horowitz—widely regarded as one of the world's largest venture capital funds (Schonfield, 2011)—compares Bitcoin to other historically disruptive technologies in a cri de coeur featured by the *New York Times*:

> Eventually mainstream products, companies and industries emerge to commercialize it; its effects become profound; and later, many people wonder why its powerful promise wasn't more obvious from the start. What technology am I talking about? Personal computers in 1975, the Internet in 1993, and—I believe—Bitcoin in 2014. (Andreessen, 2014a)

Elsewhere, Andreessen's words seem to resonate with the idea that extremist technologies shed their political skin as they grow:

> I think the relevant comparison point for Bitcoin is actually 1994 for the consumer Internet. . . . [I]t was really fringe, and really weird, and really new, and really scary, and really odd. . . . I don't know how you get fringe technology without fringe politics and fringe characters. You just have to go through a maturation process where you come out the other end and the fringe technology goes mainstream and gets widely adopted. Along the way, the fringe characters and fringe politics tend to get alienated and move onto the next fringe technology. (Andreessen, 2014b)

Andreessen is a highly influential developer, entrepreneur, and investor, gaining renown as a pioneer during the early Internet revolution by founding a number of successful companies such as Netscape. His words thus carry significant weight in Silicon Valley and around the world. The quotation just cited, for example, formed part of a fireside chat at CoinSummit, an invitation-only conference designed to "connect virtual currency entrepreneurs, angel and VC investors, hedge fund professionals and Bitcoin enthusiasts" (Rizzo, 2014). Quite clearly, Andreessen Horowitz is a centre of calculation for successful investing with enormous resources and intel not available to smaller venture capitalists. To use a metaphor from Bruno Latour (1987), Andreessen acts like a "mouthpiece" for a collection of experts who have a track record for making informed and profitable decisions (see also Tkacz, 2015). Key figures like this play an important role as global signallers, highlighting the upcoming success of technology start-up companies.

Examples abound. Atlanta-based BitPay was not looking for investment when Silicon Valley's Founders Fund came knocking. However, the company decided the opportunity to have experienced entrepreneurs like Peter Thiel, Ken Howery, Luke Nosek, and Brian Singerman come on board was something they could not afford to miss out on (Lunden, 2013). Similarly, Greylock Partners—whose investment team includes Max Levchin (investor in Pinterest, Yammer, and Yelp) and Reid Hoffman (cofounder of LinkedIn and investor in Zynga, Facebook, Airbnb, and Flickr)—joined Index Ventures in a $20 million USD Series A round to finance wallet company Xapo, along with previous key investors Benchmark, Fortress Investment Group, and Ribbit Capital (del Castillo, 2014). When high-profile venture capitalists make public investment rounds like this, they act as votes of confidence for Bitcoin and related companies, encouraging other investors to follow suit. As Bitcoin start-ups become ever more embedded in Silicon Valley through investment linkages, the underlying technology is rendered legitimate on the global stage.

Embedding Agents

Risk-taking is normal, encouraged, and even glorified in Silicon Valley thanks to an endless list of success stories from pioneering companies such as Apple, Intel, and Facebook. Employees willing to break off from technology giants and start their own projects are endowed with a certain amount of social value. This is exactly how Bitcoin wallet and exchange company Coinbase was formed. As a seasoned web entrepreneur, cofounder, and CEO, Brian Armstrong was no stranger to starting his own company—cofounding UniversityTutor.com in 2004 and founding BuyersVote.com and FreedmailPro.com in 2009. Armstrong was working at Airbnb in San Francisco, where he was one of the first 100 employees, before he left to form Coinbase in 2012 (Epicenter Bitcoin, 2015). That year he met Adam Draper at a coffee shop in Mountain View to pitch his company for financing. Impressed by Armstrong's vision, Draper contributed towards a $600,000 USD seed round investment (Draper University, 2014). Since then, Coinbase has received a total of $547.3 million USD from investors including Andreesen Horowitz, Ribbit Capital, and the New York Stock

Exchange (Crunchbase, 2019). Following the surge in a bitcoin's market value in 2017 (from $997 to $19,343 USD) the company had to ward off other interested investors who were approaching employees to buy their shares (Raza, 2018). Coinbase was last valued at $8 billion USD (Russell, 2018).

The dense concentration of venture capital in Silicon Valley not only helps cultivate native companies but also pulls technology start-ups to the area (Hall & Markusen, 1985; Zook, 2002; Hellmann & Puri, 2002; Sturgeon, 2003; Harris & Junglas, 2013).[21] Some of the smaller Bitcoin enterprises I spoke to had moved to the Valley specifically to find capital. Venture capital firms, in turn, act as "embedding agents" in the local economy (Ferrary & Granovetter, 2009, 352). Like financial firms in global cities (Sassen, 1991; Thrift, 1994), venture capitalists run in the same circles promoting collaboration as well as competition to ensure a rising tide lifts all boats. These "strategic alliances" (Sassen, 2005, 29) are often achieved through joint ventures, as explained to me by the managing partner of an investment firm in 2015:

> We have about 15 Bitcoin CEOs as our clients and another 35 operating companies. So we have a network of 50 Bitcoin CEOs, which is kind of an unparalleled resource in the sector. We position ourselves as a blockchain-dedicated investment firm—we don't compete with other venture firms. We want to be a value-added co-investor that brings a lot of domain expertise in a given syndicate for financing. . . . So we cooperate with Boost quite a bit. We work with Pantera quite a bit. Barry Silbert at Bitcoin Opportunity Corp. We're all in a lot of the same deals. And those four groups are the only dedicated Bitcoin investors around.

The firm preferred companies to be local so they could better keep track of progress and "get a feel for the culture in their office environments." Unwinding this provinciality reveals the deep, dense, and proximate networks within which venture capitalists sit and how they use these to increase the success rate of their investments.

During the time I spent visiting Boost VC it was resoundingly clear the Drapers were connecters as much as investors (see also Ferrary & Granovetter, 2009). Adam Draper would encourage the companies in his accelerator to build strong industry networks and hosted many events with renowned figures and firms in Silicon Valley to facilitate this. The three months start-ups spent at Boost VC were not only for working on their products but for working on business relationships. Building alliances with other investors, entrepreneurs, lawyers, and consultants benefit the companies and, in turn, their financiers. More than just the monetary fuel for innovative enterprise, then, venture capitalists become partners and mentors while offering access to a secondary economy crucial for growth and prosperity (Kenney & von Burg, 2001). They connect start-ups to "universities, large firms, research laboratories, [other] VC firms, law firms, investment banks, commercial banks, certified public accountants (CPA), consulting groups, recruitment agencies, public relation agencies and media" (Ferrary & Granovetter, 2009, 335). These linkages spread like fingers across economic space. In other words,

> deeply embedded venture capitalists are embedding agents for the iso-lated entrepreneurs they back. . . . VC firms are the main hubs between entrepreneurs and the complex networks of Silicon Valley. They enable interactions between interdependent economic agents. They do this because the profitability of their investments depends on these inter-actions. Entrepreneurs have access to information, resources, service providers and business partners through their investors. (Ferrary & Granovetter, 2009, 352)

Despite Bitcoin's image as a distributed, spaceless, and self-governing algorith-mic protocol, start-up companies—already important for breaking down tech-nical barriers between blockchains and wider markets—are fundamental for embedding networked ledger practices in economies like Silicon Valley. Start-ups are, after all, dependent on other actors in the deeply situated technology industry, and venture capitalists help anchor them in this intricate spatial milieu. The concentration of these institutions in Silicon Valley highlights it as a centre of industry practice and knowledge where webs of actors can set themselves up as financial and informational silos. But as start-ups are ever more deeply embed-ded in these networks, cultures of entrepreneurship appear to be domesticating the 'libertarian hacker' and their 'disruptive technologies.' I initially demonstrate this by stepping back in time to foreshadow cryptocurrency industry develop-ments with a narrative concerning a famous precursor, PayPal. This is, perhaps, the earliest success story of a modern-day 'radical' FinTech company.

Remembering PayPal

In 1998, amidst the frenzy of the dotcom bubble, Peter Thiel and Max Levchin launched a start-up called Fieldlink designed to facilitate digital payments based on cryptographic software applied to personal digital assistant devices (Jackson, 2004). It would later merge and evolve to become PayPal. CEO, Peter Thiel, had built a wariness of concentrated government power as he grew up in the Bay Area and built the company's mission statement around a libertarian-fuelled dis-ruption of the banking sector (Packer, 2011; see Appendix 23). Such distrust in fiat currency revolved around its vulnerability to nation-state corruption. Thiel's politically charged tone bears a striking resemblance to early posts on the Bitcoin Forum and there has even been speculation that Satoshi Nakamoto could be any number of PayPal's old employers (Hacker News, 2013). Indeed, the management team drank from the same anti-statist cup as the cypherpunks and shared similar literature: required reading "among the group was Cryptonomicon, written by the cyber-punk author Neil Stephenson—a cult novel among hackers, which imagines an anonymous internet banking system using electronic money" (Brown, 2014).

With the rise of copycat competitors, Thiel unleashed an aggressive marketing campaign in an attempt to achieve the 'network effect'—a theory where "the more numerous the users who use a platform, the more valuable that platform becomes for everyone else" (Srnicek, 2017, 45)—as quickly as possible. Here, a "large, established network is very valuable to enter and very costly to leave; in essence it locks in its members and prevents would-be competitors from getting off the ground" (Jackson, 2004, 41). This was a turbulent time for the ambitious company and libertarian politics started to take a back seat as they became secondary to survival and expansion.[22] Some growing pains included "[s]cheming Mafioso, capricious regulators, opportunistic lawyers, savvy online identity thieves, volatile capital markets, [and] antagonistic press" (Jackson, 2004, 3). As the company turned to face these pressures they were forced to respond with increasing standardisation procedures.

Both PayPal and its customers became victims of fraudulent activity and the company responded by implementing sophisticated fraud deterrent and detection mechanisms, which were more than welcomed by its user base (Jackson, 2004). From a different direction, increased pressure came via Mastercard and Visa—with which PayPal still dealt behind the scenes—to tighten up regulation compliance (Brown, 2014). Elsewhere, legal battles with state jurisdictions demanded a degree of accountability, and when the company pushed for an initial public offering in a volatile climate (following the collapse of the dotcom bubble) it was forced to start playing by the institutional rules laid out by investment banks, legal firms, and the Securities and Exchange Commission (Jackson, 2004). On completion of the public offering, business interests also had to start reflecting new shareholder interests. Then, in 2002, PayPal was bought by eBay for $1.5 billion USD. From then on it was enveloped into a more rigid and bureaucratic corporate structure lacking the same "audacious goal of empowering individuals by revolutionizing world currency markets" (Jackson, 2004, 256). As the company grew it neglected its "original vision of global currency liberation" (Jackson, 2004, 226): disruption had been softened and sidelined for the boardrooms of big business. This is a common trend as most entrepreneurial activities "rely on bureaucratic routines for sustenance, whether these are embedded in software packages, organizational knowledge, or highly complex logistics" (Clark & Thrift, 2005, 239).

This narrative demonstrates the presence of an alternative culture of entrepreneurial payment systems on the US West Coast predating Bitcoin. More important for my argument, it shows how watered-down technological radicalism is a byproduct of companies becoming amenable, acquiescent, and submissive to the business interests of complex networks within which they are increasingly embedded. This diffusion of culture between disruptive pioneers and experienced bureaucrats is not the exception but the rule in Silicon Valley and other global technology hubs. Radical politics are made malleable to fit the moving trajectory of a company that ultimately submits to a desire for making profit. While PayPal was, on one level, revolutionary—it indeed "empowered millions around the globe to move money with the click of a mouse" (Jackson, 2004, 312)—it overcame its growing pains by scaling into an(other) accountable corporate structure. In the process it mutated from 'disruption' to 'disruption lite.'

Normalised disruption again shares lineages and genealogies with ideals and juxtapositions that have commonly been referred to as the Californian Ideology. Bitcoin, as both a concept and an industry, is caught within this prolonged schizophrenic arm-wrestle. This was personified by a venture capitalist I interviewed at a San Francisco-based firm:

Venture Capitalist: We think we're in a pretty important part of history in terms of the innovation that's happening—the innovation that's happening right here in our backyard. And we're all California guys, born and raised in the Bay area. So it's a pretty, maybe Renaissance is too hokey of a term, but there is a special thing happening in Silicon Valley right now . . . and that's just Silicon Valley in general. If you take a look at Bitcoin or the blockchain over that, it's an incredibly disruptive technology, tons of innovation going on with it. So within the wider world we're in a very important part of the country and the state, and then in Silicon Valley. And within Silicon Valley the best and the brightest are interested in the blockchain, so we feel that we are on the vanguard of a really important technology that has the possibility to change the world. So there is kind of a social and political mission embedded into Bitcoin in our investment activity that we feel passionate about.

Entrepreneur in Residence: And it's an opportunity to make a lot of money.

Venture Capitalist: Yeah. We're not just doing this because we think banks suck and we want to revolutionise financial services. We want to change the world and make a lot of money doing it. Those are the dual mandates.

There is excitation and adrenaline behind Bitcoin's innovative potential made visceral by a feeling of being at the forefront of global innovation (also described in the Preface of this book). The double-bottom line in the quoted interview is clear: "we want to change the world and make a lot of money doing it" (see also Nelms et al., 2017; Herian, 2018). This is a powerful worldview where the dual mandates are not seen as contradictory but, contrastingly, as being achieved through each other. As entrepreneurial practices play out to fulfil this ideology, innovation on the 'political periphery' is absorbed into the 'standardised centre.' At the same time, reincarnations of PayPal—centralised companies subject to market forces and state regulation—built on top of Bitcoin and other blockchains create a (more) manageable economy of transactions. Within this ecosystem, technology is normalised and re-politicised in an all-too-familiar way: although "new frontiers may be opened up by enterprising individuals, the original pioneers are quickly replaced by more collective forms of organization, such as joint-stock companies" (Barbrook, 2001, 53).

As more actors align with a start-up company, higher levels of bureaucracy are incorporated. Here, the "desire to attract a mass audience can be a far more effective method of inhibiting political radicalism and cultural experimentation than any half-baked censorship provisions" (Barbrook, 2001, 54–55); indeed, from a consumer perspective, many "people will happily accept corporate control over cyberspace if they are provided with well-produced online services" (Barbrook, 2001, 55). In other words, the demand for market security via authoritative bodies welcomes a degree of accountable centralisation in order to cope with the 'real world' of risk and regulation. Perhaps then, through entrepreneurial practice, the "technologies of freedom" really are "turning into the machines of dominance" (Barbrook & Cameron, 1996, 13). Or, rather, as John Perry Barlow suggested at the Blockchain Global Impact Conference, the practices of entrepreneurship surrounding cryptographic systems ensure the two will always be in perpetual conflict.

States of Embeddedness

The rise of the Internet posed the "problem of squeezing transnational activity into the national legal straightjacket (*sic*)" (Kohl, 2007, 4). Contemporary decentralised architectures currently being built on top of the TCP/IP protocol are complicating this dilemma. In terms of Bitcoin, governments were initially wary of, and even hostile towards, the network because it provided avenues of (cross-border) monetary practice outside of state control. While they could certainly discourage citizens, there was little regulators could do to actually prevent them from using the Bitcoin network. Consequently, start-ups revealed themselves as key loci for control. Because Bitcoin enterprises exist in nation-state boundaries, they must compete with well-established institutions in the most regulated industry in the world: finance. Compliance is thus critical to survival. To prove this point, BitInstant was dismantled in the United States after its CEO was found guilty of "aiding and abetting the operation of an unlicensed money transmitting business" (Spaven, 2015). Contrastingly, at the Coinbase Headquarters in San Francisco I was introduced to their Head of Risk, who stressed to me how seriously the company took compliance. This conformity has allowed Coinbase to grow into an international powerhouse (Roberts, 2020). For regulators, encouraging compliant start-up growth within state borders like this gives them a grip on an otherwise 'vaporous' protocol.

During the time of my research, on the other side of the country, the New York State Department of Financial Services was shaping the cryptocurrency economy by introducing legislation known as the BitLicense (NYDFS, 2015). This meant companies conducting business in the state of New York that transmitted, stored, held, or maintained custody over virtual currencies on the behalf of others were legally required to apply for this license. Some companies, like Circle and Bitstamp, acquiesced by paying the $5,000 USD application fee to obtain a BitLicense—although Bitstamp explained how the process actually cost "roughly $100,000, including time allocation, legal and compliance fees" (Perez, 2015). Others, especially smaller firms not able to afford the license, stopped doing business in New York altogether or moved their headquarters out of the state—what *New York Business Journal* called the "Great Bitcoin Exodus" (del Castillo, 2015). Kraken (Young, 2015b), Shapeshift.io (Roberts, 2015), and BitFinex (Young, 2015c) were vocal about the added regulation, saying it stifled innovation, created unnecessary friction to their services, and invaded customer privacy. Meanwhile the fear in Silicon Valley was that other states, or worse, the Federal government, might follow the example of the BitLicense and stifle progress in the sector—a petition to withdraw the BitLicense on change.org was even brought to the attention of attendees of the San Francisco Bitcoin Meet-up Group while I was there.

The BitLicense helps demonstrate the spatial linkages start-up companies can facilitate between Bitcoin users and governments. What this reinforces is even in FinTech/blockchain economies, "the largely digitized global market for capital is embedded in a thick world of national policy and state agencies" (Sassen, 2004, 243). As start-ups actively attach identity to pseudonymous cryptographic strings they amalgamate financial practice into a centre of calculation/control. This not only affords them economic power in a growing sector but also allows blockchain architectures to conjoin more tightly with other networks such as state modes of legislation. In other words, algorithmic decentralisation becomes deeply attached to geographies of compliance.

With its concentration of cryptocurrency companies, Silicon Valley has become the largest hotspot for prospective company regulation in the world. Through Know Your Customer (KYC) and Anti Money Laundering (AML) regulations—both of which I was rigorously tested on before I was allowed to work at a cryptocurrency firm—governments can better monitor the Bitcoin economy, reattaching identity back to cryptographic strings. This is seen by some in the community as a crucial step for the growing legitimacy of cryptocurrencies but, for others, it too closely resembles traditional banking procedures. Not for the first time, parallels can be drawn between Bitcoin and the maturation of the Internet.

In the 1990s, companies began to superimpose star-shaped business models on top of the mesh network of the Internet (see Figure 2.1). The global connectivity of the TCP/IP protocol allowed enterprises to extend services to a larger market by connecting people to their central hubs and thus enclose parts of its decentralised network for themselves—modern examples include Spotify, ASOS, Facebook, NASDAQ, and PayPal. These institutions, along with network providers, offer chokepoints for networked practice and so governments began using them to monitor citizens and enforce legislation (Goldsmith & Wu, 2006; De Filippi & Wright, 2018). The same is now true for blockchain economies: pockets of control afforded by start-ups are attractive for law enforcement because they increase the visibility and accountability of transactors. The trade-off between centralised usability and decentralised anonymity is an ongoing tension in the industry.

Clearly, blockchains "are capable of both circumventing and complementing the law" (De Filippi & Wright, 2018, 52). So far legislators have mostly retrofitted existing regulation to reduce the risk of cryptocurrencies being used for money laundering, terrorism, and other organised crime (The Law Library of Congress, 2018). Inevitably the stances taken by governments differ: a few (Spain, Belarus, the Cayman Islands, Malta, and Luxembourg) have created an inclusive regulatory environment to harness innovation; some (Bangladesh, Iran, Thailand, Lithuania, Lesotho, China, and Colombia) allow citizen investment but have banned financial institutions facilitating transactions; whereas others (Algeria, Bolivia, Morocco, Nepal, Pakistan, and Vietnam) have barred activity altogether (The Law Library of Congress, 2018). Evidently, there are geographic factors at the level of state legislation that transform cryptocurrency practice.

More important for this chapter, however, pioneering start-up companies reveal themselves as important cultural sites for understanding modes of algorithmic decentralisation. As companies grow they become enrolled into legal frameworks, which often turns them into more bureaucratic machines at the expense of anarchist philosophies. However, this process of centralisation is not always clear-cut. The wallet company Blockchain.info, for example, does not store private keys but, by employing client-side encryption, provides a web-based software package that allows its users to do so (more easily) themselves. Consequently, Blockchain.info has created a proprietary software layer that maintains privacy and leaves financial control in the hands of its customers. Here, centralisation is not necessarily antonymous with financial subordination. Even with levels of resistance like this, the most control a nation-state can hope to have over blockchain technologies is to allow start-ups to operate within their jurisdictions. Malta, for example, is earning the name "Blockchain Island" after creating a hospitable regulatory environment for businesses dealing with distributed ledgers and crypto-assets (Aitken, 2018). As start-ups flock to the country to take advantage of its accommodating legal frameworks, it becomes a centre of knowledge and practice for global blockchain activity.

Conclusion

This chapter has brought together a number of actors in the San Francisco Bay Area whose interactions affect how transactions are conducted on the Bitcoin blockchain. Silicon Valley is increasingly a place where the algorithmic mechanisms and metrics of cryptocurrency protocols are both made and made sense of. Here, the Californian Ideology seems to persist, not via a singular monolithic worldview, but through the segmented entrepreneurial practices of different start-up company stakeholders. Certain centralised institutions/investors redirect information and the management of transactions into bottlenecks of control and capital accumulation. In the process, radical politics becomes watered down. Algorithmic decentralisation, then, is deeply affected by cultures of entrepreneurial activity that lend themselves to centralisation and bureaucracy: if economic transactions are surrendered to layers of proprietary software they usually become important islands of control across a decentralised algorithmic network.

Despite encapsulating a decentralist vision, blockchain economies do not eradicate centres of calculation. Bitcoin, for example, only provides a transactional base of decentralised (monetary) information, whereas added applications remain market-driven data silos.[23] In other words, distributed ledgers are relatively simple structures upon which centralised revenue models can be built, offering more complex (capital accumulating) services. Here, "[c]entralization reasserts itself . . . in the form of start-ups and tech companies, themselves ever consolidating into larger and more centralized corporations, whose governance structure is rooted primarily and unilaterally in End User License and Terms of Service agreements" (Nelms et al., 2017, 27). Bitcoin might allow for more autonomous finance but, regarding its mainstream usage, centralised companies often creep back into the picture.

Elsewhere, cryptocurrencies with stronger privacy models, such as Zcash and Monero, have been developed to counteract some of the de-anonymising effects of Bitcoin. These protocols attempt to use additional cryptographic functions to obscure wallet addresses so that (pseudo)identity is not publicly linked to the flow of funds. This reduces the amount third parties can know about transactions when operating on the behalf of individuals. Consequently, entrepreneurship does not necessarily represent a straightforward transition from unknowable to more knowable transactions; tensions between centralisation and distribution certainly still exist when examining the role of start-up companies in employing algorithmic (de)centralisation. What this chapter shows, however, is understanding the relational (dis)connections of third-party institutions and their embedded relationships is crucial for understanding the intricacies of blockchain economies. In short, processes of embedding deeply affect processes of decentralisation.

8

Blueprinting Blockchains

Introduction

So far, this book has critically analysed the first instantiation of a fully functioning blockchain, Bitcoin, accounting for its political motivations, modes of
governance, material architecture, and start-up economy. Throughout, it has
paid particular attention to contradictions at play and how these affect Bitcoin's
geographies of algorithmic (de)centralisation. As I followed Bitcoin, however, it
morphed into something—or, rather, many things—new. What I mean by this
is its blockchain architecture started being repurposed to financialise and decentralise countless other things. "By 2015, hype about the blockchain seemed to
have fully subsumed that of bitcoin" (Swartz, 2017, 85). Indeed, when I followed Bitcoin into Silicon Valley my ethnographic research 'strayed' into different spaces such as Blockchain University, Ethereum meet-up groups, and other
cryptocurrency start-ups. These environments helped further delineate the discrepancies between crypto/spaces of hope and crypto/spaces of practice.

This substantial shift in focus is often referred to by cryptocurrency communities as Bitcoin 2.0, capturing a partial yet significant drift. In corporate circles
there has been a move to "replace the word 'Bitcoin' with 'blockchain' or, even
better, 'distributed ledger' in one's presentations" (Maurer, 2016, 87). On some
level, this is a means for professionals to dissociate themselves with Bitcoin's
anarchist past/path—for example, a Silicon Valley venture capitalist I met in the
field had dropped the word 'cryptocurrency' from his firm name and replaced
it with 'blockchain' because he felt it was "cleaner." There are evidently differences between these terms. Bitcoin is now just one example of a cryptocurrency,
blockchain, and distributed ledger technology, all of which have the potential to
"enable new types of economic activity" (Davidson et al., 2018, 654). On this
note, I look at how alternative blockchains are being used as blueprints for reor-
ganising finance in various ways. The term 'blueprinting' is used in automotive
slang to mean the procedure of improving engine performance by dismantling

Money Code Space. Jack Parkin, Oxford University Press (2020). © Oxford University Press.
DOI: 10.1093/oso/9780197515075.001.0001.

and rebuilding its components to different specifications. The title of this chapter, "Blueprinting Blockchains," thus captures how these architectures are being tweaked to meet the exact tolerances of different tasks and markets.

In the process, the chapter contributes towards an understanding of algorithmic decentralisation by examining the (socio)technical affordances of blockchains. The word "affordance" was first introduced by James Gibson (1979) to describe the possible actions available to organisms in the physical world. For example, a cave can provide the affordance of shelter to humans. This concept was later applied to human-machine interaction by Donald Norman (1988) who used it to understand how technologies can be designed to prescribe human behaviour (and the times when this fails). Later, affordances were extrapolated to relate more directly with how technologies enable and constrain forms of social interaction (Gaver, 1996; Wellman et al., 2003). More recently, there has been a deluge of work demonstrating the agency of humans in reappropriating technologies originally designed to function in specific ways (Bucher & Helmond, 2017). There can even be dislocations between what stakeholders think a technology does and how it actually operates in practice (Nagy & Neff, 2015).

Clearly, there is no singular definition of affordance so it risks becoming an elusive term. What is obvious, though, is that humans and machines affect and direct each other in various ways from different directions (Bucher & Helmond, 2017). With this in mind, I use the word "affordance" here to show how blockchains provide their users certain capabilities and limitations while their users also create capabilities and limitations for the architectures themselves. In other words, I explore where human and non-human agency exists through a variety of blockchains and use this to demonstrate when discrepancies appear between how they are imagined and how they play out in practice. Additionally, when dealing with software platforms (i.e., blockchains), affordances often stretch outside of their own environments, so this approach must cater for "how they may be integrated in other platforms and services as well as how these activities afford back to the platform and its multiple users" (Bucher & Helmond, 2017, 249). In short, multiple stakeholders affect and are affected by distributed ledger technologies in a context-specific manner.

The chapter begins by building on a recent body of knowledge known as platform capitalism that looks at how online engagements are becoming increasingly financialised and how the gatekeepers of popular software packages control more and more citizen data. From the point of view of the platform capitalist, "apps are for capital simply a means to 'monetize' and 'accumulate' data about the body's movement while subsuming it ever more tightly in networks of consumption and surveillance" (Terranova, 2014). A typology of blockchains, with their multiple visions of decentralisation, are then laid out to understand how they reflect stakeholder interests. I then adapt the term 'platform capitalism' to see what blockchain capitalism is starting to look like. Inevitably, it is realised in a number of ways but obligatory passage points are often formed through or around their architectures to create points of control across networked economies. These illustrations demonstrate the levels of power in blockchain ecosystems, the mutability of data in certain circumstances, and the role of distributed ledgers as tools of capital accumulation.

Platform Capitalism

The etymological roots of the word "platform" come from 16th-century Middle French *plateforme*, which literally means flat (*plate*) form (*forme*). While it can be applied to different phenomena, it is usually used to describe a standardised, uniformed, or levelled surface (structural, geological, political, theatrical, theoretical, etc.) as a foundation upon which something else can act or be constructed. A platform, therefore, is "an object, system or process that . . . provides the basis for practice of some kind" (Neilson, 2016, 1). Today, the term is increasingly used in the digital context to describe company-owned software or computational services that "afford an opportunity to communicate, interact or sell" (Gillespie, 2010, 351). As Anja Kanngieser et al. (2014) explain:

> Within technological disciplines and fields the term 'platform' was originally synonymous with operating systems, however the acceleration of social networking services such as Facebook, Twitter, tumblr, Weibo and Renren reconfigured the notion of the platform as a catalysing method for internet user participation, content sharing and clustered organisation. (305–306)

The upsurge of platforms has been coupled with ideas of progression where producers and consumers can conduct transactions more directly and seamlessly. From this perspective, citizens are provided with an avenue to profit from assets that would otherwise be difficult—for example, cars (Uber) or spare rooms (Airbnb). Enter a "proliferation of new terms: the gig economy, the sharing economy, the on-demand economy, the next industrial revolution, the surveillance economy, the app economy, the attention economy, and so on" (Srnicek, 2017, 37). The word 'sharing' has been particularly popular. However, while the builders of platforms promote a "seemingly flatter and more participatory model" of commerce (Morozov, 2015), critics have described a "confused usage": "helping each other out by sharing resources is one thing while commodifying these resources by charging a fee for their use is quite another" (Olma, 2014).

Claims of disintermediation have also been debunked: middle(wo)men are merely camouflaged by platforms (Lobo, 2014). Software companies act like "digital bridge builders" (Scholz, 2017, 159) and thus re-coordinate the connectivity between supply and demand by replacing more traditional intermediaries with new digital architectures (Olma, 2014). Their owners are raised up as powerful monopolising gatekeepers of transactional bottlenecks with "unprecedented control over the markets they themselves create": "price is not the result of the free play of supply and demand but of specific algorithms supposedly simulating the market mechanism" (Olma, 2014). From this powerful position they can control the "rules of the game" (Srnicek, 2017, 47). Platform capitalists thus emerge as obligatory passage points between buyers and sellers who "reimpose hierarchical relations at the service of social reproduction and the production of surplus value" (Terranova, 2006, 33).

In essence, the platform can be understood "as a distinct mode of socio-technical intermediary and business arrangement that is incorporated into wider processes of capitalization" (Langley & Leyshon, 2016, 1). In the process, platform owners extract immense amounts of data and look to monetise it. This valuable "raw material" can be "refined and used in a variety of ways" (Srnicek, 2017, 14). Calls for greater anonymity, then, "miss how the suppression of privacy is at the heart of the business model" (Srnicek, 2017, 101). By selling access to user information—which is extremely valuable to entities like advertisers or market researchers—this data is turned into a secondary revenue stream (O'Dwyer, 2015b; Langley & Leyshon, 2016).

"Every day, one billion people in advanced economies have between two billion and six billion spare hours among them. Capturing and monetizing those hours is the goal of platform capitalism" (Srnicek, 2017, 4). By orchestrating this untapped labour, the platform capitalist takes a cut. Often this involves taking advantage of labour in "grey zones" or "regulation gaps" (Lobo, 2014). By legally defining their workers as independent contractors, platform capitalists can cut costs by utilising a workforce with no employer-paid health insurance, sick leave, paid overtime, holiday leave, pension plan, or basic worker protections against discrimination (Calloway, 2016; Scholz, 2017; Srnicek, 2017). Behind the facade of job creation, then, is unpredictable employment with no livable wage, contributing to the increasing disparity between rich and poor and the decline of median income (Brynjolfsson & McAfee, 2016). This is not John Maynard Keynes's (1930b) vision of technology automating labour to cull the hours of the working week but a suggestion of menial and meaningless jobs for those lucky enough to have them (Graeber, 2015).

Blockchains, as distributed platforms, have been offered as vehicles for creating a more legitimate sharing economy. In other words, blockchains can supposedly remove the need for third parties when conducting transactions, thus affording fairer market conditions for both producers and consumers. However, perhaps the failures of blockchain predecessors should warrant a more critical investigation:

> Like the 'sharing economy' before it, which began with visions of peer-to-peer commerce and quickly became platforms for on-demand task work, it's easy to see how [blockchain] start-ups with utopian visions might 'pivot' (to use industry parlance) toward business models different from or even in opposition to their original goals. (Swartz, 2017, 87–88)

I continue this chapter by examining how blockchain capitalism is beginning to take shape and how it affects modes of algorithmic decentralisation. Firstly, I describe some common themes across a plurality of blockchains.

Dissecting Blockchains

As "early as 2011, people were using the lower digits of Bitcoin transactions as a way of encoding messages within the blockchain" (Buterin, 2012b).[1] This was the start of blockchains being used for more than just money. In December 2013, nearly five years after Bitcoin's original release, Vitalik Buterin (2013b) published a white paper titled "Ethereum: A Next Generation Smart Contract and Decentralized Application Platform." Bitcoin's lack of a robust scripting language for developing applications led Buterin to design the blueprint for Ethereum. This blockchain differs from Bitcoin because it runs as a virtual machine following Turing-complete rules meaning, given enough time, the system can theoretically be used to compute anything. In this system "transactions may be either hashes of accounts (like Bitcoin) or hashes that link to executable code. This ability to execute arbitrary code is why Ethereum is a general-purpose computing environment" (DuPont, 2019, 86). In other words, Ethereum miners can operate different commands for users (other than just transactions) and trigger certain actions for external software. This affords programmers a lot of creative freedom to design applications and allows Ethereum to become the Swiss army knife of blockchains.

The project attracted a large pool of talented developers from across the world, among them "two former Goldman Sachs employees—which has been a matter of some dismay in the heavily libertarian, anti-establishment [early] cryptocurrency community" (Schneider, 2014). The team raised $18 million USD worth of funding in bitcoins to start working on the project.[2] Nineteen months after Buterin's paper was published, in July 2015, Ethereum was released. Over this time, the global interest in blockchains had transformed into hype. The opening paragraph of Melanie Swan's (2015) book, *Blockchain: Blueprint for a New Economy*, exemplifies this enthusiasm:

> We should think about the blockchain as another class of thing like the Internet—a comprehensive information technology with tiered technical levels and multiple classes of applications for any form of asset registry, inventory, and exchange, including every area of finance, economics, and money; hard assets (physical property, homes, cars); and intangible assets (votes, ideas, reputation, intention, health data, information, etc.). But the blockchain concept is even more; it is a new organizing paradigm for the discovery, valuation, and transfer of quanta (discrete units) of anything, and potentially for the coordination of all human activity at a much larger scale than has been possible before. (vii)[3]

Euphoric descriptions like this quickly became the norm and new businesses began flowering to bring about this brave new world. Even *The Economist* (2015) noted blockchain's potential to "transform how the economy works."

Different stakeholders are imagining blockchains in various ways, giving rise to an assortment of (proto)types. Some architectures of decentralisation don't even use blocks or chains at all, hence the umbrella term "distributed ledger technology." Three broad categorisations have been outlined. First, *public ledgers* are open in their design allowing anyone to conduct transactions, view records, or join the consensus process (e.g., Bitcoin, Litecoin, or Ethereum). Second, *private ledgers* are closed in their design, constraining write permissions to one entity whereas read permissions may be made public or restricted to certain actors (e.g., Multichain or MONAX). Usually, they are "internal to a single company, and so public readability may not be necessary in many cases at all, though in other cases public auditability is desired" (Buterin, 2015). Private ledgers, then, "should be considered for any situation in which two or more organizations need a shared view of reality, and that view does not originate from a single source" (Greenspan, 2016). Third, *consortium ledgers* lie somewhere between the two: write permission is controlled by a pre-selected set of nodes whereas read permission might be open or closed depending on preference (e.g., Hyperledger Fabric, Libra, or R3). For example, "one might imagine a consortium of 15 financial institutions, each of which operates a node and of which 10 must sign every block in order for the block to be valid" (Buterin, 2015).

Amongst all this innovation, blockchains can often appear to be a "solution in search of a problem" (Swartz, 2017, 97). Indeed, in Silicon Valley, I spent time with people who treated every problem as a nail and every solution as a blockchain hammer. Or, put differently, blockchain was being flung at the pro-verbial wall to see where it stuck. I was given a BitPay sticker at the Blockchain University demo night that exemplified this mindset, reading: "Decentralize all the things." When blockchain is the given answer, but the question remains unknown, there are few limits to the power of algorithmic decentralisation.

Blockchain hype was personified by the rise in share price of a company called On-line Plc by 394% when it changed its name to Online Blockchain Plc (Pham, 2017). This process has been referred to as "chainwashing" (Swanson, 2017a). On the other hand, overenthusiasm has also been countered with a more criti-cal outlook by others in the industry: "you don't need blockchain per se, you need a solution to some problems that eventually could become a blockchain" (Meunier, 2016). Often, however, a traditional database will do (Meunier, 2016). Gideon Greenspan (2015), CEO of MulitChain, echoes this sentiment:

> Here's how it plays out. Big company hears that blockchains are the next big thing. Big company finds some people internally who are interested in the subject. Big company gives them a budget and tells them to go do something blockchainy. Soon enough they come knocking on our door, waving dollar bills, asking *us* to help *them* think up a use case.

Greenspan warns interested parties away from the idea of blockchain for block-chain's sake. Others critique the functional efficacy of private and consortium blockchains entirely. For example, Andreas Antonopoulos, a famous Bitcoin advocate and blockchain purist, sees any closed architecture as worthless:

> Not only is decentralization, open protocols, open source, collaborative development and living in the wild a feature of Bitcoin, that's the whole point. And if you take a permissioned ledger and say, that's all nice, we like the database part of it, can we have it without the open decentral-ized P2P open source non-controlled distributed nature of it, well you just threw out the baby with the bathwater. (cited in O'Connell, 2016b)

He states elsewhere:

> This is the big argument of 2015. It's the 'let's take bitcoin, cut off its beard, take away its piercings, put it in a suit, call it blockchain, and pres-ent it to the board.' It's safe. It's got borders. We can apply the same regulations. We can put barriers to entry and create anti-competitive environment to control who has access. (cited in Frauenfelder, 2016)

For Antonopoulos, the disruptive potential of distributed ledger technologies lies in openness and reduced central oversight. From this point of view, blockchains are a trade-off between freedom and efficiency where the most efficient system is a database that can "process billions of transactions per second, as long as you give all the authority and trust to a single party" (cited in Frauenfelder, 2016). So Bitcoin, as opposed to Visa, is "paying an efficiency price in order to maintain neutrality of the network . . . [and] decentralization of trust" (cited in Frauenfelder, 2016).

Indeed, "if the price of centralisation is trust (as users need to trust centralised operators with their data), decentralisation comes at the price of transparency (as everyone's interactions are made visible to all [of the] network's nodes)" (De Filippi, 2015). When coupled with public transactions, then, blockchains may "end up being more vulnerable to governmental agencies or corporate scrutiny than their centralised counterparts" (De Filippi, 2015).[4] While "it might be harder to implement a decentralised system that is fully privacy-compliant, transparency and privacy should, however, not be regarded as being in a fundamental conflict" (De Filippi, 2015). After all, there are many inventive experiments going on in the sector looking to weld these qualities together.

The Ethereum Network

Different incantations of blockchains are important for understanding how algorithmic (de)centralisation plays out. I outline two examples of projects built on top of the Ethereum blockchain to show how 'distributed' economies are starting to function. The first is Storj: a platform and token (STORJ) designed to decentralise data storage across the Internet. Today, the majority of the world's hard drive space goes unused on millions of people's devices—to Storj this is, quite literally, a waste of space. Almost exclusively, cloud storage is facilitated by giant platform monopolies such as Google, Apple, or Amazon, and relies on enormous data centres owned by companies like Digital Reality Trust, Equinix, and Global Switch. In their own words, Storj is a "peer-to-peer cloud storage network implementing client-side encryption" allowing "users to share data without the reliance on a third party storage provider" (Wilkinson et al., 2016, 1). In short, the system allows people to rent out their unused hard drives in return for a cryptographic token, which can be exchanged for more space or for other (crypto)currencies. The idea is to "mitigate most traditional data failures and outages, as well as significantly increase security, privacy, and data control" (Wilkinson et al., 2016). In a promotional video, Storj explains:

[E]ach file is shredded, encrypted, and spread across the network until you're ready to use it again. And you can be sure the files are safe because the keys are in your pocket not a company's. Only you have access to your stuff. Because the network is shared, you don't have to worry about slow download speeds coming from one place: we're all helping to make the system blazing fast. And if you have some extra space lying around you'll get paid by users who need more than they can share. It's like renting out your empty hard drives. A cloud with security, no downtime, and speed at a fraction of the cost. (Storj, 2018)

This is not only a company with a different mentality to platform capitalism but one that seeks to abolish many of its disadvantages, such as the centralisation and commodification of information associated with data mining.

The second example is Arcade City, a blockchain ride-sharing application. It was designed to create "decentralized marketplaces owned and operated by the participants themselves" (David, 2017). The company is a response to Uber, which it vilifies for being a "corporate overlord" (Arcade City, 2018):

Tech companies like Uber and AirBnB have seized on this 'sharing economy' trend to build billion-dollar corporations facilitating pseudo peer-to-peer transactions at global scale. As central intermediaries and gatekeepers, they restrict access to their marketplaces and dictate the terms of each transaction. (David et al., 2016, 1)

In place of platform capitalism, Arcade City tries to install platform coopera- tivism with open source development, blockchain transactions, crypto-equity, and a swarm model of governance, where service providers can create their own autonomous groups (David et al., 2016). When Uber and Lyft lost a legal battle (concerning driver background checks) with the city of Austin, Texas, they were forced to withdraw operations from the area (Hern, 2016). This left a vacuum for Arcade City, which quickly commanded a presence there (Woolf, 2016; Wistrom, 2017; Koebler, 2017). The platform allows users to pay with Arcade City tokens, bitcoins, credit cards, "cash, Venmo, or hugs" (Tepper, 2016). As drivers started using the system they spontaneously assembled themselves into 'pods' providing specialised services, such as a "group of female Arcade City drivers who take special care to get women home safely late at night" (Arcade City Hall, 2016). This inspired the company to encourage self-organisation between their users while allowing stakeholders to 'own' equity in the network by allocating tokens to the public, development team, existing investors, found- ers, swarmers, and as future rewards (David et al., 2016).

Both case studies demonstrate how certain economic affordances are enabled by blockchains because they connect platform builders, producers, and consumers in new ways. Both applications are built on top of Ethereum, which they use as a trusted foundational layer. Each Ethereum node includes a virtual machine, which means it can undertake computational work for its users. Certain actions require different amounts of computing power, measured by a unit called gas. Users must pay miners a gas fee with Ethereum's in-built cryptocurrency, ether (ETH), in order to utilise the virtual machine. Because anyone from anywhere can ask Ethereum to execute lines of code, it is often referred to as a "World Computer" used to run decentralised applications (Dapps).

Storj and Arcade City are two examples of Dapps. Both also use a standardised specification in Ethereum called ERC20: a prefabricated smart contract used to create new cryptocurrencies running on top of its blockchain. This functionality allows third parties to create their own tokens with ease as long as they can pay for enough gas to run their operations. Evidentially, then, Ethereum is a rented platform. The very demand for gas is what encourages miners to secure the network for cryptocurrency rewards (cryptoeconomics). It is important to note this is inherently a capitalistic process: Storj and Arcade City are not necessary harbingers of a 'sharing' economy because they still commodify cloud storage and spare seats. However, they do attempt to transform the dynamics of these markets to reduce the consolidated wealth and power of platform capitalists— or, at least, they promote this vision. But how does blockchain capitalism play out in practice?

Blockchain Capitalism

If Bitcoin is meant to be digital gold for transacting value, then ether is a digital fuel for running Dapps. The fee-based model of the Ethereum blockchain means application builders must acquire ether before they can utilise its virtual machine. Application currencies and ether both float on the market via exchanges so they can be traded for one another. In this way, Storj consumers are indirectly paying Ethereum miners as an intermediary through a series of steps (see Figure 8.1). Thus, the same capitalistic logic of a fee-based service applies for this instantiation of blockchain capitalism as it does for platform capitalism, only with a different payment framework. Companies that build currencies on top of Ethereum take a fee for their service to pay for access to its blockchain (while generating profit).

The manifestation of blockchain capitalism, as played out by Ethereum, demonstrates how miners are randomised third parties paid for facilitating

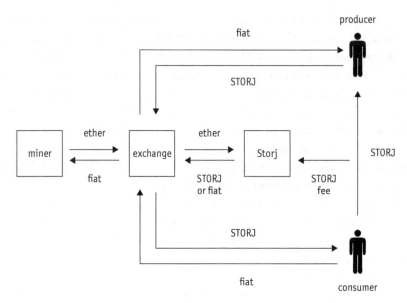

Figure 8.1 Flow of currencies (fiat, ether, and STORJ) between different actors in the Storj economy.

transactions on the underlying blockchain layer. Ignoring mining pool cen-tralisation for a moment, this could still reduce the monopolistic tendencies of platform capitalism by ensuring dispersed and irregular miners are paid as opposed to one centralised institution, while keeping certain data cryptograph-ically sealed. In this way miners do not control the information of applications using Ethereum, making the middle(wo)man, to some degree, more indirect (and unable to profit from data appropriation). But this does not eradicate third parties entirely.

While institutions that build applications on top of Ethereum cannot directly alter the underlying blockchain—which operates under its own model of sena-torial governance (see Chapter 5)—they certainly are in a position to influence the codified parameters of their own currencies. Monetary policy, for example, can be predetermined: Storj decided to withhold 245 million tokens ($300 mil-lion USD) and release them incrementally with the view of creating economic stability (Dale, 2017). Other projects often choose to release their tokens all at once. The common method for doing so is an Initial Coin Offering (ICO). This is a new funding model where investors buy cryptocurrencies for certain plat-forms in the hope their value will appreciate while the builders of platforms raise capital for their projects. As Arcade City (2018) explained in a promotional video: "we are not accepting traditional venture capital where we would need to trade control for money. Instead we are going directly to the people with a public token sale in 2018. . . . That value will be held directly by you, the participants of the Arcade City network." The ICO model was also used to build Ethereum itself. As of 2019, the total cumulative funding of ICOs was $22 billion USD (CoinDesk, 2019).

The result of the Arcade City ICO shows how they can become troublesome and subject to bureaucracy. In forming the Arcade City Council, intended to act as a temporary committee for decision-making, the company aimed to make a democratic political system where ether, collected from a token sale, was placed in a smart contract requiring the signatures of 5 of the 7 members in order for funds to be released (David et al., 2016). This budget was intended to go towards software development (15%), operations (35%), market balancing (25%), contingency (15%), and marketing and community outreach (10%). However, internal disagreements saw the company split in two and the council went on to form a new venture called Swarm City, taking the 77,687.45 ETH from the token sale funds with them (worth $570,000 USD at the time but rising to $112.5 million in 2017). This was all technically a legitimate process thanks to the algorithmic rules already laid out by smart contracts.

Decentralised ride-sharing platforms may also fail to comply with state legis-lation like Uber and Lyft before them. Background checks for drivers are impor-tant to keep riders safe. Arcade City pushed this responsibility to drivers who were able to embed credentials or proof of insurance on their profile. Not only is such information easily faked but, under this model, riders are still able to pick drivers without certain criteria and could thus theoretically choose driv-ers without insurance or even a licence (Tepper, 2016). Without a centralised audit system, decentralised ride-sharing could thus create unaccountable market transactors, enable miscreant activity, and struggle to follow the law. The activity of both Arcade City and Swarm City has become much more opaque in recent years—they may be finding it difficult to get off the ground for reasons similar to this.

ICOs are another important point of interest for blockchain capitalism as they expose applications to the open market. Tokens can behave like a currency, share, and fuel for a platform all at the same time. The UK Financial Conduct Authority (2019) has thus created three regulatory definitions: exchange token, security token, and utility token. Cryptocurrencies can be any combination of the three. For example, Storj coins afford owners the ability to trade them for other currencies (exchange), have a stake in the future value of the platform (security), and/or use them to store data in a distributed file storage system (utility).

For the most part, however, these coins are traded publicly as speculative assets. With little prior knowledge as to how crypto-assets should be valued, price discovery remains extremely volatile (Garcia et al., 2014; Fry & Cheah,

2016). Cryptocurrencies have thus proven to be spectacular bubble machines. All of this creates a great deal of uncertainty: as value moves through space in new ways, blockchains intersect awkwardly with existing financial regulation, raising all sorts of issues for state legislators. "Indeed, from the outside, the distinction between insider trading, venture capital funding, and crypto trading is very blurry and problematic" (DuPont, 2019, 137).

At the same time, the industry is starting to mirror traditional finance in many ways. In her article "Why crypto looks a lot like Wall Street," Jill Carlson (2017) expresses this eloquently. Instead of the distributed dream that was promised, she explains how

> we have constructed around crypto a warped version of the legacy financial system, with all the familiar players: issuers, broker dealers, exchanges and custodians. Along with these players come the legacy problems of centralized control, intermediation, systemic risk, market malpractice and—importantly—short-term greed. (Carlson, 2017)

In this sense, blockchain technology has truly "created more intermediaries than it has displaced" and, more poignantly, cryptocurrencies are equally as "exposed to each other as banks, exchanges, and custodians were in 2008" (Carlson, 2017). The "[c]ommingling of funds within wallets and exchanges, opaque accounting, cross-exchange exposure and unclear margin requirements are a few of the sources of institutional risk in the market" (Carlson, 2017). Similarly, "[m]arket manipulation, insider trading, shilling, spoofing, pumping-and-dumping and conflicts of interest [are] abound in cryptocurrency markets" (Carlson, 2017).

On this last note, power is often consolidated within large companies that have a great deal of influence over the market. When Coinbase launched a service for Bitcoin Cash via their platform the value of the cryptocurrency rocketed as it was deemed legitimised by one of the world's largest exchanges. Perhaps more interestingly, the price had already experienced a dramatic spike some hours before, which caused a degree of suspicion concerning possible insider trading practices at the company, leading to an internal investigation (Russell & Tepper, 2017; Koetsier, 2017). Apparently, old forms of (centralised) market manipulation are not necessarily absent from blockchain economies.

Only the macro movements of information can be seen on the Ethereum blockchain so applications (depending on how they are built) can become opaque data silos where malpractice can occur. These pockets of information are also susceptible to monetisation and regulation, particularly when identity verification is a prerequisite for use. In other words, transparency is just an option for companies to consider and they can choose to operate behind closed doors like their predecessors if they so wish (see Pasquale, 2015). So while miners cannot see application data, its builders can install measures to do so. As Carlson (2017) argues, the "intent was to give people direct control of their funds, free from seizure from banks and governments. Instead, people are handing over that control to a new class of actors—who are frequently even less accountable than their old school counterparts." Often, "[w]e may think that we are down the crypto rabbit hole, but really we are through the Wall Street looking glass" (Carlson, 2017).

An important characteristic of code is its need to evolve within a forever-changing sociological, political, technological, and economic landscape. Mutations are necessary when bugs appear or when new services are required to increase functionality (e.g., Uber Eats turned ride-sharing into a delivery service). Programmers need to earn a living and venture-backed start-ups, that exist to chase profit, remain the key model for organising labour in order to create software (see Chapter 7). Consequently, application builders become rule makers and capital accumulators. At the same time, problems associated with informal labour are not (yet) solved with blockchain capitalism. If cryptocurrencies become a mode of income for producers, then who provides pensions, holiday pay, sick leave, health insurance, paid overtime, or worker protection? While legislation could be introduced to hold blockchain capitalists accountable for labour rights, is it really possible for them to influence the users of decentralised architectures in this way? Further still, should it be the application builders or miners who pay for this? Can worker protection really be programmed into the mechanisms of code? And when version forks occur, should it be the users or the code builders who decide which version of reality to take on? These issues of algorithmic decentralisation deeply affect processes of blockchain capitalism and vice versa.

Finally, what happens if a critical mass of economic activity is directed through a single distributed architecture like Ethereum? This would render it one big obligatory passage point for accessing the economy and beget its own form of centralisation, albeit one built upon a distributed architecture (see also De Filippi & Wright, 2018). If all services branch off from this blockchain, they become completely dependent on it and thus, if compromised, the whole system could come tumbling down. Suddenly, the traditional financial system appears strangely resilient. When mortgage derivatives at investment banks failed during the 2008 financial crisis, interdependent risk between centralised firms threatened to pull the entire system down in a domino effect. However, governments were able to prop up failing banks with a bailout, 'fixing' them in a modular manner with taxpayer money. While some pieces were removed, and all suffered, the financial system survived, albeit at a devastating cost to many citizens across the world.

With this in mind, what would happen to an Ethereum-dependent economy if the value of ether disintegrated following a 51% attack? Could the whole thing grind to a halt without a modular piece to fix? Ethereum smart contracts are also "susceptible to invalidity through obsolescence and boredom. If the electronic network were shut off, or if everyone moved on to a new system, there is no paper-based backup archiving the[ir] existence (or execution)" (DuPont & Maurer, 2015). Of course, some of these risks may be lessened by using a multitude of blockchains to cater for different transactions, but does this not create another web of interlinked networks that are both integrated and codependent? And if changes do need to be made, will they be done so under models like senatorial governance that might cause a split in a financial ledger record similar to Bitcoin? These affordances and limitations raise very real problems for an emerging industry at micro and macro scales. The next section better captures some of the tensions, conflicts, and contradictions at stake for blockchain capitalism when distributed architectures are coerced around a singular decision.

The Decentralised Autonomous Organisation

It should be clear by now that blockchains are not necessarily the holy grail of distribution, but rather different levels and modes of (de)centralisation are played out at a number of scales through their architectures. As the Internet promised and failed to bring about a distributed society, blockchains seem to be following a similar path. The centralising tendencies of distributed networks are personified by 'The DAO': a now famous example of a Decentralised Autonomous Organisation. The DAO was an application designed to self-organise between participants based on smart contracts that rested upon the Ethereum blockchain. "The general objectives of smart contract design are to satisfy common contractual conditions (such as payment terms, liens, confidentiality, and even enforcement), minimize exceptions both malicious and accidental, and minimize the need for trusted intermediaries" (Szabo, 1994). The aim here is to "collapse contract formation and enforcement into a single instrument" (Levy, 2017, 3). Blockchains have become instrumental to the development of smart contracts because they are meant to act like 'unforgeable' databases that can trigger their execution. Consequently, smart contracts are supposed to "carry out corporate functions in accordance with the will of their shareholders, while being constrained by programmatic bylaw" (Mark et al., 2016, 2).

"As an alternative form of governance, proponents claim that through blockchain technologies autonomous individuals are capable of creating a self-governing community (or multiple communities) with enforceable rules of interaction without the requirement of any centralized (hierarchical) power structures" (Reijers et al., 2016, 140). The concept of a DAO, in general, is "to codify the rules and decision making apparatus of an organization, eliminating the need for documents and people in governing, creating a structure with decentralized control" (Siegel, 2016). The particular DAO in this case study "was meant to operate like a venture capital fund for the crypto and decentralized space" (Madeira, 2016):

> The DAO operates somewhat like a venture capital firm, in that it collects a pool of funds to invest in worthy proposals, but it differs in that all the individual investors are able to vote, in proportion to the size of their investment, on each investment proposal put forward to the fund. The aspirational goals for The DAO are to utilize the wisdom of the crowds for this decision-making process, and to eliminate the risks posed by middlemen using a programmatic approach to corporate management. (Mark et al., 2016)

A white paper emerged with The DAO explaining how, thanks to blockchains, organisations could be created for the first time where: "(1) participants maintain direct real-time control of contributed funds and (2) governance rules are formalized, automated and enforced using software" (Jentzsch, 2016). "The proposal was enticing to many investors because it used many aspects of blockchain technology to accomplish its primary function, such as payment and granular management of access . . . in an open, immutable, and verifiable manner" (DuPont, 2018, 161).

The project was created on 30th April 2016 and became, at the time, the largest crowdsourcing campaign in history when $150 million USD worth of ether was invested in its token sale (Siegel, 2016; Waters, 2016).[5] On the 27th May, one day before the crowd-sale closed, a scientific paper was released disclosing seven possible attacks on The DAO (Mark et al., 2016), which caused a dip in the price of ether, devaluating The DAO funds from $150 to $132 million USD (Slashdot, 2016).[6] The real trouble came, however, on the 17th June when someone was found to be hacking The DAO and draining the investors' ether into a different account (Buterin, 2016). A total of 3.6 million ETH ($70 million USD) was syphoned off from the pool of investor funds.

The smart contract of The DAO was codified on top of the 'immutable' Ethereum blockchain and so, theoretically, the investors should not have been able to get this money back. After all, the code was designed to be rigid so the organisation could govern itself via strict, predetermined rules. Such inflexibility may overlook the social messiness inherent in certain transactions, which traditional legal contracts and courts can better cater for (Levy, 2017). In this case, the only possible way of revoking the fraudulent transaction was to alter the underlying Ethereum backbone—something antithetical (and even anti-ethical) to blockchain philosophy. After all, "The DAO was supposed to represent a turning point in legal authority, where code really does form a new legal regime" (DuPont, 2018, 169). In this sense, hacked transactions should be as permanent as 'legitimate' ones and recognised as a price that must be paid for a 'fair' network with 'distributed' control. But 15% of all ether in existence was then 'locked' within The DAO and a large proportion was suddenly in the hands of a 'miscreant.'

Although the bug exploited was unique to The DAO and nothing to do with Ethereum, the success of this project was seen as imperative for the success of the underlying network as a whole. Similar to the resolution process of Bitcoin's 2013 accidental hard fork (see Chapter 5), a group of Ethereum developers gathered online to formulate a strategy for resolving the problem (DuPont, 2018). Led by Vitalik Buterin, they decided to "hack the hacker" (Kar, 2016). The programmers managed to move the stolen funds temporarily into another smart contract, which would be frozen for 28 days while they came up with another plan. When all other ideas failed, an intentional hard fork was proposed, which meant convincing Ethereum miners to go back to an old block predating the hack and to begin building on top of it (to mine into existence another version of reality). This strategy completely undermines the idea of blockchains acting as permanent records by re-mining the supposedly 'singular' account of history. The decision generated a great deal of backlash on Reddit from purists who regarded Ethereum as a

> foundational infrastructure upon which a flurry of projects and experiments are supposed to blossom, and in order for them to blossom they need a foundation that is strong, and that has integrity in the face of challenges. The hard fork proposal is a compromise that ruins that integrity and signals that projects like the DAO can influence the underlying foundation to their own advantage. To me that is totally unacceptable and is a departure from the principles that drew me to Ethereum.... The fact that the Ethereum foundation has been involved in and promoted the DAO project has been an error and it only usurps the trust that people have in Ethereum as a foundational infrastructure for other projects. (nustiudinastea, 2016; see also thehighfiveghost, 2016)

Ultimately, it was put down to a vote: ether holders were able to send transactions to a platform that acted like a ballot box. The supermajority of people sided with the hard fork (89%)—many of which were DAO stakeholders and thus affected by the hack (Madeira, 2016). Like banks during the 2008 financial crisis, The DAO was deemed too big to fail for the Ethereum ecosystem

(Siegel, 2016)—although this time the decision was made democratically by all of its stakeholders. On the 20th July the majority of miners rolled back to block 1,920,000 to rewrite the historical records of Ethereum, thus omitting The DAO hack.[7]

The Ethereum website described its blockchain as a "decentralized platform that runs smart contracts: applications that run exactly as programmed without any possibility of downtime, censorship, fraud or third party interference" (Ethereum, 2016). However, the human intervention that saved The DAO proves blockchains are theoretically and practically mutable if enough of their actors align. Some have gone so far as to say this turns "the bright prospect of a de-centralized autonomous market into a gloomy centralized dictatorship" (Dovey, 2016).[8]

A collection of miners, however, put their blockchain purist philosophy ahead of profits and refused to accept the changes. Strictly speaking, if miners are operating purely for financial gain, the longest side of a forked blockchain should end up being the only version because it contains more cryptographic proof and encourages them to gather cryptocurrency rewards exchangeable with the many others using that chain. Evidently, however, political motivations can cause a rift in cryptoeconomics: to this day, a smaller group have continued mining the 'old' Ethereum chain, now known as Ethereum Classic. This creates a permanent bifurcation: a fragmentation of communities who do not see the same 'truth' (see Chapter 5). Ethereum Classic has "refused to die despite the Ethereum Foundation's repeated attempts to kill it" (Coppola, 2016). Consequently, two competing views of legitimacy and authenticity can be found on either side of the fork. More moderate stakeholders "saw the hard fork as evidence of the flexibility and practicality of Ethereum and its leaders, while the more ideological saw the hard fork as censorship by a powerful cabal, or proof that blockchain technology was unable to live up to its idealistic promises" (DuPont, 2018, 165).

Another hard fork occurred on the 24th November when two of Ethereum's clients, Geth and Parity, "slipped out of synch" but was later fixed when the Ethereum developer team warned miners if they did not update their systems they would be working on an invalid chain with no support (DuPont, 2018): "[s]o much for the old chain dying out naturally because everyone freely decides to use the new one. This is more like Microsoft: 'old versions of Windows are no longer supported'. Devs rule, ok" (Coppola, 2016).[9] Although the The DAO was always supposed to be a hybrid mode of human-machine governance (code actualising the votes of stakeholders), these issues clearly demonstrate how forms of collective action can unravel the promise of non-repudiation. In other words, "social actors fell back to traditional strong network ties. In doing so, governance of The DAO discredited its ideological underpinnings" (DuPont, 2018, 172).

"The Empire Strikes Back"

Broader technical innovations in FinTech are tweaking existing economic systems to create efficiency gains as well as producing completely new models of business such as crowdfunding and peer-to-peer lending. These evolutions threaten the embedded and, some would say, 'outdated' financial industry. The majority of disruptors are platform capitalists who look to connect people through their own centralised systems (PayPal, Venmo, TransferWise) as opposed to traditional banking behemoths. Unsurprisingly, banks and other financial services are responding by developing their own financial innovations. Nick Shalek, a partner at Ribbit Capital, refers to this as "The Empire Strikes Back" (VLAB, 2015). Here, financial firms have had no choice but to *partner* or *compete* with emerging FinTech start-ups and, if that does not work, *acquire* or *co-opt* them (VLAB, 2015).[10] Nationally and globally, regional control over the FinTech ecosystem is dominated by Silicon Valley but New York has become the fastest growing FinTech centre in the world as Wall Street recognises the danger of being left behind (Accenture, 2014). Consequently, "[t]he visions and aspirations of Wall Street and Silicon Valley are merging. Start-ups are now looking to innovate at the level of money, payment and funding, while financial companies innovate through technology" (Lovink & Tkacz, 2015, 16).

Existing powerhouses in the banking industry are also looking to benefit from their own forms of blockchain capitalism. Many of these banks attempt to enclose ideas developed in the open source software 'commons' (initially posed as public tools for decentralisation) with aggressive patenting. This is a relatively unique vision for decentralisation: consortium blockchains are generally being produced by the powers that be to maintain their hold on the capitalist market. For example, as a response to their ageing and slow-paced means for facilitating trans-bank payments (see Appendix 12), SWIFT has included blockchain technology in its global payments innovation initiative (Prisco, 2015b). SWIFT subsequently stepped up their exploration in distributed ledger technologies by designing a proof of concept (POC) to reconcile bank nostro databases in real time (SWIFT, 2017; Finextra, 2017). To do this, it has started building a blockchain application leveraging the open source Hyperledger Fabric codebase to simplify cross-border payments by synchronising databases and optimising the global liquidity of banks (del Castillo, 2017). Here, "only authorized members will be able to access the POC, which will be integrated with Swift's own identity management platform and its public key infrastructure" (del Castillo, 2017). SWIFT claims that distributed ledger technologies can generate trust in a disseminated system, efficiency in broadcasting information, complete traceability of transactions, simplified reconciliation, and high resiliency (SWIFT,

2016). Hyperledger Fabric itself is an open umbrella project initiated by the Linux Foundation collating open source blockchains and related tools such as Digital Asset Holdings, Blocksteam's libconsensus, and IBM's OpenBlockchain. Blockchains are partly, but clearly, moving from an anarchist tool of economic dissent towards the apparatuses of embedded centralised powers in already existing Financial Empires.

Many other banking powerhouses have been investing time and money into understanding the potential impact of blockchains on the world economy. For example, while I was working out of Level39 in Canary Wharf, I met with UBS's Blockchain Innovation Lab, which had created an office there. As Switzerland's highest grossing bank, they had set up this enterprise in Europe's largest FinTech accelerator to keep a finger on the pulse of an emerging industry (Level39, 2015; Irrera, 2015; Prisco, 2015a). Similarly, I interviewed the founder and director of a cryptocurrency company situated in an accelerator set up by Barclays in Notting Hill, London, where they were given free office space. He recalled to me how a member of the bank had told him: "you're our tentacles out there." It was his belief that banks were suddenly realising they were going to have to work more closely with new start-ups because they themselves were "bereft of ideas and moved at a snail's pace of innovation due to their bureaucratic structures." Back in Silicon Valley, I attended a Retail and FinTech Expo at Plug and Play, where hordes of traditional investors were looking to take advantage of ideas in the emerging technology industry by listening to start-up pitches and investing in those they saw as potentially disruptive.

New ventures are also forming to become the connector between traditional institutions. R3 is a "financial innovation firm that leads a consortium partnership with over 80 of the world's leading financial institutions and regulators . . . work[ing] together to design and deliver advanced distributed ledger technologies to the global financial markets" (R3, 2017). The firm was created by former Wall Street executive David Rutter in 2015 and included stakeholders Goldman Sachs, Barclays, BBVA, Commonwealth Bank of Australia, Credit Suisse, JP Morgan, Royal Bank of Scotland, State Street, and UBS (Vigna, 2015; Allison, 2015; Kelly, 2015; Williams-Grut, 2015). Goldman Sachs pulled out in 2016 (Hackett, 2016), yet remained investors in other blockchain start-ups such as Digital Assets Holdings (McLannahan, 2016).[11] IBM, Chain, Ethereum, Eris Industries, and Intel helped run tests on the R3 project, marking "an unprecedented scale of institutional collaboration between the financial and technology communities" (Buitenhek, 2016, 115).

While this consortium is related to the rise of blockchains, they, like many others, have moved towards the term 'distributed ledger technology' to describe the subject of their "research, experimentation, design and engineering" (R3, 2017). Their three strategic pillars are: 1) to develop "the base layer reference architecture to underpin a global financial-grade ledger"; 2) to deploy a "secure, multi-institution collaborative lab to test and benchmark blockchain technologies," and; 3) to run "use cases to identity and design 'up the stack' commercial applications" (R3, 2017). R3 boasts a myriad of seasoned finance professionals such as investment banker Jesse Edwards and FX trading manager Todd McDonald, technology professionals such as Richard Brown from IBM, and ex-Bitcoin Core developer Mike Hearn (for the more radical Bitcoiners, the relocation of programmers once involved in the 'Bitcoin movement' has been branded as 'switching sides'). R3 state how their distributed ledger platform, Corda, was designed to "record, manage and synchronise financial agreements between regulated financial institutions. It is heavily inspired by and captures the benefits of blockchain systems, without the design choices that make blockchains inappropriate for many banking scenarios" (Brown, 2016).[12] Managing Director, Charlie Cooper, explains how "changes must be made to satisfy regulatory, privacy and scalability concerns" (Peyton, 2017).

An introductory white paper describes Corda as taking "a unique approach to data distribution and transaction semantics while maintaining the features of distributed ledgers which first attracted institutions to projects such as R3, namely reliable execution of financial agreements in an automatable and enforceable fashion" (Brown et al., 2016, 15). Chief Technology Officer, Richard Brown (2016), in his equally optimistic yet sobering R3 blogpost, describes five characteristics offered by the "blockchain bundle": consensus, validity, uniqueness, immutability, and authentication. The culmination of these characteristics and the "thing that is *genuinely new* is the emergence of platforms, shared across the Internet between mutually distrusting actors, that allow them to reach consensus about the existence and evolution of facts shared between them" (Brown, 2016). Brown explains how the financial industry is defined by these arrangements but firms share a common problem costing tens of billions of dollars a year to rectify: "the agreement is typically recorded by *both* parties, in *different* systems" (Brown, 2016).

In a technical Corda white paper, Mike Hearn (2016b) explains how the solution offered by blockchains is to "trade performance and usability for security and global acceptance." This makes sense for a cryptocurrency, but for an interbank management system (i.e., an operational database) it is far from optimal. Rather than using a standardised blockchain architecture as a one-size-fits-all solution, the Corda team designed their platform "from the ground up to address the specific needs of the financial services industry" (Rutter, 2017). As such, Corda is a system that looks to share the management of financial agreements across firms that "record the agreement consistently and identically," is "visible to the appropriate regulators," and is "built on industry-standard tools, with a focus on interoperability and incremental deployment" without "leak[ing] confidential information to third parties" (Rutter, 2017). And so, Corda directly applies "the 'authentication', 'immutability' and 'uniqueness service' features of blockchains" but radically departs "when it comes to the scope of 'consensus' (parties to individual deals rather than all participants) and 'validation' (the legitimate stakeholders to a deal rather the whole universe or some arbitrary set of 'validators')" (Rutter, 2017). Crucially, then, Corda "restricts access to data within an agreement to only those explicitly entitled to it, rather than the entire network . . . [while] linking business logic and data to associated legal prose in order to ensure that the financial agreements on the platform are firmly rooted in law" (Rutter, 2017).

One of the reasons the banking world has become so transfixed on blockchain technologies is because of the pace and security they promise in terms of clearing and settling interbank trades. In short, this allows bankers "to get back to trading in risk. The blockchain is exciting precisely because it can permit a new, re-risking of finance" (Maurer, 2016, 90). "By facilitating speed-up, reducing latency, and maintaining a persistent and verifiable record, distributed ledgers have the potential to reactive pre-2008 practices of making and managing risk-stratified products" (Maurer, 2016, 93). Coming from another angle, what

> cryptocurrency and blockchain enthusiasts potentially miss in the race for highspeed capital flows . . . is that existing infrastructure is often slow on purpose. Slow clearance and settlement procedures, for instance, function as a speedbump, to lower overall velocity and give actors time to react, fix mistakes, and make rational decisions. In other words, slowness itself is a form of regulation (DuPont, 2019, 157).

The space-times of finance will no doubt require further negotiation as processes of algorithmic (de)centralisation unfold.

Going Full Circle

R3 is also involved in a venture called 'FedCoin.' This term started being used in the blogosphere during 2013 to describe the possibility of creating central bank cryptographic tokens, which could be pegged to the currencies of specific nation-states (Koning, 2013, 2014; Motamedi, 2014; Sams, 2015; Andolfatto, 2015). In a discussion paper released in 2015, the Bank of England reviewed the benefits and challenges of adopting a form of national digital currency similar to Bitcoin. Previously, the Bank of Canada embraced the possibilities of cryptocurrencies after Andreas Antonopoulos famously addressed the Canadian Committee on Banking, Trade, and Commerce in 2014 (Senate of Canada, 2014; Weber, 2016; Fung & Halaburda, 2016). They have since been working with R3 on central bank digital currency projects, as have the Monetary Authority of Singapore (Swanson, 2017b). Other countries conducting similar projects include China, the Bahamas, Thailand, Uruguay, Sweden, and India (Helms, 2019). Each initiative could reduce the need for citizens to carry coins and banknotes in their pockets.

The idea of a 'cashless society' is increasingly (and intentionally) painted as 'progressive' by commercial and central banks but also threatens to create ubiquitous forms of economic surveillance over populations (Scott, 2018). Digital 'paper trails' would afford governments greater control over the informal economy at the cost of confidentiality for everyday people. The International Monetary Fund (2019) outlines the main reasons for employing central bank digital currencies: "lowering costs, increasing efficiency of monetary policy implementation, countering competition from cryptocurrencies, ensuring contestability of the payment market, and offering a risk-free payment instrument to the public." Private blockchains are more conducive for legal compliance and "allow for faster payments, transaction throughput and settlement speed" (Koning, 2016). On the other hand, public blockchains might recreate "some of the unique qualities of coins and banknotes, particularly their ability to provide anonymity and censorship resistance" (Koning, 2016). Ultimately, design choices will help produce different money/code/spaces and affect the affordances of central banks and their citizens.

Blockchains are also being envisioned as powerful mechanisms for organising other nation-state operations (see Appendix 24). Honduras, Sweden, and the Republic of Georgia have all considered using distributed ledgers for securing land title registration in a manner where data cannot be tampered with (Shin, 2017). Honduras, for example, has a long history of dispute concerning land ownership, which has seen large companies dispossess poor indigenous populations (Council of Hemispheric Affairs, 2014).

> The intersection between profit-seeking multinational companies, the war on drugs, a broken judicial system, private security guards, and a repressive and corrupt military and police comes down to a doleful reality in which innocent people and communities reclaiming their lands are murdered, threatened, and displaced. (Council of Hemispheric Affairs, 2014)

The majority of land ownership remains undocumented, exasperating this problem further. That which is legally accounted for has often been altered by corrupt officials to allow for business expansion (Chavez-Dreyfuss, 2015). A blockchain company called Factom entered a partnership with the Honduras government to pursue the idea of recording land titles on distributed ledgers, with the aim of providing an incorruptible, transparent, chronological chain of ownership through time. While this might seem, at first glance, like blockchain to the rescue, there is a deeply political choice to be made when initially entering the deeds to property in such a system. Blockchains are supposed to represent a single, objective, shared record of truth. But land dispute is fundamentally a problem of subjectivity. So what happens if a country sets up a blockchain omitting a person's claim to a piece of land? Is their point of view, their reality, omitted forever?

Approaching this dilemma from another angle, why should anyone trust the records of a database in the first place? They are, after all, merely carriers of information. In order for that data to hold weight, blockchains must be recognised as legitimate by all involved stakeholders; otherwise they are just another matter of dispute, or worse, meaningless databases too easily ignored. Traditionally, the most effective way for documents, digital or otherwise, to be taken seriously is for them to be enrolled into judiciary networks backed up by courts and law enforcement. In other words, paperwork must be afforded its power by humans in order for it to constrain and 'dictate' action. The same is true for digital information.

For many smart contracts to operate there must also be a constant and reliable source of data, aside from blockchains, to trigger their execution. This often comes from third parties (individuals, machines, or organisations) referred to as oracles. For example, the London Interbank Offered Rate (LIBOR) taken from a consortium of banks could be used to activate an interest rate derivative payoff (De Filippi & Wright, 2018), or temperature readings taken from thermometers could prompt a financial reward for governments participating in climate change action. External data feeds, however, remain vulnerable to manipulation (DuPont, 2019). Here, centralised corporations and state regulators are not absent from blockchain governance but play a perpetual part in directing transactions. Consequently, 'consulting the oracle' might be an integral part of trusting smart contracts built on top of distributed ledger technologies. Centralisation and distribution remain in an ongoing tension.

Conclusion

Blockchain ecosystems are extremely important for understanding the wider relationships between money, code, and space, increasingly so as the technology is further absorbed within the global economy. This chapter described some of the ways different entities are (re)appropriating Bitcoin's blockchain architecture to 'program' new economic realities. Not only is decentralisation imagined and practised with variation, but many instantiations are now becoming tangled up in an interdependent web. Blockchains show it no longer makes sense (if it ever did) to think about centralisation and decentralisation as a binary system. Instead, these terms should be understood as two spatial patterns that occur in different connective networks. After all, multiple actors attempt to employ these two arrangements in competing ways. Consequently, calling something centralised or decentralised as a whole is almost meaningless without tracing the contextual, relational, and spatial patterns of sociotechnical practice that shape (and are shaped by) economies.

Quite evidently, blockchain knowledge is being carried forward to build new infrastructures (central bank settlement systems, global supply chains, nation-state voting, etc.). Here, there are contrasting ideologies and practices that highlight practical and theoretical limitations to distributed economies. As the technology is normalised, it is subject to bureaucratic routines that include "diligence on investors, book-building, addressing compliance concerns and handling the legal process. On the one hand, this marks an important initiative in maturing the market. On the other, it is recreating Wall Street's system around this new asset class" (Carlson, 2017). There are, of course, exceptions to the rule but for the most part architectures are constrained by processes of blockchain capitalism.

It is important to remember there is often a "homologous spectrum of support" for political-technological modes of organisation "ranging from liberal capitalists to an assortment of anti-capitalist positions" (Taffel, 2015c, 57). With this in mind, blockchains should not be thought of as monolithic data structures moving in one direction: although they may share things in common, there is no such thing as a singular or universal blockchain standard. The politics of individual chains are complex and vary according to their design and uptake. Here, contingent subtleties of power emerge. More often than not, however, blockchains are being utilised as a mode of technological disruption *and* capital accumulation (see Chapter 7). The term 'blockchain capitalism' describes a subcategory of platform capitalism—which could become its dominant form if their builders succeed in 'decentralising everything'—where the quest to enhance profit bends distributed architectures around certain revenue streams. Here, capitalistic tendencies have filtered into private, public, and consortium blockchains, each harnessing different affordances (for their users, builders, and the architectures themselves). While blockchains can certainly be grouped like this, it is important to remember affordances arise through practice and thus new and unpredictable powers can appear.

Ultimately, blockchains, in their current form, do not bring about a world without concentrated power but reshuffle the tensions between centralised and distributed aspects of socioeconomic networks as they are constantly reassembled. This suggests the impossibility of a fully distributed world, but more than that: competing visions for different blockchains reiterate how achieving a 'singular' utopia is impossible due to the diversity of human desires (Jameson, 2005; Moylan & Baccolini, 2007). In other words, understanding utopia as a final destination, or blueprint, is always a contradiction, a forlorn hope, thanks to an inherent concreteness of prescriptive ideas that excludes competing visions of 'paradise.' Utopianism, then, is forever incomplete, in motion, a trial-and-error process resisting fixity. Indeed, the explosion of distributed ledgers showcases an array of imagined futures as well as the proposed roads leading towards them. Subjectivity ensures that distributed utopias will always simultaneously be distributed dystopias (for others). Perhaps, then, the definition of *utopia as blueprint* should be shed in favour of *utopia as method* or *process*: this is "the imaginative capacity to resist a complex and all-consuming system which forecloses on the possibility of imagining a different future" (Drage, 2019, 157; see also Tally, 2011). In this sense, Bitcoin should not be championed as a definitive answer to central banks but can, instead, be applauded for asking questions in the first place.

Conclusion

Drawing from a diverse set of literatures, the aim of this book has been to trace diligently the cultural, political, material, economic, and spatial networks of Bitcoin and other blockchains in order to understand how power is manifested across their architectures between humans and non-humans. The five empirical chapters deal with different theoretical strands that represent overlapping but distinct component parts of the Bitcoin/blockchain cultural economy. The main focus has been to explore how Bitcoin's apparently distributed network infrastructure becomes materialised, socialised, and centralised at different levels.

Thus far, the price of Bitcoin has largely remained beyond the analytical scope of this book because it can become extremely distracting for academics and other commentators: hysteria fills the rhetoric of proponents and sceptics alike as the value fluctuates between highs and lows. In other words, for pundits, a rising price often reflects success and a falling price reflects failure. I first became involved with Bitcoin in the summer of 2013, at the foot of its third bubble: soon after, a single bitcoin rocketed from around $68 to $1,163 USD.[1] When the price began to fall slowly towards a low of $151 in 2015, many of my peers would confidently tell me: "Bitcoin is dead." Bitcoin communities are used to pessimistic accounts, often to the point of amusement. This is represented by the webpage Bitcoin Obituaries (99bitcoins.com/bitcoin-obituaries), which lists accounts of its death and has become a popular cultural meme—at the time of writing, Bitcoin has been declared dead 380 times by various journalists and other commentators. The first announcement was in 2010 when the currency was valued at just 23 US cents. It is important to remember the price of Bitcoin is not necessarily indicative of, and certainly not directly proportional to, its success as a decentralising phenomenon. In many cases the stability of currencies is preferable to both volatility or increasing value (see Chapter 2).

However, the price is still relevant and intersects with other geopolitical events. For example, the value of a bitcoin, like gold, often spikes during times of geographically specific uncertainty—for example, the Cypriot financial bail

Money Code Space. Jack Parkin, Oxford University Press (2020). © Oxford University Press.
DOI: 10.1093/oso/9780197515075.001.0001.

in, the UK Brexit vote, and the US presidential election of Donald Trump—because the protocol can be used as a tool for capital flight (as with other financial markets, what proportion of trades this accounts for remains murky).[2] This realises a core tenet of Bitcoin's development: providing the power for individual citizens to opt out of fiat currencies in times of crisis. Yet it also means external speculators can profit from the flow of other people's money conversions, piggybacking profits from crises. While it could be argued this is nothing new, Bitcoin is certainly a novel means for doing so.

The point of this book has been to stress: while blockchains may offer more distributed modes of money and finance, it is important to account for contours of power that form between its actor-networks. Upon closer examination, the role of centralised obligatory passage points in blockchain architectures is significant and often necessary for their formation and maintenance. Even the price of a bitcoin is not given but is 'discovered' and 'changed' via market mechanisms assembled through centralised exchanges via bids and asks—themselves constituted by a range of social factors (capital flight, investment, remittances, etc.). These bottlenecks 'collect' aggregated speculation as centres of calculation (Latour, 1987). At the same time, they influence cryptocurrency and blockchain economies as centres of performance.

This analysis echoes depictions of nomadic global monetary flows (Leyshon & Thrift, 1997). As value materialises and circulates through different intermediaries—banknotes, digital balances, derivatives, stocks, property—it is only temporarily tied to particular things, people, and places yet forcefully participates in assembling their cultural and economic geographies (Leyshon & Thrift, 1997). As time goes on, these money/spaces are increasingly mediated by code, which plays a powerful role in modulating "the conditions under which sociospatial processes operate" (Kitchin & Dodge, 2011, 65). Consequently, it is appropriate to understand contemporary economic geographies as money/code/spaces. This theoretical understanding requires methodologies able to trace the material-semiotic connections between things and people that enact and sustain codified data structures like Bitcoin, blockchains, and other digital currencies.

Traditionally, transaction processors within monetary networks have elevated themselves into positions of power not only by accumulating capital (syphoning off value from the flows of money) but by becoming the gatekeepers of information where data can be interpreted to make informed economic actions or be monetised itself (Leyshon & Thrift, 1997). Cryptographic money, as offered by blockchains, is administered by distributed ledgers, often reflecting motivations to separate money from centralised institutions. In Chapter 6, I showed on a technical level (in terms of node dispersion and the logic of its algorithmic architecture) how the networked protocol of Bitcoin is certainly distributed: there is no in-built hierarchy amongst peers and any node is free to join any other (see Figure 2.1). However, the different cultural-economic practices of actors intersecting with the protocol work to apply obligatory passage points and centralise certain pieces to form an overall decentralised network state: the senatorial governance of code development, the concentration of private key management under start-up companies, and the coalescence of miners in pools. So while the technical architecture may look perfectly distributed, the economy and monetary policy are decentralised (that is, working through many centres). In other words, hierarchy is (re)formed through human-machine (inter)action.

Following geographies of algorithmic (de)centralisation not only pulls to the surface the cultural, economic, material, and political relationships of money/code/space on an empirical level, but also makes advances towards a conceptual terrain. Bitcoin's attempt to homogenise and flatten monetary networks with its blockchain architecture only shows how there will always be multiple incantations and hierarchies of money as they fill different political spaces. The fragmentation of the Bitcoin project personifies this: altcoins, hard forks, private blockchains, and so on. Now, with open source blueprints for cryptographic code/money at everybody's fingertips—alongside many ideas for how they should be tweaked in order to function correctly, satisfy applications, or fulfil political agendas—the sheer quantity of world currencies is growing. So while money homogenises everything under its quantifiable scale (Marx, 1867; Simmel, 1900), not everything is homogenised under the same money.

As Alexander Galloway (2004) uncovered hierarchy and power through the Internet, and as Nathanial Tkacz (2015) exposed bureaucracy and closure in Wikipedia, my investigation finds centralisation in Bitcoin. Tracing the material-semiotic connections between the things and people that enact and sustain the codified data structures of blockchains has demonstrated how their geographies are never isotropic. In other words, while blockchains certainly work to (re)distribute practices on some level, examining their networks from different social, spatial, and material angles reveals subtleties of uneven power. Framing obligatory passage points as socio-spatial 'structures' or 'zones' through which certain cultural-economic practices are enrolled works to redefine centralisation and decentralisation (currently terms used far too ambiguously to carry any real potency) into relational and contingent processes. Multiplications of passage points represent decentralised systems but these bottlenecks do not always afford the same control to all actors—as outlined by senatorial governance and the material infrastructure of Bitcoin. To arrive at such conclusions, the trajectories of networked practice were traced in order to uncover their cohesion in different places. Through empirical analysis and theoretical critique, it was found that many centres of Bitcoin shape (and are shaped by) the network in distinctive fashions. The politics and affordances of Core developers, for example, differ to the politics and affordances of start-up companies.

With this in mind, blockchains will not become ubiquitous modes of democratisation but, equally, will not disappear (at least overnight) from modes of societal organisation. Instead, they are likely to form complex patterns of relatively centralised networked practice (funnelled through obligatory passage points) and relatively distributed connectivity (at a technical level) like the Internet before it. After all, they live in the same cultural-economic world. The Bitcoin governance structure is decentralised when observing the many clients that can be built on top of the network (with the possibility of forking their own rules) but the development of different software rules requires degrees of centralised coordination (see Chapter 5). Miners must be relied upon for voting on decisions, who seem distributed until the cohesion of mining pools are observed; yet the fact that individual miners can move between pools provides another decentred pattern of governance. Similarly, start-up companies build centralised bottlenecks of control (over private keys, for example) but the option still remains for individuals to download a Bitcoin client software themselves and become their own self-regulating node in a financial network. Consequently, algorithmic decentralisation is piecemealed ideologically and operationally among a mismatch of stakeholders so that it becomes a cultural-economic multiplication.

While the analytical framework of obligatory passage points can be used to unravel unequal power relations in other social, technical, and economic networks, it is important to remember that each is highly contextual. So, while the specific structure of senatorial governance *may* be used as a template for other proof-of-work blockchains, there are now a plethora of decentralised architectures adopting various protocol mechanisms for reaching network consensus. Each must be studied in(ter)dependently to understand their nuanced modes of power. For example, the now highly anticipated blockchain-based Libra currency announced by Facebook will not have the same protocological rules to Bitcoin in terms of node participation and will thus produce a different governance system (i.e., where transaction validators are elected by a consortium). Additionally, more centralised models of cryptocurrency proposed by central banks may be much less 'senatorial' and carry even greater authoritarian and monopolistic potential than proof-of-work blockchains ever have. Ultimately, the logic and labour of both humans and machines will inevitably vary in distinctive networks; it is the patterns in which they interlock that are important for delineating control.

For the most part, radical distribution appears to be a stark impossibility on both a technical and capitalistic level: platforms need to be built under some form of centralised governance whereas the quest for capital accumulation demands a degree of conglomeration in economic systems. This is put poignantly by Steve

Wilson, vice president and principal analyst of Constellation Research: "[t]here is no utopia in blockchain. The harsh truth is that when we fold real world management, permissions, authorities and trust, back on top of the blockchain, we undo the decentralisation at the heart of the design" (Wilson, 2016). The same pattern was seen during the maturation of the Internet as different entities enrolled its new spatial connectivity into hierarchal channels of revenue. Profit, after all, is nothing if not the centralisation of wealth. Evidentially, code struggles to eradicate the asymmetries produced by cultures and economies.

The specific organisational structure outlined in the case of Bitcoin also speaks back to the actor-network approach used to analyse it. Such thinking is often championed for "complicating the distinctions between human and non-human, social and material" (Whatmore, 2002, 1). For some this is a double-edged sword: while it gives non-humans a voice it can be accused of relegating human agency to the same potency as that of objects and ideas (Collins & Yearley, 1992). In other words, a flat ontology is formed that fails to attend to power structures in society by losing itself in an endless web of description (Amsterdamska, 1990; Whittle & Spicer, 2008). Conversely, this book has shown how actor-network thinking can be used to illuminate human agency among complex entanglements of non-humans—understanding hierarchy from the inside-out in order to bring it to the surface. In fact, what this framework demonstrates is how hierarchy is not imposed from upon high by a preceding, external, all-powerful force (like the state, capitalism, or an algorithmic protocol) but rather coercive actors are held and maintained within complex networks of everyday material practice (that might produce aspects of statist, capitalistic, or protocological control). It is these hybrid ensembles that can be unraveled to reveal localities of power.

Consequently, actor-network thinking should not encourage a flat ontology but be administered to help researchers enter a fray of knowns and unknowns where power structures can be traced out *between* people and things. It is by understanding these relationships that the roles of humans and non-humans can be mapped, or positioned, within asymmetric conditions, thus becoming accountable for varying degrees of control. In other words, actor-network thinking can highlight when humans and non-humans, or rather groups of both, are (mis)aligned to dominate each other.

Blockchain Tensions

Bitcoin arose in opposition to centralised forms of monetary policy and posed challenges to established norms of international financial transactions. In Chapter 1, the many promises and problems of blockchains were unpacked to delineate the apparent contradictions produced by their architectures. I described the growth of Bitcoin and problematised it amongst its many stakeholders. The concepts of money, code, and space, as they are (re)defined through the organisational lens of the Bitcoin blockchain, were developed in Chapter 2. Here, money/code/space was used as an analytical framework for understanding the geographies of blockchains and approaching the concept of the algorithmic decentralisation of (crypto)currency. Taking inspiration from actor-network theory, I started to shed the centralisation-decentralisation dualism by adapting obligatory passage points as a way of understanding centralised control in 'distributed' networks (Callon, 1986; Musiani et al., 2018). Throughout, the specific practices constituting money/code/spaces were articulated so that understandings of Bitcoin and blockchain technology would encapsulate their complex cultural relationships.

The investigation set out in Chapter 3 was designed to carve through the imaginaries of blockchain decentralisation as they intersect with the materialities of infrastructure and high technology economies. This involved redefining a follow the thing methodology around the spatial traces of blockchains, with specific attention paid to Bitcoin, to interrogate their algorithmic architectures as socioeconomic organisational mechanisms. Throughout the rest of the book, the definition of the Bitcoin blockchain as a *thing* changed to offer an array of perspectives, which helped reveal varying modes of (de)centralisation: Chapter 4 as ideology; Chapter 5 as open source code; Chapter 6 as infrastructure; Chapter 7 as entrepreneurship, and; Chapter 8 as precursor for a range of decentralised forms. Harnessing an ethnographic sensitivity, I traced certain spatial trajectories to illuminate the (dis)connections formed through emerging practices as they coalesced at different geographical points.

Blockchains, as management systems, are (generally) designed to obscure user identity through public key cryptography and so pursuing certain connections proved to be a challenging endeavour. It seems quite fitting, then, given the community's references to *Alice in Wonderland* in terms of 'going down the Bitcoin rabbit hole,' that this task, at times, felt like I was 'following the white rabbit'; a frenetic pursuit of an alluring, allusive, and illusive entity into strange places. Such is a common feeling for thing followers: "[t]his kind of research can involve exciting but risky ventures. And it can do your head in. So many things that aren't supposed to go together in theory come together in practice" (Cook et al., 2006, 657). The feeling is bittersweet as "direct connections [can't always] be traced, between . . . places and people" (Cook & Harrison, 2007, 58). This is the same for "any thing you could try to follow. Unravelling and becoming more entangled in the process" (Cook et al., 2004, 662).

Methodological exasperations are only exaggerated in this case by the slipperiness of digital things and the dead ends provided by cryptographic concealment. But these "linkages do not just stop at a certain point . . . they just get flimsier, more difficult to discern" (Miller, 1998, 363). What is more, spatial disconnections are just as important to blockchain ontologies as are the connections that can be more easily followed. Severed ties and gaping chasms *make* space as much as connected paths that neatly align and converge: the resilience and deterioration, welding and breaking, of trajectories are the enactments and characteristics of overlapping (blockchain) geographies. So the spatial disconnections presented by blockchains are not only methodological hurdles but also an important part of their very being—stumbling across impasses says something about the character of architectures. Blockchains, then, simultaneously expose and mask their own spatial connections by cryptographic design: their transactional spatiality is inherently one of (dis)connection.

Follow the thing work opens up more boxes than it closes but this is precisely the point: as a tool for locating uneven political relationships at different scales it illuminates points of interest for future researchers. By debunking imaginaries of blockchains as homogenising platforms that can flatten all power in monetary (and other) networks, and instead revealing them as complex and contingent digital-material architectures that bind humans and non-humans together in asymmetrical ways, my follow the thing work has attempted to cut through Bitcoin (and blockchain) cultural economies; in doing so, it has been like looking at a cross-section of bedrock to determine the strata of a geological system. In other words, the ethnographer, "renegotiating identities in different sites . . . learns more about a *slice* of the world system (Marcus, 1995, 113, my emphasis). This is both a strength and a limit to all ethnographic research: it is not necessarily representative but also helps reject overarching theoretical generalisations that shroud complexity and, in this case, power. Blockchains, then, should not succumb exclusively to overarching investigations but become subject to more detailed and nuanced cultural studies that unpick and unpack their algorithmic fabrics (made up of people, places, and machines) to reveal unique and inherent spatial arrangements.

In this case, a geographic attentiveness helped reveal the different worldviews surrounding the algorithmic architectures of blockchains from various stakeholders (venture capitalists, governments, libertarians, regulators, hackers, etc.). Interestingly, these visions proved to be in a state of political tension and friction. This resonates with the point: "what an algorithm is designed to do in theory and what it actually does in practice do not always correspond due to a lack of refinement, miscodings, errors and bugs" (Kitchin, 2017, 25). From my own analysis, I would also add *political struggle* to this list. The research process I laid out was an attempt to encompass this understanding, looking to debunk the ideological claims of decentralisation saturating online discourse pertaining to blockchains. The manner in which algorithms do work in the world cannot be

> simply denoted from an examination of the algorithm/code
> alone . . . [because] algorithms perform in context—in collaboration
> with data, technologies, people, etc. under varying conditions—and
> therefore their effects unfold in contingent and relational ways, produc-
> ing localised and situated outcomes. (Kitchin, 2017, 25)

It was by recognising this multifariousness that I decided not only to rely on the Bitcoin code to tell its own story but allowed different narratives to emerge by following the trajectories of a host of other actors that propel it into being.

The historical and perpetuating ideologies that fuelled the creation of Bitcoin, outlined in Chapter 4, demonstrated how the idea of decentralisation has been welded to that of technological development/determinism and perpetuated as an optimal model for economic organisation. While a core strand of right-wing extremism certainly exists in these cultures (Golumbia, 2015, 2016b), this book showed how code and other infrastructures do not wholly encom-pass the politics of their (original) makers. Instead, they become wrapped up in a storm of competing trajectories that carry them off in different directions. Bitcoin infrastructure represents a struggle between different groups of people wishing to subvert or control points in its architecture for different cultural, political, ideological, or economic reasons: for example, start-ups to accumu-late capital or coin tumblers to enhance anonymity.[3] As such, Bitcoin is torn at its algorithmic seams: a reminder that architectures are politically polysemous in their becoming, carrying multiple affordances and destinies. This makes any future alignments of money/code/space (not limited to blockchains) poignant foci of research as each component collides in different ways, presenting spatio-political struggles amongst various stakeholders performing (and profiting from) economic practices.

The plurality of identities that saturated Bitcoin communities was once fairly cohesive because members were bound by the unified goal of developing and normalising the protocol within the global economy. However, as the network has scaled it has become clear how a singular open source codebase, and its (de) centralised mode of governance, cannot fulfil the desires of all its diverse propo-nents. The growing number of Bitcoin stakeholders, personified by numerous forks, reflects this while the diversity of altcoins, blockchains, start-up compa-nies, mining pools, and meet-up groups exhibits fragmentation. Quite clearly there is no singular blockchain worldview yet the quest for (some level of) decentralisation unites them all, whether this is to increase efficiency (central bank blockchains) or to disrupt the entire economic order (Bitcoin). The key lesson in Chapter 5 is that code builders retain a certain degree of power over the digital infrastructures they create (even under open source models and a 'decentralised' miner-voting governance mechanism). While there are avenues

for dissent, these must come in the form of competing (de)centralised parties who can only hope to hijack the system, partly, for themselves. This is not
a scathing critique of decentralised governance, as it certainly generates a new
organisational model where power to make decisions for change can be jostled
for amongst different actors. But the presence of centralised governors should
never be overlooked.

In Chapter 6, I demonstrated how Bitcoin unavoidably has a material and
spatial fabric despite popular ethereal imaginaries of the digital. At the same
time, however, I showed how cryptography and a peer-to-peer architecture are,
on some level, employed to veil Bitcoin's material and spatial processes. The
cryptographic techniques shroud the specificity of space in mathematical obscurity. Money under the Bitcoin blockchain, in effect, appears dematerialised and
despatialised as it enters a 'foggy' digital nebula that negates the possibility of
following some of its footprints. In other words, the material and spatial mechanisms are still whirring away under the hood but the inability to trace them renders the Bitcoin network a somewhat impalpable entity because transactions, by
design, enter a cryptographically sealed black box.

By following a bitcoin 'through space' it became evident how technically distributed blockchains rely on centralised cultural-economic components where
information is bottlenecked into certain infrastructural spaces (undersea network cables, data centres, ISPs, etc.). The builders of Bitcoin have attempted
to overcome these material limitations by polyfurcating its database capability
across many nodes and obscuring certain data metrics behind cryptographic
algorithms. However, when looking at individual wallet services or exchanges
in the industrial economy, information and practices are (re)concentrated in
centralised locations and become subject to internal weaknesses and hacks, as
with any other financial system. While cryptography exists to mask transactions,
technical barriers to entry push user practices through these bottlenecks, affording their owners the ability to act as centres of calculation who emerge, via this
very process, as the gatekeepers of information and the administrators of transactions. These centres are consequently enrolled as powerful actors within the
money/code/spaces of blockchains. Here, start-up companies play a role in reattaching some of the 'ethereal' algorithmic processes of cryptocurrencies back to
locatable space; while the Bitcoin blockchain architecture may be distributed
and opaque, for start-ups the Bitcoin economy of transactions is anything but.

Similarly, the process of cryptoeconomics necessitates 'built in' competition,
giving rise to centralised mining practices. The scaling of such operations, by
people all over the world investing in more efficient machines, raises the difficulty of receiving block rewards. This competition has given rise to mining
pools: centralised bottlenecks through which miners, separated through space,
can collectively funnel their power together to increase the likelihood of a block

reward being shared among participants (proportional to their contributions of hashing power). With an oligopoly of large mining pools, miner voting is consolidated among a few small parties (effectively being raised as political representatives for individual miners). Such activities obey the codified rules of the Bitcoin protocol, demonstrating how centralisation can certainly linger within blockchain modes of operational governance. The *material* logic of code, then, is essential for pinpointing control in any digital infrastructure including the subtle hierarchies of distributed cryptographic systems.

Bitcoin has provided an opportunity for pioneers to carve different business models out of its distributed architecture, creating a vibrant industry in technology hubs like Silicon Valley. In these spaces, the axioms are of a forthcoming and democratising disruption marching forward under the banner of technological decentralisation. In Chapter 7, I showed how the production of Bitcoin and blockchain companies encapsulates a plurality of desires but these are ultimately underpinned by a relentless faith in technological determinism. The idea is to bring forth disruption and profit simultaneously with decentralised architectures. Here, (blockchain) technology becomes a tool that can satisfy the dreams of all stakeholders from hackers to venture capitalists, the left to the right. The internal wrestle of worldviews entrapped in blockchains can be seen, in many cases, as the Californian Ideology in practice. As start-up companies scale, they are enrolled into an embedding and centralising process exposing themselves to external pressures like venture capitalists, legal firms, and nation-state governments. This transforms start-ups from small, flexible, disruptive projects run by a select few technocrats into larger political melting pots, succumbing to multiple modes of bureaucracy. The varied cultures of these different players, far from being irrelevant, are extremely important to cryptocurrency and blockchain economies. Promises of human disintermediation are again shown to be a fantasy as certain parts of Bitcoin become susceptible to hacks, manipulation, incompetencies, insider trading, and other 'faults' supposedly antithetical to cryptosystems. All of these tend to creep back through their centralised pieces. The overall trend: capitalistic best interests of centralised proprietary software companies win out over anarchist philosophies in a familiar pattern of normalisation.

Finally, Chapter 8 started to unpack the branching out of blockchain projects from Bitcoin while ensuring their political mutuality was not lost entirely. This focused predominantly on the contradiction of how blockchains are set up as a tool for both radical decentralisation *and* capital accumulation. In many ways, this chapter acted as an overview but also pinpointed the varying money/code/ spaces emerging from algorithmic decentralisation as blockchains are further co-opted among a myriad of stakeholders. So while code certainly transduces the spaces of everyday life (Kitchin & Dodge, 2011), it is also remoulded by cultural practice not limited to the updates made by programmers. Code/spaces, then, are continually processual so that power achieved through their digital-material architectures evolves over time. As such, the money/spaces of blockchains are not fixed, but are continually unfolding and splintering.

Value creation and transference via blockchains continue to be performed through dense social networks but the transformational relationship with code deeply affects their layered and connective spatial make-up. Consequently, the cultural-economic busyness of money/code/space must garner attention: while political monetarist desires can be embedded in software, these rules are not necessarily set in stone. The algorithmic configuration of Bitcoin may, on the surface, appear to be perfectly distributed but, in practice, it becomes socialised and materialised around specific centres. So, on one hand, code "does what it says" in the sense that software materially executes what is written in its programming language (Galloway, 2004, 193) but, on another, it does not because its rules can be manipulated or bent around cultural, economic, and political practice. Future theorisations of money/code/space should be aware of these nuances as value is transacted across ever-changing algorithmic geographies.

Appendices

For the sake of space, the appendices for this book can be downloaded free of charge by visiting www.jackparkin.com.

Notes

Preface

1. This is, at least, the popular contemporary usage of the term 'cryptography' (DuPont, 2014; see Chapter 3).

2. In this book, I use double quotation marks for excerpts taken directly from speech or external references and single quotation marks to represent rhetorical words or phrases—for example, figures of speech or instances where the terms are questionable and do not necessarily reflect my personal point of view.

3. Due to the nascency of Bitcoin and blockchain technology many of the resources in this book are online texts and do not have page numbers. Instead of writing "n.p." after each quotation, I state here that if no page number is shown then it can be taken to be a source without pages.

4. While certain journalists claim both the network and the currency can be referred to as "Bitcoin" (capitalised), I maintain the aforementioned distinction because this better reflects the cultural norms of the community from which it originated (see also Lustig & Nardi, 2015). Additionally, it is often useful to distinguish between the Bitcoin network itself and the currency it brings into being—although it will become clear these two 'things' are interlaced and codependent.

5. China Fortune Land Development is a publicly traded Chinese real estate company, demonstrating the international links/investments maintained by Silicon Valley's regional technology economy (Saxenian, 2002).

6. Squirrel, as a builder of smart contracts, would receive a fee but the code of the smart contract predetermined by all parties would execute the transaction 'independently.' So, Squirrel becomes a new kind of third party as a cooperative rule builder. However, once the parameters of the contract are written they cannot be undone (unless those changes are agreed upon by all parties before it executes).

7. Plug and Play is a venture capitalist and incubator firm that invests a small amount of money in a large amount of companies, housing them in an enormous space in Sunnyvale, Silicon Valley. Their business model is such that when a small number of companies succeed, such as Dropbox or Zoosk, the payoffs more than cover the costs of their other ventures. The group has provided a number of Bitcoin and blockchain companies with venture capital and has also hosted the Silicon Valley Bitcoin Meet-up Group.

Introduction

1. I empathise with David Golumbia's (2016a) frustration with the neologism 'hacker': it "has so many meanings, and yet it is routinely used as if its meaning was unambiguous ... [and]

as if these ambiguities are epiphenomenal or unimportant" (124). The nuances of how I use the term will become clear as the book develops.

2. At the same time, I recognise humans are constructed from, and embody their own form of, materiality.

3. I use architecture to mean the mathematical and algorithmic structure of code (akin to software) whereas infrastructure relates to the material networks of silicon chips, cables, wires, and electricity (akin to hardware) that allow computer programs to run. It will become clear throughout the book that this is not a binary distinction.

4. The rhetoric of TED Talks, for example, often reverberate notions of technological sensationalism. In a presentation entitled "The Future of Money," Neha Narula (2016) claims: in a "programmable world we remove humans and institutions from the loop."

5. Incidentally, blockchains have also been posed as a basis for distributed memory from which to build artificial intelligence (Volpicelli, 2017; Corea, 2017; Marr, 2018).

Chapter 1

1. As Satoshi Nakamoto is a pseudonym, there is no way to know for sure whether they are male, female, or a group of people. Various claims and educated guesses have been made as to who Nakamoto is yet there is no overriding evidence that can conclude this identification. Tom Boellstorff (2008) argues that the "actual world" identities of people behind their online avatars are relatively unimportant to the virtual settings that they perform in. In this sense, it is not crucial to determine who Satoshi Nakamoto is underneath the pseudonym/avatar/screen name but rather to take into account how this anonymity enacts the situations to which he/she/they contribute. Satoshi Nakamoto, then, is taken to be an anonymous cultural actor without speculation over identity.

2. In these online spaces Bitcoin began resonating strongly with libertarians, cryptoanarchists, and cypherpunks who revelled in the idea of a monetary alternative to fiat currency that claimed to obliterate trust in banks and governments (see Chapter 3).

3. The term 'cryptocurrency' was first conceived by a user on the Bitcoin Mailing List in reference to the cryptographic functions that allow it to run (Popper, 2015a). Nakamoto and Malmi approved of the terminology and began using it themselves. Vires in Numeris was proposed by a user of the Bitcoin Forum during a discussion about logos/mottos (see https://bitcointalk.org/index.php?topic=4994.msg140770#msg140770).

4. When the Bank of England and the Federal Reserve propped up failing banks in 2008 with injections of money, it was a decision made and shared between these central banks and their governments.

5. This is like watching people in a room wearing balaclavas passing fiat money around: it is clear where the money is moving and how much money each person is holding and/or passing, yet it is not clear who the specific people exchanging the currency are. This analogy is, however, oversimplified as users can in fact have multiple addresses.

6. Each bitcoin is divisible to the increment of 0.00000001, named a satoshi after the pseudonym of its inventor(s).

7. This meet-up is a community of enthusiasts, programmers, and entrepreneurs who gather to discuss and develop concepts concerning the blockchain Ethereum and its inbuilt cryptocurrency, ether.

8. It is worth noting there are now other consensus mechanisms, like proof-of-stake and proof-of-space, that can be used to build blockchains.

9. Technically speaking, it is the chain that can provide proof of the most work that is always trusted as opposed to the longest chain because longer chains could theoretically be made with less work done upon them. This was not taken into account by Satoshi Nakamoto's white paper but has since been incorporated by the Bitcoin Core developers. In this book, 'longest chain' refers to 'the chain with the most proof-of-work.'

10. When a coffee is purchased with bitcoins a merchant may accept the transaction entering the mempool as standing, whereas a car salesman selling a Ferrari may wait for six or more confirmations to be sure the network has reached a consensus on that transaction and the coins now 'officially' belong to the garage.

11. Block rewards can only be spent by miners after 100 confirmations have been made on top of their new block to account for forks and to further incentivise the mining of longest chains (dishonest nodes would not be able to spend any block rewards on shorter chains).

12. The 22nd of May has since become a significant cultural event in the Bitcoin community, where many will eat pizza to commemorate the transaction.

13. This means if someone were to have bought $10 USD worth of bitcoins on this day, they would have had around $259 million USD worth at the 2017 peak.

14. McCaleb had the domain mtgox.com left over from a failed project titled *Magic: The Gathering Online eXchange*, a website designed for trading cards associated with the role-playing game. He decided to repurpose the acronym for his Bitcoin exchange.

15. These bitcoins would have cost somewhere in the region of $15 billion USD during the 2017 price peak.

16. This mirrors the romantic Silicon Valley genesis stories of hardware companies like Apple and Intel set up by two men in a garage and software companies like Google and Facebook created by students in dormitory rooms.

17. As Amazon, Google, and eBay were following the dotcom crash.

18. It is worth noting, however, that a vast proportion of the 97% of bitcoins lying in 4% of addresses are now likely 'dead' and can never be used again due to the loss of private keys, although there is no way of telling for sure how much.

19. This amount of bitcoins would have been worth $19.1 billion USD around the 2017 price peak.

20. Other estimates suggest network control can even be achieved with much less than 51% of hashing power (Eyal & Sirer, 2014; Heilman et al., 2015).

Chapter 2

1. Of course, there is always some 'use value' to material currencies—a banknote could be used for writing upon or a coin used as a paperweight—but this is not tied to its 'monetary value.' Commodity monies, however, like the historical usage of precious metals for coinage (which could be melted down to make jewellery) might provide an example where 'monetary value' and 'use value' are somewhat reconciled.

2. Arguably, this analysis is most prevalent to modern fiat currencies as, historically, commodity monies like gold, coffee beans, and cigarettes can be seen to have their own significant use values.

3. Historically, in the United States, lowered taxation rates on payments made to the state with sovereign currency encouraged its rise as the dominant form of money (Agha, 2017).

4. The practice of clipping coins in the Middle Ages demonstrates a bottom-up attempt to detach metallist and chartalist value: miscreants would cut pieces of silver or gold from the outside of their coins in the hope they could still be spent at face value while the clipper kept the extra bits for themselves. Debasement represents a similar move from the top-down: rulers have often compromised the purity of their coinage by reducing the quantity of precious metal in each unit. This allowed them to pay for rising government expenses with less commodity reserves.

5. The "M" in "M-Pesa" stands for mobile, whereas "pesa" is Swahili for money.

6. Equally, however, Daivi Rodima-Taylor and William Grimes (2018) show how "Bitcoin-based remittance services continue to operate along the 'last mile' rails of traditional remittance outlet that have no incentive to lower their fees for cryptocurrency transfers" (122).

7. Jevons (1875) also included *standard of deferred payment* to form four functions but this has been, more often than not, dropped by economists in a belief that the characteristic is subsumed by the other functions.

8. Away from the negative press that surrounded Bitcoin's link to Silk Road, an article in the *International Journal of Drug Policy* described how this system created a safer market with responsible vendors, intelligent consumers, high-quality narcotics, and a transaction process with none of the dangers associated with face-to-face contact (van Hout & Bingham, 2014).

9. From another perspective, because Bitcoin harbours no physical coin it may work to illuminate "the centrality of money of account in that it depends on a computationally derived system of record keeping that warrants its own moneyness" (Maurer, 2017b, 227).

10. This is on some level excusable if such discourse is intended as a metaphorical hyperbole but does not work ontologically.

11. While I take this point from Henri Lefebvre (1991), I do not adopt his trialectic segmentation of space into physical, mental, and social fields in fear of its prescriptiveness.

12. The bailing out of banks after the 2008 global financial crisis and the scandal presented by the NSA PRISM data mining network have only fuelled this distrust in central government despite the key role of corporations in both of these events.

13. From this perspective, it is also important to remember the network diagrams in Figure 2.1 are topological rather than topographical and so have limitations when imagining the precise spatial materiality of the Internet.

14. The same is true in Iran where the state imposes measures to remove anti-government websites and has installed the Telecommunications Infrastructure Company that exclusively rents out bandwidth to local Internet service providers which it uses to reduce speeds during times of political uprising, crippling online access (Akbari, 2020).

15. Many peer-to-peer software protocols, like The Onion Router (Tor) and BitTorrent, have been specifically designed to (re)decentralise and (re)anonymise the Internet.

16. In this instance, the walls that spatially constrain prisoners and render them immobile are just as important for performing cigarette-money as the use-value or fungibility of the commodity itself.

17. An example of an obligatory passage point in a decentralised infrastructural network is the Panama Canal: an artificial channel of water connecting the Atlantic and Pacific oceans between the continents of North America and South America. The control of this unique spatial conduit enables the Republic of Panama to become a powerful economic gateway in the 'decentralised' network of international maritime trade by permitting or omitting ships through a controlled point of convergence.

18. Although concentrations of gold can be reduced through debasement, tests are available to discern its purity.

Chapter 3

1. Examples of this work are collated at followthethings.com—a subversive shopping website I helped launch with Ian Cook and others (et al.), cataloguing "films, books, academic journal articles, art installations, newspaper articles and undergraduate research" (Cook, 2011a).

2. For example, Nigel Dodd (2017) describes working as a guard in the back of a Securicor lorry that "carried vast amounts of cash between banks on the south coast of England and a depot somewhere near London" (230). This fascinating snapshot into the mobile life of currency reveals the banality of the job—Dodd would lie bored on a "mattress" made from money bags, which he estimated to be worth around £4 million GBP, with the protection of a "big stick" by his side in case someone managed to get in (although he "could not imagine how")—as well as "the infrastructure of the formal cash economy and the huge effort and cost involved in moving money around" (231).

3. Tracing 'paper trails' (which are these days predominantly digital footprints) is a process used by governments to track the movement of money used for illicit purposes but access to these accounts for researchers is extremely difficult to attain, not to mention potentially unethical.

4. An example of a 'smaller thing' is a singular unit of bitcoin, which runs along the rails of a 'big thing': the Bitcoin protocol (see Chapter 6).

5. Blockchains can be referred to as software, algorithm, database, platform, or protocol. While these descriptions are sometimes interchangeable I mostly refer to blockchains as *algorithmic protocols* for semantic cleanliness.

6. I refer to this form of participant observation as having an "ethnographic sensitivity" because 'hardcore' anthropologists would most likely reject the term 'ethnography' due to the duration of time that I spent in particular environments. For example, I would sometimes only stay with a company for a few weeks, whereas the term 'ethnography' is usually reserved for participant observation developing in the field for a year or more. To some degree, then, pure ethnographies are becoming a dying art with the growing corporatisation of the neoliberal university where academics rarely ever have the chance to spend this amount of time in the field.

7. Notably, Haraway establishes "as much a metaphorical as a material sense of the things she traces" (Marcus, 1995, 108).

Chapter 4

1. Harvey's tittle mirrors Raymond Williams's (1989) *Resources of Hope*.

2. The recent developments in artificial intelligence—of which, incidentally, blockchains are becoming a viable component—may begin to complicate this statement somewhat.

3. In a fashion staying true to digital cryptography's strong statist history, this method had previously been theorised and modelled by the British Government Communications Headquarters (GCHQ) where it was referred to as "non-secret encryption" (Ellis, 1970). This work was not declassified until 1997 (Singh, 1999).

4. RSA is an acronym devised from the surnames of its three creators: Ron Rivest, Add Shamir, and Leonard Adleman.

5. Julian Assange is a cryptographer/cypherpunk known for the creation of WikiLeaks— another materialisation of decentralist and open politics—and is a vocal proponent of the mantra 'information should be free.' Assange's resistance against nation-state control, especially military activity, led to the issuance of an international warrant for his arrest. He was granted asylum by the Embassy of Ecuador in London where he resided for seven years before his eventual arrest in 2019.

6. While spaces are certainly enacted and changed by cryptographic practices, the talk of "new lands" is a hyperbolic distraction, as these remain strictly physical processes (see Chapter 6).

7. Although the cost of sending one email is negligible in this system (fractions of a cent), sending thousands starts to become expensive and thus forces attackers to pay for this form of system abuse: an economic deterrent.

8. It is worth noting that all humans (and non-humans) create space through daily hybrid interaction and digital architects are just one of many actors who apply order to social processes via their creations.

9. "The structure may be flexible; it may vary over time; it may evenly or unevenly distribute tasks, power and resources over the members of the group. But it will be formed regardless of the abilities, personalities, or intentions of the people involved" (Freeman, 2003).

Chapter 5

1. What is meant by "post-humanist" here is the more radical theoretical ideas encouraged by cybernetics. This involves technological processes that remove humans from privileged positions in cognition and decision-making (Wolfe, 2009).

2. In these particular spaces I adopt more of a participant observer role than an observant participant, as I do not develop the Bitcoin source code myself.

3. Once Satoshi Nakamoto initiated the Bitcoin code it was 'out in the open' and so, theoretically, anyone could have mined a block thereafter.

4. The BBC article was originally titled "Bitcoin creator reveals his identity" but was later changed to "Australian Craig Wright claims to be Bitcoin creator." The text was also rewritten to recognise there was still doubt about Craig Wright's claim.

5. Technical barriers to entry also exist: the majority of Bitcoin Core is written in C++ and Python, meaning contributors must often be well versed in these programming languages (Song, 2017).

6. It is a block size *limit* because miners can fill blocks with as many transactions they wish as long as they do not exceed a specific data size. Miners, for example, could mine empty blocks yet this is not in their economic interest (although it could be used as a form of political protest by stifling transactions on the network) because they would forgo receiving transaction fees.

7. It is worth noting Mike Hearn has a grand total of 2 commits out of 20,861 in the Bitcoin Core repository making his impact extremely low. However, Hearn has made valuable contributions to other Bitcoin domains like bitcoinj, a software library used by a few Bitcoin light clients.

8. It is common practice to circulate the ideas around the bitcoin-dev mailing list before submitting a pull request to gauge how it will be received and to see if others are thinking about or working on similar problems (Song, 2017).

9. However, a permanent fork in the blockchain made for political reasons, as opposed to being an accident, might allow users to trust both sides of the chain (as the rest of this chapter will explain).

10. Technically, a soft fork is a tightening of the rules (e.g., decreasing block sizes) because previously valid transactions are made invalid: while old nodes cannot utilise these new specifications, they can still accept its blocks because they play by old rules. A hard fork is a loosening of the rules (e.g., increasing block sizes) so that previously invalid transactions are made valid on the new chain and are thus rejected by old nodes.

11. The second Bitcoin client in the network's history, bitcoind, provided a command line-based daemon that replaces a graphical user interface (GUI) with JSON-RPC: the resultant application programming interface (API) is useful for integrating with third-party software and payment systems. "Beyond the reference client (bitcoind), other clients and libraries can be used to interact with the bitcoin network and data structures. These are implemented in a variety of programming languages, offering programmers native interfaces in their own language" (Antonopoulos, 2014, 56). MultiBit, and other 'thin' clients, have been designed so that users can interact with the network without having to download the whole blockchain (267 GB at time of writing).

12. To be clear, signalling is a coordination mechanism whereas enforcing new software rules is akin to voting on that implementation.

13. The transaction malleability "flaw allowed anyone to change small details that modified the transaction id (and the subsequent hash) but not the content" (Acheson, 2018). The malleable part of a transaction (witness signatures) could not be altered to change the recipient or amount of bitcoins being sent. However, malleating the witness signature created a new transaction ID, which could be used to trick the sender into thinking the transaction did not complete in the hope they would send it to the attacker again. Transaction malleability also "prevented the development of more complex features such as second-layer protocols and smart contracts" (Acheson, 2018).

14. A subsequent miner activated hard fork to increase block sizes was also mapped out (van Wirdum, 2017a).

15. Another possible reason for the reluctance of miner upgrades relates to the "AsicBoost Scandal" (van Wirdum, 2017b). After claiming to have reverse-engineered Bitmain mining

chips, Gregory Maxwell sent a message to the bitcoin-dev mailing list explaining the hard-ware was using a patented technology called AsicBoost, which allowed users to mine with 30% increased efficiency (van Wirdum, 2017b). This exploit, however, would not work following SegWit upgrades, providing economic incentive for the company to block its activation.

16. These companies could also choose to list both coins but there is a degree of risk accepting the side with less mining power: if all miners on that chain upgrade to the new node rules it will be orphaned and all the transactions wiped out. So, if an exchange pays a user for the legacy coin (old nodes) and all miners reorganise onto the new chain then they will be left holding nothing.

17. Customers, however, might apply pressure on Bitcoin exchanges to list newly forked coins. This happened after the introduction of Bitcoin Cash: initially, many companies did not list this coin but a backlash from wallet and exchange users convinced them to list the new cryptocurrency.

18. Ironically, Buterin did later "[f]orce double spends to reverse million-dollar thefts" as the 'Lead Developer' of Ethereum when an application running on top of its blockchain was hacked and funds drained from accounts (see Chapter 8).

19. To complicate matters, this date was planned to coincide with the SegWit flag day and the initiation of its user activated soft fork.

20. The Bitcoin protocol has a rule stating the mining difficulty will adjust every 2,016 blocks to account for changing accumulative network mining power. When miners join (or leave) the network, the rate of finding a nonce increases (or decreases). To keep the block rate steady (roughly every 10 minutes), mining difficulty resets to account for the new total mining power. However, when a split between two chains occurs both sides will have differ-ent mining power (depending on how many miners decide to join each) but will share the same difficulty. The side with fewer miners will take a longer time to find nonces and thus mine blocks. After 2,016 blocks the legacy chain will reset and the block rate will return to 10 minutes. In terms of Bitcoin Cash, the new chain included an added rule that stated difficulty decreases as the amount of time it takes to find a block increases. This allowed it to start mining at a normal rate relatively quickly as opposed to waiting a long time for the difficulty to reset. At the time of writing, miners often swap between Bitcoin and Bitcoin Cash depending on which is proving to be more profitable.

21. However, from the perspective of each chain there is a singular monolithic transactional record.

22. Indeed, Bitcoin and Bitcoin Cash do seem to "represent separate houses of worship" (Golumbia, 2018).

Chapter 6

1. I use the phrase "relatively static" because the material bits and pieces of the Internet are constantly shifting and mutating (i.e., servers 'going down'). It is the connectivity and com-plexity of its decentralised network that allows the Internet to continue functioning when components fail or new ones come 'online.'

2. Although, logic itself is (re)crafted through material processes involving brains, diagrams, ink-and-paper, computation, and so on.

3. Recognising the functional materiality of (digital) infrastructural networks in this way has elsewhere been described as understanding the "muscle" of the global economy (Herregraven, 2014).

4. This concept of tension between binaries—a nearness of the fictional and functional, falsity and truth, virtual and actual, immaterial and material, without them fusing completely—is drawn from John Wylie's (2007) work on landscapes.

5. This transaction alone is a function heavily reliant on a plethora of sociotechnical actors and material architectures required to facilitate the transfer of funds. One only has to

imagine the office floors, administrators, Internet service providers, computers, servers, cables, papers, office chairs, people, and materialities of other third-party companies for the Bpay transaction to be conducted.

6. At this point the transaction had 0 confirmations because subsequent blocks in the blockchain had not yet been built on top of it (see Chapter 1).

7. Scripts can also 'spend coins' from multiple public keys and send them to many others.

8. Because I do not mine or own a company I am part of the 'assembly minor' in terms of Bitcoin's senatorial governance structure (see Table 5.2).

9. Hardware and software can only ever be ideologically separated, never physically (Chun, 2006).

10. Other Bitcoin and blockchain companies working out of Level39 have included GoCoin, BitFury, Applied Blockchain, BTL, capitalDIGI, Casha, CEX.IO, Coinfirm, and Euklid.

11. Often, a secondary code is sent to a user's mobile phone or tablet (this is done through SMS or an application such as Authy or Google Authenticator). Multi-signature procedures like this increase the likelihood of the person logging in being legitimate, as an imposter would need to know the password *and* be in possession of the account user's device.

12. The 'change' from the transaction will then go into a new address controlled by the software and will become the 'newest' coins. This process is explained later in the chapter.

13. The IP packets may arrive in a different order or not at all. The recipient IP sends a signal back to the sending IP when the packet arrives. If the sending IP does not get back this 'received' signal in a certain amount of time it will resend that packet until it gets a confirmation it got there.

14. In actual fact, this is not too dissimilar to the spending of fiat currency in the form of physical cash or a digital bank balance. These are also a future claim on resources or 'unspent transactions.' It is the mechanism for spending them that differs most prominently.

15. I add the word 'machine' here because Bitcoin, as a 'programmable money,' has also been envisioned as a currency enabling machine-to-machine payments for the Internet of Things (Swan, 2015).

16. These parameters are what have led people to refer to Bitcoin as programmable money because certain rules (such as time frames) can be placed on the spending of coins.

17. The companies also illuminate the identity of people behind cryptographic strings due to strict Know Your Customer regulation within nation-state territories (see Chapter 7).

18. Ralph Merkle, a "co-inventor of public-key cryptography, calls hashes the 'duct tape' of cryptography" (Landau, 2006, 330).

19. Note the 17 zeroes at the start of the hash.

20. This space for metadata is what Satoshi Nakamoto once utilised in the genesis block to indicate how Bitcoin is a response to the 2008 global financial crisis. This was done by referencing the politically charged headline of a UK newspaper (see Chapter 1).

21. Although this tempo is often slower or faster due to miners racing to find a winning nonce to generate a block.

Chapter 7

1. This might merely represent a shift from experienced financial technocrats to inexperienced ones.

2. However, technology companies like Facebook are becoming subject to their own controversies surrounding user privacy.

3. Public polls during 2014 showed four of the top ten most disliked brands in the United States were financial services (VLAB, 2015).

4. Goldman Sachs was first described as the "great vampire squid" by Matt Taibbi (2010) in *Rolling Stone*.

5. However, "[b]anks responded by pouring resources into information technologies, and subsequently those employees who did leave for Silicon Valley often returned" (DuPont, 2019, 156).

6. For example, Islamic banking practices are conducted between certain citizens within nation-state economies (Maurer, 2005). At the same time, markets retain unique characteristics at the state level (Whitley, 1999).

7. See, for example, Silicon Alley (New York), Silicon Docks (Dublin), Silicon Roundabout (London), Silicon Beach (Sydney), Silicon Glen (Central Belt, Scotland), and Silicon Cape (Cape Town). These places brandish the capitalised version of the word "Silicon" to promote an imaginary of disruptive development, no longer referring to semiconductors directly but to high technology as a whole.

8. These buildings have otherwise been known as hacker houses or hostels (McNeill, 2016).

9. At the time of my research, there had been a number of house fires in the Mission District where some locals had lost their lives. Many blamed these fires on property owners who, not being able to profit from renovating their buildings due to strict zoning and rent control laws, were allegedly setting them alight so they could start from scratch. This exasperated the tension between long-term residents and migrating techies, whose presence was generating a demand for gentrification.

10. The 20Mission ground floor has since been turned into a retail space for local artists and manufacturers. All of the products on the floor can be purchased with bitcoins—this is how I paid for my copy of *The Age of Cryptocurrency*.

11. These included: San Francisco Bitcoin Meetup; San Francisco Bitcoin; SF Bitcoin Devs; Bitcoin/Cryptocurrency Mining Group (SF Bay Area); Digital Currency Entrepreneurship & Startups (Bay Area); Women in Bitcoin (San Francisco); SF Ethereum Meetup; Decentralized Autonomous Society Meetup (Palo Alto); Future of Payments; Buttonwood SF P2P Cryptocurrency Trading: Trade Cryptocurrencies' Proof of Drink; Berkeley Bitcoin Meetup; East Bay Bitcoin Meetup; Silicon Valley Bitcoin; Silicon Valley Ethereum Meetup, and; Stanford Bitcoin Meetup. Some of the groups had already become inactive by the time I arrived in the Bay Area but many others have popped up since.

12. Beforehand, I had only ever been to Bitcoin meet-ups held in pubs.

13. For companies actively presenting at meet-ups there is a certain trade-off between showing their cards and keeping them close to their chest. While it is beneficial for the industry as a whole if companies share knowledge and develop ideas collaboratively, the individual Bitcoin firm must also stay competitive. Even inside firms there are levels of clearance to company information for different employees, as I learnt working inside a number of Bitcoin and blockchain start-ups. This is a tightrope for every technology start-up to navigate due to the highly mobile labour coming and going from enterprise (see Saxenian, 1989a; Angel, 1991; Benner, 2003; Huber, 2011).

14. There is a degree of dislocation between this emancipatory narrative and the uptake of cryptocurrencies in the developing world (see also Rodima-Taylor & Grimes, 2018). During my time working at a Silicon Valley Bitcoin start-up, I handled a marketing scheme directing services towards countries that had experienced internal currency problems like Greece, Argentina, and Zimbabwe, as well as unbanked populations in Africa, South America, and Asia, and countries with a high proportion of migrant workers conducting remittances, such as the Philippines. However, despite efforts made by companies to promote cryptocurrencies as a solution in these countries, uptake has been extremely underwhelming. Forcing alien currencies on populations in a top-down manner neglects how perceptions of value are culturally intricate and specific (see Chapter 2). Alternatively, more successful monetary alternatives like M-Pesa have largely been driven from the bottom-up (Rodima-Taylor & Grimes, 2018).

15. The article explained there were 177 instances where Ripple and Stellar's (open) source code was identical and the word "Ripple" repeatedly appeared in Stellar's software. This was given as evidence for a copy and paste job from Ripple's open source repository on GitHub and a failed search and replace command by Stellar's developers (Craig, 2015).

16. Indeed, "the Californian ideology attracts those individuals who hope that they're smart— or lucky—enough to seize the opportunities presented by the rapid changes in the technological basis of social production" (Barbrook, 2001, 55).

17. "No-collar" is a term first used by Andrew Ross (2003) to describe employees of dotcom companies.

18. Similarly, there is a classic scene in the HBO series *Silicon Valley* (Altschuler et al., 2014), where a struggling investor, Erlich Bachman, is speaking to the CEO of a start-up he has invested in, Richard Hendricks:

> BACHMAN: When I sold my company, Aviato, I wanted to give back. That's why I started this place. To do something big. To make a difference. You know, like Steve.
> HENDRICKS: Jobs or Wozniak?
> BACHMAN: [Pause]
> HENDRICKS: Er, Steve Jobs or Steve Wozniak?
> BACHMAN: No, I heard you.
> HENDRICKS: Which one?
> BACHMAN: Jobs.
> HENDRICKS: Well, I mean, Jobs was a poser. He didn't even write code.

19. There was a certain degree of global overlap at Bitcoin meet-ups across the San Francisco Bay Area, New York City, London, Washington DC, and Sydney. As many Bitcoiners moved around they would attend groups in other cities or countries to extend their networks. Consequently, I would often bump into the same people in different parts of the world.

20. Adam Draper once had an ambitious plan to fund 100 Bitcoin companies by 2017 (Cawrey, 2014).

21. Many of these venture capitalists are equity holders of earlier successful start-ups.

22. This struggle stimulated a corybantic rotation of upper management that saw Bill Harris, Elon Musk, and Peter Thiel (twice) take the reins as CEO while other key figures, like Reid Hoffman and David Sacks, were moved within the company structure (Jackson, 2004).

23. Of course, cryptoeconomics shows how the protocol layer is also, on some level, market-driven.

Chapter 8

1. Satoshi Nakamoto was the first to encode metadata in the Bitcoin blockchain by leaving a message in the genesis block (see Chapter 1).

2. To put fees into perspective, this $18 million USD worth of investment only cost a total of $350 USD to transfer at the time.

3. A pre-published copy of this book was given to students at the first lecture of Blockchain University.

4. This was personified when two corrupt federal agents on the Silk Road task force stole vast amounts of bitcoins on the job (Haun, 2016). Although they used their agent status to destroy more vulnerable data on centralised government databases, the US government used network analysis on the Bitcoin blockchain to track the perpetrators down (Haun, 2016).

5. Quinn DuPont (2019) believes this is an undervaluation and estimates that 11,944,260.98 ETH was invested at a value of around $251 million USD.

6. It is interesting to note that Bitcoin's price surged at the same time, which could be a reflection of people jumping ship from Ethereum to Bitcoin (Bovaird, 2016).

7. The rollback was helped by the relative youth of the blockchain, which could have been much harder to achieve later on as more stakeholders joined the network to build applications on top of it.

8. The DAO did end up representing a democracy of 'majority rules' but it also broke the imaginary of immutability concerning the Ethereum chain, showing instead how key

figures can orchestrate its unravelling for the benefit of a single application (and, in the process, the historical record of all other decentralised applications also using Ethereum as a chronological database).

9. Further complications regarding forking might arise when Ethereum developers attempt to move towards a proof-of-stake consensus as they plan to (Hertig, 2017). There could, quite possibly, be a split between proof-of-work and proof-of-stake Ethereum chains.

10. Examples of partnering include Citigroup and Lending Club joining forces, whereas the actions of bank and brokerage firm Charles Schwab demonstrate competition: disclosing in a public manner their intelligent algorithmic investment strategy takes on the likes of Wealthfront and other software-based investing platforms (VLAB, 2015). Similarly, measures taken by established institutions to capture the innovation and energy in Silicon Valley include accelerators funded by banks (i.e., FinTech Innovation Lab and Inno Tribe) while the acquisition of Level Money by Capital One, Check by Intuit, and Simple by BBVA personify the "if you can't beat them buy them" strategy (VLAB, 2015).

11. Other banks that later joined the consortium include Banco Santander, Bank of America, BMO Financial Group, BNP Paribas, BNY Mellon, CIBC, Citi, Commerzbank, Danske Bank, Deutsche Bank, HSBC, ING Bank, Intesa Sanpaolo, Macquarie Bank, Mitsubishi UFJ Financial Group, Mizuho Financial Group, Morgan Stanley, National Australia Bank, Natixis, Nordea, Northern Trust, OP Financial Group, Royal Bank of Canada, Scotiabank, SEB, Société Générale, TD Bank Group, UniCredit, U.S. Bank, Wells Fargo, and Westpac Banking Corporation (Allison, 2016). However, Banco Santander, Morgan Stanley, and National Australian Bank also left the project in 2016, along with Goldman Sachs (Martin, 2016).

12. Bitcoin Core developer Peter Todd has also been hired to help build Corda.

Conclusion

1. There have been four bubbles in Bitcoin's history: 1) $1 to $32 in 2011; 2) $13 to $184 in mid-2013; 3) $68 to $1,163 in late 2013; and 4) $152 to $19,290 from 2015 to the end of 2017.

2. However, the fall of the price of bitcoins during the coronavirus outbreak suggests this may no longer be the case.

3. Coin tumblers are services that mix different cryptocurrency funds together in order to disguise the movement of money through the network and further obscure potentially trackable and identifiable coins. This represents the continued presence of an 'anarchist' or 'hacker' strand in Bitcoin/blockchain culture, where anonymity is preferred. However, they "require users to trust that the mixing service will not abscond with the funds, keep a record of users and transactions, or do a poor job of mixing" (DuPont, 2019, 64).

References

Abbate, J. (1999) *Inventing the Internet*. MIT Press.

Accenture (2014) The rise of fintech: New York's opportunity for tech leadership. The Partnership Fund for New York City.

Acheson, N. (2018, February 22) What is SegWit? *CoinDesk* <https://www.coindesk.com/information/what-is-segwit/>.

Agha, A. (2017) Money talk and conduct from cowries to Bitcoin. *Signs and Society* 5 (2): 293–355.

Aitken, R. (2018, October 29) Crypto investors flocking to 'Blockchain Island' Malta in droves. *Forbes* <https://www.forbes.com/sites/rogeraitken/2018/10/29/crypto-investors-flocking-to-blockchain-island-malta-in-droves/#6dc10be45ff9>.

Allison, I. (2015, September 18) Blockchain expert Tim Swanson talks about R3 partnership of Goldman Sachs, JP Morgan, UBS, Barclays et al. *International Business Times* <http://www.ibtimes.co.uk/blockchain-expert-tim-swanson-talks-about-r3-partnership-goldman-sachs-jp-morgan-ubs-barclays-1519905>.

Allison, I. (2016, March 3) R3 completes trial of five cloud-based blockchain technologies with 40 banks. *International Business Times* <http://www.ibtimes.co.uk/r3-completes-trial-five-cloud-based-blockchain-technologies-40-banks-1547260>.

Altschuler, J., Judge, M., and Krinsky, D. (2014) *Silicon Valley*. HBO. 3 Arts Entertainment. Altschuler Krinsky Works. Judgemental Films Inc.

Amin, A., and Thrift, N. (1994) Living in the global. In Amin, A., and Thrift, N. (eds) *Globalization, Institutions and Regional Development*. Oxford University Press.

Amin, A., and Thrift, N. (2002) *Cities: Reimagining the Urban*. Polity Press.

Amin, A., and Thrift, N. (2004) *Cultural Economy Reader*. Blackwell.

Amsterdamska, O. (1990) 'Surely you're joking, Mr Latour!' *Science, Technology, Human Values* 15 (4): 495–504.

Anand, N. (2011) Pressure: the politechnics of water supply in Mumbai. *Cultural Anthropology* 26 (4): 542–564.

Anderson, B. (2008) For Space (2005): Doreen Massey. In Hubbard, P., Kitchin, R., and Valentine, G. (eds) *Key Texts in Human Geography*. Sage.

Anderson, B., and Harrison, P. (2010) *Taking Place: Non-Representational Theories and Geography*. Ashgate Publishing Company.

Anderson, B., and Wylie, J. (2009) On geography and materiality. *Environment and Planning A* 41 (2): 318–335.

Andolfatto, D. (2015) Fedcoin: on the desirability of a government cryptocurrency. *MacroMania* <http://andolfatto.blogspot.co.uk/2015/02/fedcoin-on-desirability-of-government.html>.

Andreessen, M. (2014a, January 21) Why Bitcoin matters. *New York Times* <https://dealbook.nytimes.com/2014/01/21/why-bitcoin-matters/>.

Andreessen, M. (2014b, March 26) Video—Bitcoin fireside chat with Marc Andreessen and Balaji Srinivasan. *Weusecoins* <https://www.weusecoins.com/video-fireside-chat-about-bitcoin/>.

Androulaki E., Karame, G., Roeschlin M., Scherer T., and Capkun S. (2013) Evaluating user privacy in Bitcoin. In Sadeghi, A. (ed) *Financial Cryptography and Data Security*. LNCS 7859: 34–51. Springer.

Angel, D. (1991) High-technology agglomeration and the labor market: the case of Silicon Valley. *Environment and Planning A* 23: 1501–1516.

Angel, D. (2000) High-technology agglomeration and the labor market: the case of Silicon Valley. In Kenney, M. (ed) *Understanding Silicon Valley: The Anatomy of an Entrepreneurial Region*. Stanford University Press.

Antonopoulos, A. (2014) *Mastering Bitcoin: Unlocking Digital Cryptocurrencies*. O'Reilly Media.

Antonopoulos, A. (2015a) Mastering Bitcoin. *WIRED MONEY* <https://www.youtube.com/watch?v=A6kJfvuNqtg>.

Antonopoulos, A. (2015b) Consensus algorithms, blockchain technology and Bitcoin (University College London). *Satoshi Pollen* <https://www.youtube.com/watch?v=sE7998qfjgk&t=151s>.

Antonopoulos, A. (2016) The Internet of money. *Merkle Bloom LLC*.

Aoyama, Y., Dodge, M., Townsend, A., and Zook, M. (2004) New digital geographies: information, communication, and place. In Brunn, S., Cutter, S., and Harrington, S. (eds) *Geography and Technology*. Springer.

Appadurai, A. (1986) *The Social Life of Things: Commodities in Cultural Perspective*. Cambridge University Press.

Appadurai, A. (1990) Disjuncture and difference in the global cultural economy. *Theory, Culture & Society* 7 (2–3): 295–310.

Appelbaum, B. (2018, February 28) Is Bitcoin a waste of electricity, or something worse? *New York Times* <https://www.nytimes.com/2018/02/28/business/economy/bitcoin-electricity-productivity.html>.

Arcade City (2018) Arcade City homepage <https://arcade.city>.

Arcade City Hall (2016) Decentralization and the future of ridesharing. Arcade City Blog <https://blog.arcade.city/decentralization-and-the-future-of-ridesharing-29d8f84a4ea7>.

Arthur, W. (1994) *Increasing Returns and Path Dependency in the Economy*. University of Michigan Press.

Ash, J., Kitchin, R., and Leszczynski, A. (2016) Digital turn, digital geographies? *Progress in Human Geography* 42 (1): 1–19.

Ash, J., Kitchin, R., and Leszczynski, A. (2019) *Digital Geographies*. Sage.

Assange, J., Appelbaum, J., Muller-Maguhn, A., and Zimmerman, J. (2012) *Cypherpunks: Freedom and the Future of the Internet*. OR BOOKS.

Atlassian (2017) What is version control? *Atlassian Tutorials* <https://www.atlassian.com/git/tutorials/what-is-version-control>.

Atzori, M. (2015) Blockchain technology and decentralized governance: is the state still necessary? <http://nzz-files-prod.s3-website-eu-west-1.amazonaws.com/files/9/3/1/blockchain+Is+the+State+Still+Necessary_1.18689931.pdf>.

Audretsch, D., and Feldman, M. (2003) Knowledge spillovers and the geography of innovation. In Henderson, J., and Thisse, J. (eds) *Handbook of Urban and Regional Economics*. North Holland Publishing.

Auletta, K. (2009) *Googled: The End of the World as We Know It*. Penguin.

Australian Tax Office (2014, December 18) Tax treatment of crypto-currencies in Australia—specifically bitcoin <https://www.ato.gov.au/General/Gen/Tax-treatment-of-crypto-currencies-in-Australia---specifically-bitcoin>.

Babbie, E. (2008) *The Basics of Social Research*. Thomson Wadsworth.

Back, A. (2002) Hashcash—A denial of service counter-measure. <http://www.hashcash.org/hashcash.pdf>.

Baichwal, J. (2006) *Manufactured Landscapes*. Zeitgeist Films.

Baker, W., and Jimerson, J. (1992) The sociology of money. *American Behavioural Scientist* 35 (6): 678–693.

Balea, J. (2014, December 12) Bitcoin remittances to the Philippines have gone up. Here's why. *Tech in Asia* <https://www.techinasia.com/bitcoin-remittances-rebit-philippines>.

Ball, J., Arthur, C., and Gabbatt, A. (2013) FBI claims largest Bitcoin seizure after arrest of alleged Silk Road founder. *The Guardian* <https://www.theguardian.com/technology/2013/oct/02/alleged-silk-road-website-founder-arrested-bitcoin>.

Balmès, T. (2005) *A Decent Factory*. Margot Films. Making Movies Oy. France 2. BBC—Storyville & YLE.

Bank of Canada (2014) Decentralized E-Money (Bitcoin) *Backgrounders* <http://www.bankof-canada.ca/wp-content/uploads/2014/04/Decentralize-E-Money.pdf>.

Banse, T. (2014, April 7) Central Washington home to nation's biggest Bitcoin 'mine,' more coming. *nwnewsnetwork.org* <http://nwnewsnetwork.org/post/central-washington-home-nations-biggest-bitcoin-mine-more-coming>.

Baran, P. (1962) On distributed communications networks. The RAND Corporation.

Barber, S., Boyen, X., Shi, E., and Uzun, E. (2012) Bitter to better—How to make Bitcoin a better currency. In Keromytis, A. (ed) *Financial Cryptography and Data Security*. LNCS 7397: 399–414. Springer.

Barbrook, R. (2001) Hypermedia freedom. In Ludlow, P. (ed) *Crypto Anarchy, Cyberstates, and Pirate Utopias*. MIT Press.

Barbrook, R. (2015) *The Internet Revolution*. Network Books.

Barbrook, R., and Cameron, A. (1996) The Californian ideology. *Science as Culture* 6 (1): 44–72.

Bardhan, P., and Mookherjee, D. (2006) *Decentralization and Local Governance in Developing Countries: A Comparative Perspective*. MIT Press.

Barlow, J. (1996) The declaration of the independence of cyberspace. *Electronic Frontier Foundation* <https://www.eff.org/cyberspace-independence>.

Barndt, D. (2002) *Tangled Routes: Women, Work and Globalization on the Tomato Trail*. Lanham: Rowman & Littlefield.

Barok, D. (2011) Bitcoin: censorship-resistant currency and domain system for the people. Forum America Bar Association.

Barratt, M. (2012) Silk Road: eBay for drugs. *Addiction* 107 (3): 683–684.

Bashir, M., Strickland, B., and Bohr, J. (2016) What motivates people to use Bitcoin? In Spiro, E., and Ahn, Y. (eds) *Social Informatics*. Springer.

Bateson, G. (1972) *Steps to an Ecology of Mind*. The University of Chicago Press.

Baumann, A., Fabian, B., and Lischke, M. (2014) Exploring the Bitcoin network. 10th International Conference on Web Information Systems and Technologies (WEBIST). Barcelona, Spain.

Baur, D., Hong, K., and Lee, A. (2015) Bitcoin: medium of exchange or speculative assets? SSRN.

BBC (2016, May 2) Australian Craig Wright claims to be Bitcoin creator. *BBC Technology* <http://www.bbc.co.uk/news/technology-36168863>.

Becker, J., Breuker, D., Heide, T., Holler, J., Rauer, H., and Böhme, R. (2013) Can we afford integrity by proof-of-work? Scenarios inspired by the Bitcoin currency. In Böhme, R. (ed) *The Economics of Information Security and Privacy*. Springer.

Becker, W. (1997) Teaching economics to undergraduates. *Journal of Economic Literature* 43: 1247–1362.

Benedikt, M. (1991) *Cyberspace: First Steps*. MIT Press.

Benkler, Y. (2016) Degrees of freedom, dimensions of power. *Daedalus* 145 (1): 18–32.

Benner, C. (2003) Learning communities in a learning region: the soft infrastructure of cross-firm learning networks in Silicon Valley. *Environment and Planning A* 35: 1809–1830.

Bergstra, J., and de Leeuw, K. (2013) Bitcoin and beyond: exclusively informational money. Informatics Institute, University of Amsterdam.

Bergstra, J., and Weijland, P. (2014) Bitcoin: a money-like informational commodity. <http://arxiv.org/pdf/1402.4778.pdf>.

Bergvall-Kåreborn, B., and Howcroft, D. (2014). Amazon Mechanical Turk and the commodification of labour. *New Technology, Work and Employment* 29(3): 213–223.

Bernanke, B. (2009) *Essays on the Great Depression*. Princeton University Press.

Bernard, R. (1998) *The Corporate Intranet*. John Wiley and Sons.

Berry, D. (2011) *The Philosophy of Software*. Palgrave Macmillan.

Bershidsky, L. (2014, July 17) Trust will kill Bitcoin. *Bloomberg* <https://www.bloomberg.com/view/articles/2014-07-17/trust-will-kill-bitcoin>.

Bestor, T. (2000) How sushi went global. *Foreign Policy* 121: 54–63.

Beverungen, A., and Lange, C. (2017) Cognition in high-frequency trading: the cost of consciousness and the limits of automation. *Theory, Culture & Society* 35 (6): 75–95.

Biddle, S., and Cush, A. (2015, December 8) This Australian says he and his dead friend invented Bitcoin. *Gizmondo* <https://gizmodo.com/this-australian-says-he-and-his-dead-friend-invented-bi-1746958692>.

Biryukov, A., Khovratovich, D., and Pustogarov, I. (2014) Deanonymisation of clients in Bitcoin P2P network. ACM SIGSAC Conference on Computer and Communications Security.

Bissessar, S. (2013) Analysis of Bitcoin transaction flows to reveal usage and geographic patterns. University College London. Master's Thesis.

Bitcoin Project (2017) How does Bitcoin work? bitcoin.org <https://bitcoin.org/en/how-it-works>.

Black, R., Bollands, T., Davies, W., Charlton, K., Christie-Miller, C., Redfern, M., Stevens, J., Swan, M., Webber, L., Wheatley, M., Woolford, B. (2010) Our new commemorative £2 coin. followthethings.com <http://www.followthethings.com/commemorativecoin.shtml>.

Blackwell, M. (2007) *The Secret Life of Things: Animals, Objects and It-narratives in Eighteenth-century England*. Bucknell University Press.

Blanchard, O. (2011, March 14) The future of macroeconomic policy: nine tentative conclusions. IMF Blog <https://blogs.imf.org/2011/03/13/future-of-macroeconomic-policy>.

Blanchette, J. (2011) A material history of bits. *Journal of the American Society for Information Science and Technology* 62 (6): 1042–1057.

Blanchette, J. (2012) *Burdens of Proof*. MIT Press.

Blankenship, J. (2017) Forging blockchains: spatial production and political economy of decentralised cryptocurrency code/spaces. University of South Florida. Master's Thesis.

Blinder, A. (2000, June 1) The Internet and the New Economy. The Brookings Institution <https://www.brookings.edu/research/the-internet-and-the-new-economy>.

Bloemen, S. (2001) *T-shirt Travels*. Grassroot Pictures.

Boellstorff, T. (2008) *Coming of Age in Second Life: An Anthropologist Explores the Virtually Human*. Princeton University Press.

Böhme, R., Christin, N., Edelman, B., Moore, T. (2015) Bitcoin: economics, technology, and governance. *Journal of Economic Perspectives* 29 (2): 231–238.

Bollier, D. (2015, March 4) The blockchain: a promising new infrastructure for online commons. bollier.org <http://www.bollier.org/blog/blockchain-promising-new-infrastructure-online-commons>.

Bonabeau, E., Theraulaz, G., Deneubourg, J., Aron, S., and Camazine, S. (1997) Self-organization in social insects. *Trends in Ecology & Evolution* 12 (5): 188–193.

Bontems, V., Petit, P., and Stiegler, B. (2008) *Economie de l'hypermatériel et psychopouvoir*. Mille et Une Nuits.

Borsook, P. (2000) *Cyberselfish: A Critical Romp through the Terribly Libertarian Culture of High Tech*. PublicAffairs.

Bovaird, C. (2016, May 27) Was Ether's loss Bitcoin's gain? Traders wonder after wild week <http://www.coindesk.com/was-ethers-loss-bitcoins-gain>.

Bowker, G., and Star, S. (1999) *Sorting Things Out: Classifications and Its Consequences*. MIT Press.

Boyd, A. (2011) San Francisco's Castro district: from gay liberation to tourist destination. *Journal of Tourism and Cultural Change* 9 (3): 237–248.

Braunstein, P., and Doyle, M. (2002) *Imagine Nation: The American Counterculture of the 1960s and '70s*. Routledge.

Brekke, J. (2018) Postcards from the world of decentralized money: a story in three parts. In Gloerich, I., Lovink, G., and de Vries, P. (eds) *MoneyLab Reader 2: Overcoming the Hype*. Institute of Network Cultures.

Brewer, J. (2000) Ethnography. In Bryman, A. (ed) *Understanding Social Research*. Policy Press.

Bridges, T. (1772) *The Adventures of a Bank-Note*. Printed for T. Davies.

Brikman, Y. (2014, April 24) Bitcoin by analogy. *ybrikman.com* <http://www.ybrikman.com/ writing/2014/04/24/bitcoin-by-analogy>.

Brito, J. (2011, April 4) Online cash Bitcoin could challenge governments. *Time Magazine* <http:// techland.time.com/2011/04/16/online-cash-bitcoin-could-challenge-governments>.

Broderick, R. (2011) Bitcoin, used to purchase illegal things, has been illegally stolen. *Motherboard* <https://motherboard.vice.com/en_us/article/gvv8kj/bitcoin-currency-used-for-illegal-things-illegally-stolen>.

Brown, J., and Duguid, P. (2000) *The Social Life of Information*. Harvard Business Review Press.

Brown, M. (2014, September 19) Peter Thiel: the billionaire tech entrepreneur on a mission to cheat death. *The Telegraph* <http://www.telegraph.co.uk/technology/11098971/Peter-Thiel-the-billionaire-tech-entrepreneur-on-a-mission-to-cheat-death.html>.

Brown, R. (2016, April 5) Introducing R3 Corda™: a distributed ledger designed for financial services. The R3 Report <http://www.r3cev.com/blog/2016/4/4/introducing-r3-corda-a-distributed-ledger-designed-for-financial-services>.

Brown, R., Carlyle, J., Grigg, I, and Hearn, M. (2016) Corda: an introduction. <https://docs. corda.net/_static/corda-introductory-whitepaper.pdf>.

Brunton, F. (2015) Heat exchanges. In Lovink, G., Tkacz, N., and de Vries, P. (eds) *MoneyLab Reader: An Intervention in Digital Economy*. Institute for Network Cultures.

Brunton, F. (2019) *Digital Cash: The Unknown History of the Anarchists, Utopians, and Technologists Who Created Cryptocurrency*. Princeton University Press.

Bryant, S., Forte, A., and Bruckman, A. (2005) Becoming Wikipedian: transformation of participation in a collaborative online encyclopedia. Group'05 <https://www.cc.gatech.edu/~asb/ papers/bryant-forte-bruckman-group05.pdf>.

Brynjolfsson, E., and McAfee, A. (2014) *The Second Machine Age: Work, Progress, and Prosperity in a Time of Brilliant Technologies*. W. W. Norton & Company.

Bucher, T. (2018) *If . . . Then: Algorithmic Power and Politics*. Oxford University Press.

Bucher, T., and Helmond, A. (2017) The affordances of social media platforms. In Burgess, J., Marwick, A., and Poell, T. (eds) *The SAGE Handbook of Social Media*. Sage.

Buckingham, D., Willett, R. (2006) *Digital Generations: Children, Young People, and New Media*. Lawrence Erlbaum Associates Inc. Publishers.

Buitenhek, M. (2016) Understanding and applying blockchain technology in banking: evolution or revolution? *Journal of Digital Banking* 1 (2): 111–119.

Burniske, C., and White, A. (2017) Bitcoin: ringing the bell for a new asset class. ARK Invest & Coinbase.

Burns, D., Hambleton, R., and Hogget, P. (1994) *The Politics of Decentralisation: Revitalising Local Democracy*. The Macmillan Press Ltd.

Burrows, R., and Featherstone, M. (1995) *Cyberspace, Cyberbodies, Cyberpunk: Cultures of Technological Embodiment*. Sage.

Busk, O. (2009) £20 banknote. followthethings.com <http://www.followthethings.com/banknote. shtml>.

Bustillos, M. (2015 December 11) The bizarre saga of Craig Wright, the latest 'inventor of Bitcoin'. *New Yorker* <https://www.newyorker.com/business/currency/bizarre-saga-craig-wright-latest-inventor-bitcoin>.

Buterin, V. (2012, December 1) BitMessage: a model for a new web 2.0? *Bitcoin Magazine* <https:// bitcoinmagazine.com/articles/bitmessage-a-model-for-a-new-web-2-0-1354411679>.

Buterin, V. (2013a, March 12) Bitcoin network shaken by Bitcoin fork. *Bitcoin Magazine* <https://bitcoinmagazine.com/articles/bitcoin-network-shaken-by-blockchain-fork-1363144448>.

Buterin, V. (2013b) Ethereum: a next-generation smart contract and decentralized application platform. GitHub <https://github.com/ethereum/wiki/wiki/White-Paper>.

Buterin, V. (2015) On public and private blockchains. Ethereum Blog <https://blog.ethereum. org/2015/08/07/on-public-and-private-blockchains>.

Buterin, V. (2016, June 17) CRITICAL UPDATE Re: DAO vulnerability. Ethereum Blog <https://blog.ethereum.org/2016/06/17/critical-update-re-dao-vulnerability>.

Buterin, V. (2017, February 23) Introduction to cryptoeconomics. Ethereum Foundation <https://www.youtube.com/watch?v=pKqdjaH1dRo>.

Buy Bitcoins Worldwide (2020) UASF/ User activated softfork <https://www.buybitcoinworld-wide.com/uasf>.

Caincrross, F. (1997) *The Death of Distance: How the Communications Revolution Will Change Our Lives.* Orion Business Books.

Callon, M. (1986) Some elements of a sociology of translation: domestication of the scallops and the shermen of St Brieuc Bay. In Law, J. (ed) *Power, Action, Belief: A New Sociology of Knowledge?* Routledge.

Callon, M. (1998a) *Laws of the Market.* Wiley.

Callon, M. (1998b) An essay on framing and overflowing: economic externalities revisited by sociology. *The Sociological Review* 46 (1): 244–269.

Callon, M. (1999) Actor-network theory—the market test. In Law, J., and Hassard, J. (eds) *Actor Network Theory and After.* Blackwell Publishers.

Callon, M. (2007) What does it mean to say that economics is performative? In Mackenzie, D., Muniesa, F., and Siu, L. (eds) *Do Economists Make Markets? On the Performativity of Economics.* Princeton University Press.

Callon, M., and Latour, B. (1981) Unscrewing the big Leviathan: how actors macro-structure reality and how sociologists help them do so. In Knorr-Cetina, K., and Cicourel, A. (eds) *Advances in Social Theory and Methodology: Toward an Integration of Micro- and Macro-Sociologies.* Routledge & Kegan Paul.

Callon, M., Méadel, C., and Rabeharisoa, V. (2004) The economy of qualities. In Amin, A., and Thrift, N. (eds) *Cultural Economy Reader.* Blackwell.

Callon, M., and Muniesa, F. (2005) Peripheral vision: economic markets as calculative collective devices. *Organization Studies* 26 (8): 1229–1250.

Campbell-Verduyn, M. (ed) *Bitcoin and Beyond: Cryptocurrencies. Blockchains, and Global Governance.* Routledge.

Campbell-Verduyn, M., and Goguen, M. (2018) The mutual constitution of technology and global governance: Bitcoin, blockchains, and the international anti-money laundering regime. In Campbell-Verduyn, M. (ed) *Bitcoin and Beyond: Cryptocurrencies. Blockchains, and Global Governance.* Routledge.

Carlson, J. (2017) Why crypto looks a lot like Wall Street. *CoinDesk* <https://www.coindesk.com/growing-greed-crypto-looks-lot-like-wall-street>.

Carmody, B. (2014, December 2) Why CoinJar really relocated to the UK. Smart Company <https://www.smartcompany.com.au/startupsmart/advice/startupsmart-legal/why-coinjar-really-relocated-to-the-uk-2>.

Carmona, A. (2015) The Bitcoin: the currency of the future, fuel of terror. In Blowers, M. (ed) *Evolution of Cyber Technologies and Operations to 2035.* Springer.

Castells, M. (1989) *The Informational City: Economic Restructuring and Urban Development.* Blackwell.

Castells, M. (1993) The informational economy and the new international division of labor. In Carnoy, M., Castells, M., Cohen, S., and Cardoso, F. (eds) *The New Global Economy in the Information Age: Reflections on Our Changing World.* Pennsylvania State University Press.

Cawrey, D. (2014) Boost VC to accelerate 100 Bitcoin companies over next three years. *CoinDesk* <http://www.coindesk.com/boost-vc-accelerate-100-bitcoin-companies-next-three-years>.

CB Insights (2018) What is blockchain technology? <https://www.cbinsights.com/research/what-is-blockchain-technology>.

CB Insights (2019) Global fintech report Q1 2019. <cbinsights.com>.

Champagne, P. (2014) *The Book of Satoshi: The Collected Writings of Bitcoin Creator Satoshi Nakamoto.* e53 Publishing LLC.

Chaparro, F. (2018, January 11) 97% of all bitcoins are held by 4% of addresses. *Business Insider* <http://uk.businessinsider.com/bitcoin-97-are-held-by-4-of-addresses-2018-1>.

Charters, A. (2001) *Beat Down to Your Soul*. Penguin Books.

Chaum, D. (1983) Blind signatures for untraceable payments. In Chaum, D., Rivest, R., Sherman, A. (eds) *Advances in Cryptology*. Springer.

Chaum, D. (1985) Security without identification: transaction systems to make Big Brother obsolete. *Communications of the ACM* 28 (10): 1030–1044.

Chavez-Dreyfuss, G. (2015, May 16) Honduras to build land title registry using bitcoin technology. Reuters. <https://www.reuters.com/article/usa-honduras-technology/honduras-to-build-land-title-registry-using-bitcoin-technology-idINKBN0O01V720150515?irpc=932>.

Cheema, S., and Rondinelli, D. (2007) *Decentralizing Governance: Emerging Concepts and Practices*. Brookings Institution Press.

Chen, P. (2010) *Economic Complexity and Equilibrium Illusion: Essays on Market Instability and Macro Vitality*. Routledge.

Cheney, I., and Ellis, C. (2007) *King Corn: You Are What You Eat*. Mosaic Films (US).

Christie-Miller, J. (2009) Blood, Sweat & Takeways. Ricochet.

Christophers, B. (2011a) Follow the thing: money. *Environment and Planning D* 29: 1068–1084.

Christophers, B. (2011b) Credit, where credit's due. Response to 'Follow the thing: credit'. *Environment and Planning D* 29: 1089–1091.

Christopherson, S. (1993) Market rules and territorial outcomes: the case of the United States. *International Journal of Urban and Regional Research* 17: 274–288.

Chun, W. (1999) *Sexuality in the Age of Fiber Optics*. Princeton University Press.

Chun, W. (2006) *Control and Freedom: Power and Paranoia in the Age of Fiber Optics*. MIT Press.

Chun, W. (2011) *Programmed Visions: Software and Memory*. MIT Press.

Clark, G. (2000) *Pension Fund Capitalism*. Oxford University Press.

Clark, G. (2005) Money flows like mercury: the geography of global finance. *Geografiska Annaler B* 87 (2): 99–112.

Clark, G., and Hebb, T. (2004) Corporate engagement: the fifth stage of capitalism. *Relations Industrielles/Industrial Relations* 59: 54–79.

Clark, G., and Thrift, N. (2005) FX risk in time and space: managing dispersed knowledge in global finance. In Knorr Cetina, K., and Preda, A. (eds) *The Sociology of Financial Markets*. Oxford University Press.

Clark, G., and Wójcik, D. (2007) *The Geography of Finance: Corporate Governance in the Global Marketplace*. Oxford University Press.

Clayton, R., Murdoch, S., Watson, R. (2006) Ignoring the Great Firewall of China. In Danezis, G., and Golle, P. (eds) *Privacy Enhancing Technologies*. Springer.

Cloke, P., Cook, I., Crang, P., Goodwin, M., Painter, J., and Philo, C. (2004) *Practising Human Geography*. Sage.

Coeckelbergh, M. (2015) *Money Machines: Electronic Financial Technologies, Distancing, and Responsibility in Global Finance*. Ashgate.

Cohen, R. (2013, November 28) Global Bitcoin computing power now 256 times faster than top 500 supercomputers, combined! *Forbes* <https://www.forbes.com/sites/reuvencohen/2013/11/28/global-bitcoin-computing-power-now-256-times-faster-than-top-500-supercomputers-combined/#330504e56e5e>.

CoinDesk (2016a, February 19) Who is Satoshi Nakamoto? <http://www.coindesk.com/information/who-is-satoshi-nakamoto>.

CoinDesk (2016b) Q1 2016 state of blockchain. *CoinDesk*.

CoinDesk (2018) Blockchain venture capital <http://www.coindesk.com/bitcoin-venture-capital>.

CoinDesk (2019) All-time cumulative ICO funding. <https://www.coindesk.com/ico-tracker>.

CoinDesk (2020) Blockchain venture capital. <https://www.coindesk.com/bitcoin-venture-capital>.

CoinJar (2015, May 24) UK relocation. CoinJar Support <https://support.coinjar.com/hc/en-us/articles/202504025-UK-Relocation>.

Coleman, E. (2012) *Coding Freedom: The Ethics and Aesthetics of Hacking.* Princeton University Press.

Collins, H., and Yearly, S. (1992) Epistemological chicken. In Pickering, A. (ed) *Science as Practice and Culture.* University of Chicago Press.

Cook et al. (2004) Follow the thing: papaya. *Antipode* 36 (4): 642–664.

Cook et al. (2006) Geographies of food: following. *Progress in Human Geography* 30 (5): 655–666.

Cook et al. (2008) Geographies of food: following. In Tucker, L. (ed) *Bioneering: Hybrid Investigations of Food.* University of California, Irvine.

Cook, I. (2011) Frequently asked questions. followthethings.com <http://www.followthethings.com/faq.shtml>.

Cook et al. (2014) Fabrication critique et web 2.0: les géographies matérielles de followthethings.com. *Géographie et cultures* 91–92: 23–48.

Cook et al. (2017) From 'Follow the thing: papaya' to followthethings.com. *Journal of Consumer Ethics* 1 (1): 22–29.

Cook, I., and Crang, M. (1995) *Doing Ethnographies.* Sage.

Cook, I., and Harrison, M. (2007) Follow the thing: 'West Indian hot pepper sauce'. *Space and Culture* 10 (1): 40–63.

Coppola, F. (2016, November 26) Ethereum's latest hard fork shows it has a very long way to go. *Forbes* <https://www.forbes.com/sites/francescoppola/2016/11/26/ethereums-latest-hard-fork-shows-it-has-a-very-long-way-to-go/#3c7e9e60443a>.

Corbridge, S. (1993) Colonialism, post-colonialism and the political geography of the Third World. In Taylor, P. (ed), *Political Geography of the Twentieth Century: A Global Analysis.* John Wiley & Sons.

Corea, F. (2017, December 1) The convergence of AI and Blockchain: what's the deal? *Medium* <https://medium.com/@Francesco_AI/the-convergence-of-ai-and-blockchain-whats-the-deal-60c618e3accc>.

Cormen, T., Leirson, C., Rivest, R., and Stein, C. (1990) *Introduction to Algorithms.* MIT Press.

Council of Hemispheric Affairs (2014, March 7) Human rights violations in Honduras: land seizures, peasants' repression, and the struggle for democracy on the ground. <http://www.coha.org/human-rights-violations-in-honduras-land-grabs-peasants-repression-and-big-companies>.

Courtois, N., Grajek, M., and Naik, R. (2013) The unreasonable fundamental incertitudes behind Bitcoin mining <https://arxiv.org/pdf/1310.7935.pdf>.

Craig, M. (2015, February 5) The race to replace Bitcoin. *The Observer* <http://observer.com/2015/02/the-race-to-replace-bitcoin/>.

Crang, M. (2003) Qualitative methods: touchy, feely, look-see? *Progress in Human Geography* 27 (4): 494–504.

Crang, P. (2005) The geographies of material culture. In Cloke, P., Crang, P., and Goodwin, M. (eds) *Introducing Human Geographies.* Routledge.

Crofton, I. (2015) *Crypto Anarchy.* LULU Press.

Crump, T. (1978) Money and number: the Trojan horse of language. *Man* 13 (4): 503–518.

Crunchbase (2019) Coinbase <https://www.crunchbase.com/organization/coinbase#section-overview>.

CryptoNinjas (2017, April 21) MGTI now mining 100 bitcoins per month, ranking as one of the largest U.S. miners. cyrptoninjas.net <https://www.cryptoninjas.net/2017/04/21/mgti-now-mining-100-bitcoins-per-month-ranking-one-largest-u-s-miners>.

Curtis, A. (2011) All watched over by machines of love and grace. *BBC.*

Cusumano, M. (2014) The Bitcoin ecosystem: speculating on how the Bitcoin economy might evolve. *Communications of the ACM* 57 (10): 22–24.

Cuthbertson, A. (2014, October 7) Geothermal gold: why Bitcoin mines are moving to Iceland. *International Business Times* <http://www.ibtimes.co.uk/geothermal-gold-why-bitcoin-mines-are-moving-iceland-1468295>.

Dabbish, L., Stuart, C., Tsay, J., and Herbsleb, J. (2012) Social coding in GitHub: transparency and collaboration in an open software repository. CSCW.

Dai, W. (1998) b-money <http://www.weidai.com/bmoney.txt>.

Dalal, N. (2014) Exploring the Bitcoin system: a complex econo-sociotechnical systems (CEST) perspective. Saïd Business School, University of Oxford.

Dale, B. (2017, December 20) $300 million lockup: Storj clarifies token economics in surprise reveal. *CoinDesk* <https://www.coindesk.com/300-million-lockup-storj-clarifies-token-economics-surprise-reveal>.

Dallyn, S. (2017) Cryptocurrencies as market singularities: the strange case of Bitcoin. *Journal of Cultural Economy* 10 (5): 462–473.

David, C. (2016, December 29) In the spirit of transparency. *Medium* <https://christopherdavid.co/in-the-spirit-of-transparency-e8037d9a0bfd>.

David, C. (2017) Introducing the Arcade Token ($ARCD)—and why you probably shouldn't buy any. Arcade City Blog <https://blog.arcade.city/introducing-the-arcade-token-atx-and-why-you-probably-shouldnt-buy-any-f32f40900b1e>.

David, C., Ponnet, S., De Wachter, K., Adriaenssen, B., and Thuy, M. (2016) Whitepaper and token plan. Arcade City.

Davidson, J., and Milligan, C. (2004) Embodying emotion sensing space: introducing emotion geographies. *Social and Cultural Geography* 5 (4): 523–532.

Davidson, S., De Filippi, P., and Potts, J. (2018) Blockchains and the economic institutions of capitalism. *Journal of Institutional Economics* 14 (4): 639–658.

Davies, G. (1994) *A History of Money: From Ancient Times to the Present Day*. University of Wales Press.

Davis, J. (2011, October 10) The crypto-currency: Bitcoin and its mysterious inventor. *The New Yorker* <http://www.newyorker.com/magazine/2011/10/10/the-crypto-currency>.

Davis, M. (1992) Who killed LA? A political autopsy. *New Left Review* 197: 3–28.

Day, M. (2018) *Bits to Bitcoin: How Our Digital Stuff Works*. MIT Press.

De Filippi, P. (2014) Bitcoin: a regulatory nightmare to a libertarian dream. *Internet Policy Review* 3 (2): 1–12.

De Filippi, P. (2015) The interplay between decentralization and privacy: the case of blockchain technologies. *Journal of Peer Production* 7.

De Filippi, P., and Loveluck, B. (2016) The invisible politics of Bitcoin: governance crisis of a decentralised infrastructure. *Internet Policy Review* 5 (3): 1–28.

De Filippi, P., and Wright, A. (2018) *Blockchain and the Law: The Rule of Code*. Harvard University Press.

de Jong, E., Lovink, G., and Riemans, P. (2015) 10 Bitcoin myths. *Institute of Network Cultures* <http://networkcultures.org/moneylab/2015/11/30/10-bitcoin-myths>.

de Vera, B. (2017, October 4) World Bank sees PH remittances hitting $33 billion in 2017. *Philippine Daily Inquirer* <http://business.inquirer.net/237974/world-bank-sees-ph-remittances-hitting-33-billion-2017-remittance-dollars-peso-world-bank>.

de Vries, A. (2018) Bitcoin's growing energy problem. *Joule* 2 (5): 801–805.

Decker, C., and Wattenhofer, R. (2013) Information propagation in the Bitcoin network. Thirteenth IEEE International Conference on Peer-to-Peer Computing.

Decker, C., and Wattenhofer, R. (2014) Bitcoin transaction malleability and MtGox. In Kutyłowski, M., and Vaidya, J. (eds) *Computer Security*. Springer.

Deek, F., and McHugh, J. (2008) *Open Source: Technology and Policy*. Cambridge University Press.

del Castillo, M. (2014, July 8) "Paypal Mafia" pals welcome hot bitcoin startup to the family. *The Business Journals* <http://www.bizjournals.com/bizjournals/news/2014/07/08/old-paypal-mafia-<pals-welcome-hot-bitcoin-startup.html>.

del Castillo, M. (2015, August 12) The "Great Bitcoin Exodus" has totally changed New York's Bitcoin ecosystem. *New York Business Journal* <http://www.bizjournals.com/newyork/news/2015/08/12/the-great-bitcoin-exodus-has-totally-changed-new.html>.

del Castillo, M. (2017, January 12) Swift is building a blockchain to optimize global cash liquidity. *CoinDesk* <http://www.coindesk.com/swift-building-blockchain-app-optimize-global-cash-liquidity>.

Delbecq, A., and Weiss, J. (1990) A regional culture perspective of high technology management. In Lawless, M., and Gomez-Meija, L. (eds) *Strategic Management in High Technology Firms.* JAI Press.

Demartino, I. (2015, September 2) Who asked Wlad? What does Bitcoin's Lead Developer say about the scaling debate? (Exclusive). *CoinJournal* <https://coinjournal.net/who-asked-wlad-what-does-bitcoins-lead-developer-say-about-scaling-debate-exclusive>.

Demeritt, D. (2002) What is the 'social construction of nature'? A typology and sympathetic critique. *Progress in Human Geography* 26 (6): 767–790.

Derrida, J. (1967) *Of Grammatology.* Les Éditions de Minuit.

Dibbell, J. (2007, June 17) The life of the Chinese gold farmer. *New York Times* <http://www.nytimes.com/2007/06/17/magazine/17lootfarmers-t.html>.

DiBona, C., Ockman, S., and Stone, M. (1999) *Open Sources: Voices from the Open Source Revolution.* O'Reilly.

Dicken, P. (2015) *Global Shift: Mapping the Changing Contours of the World Economy.* Sage.

Dicken, P., and Lloyd, P. (1990) *Location in Space: Theoretical Perspectives in Economic Geography.* HarperCollins.

Dicken, P., and Thrift, N. (1992) The organization of production and the production of organization: why business enterprises matter in the study of geographical industrialization. *Transactions of the Institute of British Geographers* 17: 279–291.

Diffie, W., and Hellman, M. (1976) New directions in cryptography. *IEEE Transactions on Information Theory* 22 (6): 644–654.

Digital Currency Group (2017, March 23) Bitcoin scaling agreement at Consensus 2017. *Medium* <https://medium.com/@DCGco/bitcoin-scaling-agreement-at-consensus-2017-133521fe9a77>.

Dodd, N. (1994) *The Sociology of Money: Economics, Reason and Contemporary Society.* Cambridge: Polity Press.

Dodd, N. (1995) Money and the nation-state: contested boundaries of monetary sovereignty in geopolitics. *International Sociology* 10: 139–154.

Dodd, N. (2014) *The Social Life of Money.* Princeton University Press.

Dodd, N. (2017) Utopian monies: complementary currencies, Bitcoin, and the social life of money. In Bandelj, N., Wherry, F., and Zelizer, A. (eds) *Money Talks: Explaining How Money Really Works.* Princeton University Press.

Dodd, N. (2018) The social life of Bitcoin. *Theory, Culture & Society: Technologies of Relational Finance* 35 (3): 35–56.

Donet, J., Pérez-Solà, C., Herrera Joancomartí, J. (2014) The Bitcoin P2P network. In Böhme, R., Brenner, M., Moore, T., Smith, M. (eds) *Financial Cryptography and Data Security.* Springer.

Donnelly, J. (2014, December 28) Bitcoin 2014: Bitcoin's biggest nightmare, the collapse of Mt. Gox. *Inside Bitcoins* http://insidebitcoins.com/news/bitcoin-2014-bitcoins-biggest-nightmare-the-collapse-of-mt-gox/28074>.

Dovey, M. (2016, July 12) Blockchain & bureaucracy. Institute of Network Cultures <http://networkcultures.org/moneylab/2016/07/12/%C2%ADblockchain-bureaucracy>.

Dovey, M. (2018) Love on the block. In Gloerich, I., Lovink, G., and de Vries, P. (eds) *MoneyLab Reader 2: Overcoming the Hype.* Institute of Network Cultures.

Dowd, K. (2014) New private monies: a bit-part player. Institute of Economic Affairs.

Downey, G., and Fisher, M. (2006) Introduction: the anthropology of capital and the frontiers of ethnography. In Fisher, M., and Downey, G. (eds) *Frontiers of Capital: Ethnographic Reflections on the New Economy.* Duke University Press.

Drage, E. (2019) Utopia/dystopia, race, gender, and new forms of humanism in women's science fiction. *Università di Bologna.* PhD Thesis.

Draper University (2014) Adam Draper: Bitcoin as a utility for financial markets. *Zapchain Interview* <https://www.youtube.com/watch?v=kRwVWPDdYH8>.

Draper, W. (2011) *The Startup Game: Inside the Partnership between Venture Capitalists and Entrepreneurs*. Palgrave Macmillan.

Dubé, L., Bourhis, A., and Jacob, R. (2005) The impact of structuring characteristics on the launching of virtual communities of practice. *Journal of Organizational Change Management* 18 (2): 145–166.

Ducheneaut, N. (2005) Socialization in an open source software community: a socio-technical analysis. *Computer Supported Cooperative Work* 14: 323–368. Springer.

DuPont, Q. (2014, May 7) The politics of cryptography: Bitcoin and the ordering of machines. Humanity+ Magazine <http://hplusmagazine.com/2014/05/07/the-politics-of-cryptography-bitcoin-and-the-ordering-machines>.

DuPont, Q. (2018) Experiments in algorithmic governance: a history and ethnography of "The DAO," a failed decentralized autonomous organization. In Campbell-Verduyn, M. (ed) *Bitcoin and Beyond: Cryptocurrencies. Blockchains, and Global Governance*. Routledge.

DuPont, Q. (2019) *Cryptocurrencies and Blockchains*. Polity Press.

DuPont, Q., and Maurer, B. (2015, June 23) Ledgers and law in the blockchain. Kings Review. <http://kingsreview.co.uk/articles/ledgers-and-law-in-the-blockchain>.

DuPont, Q., and Takhteyev, Y. (2016, August 1) Ordering space: alternative views of ICT and geography. *First Monday* 21 (8) <https://firstmonday.org/ojs/index.php/fm/article/view/6724/5603>.

Dwork, C., and Naor, M. (1993) Pricing via processing, or, combatting junk mail. In Brickell, F. (ed) *Advances in Cryptology—CRYPTO '92*. Springer.

Dyson, E., Gilder, G., Keyworth, G., and Toffler, A. (1994) Cyberspace and the American Dream: a Magna Carta for the Knowledge Age. *The Information Society* 12 (3): 295–308.

Easterling, K. (2014) *Extrastatecraft: The Power of Infrastructure Space*. Verso.

The Economist (2013) Goldman versus Google: a career on Wall Street or in Silicon Valley? YouTube <https://www.youtube.com/watch?v=O6ecPxD_tV0>.

The Economist (2015, October 31) The trust machine <http://www.economist.com/news/leaders/21677198-technology-behind-bitcoin-could-transform-how-economy-works-trust-machine>.

The Economist (2016, May 2) Craig Steven Wright claims to be Satoshi Nakamoto. Is he? <http://www.economist.com/news/briefings/21698061-craig-steven-wright-claims-be-satoshi-nakamoto-bitcoin>.

Eggimann, S., Truffer, B., and Maurer, M. (2015) To connect or not to connect? modelling the optimal degree of centralisation for wastewater infrastructures. *Water Research* 84: 218–231.

Ekelund, L., and Bjurling, K. (2004) *Santa's Workshop: Inside China's Slave Labour Toy Factories*. Fair Trade Center & Lotta Films.

Elgie, R., and Thompson, H. (1998) *The Politics of Central Banks*. Routledge.

Elliott, F. (2009, January 3) Chancellor Alistair Darling on brink of second bailout for banks. *The Times* <http://www.thetimes.co.uk/tto/business/industries/banking/article2160028.ece>.

Ellis, J. (1970) The possibility of secure non-secret digital encryption. GCHQ <http://cryptocellar.org/cesg/possnse.pdf>.

England, K. (2003) Producing feminist geographies: theory, methodologies and research strategies. In Aitken, S., and Valentine, G. (eds) *Approaches to Human Geography*. Sage.

Ethereum (2016) Homepage. <https://www.ethereum.org>.

Evans, D. (2014) Economic aspects of Bitcoin and other decentralized public-ledger currency platforms. Coase-Sandor Working Paper Series 685.

Eyal, I., and Sirer, E. (2014) Majority is not enough: Bitcoin mining is vulnerable. In Böhme, R., Brenner, M., Moore, T., Smith, M. (eds) *Financial Cryptography and Data Security*. Springer.

Farlie, R., and Chatterji, A. (2013) High-technology entrepreneurship in Silicon Valley. *Journal of Economic Strategy* 22 (2): 365–389.

Farmer, J. (2003) The specter of crypto-anarchy: regulating anonymity-protecting peer-to-peer networks. *Fordham Law Review* 72 (3): 725–784.

Ferraiolo, D., Berkley, J., and Kuhn, R. (1999) A role-based access control model and reference implementation within a corporate intranet. *ACM Transactions on Information and System Security* 2 (1): 34–64.

Ferrary, M., and Granovetter, M. (2009) The role of venture capital firms in Silicon Valley's complex innovation network. *Economy & Society* 38 (2): 326–359.

Ferry, E. (2016a) Gold, Bitcoin, and financial technology. *Alchemist* 80: 14–15.

Ferry, E. (2016b) On not being a sign: gold's semiotic claims. *Signs and Society* 4 (1): 57–79.

Financial Conduct Authority (2019) CP 19/3: Guidance on cryptoassets. <https://www.fca.org.uk/publication/consultation/cp19-03.pdf>.

Finextra (2017, January 12) Swift goes deeper into the blockchain. Finextrea Research <https://www.finextra.com/newsarticle/29974/swift-goes-deeper-into-the-blockchain>.

Finney, H. (2004) RPOW—Reusable proofs of work. <https://cryptome.org/rpow.htm>.

Fisch, M. (2013) Tokyo's commuter train suicides and the society of emergence. *Cultural Anthropology* 28 (2): 320–343.

Fischer, E., and Benson, P. (2006) *Broccoli and Desire: Global Connections and Maya Struggles in Postwar Guatemala*. Stanford University Press.

Fischer, S. (1999) On the need for an international lender of last resort. *The Journal of Economic Perspectives* 13 (4): 85–104.

Fisher, M. (2006) Navigating Wall Street women's gendered networks in the New Economy. In Downey, G., and Fisher, M. (eds) *Frontiers of Capital: Ethnographic Reflections on the New Economy*. Duke University Press.

Flandreau, M., and Ugolini, S. (2011) Where it all began: lending of last resort and the Bank of England during the Overend-Gurney panic of 1866. Norges Bank Working Paper.

Fletcher, J. (2013) Currency in transition: an ethnographic enquiry of Bitcoin adherents. University of Central Florida. Master's Thesis.

Florida, R. (2008) *Who's Your City? How the Creative Economy Is Making Where You Live the Most Important Decision of Your Life*. Basic Books.

Florida, R., and Kenney, M. (1988) Venture capital-financed innovation and technological change in the USA. *Research Policy* 17 (3): 119–137.

Florida, R., and Kenney, M. (2000) Venture capital in Silicon Valley: fuelling new firm formation. In Kenney, M. (eds) *Understanding Silicon Valley: The Anatomy of an Entrepreneurial Region*. Stanford University Press.

Forbes, S. (2013) Bitcoin: Whatever it is, it's not money! *Forbes* <https://www.forbes.com>.

Forman, P. (2017, August 21) Guest post: 'Hard to follow things: natural gas'. followthethings.com <https://followtheblog.org/2017/08/21/guest-post-hard-to-follow-things-natural-gas-by-peter-forman>.

Foster, R. (2006) Tracking globalization: commodities and value in motion. In Tilley, C., Keane, W., Kuchler, S., Rowlands, M., and Spyer, P. (eds) *Handbook of Material Culture*. Sage.

Foucault, M. (1980) *Power/Knowledge: Selected Interviews and Other Writings, 1972–1977*. Pantheon Books.

Francis, M., and Francis, N. (2006) *Black Gold*. Speak-It Films. Fulcrum Productions.

Frauenfelder, M. (2016, February 19) Bitcoin is the sewer rat of currencies. *Medium* <https://medium.com/institute-for-the-future/bitcoin-is-the-sewer-rat-of-currencies-b89819cdf036#.1z0qwloag>.

Freeman, J. (2003) The tyranny of structurelessness. jofreeman.com <https://www.jofreeman.com/joreen/tyranny.htm>.

French, S., Leyshon, A., and Signoretta, P. (2008) 'All gone now': the material, discursive and political erasure of bank and building society branches in Britain. *Antipode* 40: 79–101.

Friedman, M. (1962) *Capitalism and Freedom*. University of Chicago Press.

Friedman, M. (1993) *Why Government Is the Problem*. Hoover Institution Press.

Frisby, D. (2014) *Bitcoin: The Future of Money?* Unbound.

Freud, S. (1950) Fetishism. In Strachey, J. (ed) *Sigmund Freud Collected Papers: Volume 5*. The Hogarth Press.

Fry, J., and Cheah, E. (2016) Negative bubbles and shocks in cryptocurrency markets. *International Review of Financial Analysis* 47: 343–352.

Fuller, M. (2003) *Behind the Blip: Essays on the Culture of Software*. Autonomedia.

Fuller, M. (2008) *Software Studies: A Lexicon*. MIT Press.

Fung, B., and Halaburda, H. (2016) Central Bank digital currencies: a framework for assessing why and how. Bank of Canada <http://www.bankofcanada.ca/wp-content/uploads/2016/11/sdp2016-22.pdf>.

Galloway, A. (2004) *Protocol: How Control Exists after Decentralization*. MIT Press.

Galloway, A. (2006) Language wants to be overlooked: software and ideology. *Journal of Visual Culture* 5 (3): 315–331.

GAO (2013) Financial regulatory reform: financial crisis losses and potential impacts of the Dodd-Frank Act. Report to Congressional Requesters.

Garcia, D., Tessone, C., Mavrodiev, P., and Perony, N. (2014) The digital traces of bubbles: feed-back cycles between socio-economic signals in the bitcoin economy. *Journal of the Royal Society Interface* 11 (99): 1–8.

Garfinkel, S. (1995) *PGP: Pretty Good Privacy*. O'Reilly.

Gatecoin (2017) Bitcoin: what is this 'bitcoin'? <https://gatecoin.com/bitcoin>.

Gaver, W. (1996) Situating action II: affordances for interaction: the social is material for design. *Ecological Psychology* 8 (2): 111–129.

Geiger, S. (1990) What's so feminist about women's oral history. *Journal of Women's History* 2 (1): 169–182.

Gellman, B. and Poitras, L. (2013, June 7) U.S., British intelligence mining data from nine U.S. Internet companies in broad secret program. *Washington Post*.

Gershon, L. (2014, September 13) The Origins of Silicon Valley. JSTOR Daily <https://daily.jstor.org/how-did-silicon-valley-happen>.

Gervais, A., Karame, G., Capkun, V., and Capkun, S. (2014) Is Bitcoin a decentralized currency? *IEEE Security & Privacy* 12 (3): 54–60.

Gervais, A., Ritzdorf, H., Karame, G., and Capkun, S. (2015) Tampering with the delivery of blocks and transactions in bitcoin. *Cryptology ePrint Archive* <https://eprint.iacr.org/2015/578.pdf>.

Gibson, J. (1979) *The Ecological Approach to Visual Perception*. Houghton Mifflin.

Gibson-Graham, J. K. (1996) *The End of Capitalism (as We Knew It): A Feminist Critique of Political Economy*. Blackwell.

Giddens, A. 1990. *The Consequences of Modernity*. Stanford University Press.

Gilbert, E. (2011) Follow the thing: credit. Response to 'Follow the thing: money'. *Environment and Planning D* 29: 1085–1088.

Gilbertson, A. (2015, July 14) A week inside a hacker hostel. *Bloomberg* <https://www.bloomberg.com/news/features/2015-07-14/a-week-inside-a-hacker-hostel>.

Gill, R. (2014, June 13) CEX.IO slow to respond as fears of 51% attack spread. *CoinDesk* <https://www.coindesk.com/cex-io-response-fears-of-51-attack-spread>.

Gill, S. (1992) Economic globalization and the internationalization of authority: limits and con-tradictions. *Geoforum* 23: 269–283.

Gill, S. (1993) Global finance, monetary policy and cooperation among the group of seven, 1944–92. In Cerny, P. (ed) *Finance and World Politics: Markets, Regimes and States in the PostHegemonic*. E. Elgar.

Gillespie, T. (2010) The politics of "platforms". *New Media & Society* 12 (3): 347–364.

Girard, M., and Stark, D. (2005) Heterarchies of value: distributing intelligence and orga-nizing diversity in a New Media startup. In Ong, A., and Collier, S. (eds) *Global Assemblages: Technology, Politics and Ethics as Anthropological* Problems. Blackwell.

GitHub (2019a) Homepage <https://github.com>.

GitHub (2019b) Types of GitHub accounts <https://help.github.com/articles/differences-between-user-and-organization-accounts>.

Glaser, F., Zimmermann, K., Haferkorn, M., Weber, M., and Siering, M. (2014) Bitcoin—Asset or currency? Revealing users' hidden intentions. Twenty Second European Conference on Information Systems.

Glasner, J. (2019, September 2) Blockchain and crypto deals are down sharply in 2019. *Crunchbase* <https:// news.crunchbase.com/ news/ blockchain- and- crypto- deals- are- down- sharply-in- 2019>.

Gloerich, I., Lovink, G., and de Vries, P. (2018) *MoneyLab Reader 2: Overcoming the Hype.* Institute of Network Cultures.

Goffman, E. (1959) *The Presentation of Self in Everyday Life.* Random House.

Goldsmith, J., and Wu, T. (2006) *Who Controls the Internet? Illusions of a Borderless World.* Oxford University Press.

Golumbia, D. (2009) *The Cultural Logic of Computation.* Harvard University Press.

Golumbia, D. (2015) Bitcoin as politics: distributed right-wing extremism. In Lovink, G., Tkacz, N., and de Vries, P. (eds) *MoneyLab Reader: An Intervention in Digital Economy.* Institute for Network Cultures.

Golumbia, D. (2016a) Computerization always promotes centralization even as it promotes decentralization. In Simanowski, R. (ed) *Digital Humanities and Digital Media: Conversations on Politics, Culture, Aesthetics and Literacy.* Open Humanities Press.

Golumbia, D. (2016b) *The Politics of Bitcoin: Software as Right-Wing Extremism.* University of Minnesota Press.

Golumbia, D. (2018) Zealots on the blockchain: the true believers of the Bitcoin cult. *The Baffler* 38 <https://thebaffler.com/salvos/zealots-of-the-blockchain-golumbia>.

Goodfriend, M., and King, R. (1988) Financial deregulation, monetary policy, and central banking. Federal Reserve Bank of Richmond: Economic Review.

Goodhart, C. (1991) *The Evolution of Central Banks.* MIT Press.

Goodhart, C. (2011) The past mirror: notes, surveys, debates—The changing role of central banks. *Financial History Review* 18 (2): 135–154.

Goodman, I. (2017, June 20) Bitcoin: the ascent of a borderless currency. Das Netz <http://das-netz.online/en/bitcoin-the-ascent-of-a-borderless-currency>.

Gordon, R. (2000) Does the 'New Economy' measure up to the great inventions of the past? *Journal of Economic Perspectives* 14 (4): 49–74.

Gordon, R. (2001) State, milieu, network: systems of innovation in Silicon Valley. Center for Global, International, and Regional Studies, University of California.

Gorman, S., and Malecki, E. (2002) Fixed and fluid: stability and change in the geography of the Internet. *Telecommunications Policy* 26 (7–8): 389–413.

Gousios, G., Vasilescu, B., Serebenik, A., and Zaidman, A. (2014) Lean GHTorrent: GitHub data on demand. Conference on Mining Software, 384–387.

GQ Magazine (2016, May 2) Dr Craig Wright outs himself as Bitcoin creator Satoshi Nakamoto. *GQ Magazine* <http://www.gq-magazine.co.uk/article/bitcoin-creator-satoshi-nakamoto-craig-wright>.

Graeber, D. (2011) *Debt: The First 5000 Years.* Melville House Publications.

Graeber, D. (2015) *The Utopia of Rules: On Technology, Stupidity and the Secret Joys of Bureaucracy.* Melville House.

Graf, K. (2013) On the origins of Bitcoin: stages of monetary evolution. Creative Commons <http://nakamotoinstitute.org/static/docs/origins-of-bitcoin.pdf>.

Graham, M., De Sabbata, S., and Zook, M. (2015) Towards a study of information geographies: (im)mutable augmentations and a mapping of the geographies of information. *Geo: Geography and Environment* 2 (1): 88–105.

Graham, S. (1998) The end of geography or the explosion of place? Conceptualising space, place and information technology. *Progress in Human Geography* 22 (2): 164–185.

Graham, S. (2005) Software-sorted geographies. *Progress in Human Geography* 29 (5): 562–580.

Graham, S., and Marvin, S. (1996) *Telecommunications and the City: Electronic Spaces, Urban Places.* Routledge.

Graham, S., and Thrift, N. (2007) Out of order: understanding repair and maintenance. *Theory, Culture & Society* 24 (3): 1–25.

Granovetter, M. (1985) Economic action and social structure: the problem of embeddedness. *American Journal of Sociology* 91: 481–510.

Green, M. (1974, May 26) Deciding on utilities: public or private? *New York Times* <http://www.nytimes.com/1974/05/26/archives/deciding-on-utilities-public-or-private-con-ed-has-taken-a-step.html>.

Greenberg, A. (2013, October 25) FBI says it's seized $28.5 million in bitcoins from Ross Ulbricht, alleged owner of Silk Road. *Forbes* <https://www.forbes.com/sites/andygreenberg/2013/10/25/fbi-says-its-seized-20-million-in-bitcoins-from-ross-ulbricht-alleged-owner-of-silk-road/#73e5068d2765>.

Greenberg, A. (2014, March 25) Nakamoto's neighbor: my hint for Bitcoin's creator led to a paralyzed crypto genius. *Forbes* <http://www.forbes.com/sites/andygreenberg/2014/03/25/satoshi-nakamotos-neighbor-the-bitcoin-ghostwriter-who-wasnt/#54178cbd2639>.

Greenberg, A., and Branwen, G. (2015, December 12) Bitcoin's creator Satoshi Nakamoto is probably this unknown Australian genius. *WIRED* <https://www.wired.com/2015/12/bitcoins-creator-satoshi-nakamoto-is-probably-this-unknown-australian-genius>.

Greenspan, A., and Wilcox, J. (1998) Is there a New Economy? *California Management Review* 41 (1): 74–85.

Greenspan, G. (2015, November 22) Avoiding the pointless blockchain project. MultiChain Blog <http://www.multichain.com/blog/2015/11/avoiding-pointless-blockchain-project>.

Greenspan, G. (2016) Four genuine blockchain use cases. MultiChain Blog <http://www.multichain.com/blog/2016/05/four-genuine-blockchain-use-cases>.

Greenwald, G. (2013, June 7) NSA Prism program taps into user data of Apple, Google and others. *The Guardian* <https://www.theguardian.com/world/2013/jun/06/us-tech-giants-nsa-data>.

Grigg, I. (2011) Bitcoin—the bad news. *Financial Cryptography* <http://financialcryptography.com/mt/archives/001327.html>.

Grinberg, R. (2011) Bitcoin: an innovative alternative digital currency. *Hastings Science & Technology Law Journal* 4: 159–207.

Griziotti, G. (2018) *Neurocapitalism: Technological Mediation and Vanishing Lines*. Minor Compositions.

Grubesic, T., and Murray, A. (2004) Waiting for broadband: local competition and the spatial distribution of advanced telecommunication services in the United States. *Growth and Change* 35 (2): 139–165.

Güring, P., and Grigg, I. (2011) Bitcoin & Gresham's Law—the economic inevitability of collapse. Mimeo.

Haber, S., and Stornetta, W. (1991) How to time-stamp a digital document. *Journal of Cryptology* 3 (2): 99–111.

Hacker News (2013) Why would a government have created bitcoin? <https://news.ycombinator.com/item?id=5547423>.

Hackett, R. (2016, November 22) Why Goldman Sachs and Santander are bailing on R3's blockchain group. *Fortune* <http://fortune.com/2016/11/21/goldman-sachs-r3-blockchain-consortium>.

Hajdarbegovic, N. (2014, April 16) Linguistic researchers name Nick Szabo as author of Bitcoin whitepaper. *CoinDesk* <http://www.coindesk.com/linguistic-researchers-name-nick-szabo-author-bitcoin-whitepaper>.

Hall, L. (2012) Zoom into a microchip. Science for the NISE Network. Vimeo <https://vimeo.com/48636857>.

Hall, P., and Markusen, A. (1985) *Silicon Landscapes*. Allen & Unwin.

Hall, S. (2007) Knowledge makes the money go round: conflicts of interest and corporate finance in London's financial district. *Geoforum* 38: 710–719.

Hall, S. (2011) Geographies of money and finance I: cultural economy, politics and place. *Progress in Human Geography* 35 (2): 234–245.

Hall, S. (2012) Geographies of money and finance II: financialization and financial subject. *Progress in Human Geography* 36 (3): 403–411.

Hall, S. (2012) Geographies of money and finance III: financial circuits and the 'real economy'. *Progress in Human Geography* 37 (2): 285–292.

Hall, S., and Appleyard, L. (2009) 'City of London, City of Learning?': placing business education within the geographies of finance. *Journal of Economic Geography* 9: 597–617.

Han, E. (2014, August 20) Australian Tax Office decides bitcoins are assets, not currency. *Sydney Morning Herald* <https://www.smh.com.au/technology/australian-tax-office-decides-bitcoins-are-assets-not-currency-20140820-1063gq.html>.

Haraway, D. (1991) *Simians, Cyborgs and Women: The Reinvention of Nature*. Free Association Books.

Harris, J., and Junglas, I. (2013) Decoding the contradictory culture of Silicon Valley. Accenture.

Hartwick, E. (2000) Towards a geographical politics of consumption. *Environment and Planning A* 32 1177–1192.

Harvey, C. (2014) Bitcoin myths and facts. SSRN.

Harvey, C., and Tymoigne, E. (2015, March 1) Do cryptocurrencies such as Bitcoin have a future? *Wall Street Journal* <https://www.wsj.com/articles/do-cryptocurrencies-such-as-bitcoin-have-a-future-1425269375>.

Harvey, D. (1989) *The Condition of Postmodernity: An Enquiry into the Origins of Cultural Change.* Blackwell.

Harvey, D. (1990) Between space and time: reflections on the geographical imagination. *Annals of the Association of American Geographers* 80 (3): 418–434.

Harvey, D. (2000) *Spaces of Hope.* Edinburgh University Press.

Harvey, D. (2010) *A Companion to Marx's Capital: Volume 1.* Verso.

Harvey, D. (2015) *Seventeen Contradictions and the End of Capitalism.* Profile Books.

Harvey, P. (2012) The topological quality of infrastructural relation: an ethnographic approach. *Theory, Culture & Society* 29 (4/5): 76–92.

Haun, K. (2016) How the US government is using blockchain to fight fraud. TED Talks <https://www.youtube.com/watch?v=507wn9VcSAE&t=1145s>.

Hawkins, G., Potter, E., and Race, K. (2015) *Plastic Water: The Social and Material Life of Bottled Water.* MIT Press.

Hayek, F. (1944) *The Road to Serfdom.* Routledge & University of Chicago Press.

Hearn, M. (2015, November 2) On block sizes. *Medium* <https://medium.com/@octskyward/on-block-sizes-e047bc9f830>.

Hearn, M. (2016a, January 14) The resolution of the Bitcoin experiment. Mike Hearn: Collected Essays <https://blog.plan99.net/the-resolution-of-the-bitcoin-experiment-dabb30201f7>.

Hearn, M. (2016b) Corda: a distributed ledger. R3 <https://www.corda.net/content/corda-technical-whitepaper.pdf>.

Heber, A. (2014, December 1) Australian startup CoinJar has picked up and moved to the UK to take advantage of better tax policies. *Business Insider Australia* <http://www.businessinsider.com.au/australian-startup-coinjar-has-picked-up-and-moved-to-the-uk-to-take-advantage-of-better-tax-policies-2014-12>.

Heilman, E., Kendler, A., Zohar, A., and Goldberg, S. (2015) Eclipse attacks on Bitcoin's peer-to-peer network. *USENIX Security* 15: 129–144.

Hellmann, T., and Puri, M. (2002) Venture capital and the professionalization of start-up firms: empirical evidence. *Journal of Finance* 58 (1): 169–197.

Helms, K. (2019, August 15) Central banks worldwide testing their own digital currencies. Bitcoin.com <https://news.bitcoin.com/central-banks-testing-digital-currencies>.

Herian, R. (2018) Blockchain and the distributed reproduction of capitalist class power. In Gloerich, I., Lovink, G., and de Vries, P. (eds) *MoneyLab Reader 2: Overcoming the Hype.* Institute of Network Cultures.

Hermann, G. (2006) Special money: Ithaca hours and garage sales. *Ethnology* 45 (2): 125–141.

Hern, A. (2016, May 9) Uber and Lyft pull out of Austin after locals vote against self-regulation. *The Guardian* <https://www.theguardian.com/technology/2016/may/09/uber-lyft-austin-vote-against-self-regulation>.

Herregraven, F. (2014) Geographies of avoidance. TED Talks <https://www.youtube.com/watch?v=CQR_Qp04yrg>.

Hess, M. (2004) 'Spatial' relationships? Towards a reconceptualization of embeddedness. *Progress in Human Geography* 28 (2): 165–186.

Hertig, A. (2017, January 18) Where's Casper? Inside Ethereum's race to reinvest its block-chain. *CoinDesk* <http://www.coindesk.com/ethereum-casper-proof-stake-rewrite-rules-blockchain>.

Higgins, S. (2016a, October 28) Swiss railway service to sell Bitcoin. *CoinDesk* <https://www.coindesk.com/swiss-railway-service-sell-bitcoin-ticket-kiosks>.

Higgins, S. (2016b, May 9) Swiss city to accept Bitcoin payments for government services. *CoinDesk* <https://www.coindesk.com/swiss-city-bitcoin-payments-government-services>.

Higgins, S. (2016c, March 19) How Washington State became a battleground for Bitcoin mining. *CoinDesk* <https://www.coindesk.com/bitcoin-miners-public-utility-spar-over-electrical-costs>.

Hileman, G. (2014) From Bitcoin to the Brixton pound: history and prospects for alternative currencies. In Böhme, R., Brenner, M., Moore, T., Smith, M. (eds) *Financial Cryptography and Data Security*. Springer.

Hillis, K., Petit, M., and Jarrett, K. (2013) *Google and the Culture of Search*. Routledge.

Hillis, W. (1998) *The Pattern on the Stone*. Phoenix.

Hine, C. (2000) *Virtual Ethnography*. Sage.

Hinchliffe, S. (1996) Technology, power, and space—the means and ends of geographies of technology. *Environment and Planning D: Society and Space* 14 (6): 659–682.

Hinsley, F., and Stripp, A. (1993) *Codebreakers: The Inside Story of Bletchley Park*. Oxford University Press.

Hirst, P., and Thompson, G. (1992) The problem of 'globalization': international economic relations, national economic management and the formation of trading blocs. *Economy and Society* 21: 357–396.

HM Treasury (2015) Digital currencies: response to the call of information. Crown Copyright.

Hochstein, M. (2015, October 5) Fintech (the word, that is) evolves. *American Banker* <https://www.americanbanker.com/opinion/fintech-the-word-that-is-evolves>.

Holley, E. (2015, September 23) Digitalisation will double bank IT spending next four years. *Banking Technology* <http://www.bankingtech.com/374051/digitalisation-will-double-bank-it-spending-says-gartner>.

Hu, T. (2015) *A Prehistory of the Cloud*. MIT Press.

Hubbard, P., Bartley, B., Fuller, D., and Kitchin, R. (2002) *Thinking Geographically: Space, Theory and Contemporary Human Geography*. Bloomsbury.

Huber, F. (2011) Do clusters really matter for innovation practices in Information Technology? Questioning the significance of technological knowledge spillovers. *Journal of Economic Geography* 12 (1): 107–126.

Huckle, S., and White, M. (2016) Socialism and the blockchain. *Future Internet* 8 (49): 1–15.

Hudson, R. (2005) *Economic Geographies: Circuits, Flows and Spaces*. Sage.

Hughes, A. (2004) Retailers, knowledges and changing commodity networks: the case of the cut flower trade. In Amin, A., and Thrift, N. (eds) *Cultural Economy Reader*. Blackwell.

Hughes, E. (1993) A cypherpunk's manifesto. *The Cypherpunk Mailing List* <https://www.activism.net/cypherpunk/manifesto.html>.

Hughes, K. (2008) *Jamelia: Whose Hair Is It Anyway?* Minnow Films.

Hütten, M., & Thiemann, M. (2018) Moneys at the margins: from political experiment to cashless societies. In Campbell-Verduyn, M. (ed) *Bitcoin and Beyond: Cryptocurrencies. Blockchains, and Global Governance*. Routledge.

Hynes, C. (2017) Meet the cryptocurrency startups targeting the $26 billion remittance industry in the Philippines. *Forbes* <https://www.forbes.com/sites/chynes/2017/09/15/meet-the-cryptocurrency-startups-targeting-the-26-billion-remittance-industry-in-the-philippines/#494b1b2d5510>.

iFixit (2017) MacBook Air 13" mid 2012 teardown. iFixit.com <https://www.ifixit.com/Teardown/MacBook+Air+13-Inch+Mid+2012+Teardown/9457>.

Indergaard, M. (2004) *Silicon Alley: The Rise and Fall of a New Media District.* Routledge.

Ingham, G. (2001) Fundamentals of a theory of money: untangling Fine, Lapavitsas and Zelizer. *Economy and Society* 30: 304–323.

Ingham, G. (2004) *The Nature of Money: New Directions in Political Economy.* Polity Press.

Ingold, T. (2000) *The Perception of the Environment: Essays on Livelihood, Dwelling and Skill.* Routledge.

Ingold, T. (2010) Bringing things to life: creative entanglements in a world of materials. ESRC National Centre for Research Methods <http://eprints.ncrm.ac.uk/1306/1/0510_creative_entanglements.pdf>.

Investopedia (2018a) Soft fork <https://www.investopedia.com/terms/s/soft-fork.asp>.

Investopedia (2018b) Hard fork <https://www.investopedia.com/terms/h/hard-fork.asp>.

Irrera, A. (2015, April 2) UBS to open Blockchain research lab in London. *Wall Street Journal* <http://blogs.wsj.com/digits/2015/04/02/ubs-to-open-blockchain-research-lab-in-london>.

IRS (2014) IRS virtual currency guidance: virtual currency is treated as property for U.S. federal tax purposes; General rules for property transactions apply. IRS Virtual Currency Guidance <https://www.irs.gov/newsroom/irs-virtual-currency-guidance>.

Jackson, E. (2004) *The PayPal Wars: Battles with eBay, the Media, the Mafia and the Rest of Planet Earth.* World Ahead Publishing Inc.

Jacob, J., Brinkerhoff, M., and Jovic, E., Wheatley, G. (2004) The social and cultural capital of community currency: an Ithaca HOURS case study survey. *International Journal of Community Currency Research* 8: 42–56.

Jaffe, A., Trajtenberg, M., and Henderson, R. (1993) Localization of knowledge spillovers as evidenced by patent citations. *The Quarterly Journal of Economics* 108 (3): 577–598.

James, P. (2006) *Globalism, Nationalism Tribalism: Bringing Theory Back In—Towards a Theory of Abstract Community: Volume 2.* Sage.

Jameson, F. (2005) *Archeologies of the Future: The Desire Called Utopia and Other Science Fictions.* Verso.

Jansson, J. (2011) Emerging (Internet) industry and agglomeration: Internet entrepreneurs coping with uncertainty. *Entrepreneurship & Regional Development* 23 (7-8): 499–521.

Jeftovic, M. (2017, December 20) Bitcoin is deflationary, transparent, and antifragile. *Foundation for Economic Education* <https://fee.org/articles/bitcoin-is-deflationary-transparent-and-antifragile>.

Jentzsch, C. (2016) Decentralized Autonomous Organization to automate governance. <https://download.slock.it/public/DAO/WhitePaper.pdf>.

Jevons, W. (1875) *Money and the Mechanism of Exchange.* D. Appleton and Company.

Jia, K., and Zhang, F. (2018) Between liberalization and prohibition: prudent enthusiasm and the governance of Bitcoin/blockchain technology. In Campbell-Verduyn, M. (ed) *Bitcoin and Beyond: Cryptocurrencies. Blockchains, and Global Governance.* Routledge.

Johnson, C. (2001) A survey of current research on online communities of practice. *Internet and Higher Education* 4: 45–60.

Johnson, D., and Post, D. (1996) Law and borders: the rise of law in cyberspace. *Stanford Law Review* 45: 1367–1402.

Johnstone, C. (1760) *Chrysal; or The Adventures of a Guinea.* Printed for T. Becket.

Jones, A., Boivan, N. (2010) The malice of inanimate objects: material agency. In Hicks, D., and Beaudry, M. (eds) *The Oxford Handbook of Material Culture Studies.* Oxford University Press.

Kaiser, B., Jurado, M., and Ledger, A. (2018) The looming threat of China: an analysis of Chinese influence on Bitcoin. <https://arxiv.org/abs/1810.02466>.

Kanngieser, A., Neilson, B., and Rossiter, N. (2014) What is a research platform? Mapping methods, mobilities and subjectivities. *Media, Culture & Society* 36 (3): 302–318.

Kantor, T. (2015) *Ulterior States*. IamSatoshi Production.

Kar, I. (2016, June 21) The developers behind Ethereum are hacking the hacker that hacked it.
Quartz <https://qz.com/713078/the-developers-behind-ethereum-are-hacking-the-
hacker-that-hacked-it>.

Karatani, K. (1995) *Architecture as Metaphor: Language, Number, Money*. MIT Press.

Karlstrøm, H. (2014) Do libertarians dream of electric coins? The material embeddedness of
Bitcoin. *Distinktion: Journal of Social Theory* 15 (1): 23–36.

Kashi, E., and Watts, M. (2008) *Curse of the Black Gold: 50 Years of Oil in the Niger Delta*.
Powerhouse.

Kauffman, B. (2008) Decentralism. In Hamowy, R. (2008) *The Encyclopaedia of Libertarianism*.
Sage.

Kelly, J. (2015, September 15) Nine of the world's biggest banks join to form blockchain partnership.
Reuters <http://www.reuters.com/article/us-banks-blockchain-idUSKCN0RF24M20150915>.

Keneally, M. (2014) Tim Draper bought the auctioned bitcoins seized from Silk Road. *ABC News*
<http://abcnews.go.com/US/tim-draper-bought-auctioned-bitcoins-seized-silk-road/
story?id=24399619>.

Kenney, M. (2000) *Understanding Silicon Valley: The Anatomy of an Entrepreneurial Region*.
Stanford University Press.

Kenney, M., and von Burg, U. (2001) Paths and regions: the creation and growth of Silicon Valley.
In Garud, R., and Karnøe, P. (eds) *Path Dependence and Creation*. Lawrence Erlbaum.

Keynes, J. (1930a) *A Treatise of Money*. Harcourt, Brace and Company.

Keynes, J. (1930b) *Economic Possibilities for our Grandchildren*. R. & R. Clark Limited.

Khan, D. (1967) *The Codebreakers: The Story of Secret Writing*. Weidenfeld and Nicolson.

Khoshaba, C. (2014, January 20) 20Mission, a live/work space for tech workers. *MissionLocal*
<http://missionlocal.org/2014/01/20mission-a-livework-space-for-tech-workers>.

Kienzle, J., and Perrig, A. (1996) Digital money: A divine gift or Satan's malicious tool? STS
Project <https://users.ece.cmu.edu/~adrian/projects/memoire1/memoire1.pdf>.

Keneally, M. (2014) Tim Draper bought the auctioned bitcoins seized from Silk Road. *ABC News*
<http://abcnews.go.com/US/tim-draper-bought-auctioned-bitcoins-seized-silk-road/
story?id=24399619>.

Kinsley, S. (2013a) The matter of 'virtual' geographies. *Progress in Human Geography* 38 (3): 1–21.

Kinsley, S. (2013b) Beyond the screen: methods for investigating geographies of life 'online'.
Geography Compass 7 (8): 540–555.

Kirschenbaum, M. (2008) *Mechanisms: New Media and the Forensic Imagination*. MIT Press.

Kitchin, R. (2011) The programmable city. *Environment and Planning B* 38: 945–951.

Kitchin, R. (2017) Thinking critically about and researching algorithms. *Information, Communication
& Society* 20 (1): 14–29.

Kitchin, R. (2019) The timespace of smart cities. *Annals of the American Association of Geographers*
109 (3): 775–790.

Kitchin, R., and Dodge, M. (2004) Flying through code/space: the real virtuality of air travel.
Environment and Planning A 36 (2): 195–211.

Kitchin, R., and Dodge, M. (2005) Code and the transduction of space. *Annals of the Association of
American Geographers* 95 (1): 162–180.

Kitchin, R., and Dodge, M. (2011) *Code/Space: Software and Everyday Life*. MIT Press.

Kitchin, R., and Perng, S. (2016) *Code and the City*. Routledge.

Kittler, F. (1995, Oct) There is no software. *C-Theory: Theory, Technology, Culture* 32.

Klein, J. (2019, April 15) "Money was the sizzle": Blockchain pioneer W. Scott Stornetta assesses
Satoshi's work. *Breaker Magazine* <https://breakermag.com/money-was-the-sizzle-
blockchain-pioneer-w-scott-stornetta-assesses-satoshis-work>.

Knapp, G. (1924) *The State Theory of Money*. Macmillan & Company Limited.

Knoespel, K., and Zhu, J. (2008) Continuous materiality through a hierarchy of computational
code. *Théorie, Littérature, Epistémologie* 25: 235–247.

Knorr Cetina, K., and Bruegger, U. (2002) Traders' engagement with markets: a postsocial relationship. *Theory, Culture & Society* 19: 161–185.

Knorr Cetina, K., and Preda, A. (2005) *The Sociology of Financial Markets*. Oxford University Press.

Knox, P., and Agnew, J. (2008) *The Geography of the World Economy*. John Wiley and Sons.

Kobie, N. (2017, December 2) How much energy does bitcoin mining really use? It's complicated. *WIRED* <http://www.wired.co.uk/article/how-much-energy-does-bitcoin-mining-really-use>.

Koebler, J. (2017, June 22) An update to your Motherboard: Motherboard is under new management. *Motherboard* <https://motherboard.vice.com/en_us/article/xw8ja7/an-update-to-your-motherboard>.

Koepp, R. (2002) *Clusters of Creativity: Enduring Lessons on Innovation and Entrepreneurship from Silicon Valley and Europe's Silicon Fen*. John Wiley & Sons.

Koetsier, J. (2017, December 25) Alleged: Bitcoin cash insider trading discovered via CoinBase with potential 8X return. *Forbes* <https://www.forbes.com/sites/johnkoetsier/2017/12/25/alleged-bitcoin-cash-insider-trading-discovered-via-coinbase-with-potential-8x-return/#57f0c31e6f20>.

Kohl, U. (2007) *Jurisdiction and the Internet: Regulatory Competence Over Online Activity*. Cambridge University Press.

Kondor, D., Pósfai, M., Csabai, I., and Vattay, G. (2014) Do the rich get richer? An empirical analysis of the Bitcoin transaction network. *PLoS One* 9 (2): 1–10.

Koning, J. (2013) Why the Fed is more likely to adopt bitcoin technology than kill it off. Moneyness <http://jpkoning.blogspot.com.au/2013/04/why-fed-is-more-likely-to-adopt-bitcoin.html>.

Koning, J. (2014) Fedcoin, moneyness <http://jpkoning.blogspot.com.au/2014/10/fedcoin.html>.

Koning, J. (2016) Fedcoin: a central bank-issued cryptocurrency <https://static1.squarespace.com/static/55f73743e4b051cfcc0b02cf/t/58c7f80c2e69cf24220d335e/1489500174018/R3+Report-+Fedcoin.pdf>.

Kopfstein, J. (2013, December 12) The mission to decentralise the Internet. *The New Yorker* <http://www.newyorker.com/tech/elements/the-mission-to-decentralize-the-internet>.

Kostakis, V., and Giotitsas, C. (2014) The (a)political economy of Bitcoin. *Triple C* 12 (2): 431–440.

KPMG (2019) The pulse of fintech 2018: biannual global analysis of investment in fintech. <https://assets.kpmg/content/dam/kpmg/xx/pdf/2019/02/the-pulse-of-fintech-2018.pdf>.

Kroll, J., Davey, I., and Felten, E. (2013) The economics of Bitcoin mining or, Bitcoin in the presence of adversaries. The Twelfth Workshop on the Economics of Information Security.

Kubrak, A. (2015) Geographies of imagination. Institute of Network Cultures <http://network-cultures.org/moneylab/2015/10/28/geographies-of-imagination>.

Kutler, J. (2015) Friday flashback: did Citi coin the term 'fintech'? *American Banker* <https://www.americanbanker.com/opinion/friday-flashback-did-citi-coin-the-term-fintech>.

Laclau, E. (1990) *New Reflections on the Revolution of Our Time*. Verso.

Lamport, L., Shostak, R., and Pease, M. (1982) The Byzantine generals problem. *ACM Transactions on Programming Languages and Systems* 4 (3): 382–401.

Lanchester, J. (2016) When Bitcoin grows up. *London Review of Books* 38 (8): 3–12.

Landau, S. (2006) Find me a hash. *Notices of the AMS* 53 (3): 330–332.

Langley, P., and Leyshon, A. (2016) Platform capitalism: the intermediation and capitalisation of digital economic circulation. *Finance & Society* 3 (1): 11–31.

Larkin, B. (2013) The politics and poetics of infrastructure. *Annual Review of Anthropology* 42: 327–343.

Lash, S., and Urry, J. (1994) *Economies of Signs and Space*. Sage.

Latour, B. (1986) The powers of association. In Law, J. (ed) *Power, Action, Belief: A New Sociology of Knowledge?* Routledge.

Latour, B. (1987) *Science in Action*. Harvard University Press.

Latour, B. (1988) *The Pasteurization of France*. Harvard University Press.

Latour, B. (1996) *Aramis, or, The Love of Technology*. Harvard University Press.

Latour, B. (1999a) On recalling ANT. In Law, J., and Hassard, J. (eds) *Actor Network Theory and After*. Blackwell.

Latour, B. (1999b) *Pandora's Hope: Essays on the Reality of Science Studies*. Harvard University Press.

Latour, B. (2007) *Reassembling the Social: An Introduction to Actor-Network Theory*. Oxford University Press.

Latour, B., and Woolgar, S. (1979) *Laboratory Life: The Construction of Scientific Facts*. Sage.

Law, J. (1986) On the methods of long distance control: vessels, navigation and the Portuguese route to India. In Law, J. (ed) *Power, Action and Belief: A New Sociology of Knowledge?* Routledge.

Law, J. (2007) Actor Network Theory and Material Semiotics. <http://www.heterogeneities.net/publications/Law2007ANTandMaterialSemiotics.pdf>.

Law, J. (2009) Actor-network theory and material semiotics. In Turner, B. (ed) *The New Blackwell Companion to Social Theory*, 141–158. Blackwell.

Lea, T. (2016) *Blockchain: Down the Rabbit Hole: Discover the Power of the Blockchain*. 54 Days Pty Ltd.

Lee, C., Miller, W., Hancock, M., and Rowen, H. (2000) *The Silicon Valley Edge: A Habitat for Innovation and Entrepreneurship*. Stanford Business Books.

Lee, R. (2006) The ordinary economy: tangled up in values and geography. *Transactions of the Institute of British Geographers* 31 (4): 413–432.

Lefebvre, H. (1976) *The Survival of Capitalism*. New York.

Lefebvre, H. (1991) *The Production of Space*. Blackwell.

Leroux, R. (2012) *French Liberalism in the 19th Century*. Routledge.

Leslie, S. (1993) How the west was won: the military and the making of Silicon Valley. In Aspray, W. (ed) *Technological Competitiveness: Contemporary and Historical Perspectives on the Electrical, Electronics and Computer Industries*. Institute of Electronics and Electrical Engineers.

Leslie, S. (2000) The biggest "angel" of them all: the military and the making of Silicon Valley. In Kenney, M. (2000) *Understanding Silicon Valley: The Anatomy of an Entrepreneurial Region*. Stanford University Press.

Lessig, L. (1999) *Code and Other Laws of Cyberspace*. Basic Books.

Level39 (2015, April 2) UBS, the first global bank to create an innovation lab at Level 39, to focus on blockchain and fintech innovations. Canary Wharf Group PLC <http://www.level39.co/news/ubs-first-global-bank-create-innovation-lab-level39-focus-blockchain-fintech-innovations>.

Levi, M. (2014) The Bureau de Change. In Thrift, N., Tickell, A., Woolgar, S., and Rupp, W. (eds) *Globalization in Practice*. Oxford University Press.

Levy, K. (2017) Book-smart, not street-smart: Blockchain-based smart contracts and the social workings of law. *Engaging Science, Technology, and Society* 3: 1–15.

Levy, S. (1993, February 1) Crypto rebels. *WIRED* <https://www.wired.com/1993/02/crypto-rebels>.

Levy, S. (1994, December 1) e-money (that's what I want). *WIRED* <https://www.wired.com/1994/12/emoney>.

Levy, S. (2001) *Crypto: How the Code Rebels Beat the Government—Saving Privacy in the Digital Age*. Penguin Books.

Lewis, T. (2015, April 20) SF Bitcoin Devs seminar: advanced Stellar development for Bitcoin developers. YouTube <https://www.youtube.com/watch?v=mMEEZBKGcu0&t=2465s>.

Leyshon, A. (1993) Crawling from the wreckage: speculating on the future of the European exchange rate mechanism. *Environment and Planning A* 25: 1553–1557.

Leyshon, A. (1995) Geographies of money and finance I. *Progress in Human Geography* 19 (4): 531–543.

Leyshon, A. (1997) Geographies of money and finance II. *Progress in Human Geography* 21 (3): 381–392.

Leyshon, A. (1998) Geographies of money and finance III. *Progress in Human Geography* 22 (3): 433–446.

Leyshon, A., and Thrift, N. (1994) Access to financial services and the process of financial infrastructure withdrawal: problems and policies. *Area* 26: 268–275.

Leyshon, A., and Thrift, N. (1995) Geographies of financial exclusion: financial abandonment in Britain and the United States. *Transactions, Institute of British Geographers, New Series* 20 (3): 312–341.

Leyshon, A., and Thrift, N. (1996) Financial exclusion and the shifting boundaries of the financial system. *Environment and Planning A* 28 (7): 1150–1156.

Leyshon, A., and Thrift, N. (1997) *Money/Space: Geographies of Monetary Transformation.* Routledge.

Leyshon, A., and Tickell, N. (1994) Money order? The discursive construction of the Bretton Woods and the making and breaking of regulatory space. *Envionment and Planning A* 26: 1861–1890.

LiPuma, E. (2017) *The Social Life of Financial Derivatives.* Duke University Press.

Lischke, M., and Fabian, B. (2016) Analyzing the Bitcoin network: the first four years. *Future Internet* 8 (1): 1–40.

Lobo, S. (2014, September 3) Auf dem Weg in die Dumpinghölle. Spiegel Online <http://www.spiegel.de/netzwelt/netzpolitik/sascha-lobo-sharing-economy-wie-bei-uber-ist-plattform-kapitalismus-a-989584.html>.

Lodge, G., Zhang, H., and Jegher, J. (2015, February 5) IT spending in banking: a global perspective. Celent <http://celent.com/reports/it-spending-banking-global-perspective-2>.

Loomis, M. (2005) *Decentralism: Where It Came From—Where Is It Going?* Black Rose Books.

Lotti, L. (2016) Contemporary art, capitalization and the blockchain: on the autonomy and automation of art's value. *Finance and Society* 2 (2): 96–110.

Lovink, G. (2002) *Dark Fiber: Tracking Critical Internet Culture.* MIT Press.

Lovink, G., and Tkacz, N. (2015) MoneyLab: sprouting new digital-economic forms. In Lovink, G., Tkacz, N., and de Vries, P. (eds) *MoneyLab Reader: An Intervention in Digital Economy.* Institute for Network Cultures.

Lovink, G., Tkacz, N., and de Vries, P. (2015) *MoneyLab Reader: An Intervention in Digital Economy.* Institute for Network Cultures.

Ludlow, P. (2001) *Crypto Anarchy, Cyberstates, and Pirate Utopias.* MIT Press.

Ludwig, S. (2013, April 29) Hotshot investor Chris Dixon says 'second wave' of Bitcoin startups is on the way. VentureBeat <https://venturebeat.com/2013/04/29/chris-dixon-second-wave-bitcoin-startups>.

Lunden, I. (2013, May 16) With PayPal-like ambitions for Bitcoin, BitPay raises $2M led by Founders Fund. *TechCrunch* <https://techcrunch.com/2013/05/16/an-offer-you-cant-refuse-bitcoin-startup-bitpay-raises-2m-led-by-founders-fund-the-vc-run-by-the-paypal-mafia>.

Lupton, C. (2006) Authors, it-narratives, and objectification in the eighteenth century. *A Forum on Fiction* 39 (3): 402–420.

Lustig, C., and Nardi, B. (2015) Algorithmic authority: the case of Bitcoin. Hawaii International Conference on System Sciences.

Mackenzie, A. (2005) The performativity of code: software and cultures of circulation. *Theory, Culture & Society* 22 (1): 71–92.

Mackenzie, A. (2006) *Cutting Code: Software and Sociality.* Peter Lang.

Mackenzie, A. (2018) 48 million configurations and counting: platform numbers and their capitalization. *Journal of Cultural Economy* 11 (1): 36–53.

Mackenzie, D. (2004) Physics and finance: S-terms and modern finance as a topic for science. In Amin, A., and Thrift, N. (eds) *Cultural Economy Reader.* Blackwell.

Mackenzie, D. (2006) *An Engine, Not a Camera: How Financial Models Shape Markets.* MIT Press.

Madden, D. (2010) Urban ANTs: a review essay. *Qualitative Sociology* 33: 583–599.

Madeira, A. (2016) The DAO, the hack, the soft fork and the hard fork. CryptoCompare <https://www.cryptocompare.com/coins/guides/the-dao-the-hack-the-soft-fork-and-the-hard-fork>.

Mak, K. (2008) *Red Dust*. Independent Production.

Malecki, E. (1981) Science, technology and regional economic development: review and prospects. *Research Policy* 10 (1): 312–334.

Mallard, A., Méadel, C., and Musiani, F. (2014) The paradoxes of distributed trust: peer-to-peer architecture and user confidence in Bitcoin. *Journal of Peer Production* 4: 1–10.

Malmo, C. (2015, June 29) Bitcoin is unsustainable. *Motherboard* <https://motherboard.vice.com/en_us/article/ae3p7e/bitcoin-is-unsustainable>.

Manusu, A. (2014) Factors affecting the adoption of cryptocurrencies by small businesses. University of New South Wales. Master's Thesis.

Mann, A., and Luo, T. (2010) Crash and reboot: Silicon Valley high-tech employment and wages, 2000–08. *Monthly Labor Review* (January): 59–73.

Manne, R. (2011) The cypherpunk revolutionary: Julian Assange. *The Monthly* <https://www.themonthly.com.au/issue/2011/february/1324596189/robert-manne/cypherpunk-revolutionary>.

Manor, J. (1999) *The Political Economy of Democratic Decentralization*. The World Bank.

Manovich, L. (2001) *The Language of New Media*. MIT Press.

Manovich, L. (2008) *Software Takes Command*. Bloomsbury.

Marcus, G. (1995) Ethnography in/of the world system: the emergence of multi-sited ethnography. *Annual Review of Anthropology* 24: 95–117.

Marino, M. (2006) Critical code studies. *Electronic Book Review* <http://www.electronicbookreview.com/thread/electropoetics/codology>.

Mark, D., Zamfir, V., and Sirer, E. (2016) A call for a temporary moratorium on the DAO. Hacking, Distributed <http://hackingdistributed.com/2016/05/27/dao-call-for-moratorium>.

Marr, B. (2018, March 2) Artificial intelligence and blockchain: 3 major benefits of combining these two mega-trends. *Forbes* <https://www.forbes.com/sites/bernardmarr/2018/03/02/artificial-intelligence-and-blockchain-3-major-benefits-of-combining-these-two-mega-trends/#388983844b44>.

Marriott, J., and Minio-Paluello, M. (2012) *The Oil Road: Journeys from the Caspian Sea to the City of London*. Verso Books.

Marshall, J. (2004) Financial institutions in disadvantaged areas: a comparative analysis of policies encouraging financial inclusion in Britain and the United States. *Environment and Planning A* 36: 241–261.

Martin, J. (1978) *The Wired Society: A Challenge for Tomorrow*. Prentice Hall.

Martin, A. (2016, November 26) R3 four flew: what's driving banks to flee blockchain consortium. *The Register* <https://www.theregister.co.uk/2016/11/29/banks_leave_r3_blockchain_consortium>.

Marx, K. (1867) *Capital: A Critique of Political Economy Volume 1: The Process of Production of Capital*. Verlag von Otto Meissner.

Marx, K. (1970) *A Contribution to the Critique of Political Economy*. International Publishers.

Marx, K. (1975) On the Jewish question. In Marx, K., and Engels, F. (eds) *Marx & Engels Collected Works: Volume 3*. Lawrence & Wishart.

Marx, K., and Engels, F. (1965) *The German Ideology*. Lawrence and Wishart.

Massey, D (1991) A global sense of place. *Marxism Today* 38: 24–29.

Massey, D. (1995) Masculinity, dualisms and high technology. *Transactions of the Institute of British Geographers* 20: 487–499.

Massey, D. (2005) *For Space*. Sage.

Massumi, B. (2002) *Parables for the Virtual: Movement, Affect, Sensation*. Duke University Press.

Massumi, B. (2018) *99 Theses on the Revaluation of Value: A Postcapitalist Manifesto*. Minnesota Press.

Mateas, M., and Montfort, N. (2005) A box, darkly: Obfuscation, weird languages, and code aesthetics. Digital Arts and Culture, Copenhagen.

Matonis, J. (2012, August 20) WikiLeaks bypasses financial blockade with Bitcoin. *Forbes* <https://www.forbes.com/sites/jonmatonis/2012/08/20/wikileaks-bypasses-financial-blockade-with-bitcoin>.

Maurer, B. (2005) *Mutual Life, Limited: Islamic Banking, Alternative Currencies, Lateral Reason.* Princeton University Press.

Maurer, B. (2006) The anthropology of money. *Annual Review of Anthropology* (35): 15–36.

Maurer, B. (2011) Money nutters. *Economic Sociology: The European Electronic Newsletter* 12 (3): 5–12.

Maurer, B. (2015) *How Would You Like to Pay? How Technology is Changing the Future of Money.* Duke University Press.

Maurer, B. (2016) Re-risking in realtime: on possible futures for finance after the blockchain. *BEHEMOTH A Journal on Civilisation* 9 (2): 82–96.

Maurer, B. (2017a) Money as token and money as record in distributed accounts. In Enfield, N., and Kockelman, P. (eds) *Distributed Agency*. Oxford University Press.

Maurer, B. (2017b) Blockchains are a diamond's best friend: Zelizer for the Bitcoin moment. In Bandelj, N., Wherry, F., and Zelizer, A. (eds) *Money Talks: Explaining How Money Really Works*. Princeton University Press.

Maurer, B., Nelms, T., and Swartz, L. (2013) "When perhaps the real problem is money itself!": the practical materiality of Bitcoin. *Social Semiotics* 23 (2): 261–277.

Maurer, B., and Swartz, L. (2015) Wild wild west: a view from two Californian schoolmarms. In Lovink, G., Tkacz, N., and de Vries, P. (eds) *MoneyLab Reader: An Intervention in Digital Economy*. Institute for Network Cultures.

May, T. (1992) The crypto anarchist manifesto. Cypherpunk Mailing List <https://www.activism.net/cypherpunk/crypto-anarchy.html>.

May, T. (1994) Crypto anarchy and virtual communities. hackbloc.org <http://groups.csail.mit.edu/mac/classes/6.805/articles/crypto/cypherpunks/may-virtual-comm.html>.

Mayer, R. (2015) Localized complementary currencies: the new tool for policymakers? The Sardex Exchange System, UCL.

McCracken, G. (1988) *The Long Interview*. Sage.

McHugh, G. (2013) The reality of the German bitcoin utopia: more sobering than bitcoiners would like to admit. *BTC Global* <https://btcglobal.net/blog/post/reality-of-the-german-bitcoin-utopia>.

McKemey, K., Scott, N., Souter, D., Afullo, T., Kibombo, R., and Sakyi-Dawson, O. (2003) Innovative demand models for telecommunications services. Department for International Development.

McLannahan, B. (2016, November 22) Goldman Sachs quits R3 blockchain consortium. *Financial Times* <https://www.ft.com/content/598934e0-b010-11e6-9c37-5787335499a0>.

McLeay, M., Radia, A., and Thomas, R. (2014) Money creation in the modern economy, quarterly bulletin 1. The Bank of England.

McNeill, D. (2016) Governing a city of unicorns: technology capital and the urban politics of San Francisco. *Urban Geography* 37 (4): 494–513.

McNeill, D. (2017) *Global Cities and Urban Theory*. Sage.

McQueen, S. (2007) *Gravesend*. Nottingham Contemporary Gallery.

Meiklejohn, S., Pomarole, M., Jordan, G., Levchenko, K., McCoy, D., Voelker, G., Savage, S. (2013) A fistful of Bitcoins: characterizing payments among men with no names. ACM SIGCOMM Internet Measurement Conference 127–139.

Menezes, A., van Oorschot, P., and Vanstone, S. (1996) *Handbook of Applied Cryptography*. CRC Press.

Merkle, R. (1978) Secure communications over insecure channels. *Communications of the ACM* 21 (4): 294–298.

Merleau-Ponty, M. (1963) *Phenomenology of Perception*. Routledge.

Metz, C. (2015) The Bitcoin schism shows the genius of open source. *WIRED* <https://www.wired.com/2015/08/bitcoin-schism-shows-genius-open-source>.

metzdowd.com (2020) The cryptography and cryptography policy mailing list <http://www.metzdowd.com/mailman/listinfo/cryptography>.

Meunier, S. (2016, August 4) When do you need blockchain? Decision models. *Medium* <https://medium.com/@sbmeunier/when-do-you-need-blockchain-decision-models-a5c40e7c9ba1#.9c3pa9dt7>.

Meyer, D. (2017, September 12) This place lets you pay your taxes in Bitcoin. *Fortune* <http://fortune.com/2017/09/12/switzerland-chiasso-bitcoin-tax-zug>.

Mezrich, B. (2019) *Bitcoin Billionaires: A True Story of Genius, Betrayal, and Redemption.* Little Brown.

Mezzadra, S., and Neilson, B. (2013) *Border as Method, or, the Multiplication of Labour.* Duke University Press.

Miller, D. (2010) *Stuff.* Polity Press.

Miller, D. (2011) *Tales from Facebook.* Wiley.

Miller, D., and Slater, D. (2000) *The Internet: An Ethnographic Approach.* Bloomsbury Academic.

Miller, P. (1998) The multiplying machine. *Accounting, Organisations and Society* 22 (3–4): 355–364.

Miller, R., and Côté, M. (1985) Growing the next Silicon Valley. *Harvard Business Review* (Jul–Aug): 114–123.

Mintz, S. (1986) *Sweetness and Power: The Place of Sugar in Modern History.* Penguin.

Miranda Nieto, A. (2018) *Musical Mobilities: Son Jarocho and the Circulation of Tradition across Mexico and the United States.* Routledge.

Mitchell, J. (1990) Access to basic banking services: the problems of low-income American consumers. Providence, Rhode Island Consumers Council.

Mittal, S. (2012) Is Bitcoin money? Bitcoin and alternative theories of money. SSRN <http://ssrn.com/abstract=2434194>.

Miyazaki, S. (2012) Algorhythmics: understanding micro-temporality in computational cultures. *Computational Culture: A Journal of Software Studies* 2 <http://computationalculture.net/algorhythmics-understanding-micro-temporality-in-computational-cultures>.

Mol, A. (1999) Ontological politics: a word and some questions. In Law, J., and Hassard, J. (eds) *Actor Network Theory and After.* Blackwell Publishers.

Mol, A. (2010) Actor-network theory: sensitive terms and enduring tensions. *Kölner Zeitschrift für Soziologie und Sozialpsychologie. Sonderheft* 50: 253–269.

Mollin, R. (2000) *An Introduction to Cryptography.* Chapman & Hall/CRC.

Money & Tech (2014) Adam Draper talks about Boost VC. YouTube <https://www.youtube.com/watch?v=ZyuJL0uovWE>.

Montfort, N. (2004, December 28) Continuous paper: the early materiality and workings of electronic literature. Talk given at the Modern Language Association Convention.

Moore, D. (2016, January 6) How life in San Francisco will change after the tech bubble bursts. *The Bold Italic* <https://thebolditalic.com/how-life-in-san-francisco-will-change-after-the-tech-bubble-bursts-the-bold-italic-san-francisco-75972018b5d1#.7h959h5ml>.

Moore, T., and Christin, N. (2013) Beware the middleman: empirical analysis of Bitcoin-exchange risk. In Sadeghi, A. (ed) *Financial Cryptography and Data Security.* LCNS 7859: 25–33.

Moreno, F. (2013, July 25) Erik Voorhees: 'Bitcoin is the new frontier'. *Bitcoin Magazine* <https://bitcoinmagazine.com/articles/erik-voorhees-new-frontier-1374794545>.

Morozov, E. (2015, June 7) Where Uber and Amazon rule: welcome to the world of the platform. *The Observer* <http://www.theguardian.com/technology/2015/jun/07/facebook-uber-amazon-platform-economy>.

Morris, C. (2015) Gold and the blockchain. *Alchemist* 79.

Motamedi, S. (2014, July 21) Will bitcoins ever become money? A path to decentralized central banking. Tannu Tuva Initiative <http://tannutuva.org/blog/2014/7/21/will-bitcoins-ever-become-money-a-path-to-decentralized-central-banking>.

Motherboard (2015) Life inside a secret Chinese Bitcoin mine. Vice Media LLC <https://www.youtube.com/watch?v=K8kua5B5K3I>.

Mougayar, W. (2016) *The Business Blockchain: Promise, Practice and Application of the Next Internet Technology*. John Wiley & Sons.

Moylon, T., and Baccolini, R. (2007) *Utopia Method Vision: The Use Value of Social Dreaming*. Peter Lang.

Mross, D. (2014) *The Rise and Rise of Bitcoin*. 44th Floor Productions. DARONIMAX Media. Fair Acres Media.

Mu, E. (2015, June 8) My life inside a remote Chinese Bitcoin mine. *CoinDesk* <https://www.coindesk.com/my-life-inside-a-remote-chinese-bitcoin-mine>.

Munt, S. (2001) *Technospaces: Inside the New Media*. Continuum International Publishing Group Ltd.

Murillo, E. (2008) Searching Usenet for virtual communities of practice: using mixed methods to identify the constructs of Wenger's theory. *Information Research* 13 (4): 1–36 <https://files.eric.ed.gov/fulltext/EJ837276.pdf>.

Musiani, F., Mallard, A., and Méadel, C. (2018) Governing what wasn't meant to be governed: a controversy-based approach to the study of Bitcoin governance. In Campbell-Verduyn, M. (ed) *Bitcoin and Beyond: Cryptocurrencies. Blockchains, and Global Governance*. Routledge.

Nagy, P., and Neff, G. (2015) Imagined affordance: reconstructing a keyword for communication theory. *Social Media + Society* 1 (2): 1–9.

Nakamoto, S. (2008) Bitcoin: a peer-to-peer electronic cash system. <https://bitcoin.org/bitcoin.pdf>.

Nakamoto, S. (2009, February 11) Bitcoin open source implementation of P2P currency. P2P Foundation <http://p2pfoundation.ning.com/forum/topics/bitcoin-open-source>.

Nakamoto, S. (2010a, December 5) Re: Wikileaks contact info? Bitcoin Forum <https://bitcointalk.org/index.php?topic=1735.msg26999#msg26999>.

Nakamoto, S. (2010b, December 11) Re: PC World article on Bitcoin. Bitcoin Forum <https://bitcointalk.org/index.php?topic=2216.msg29280#msg29280>.

Narayanan, A. (2013) What happened to the crypto dream? Part 1. *EEE Security and Privacy Magazine* (Mar/Apr) <http://randomwalker.info/publications/crypto-dream-part1.pdf>.

Narula, N. (2016) The future of money. TED Talks <https://www.ted.com/talks/neha_narula_the_future_of_money#t-380133>.

Negroponte, N. (1995) *Being Digital*. Vintage.

Neilson, B. (2016) Platform research. *Western Sydney University* <https://www.westernsydney.edu.au/__data/assets/pdf_file/0005/1149881/Platform_Research.pdf>.

Neilson, B. (2018) Follow the software: reflections on the logistical worlds project. In Neilson, B., Rossiter, N., & Samaddar, R. (eds) *Logistical Asia: The Labour of Making a World Region*. Palgrave Macmillan.

Nel, E., and Binns, T. (2003) Decentralising development in South Africa. *Geography* 88 (2): 108–116.

Nelms, T., Maurer, B., Swartz, L., and Mainwaring, S. (2017) Social payments: innovation, trust, Bitcoin, and the sharing economy. *Theory, Culture & Society* 35 (3): 13–33.

Nelson, A. (1999) *Marx's Concept of Money: The God of Commodities*. Routledge.

Nelson, T. (2013) I think I know who Satoshi is. YouTube <https://www.youtube.com/watch?v=emDJTGTrEm0&feature=youtu.be>.

Norman, D. (1988) *The Psychology of Everyday Things*. New York: Basic Books.

Norris, P. (2001) *Digital Divide: Civic Engagement, Information Poverty, and the Internet Worldwide*. Cambridge University Press.

North, P., and Longhurst, N. (2013) Grassroots localisation? The scalar potential of and limits of the 'transition' approach to climate change and resource constraint. *Urban Studies* 50 (7): 1423–1438.

Noyen, K., Volland, D., Worner, D., and Fleisch, E. (2014) When money learns to fly: towards sensing as a service applications using bitcoin, ETH. Zurich and University of St. Gallen.

nustiudinastea (2016) Critical update RE: DAO vulnerability. Reddit <https://www.reddit.com/r/ethereum/comments/4oiqj7/critical_update_re_dao_vulnerability>.

NYDFS (2015) Virtual currencies, New York codes, rules and regulations. NYDFS <http://www.dfs.ny.gov/legal/regulations/adoptions/dfsp200t.pdf>.

Oates, J. (2013, May 20) Has Ted Nelson named the real Satoshi Nakamoto? *CoinDesk* <http://www.coindesk.com/ted-nelson-names-the-real-satoshi-nakamoto>.

O'Brien, M. (2015, January 14) Bitcoin revealed: a Ponzi scheme for redistributing wealth from one libertarian to another. *Washington Post* <https://www.washingtonpost.com/news/wonk/wp/2015/01/14/bitcoin-is-revealed-a-ponzi-scheme-for-redistributing-wealth-from-one-libertarian-to-another/?utm_term=.9a0c6d31ffa0>.

O'Brien, R. (1992) *Global Financial Integration: The End of Geography.* Royal Institute of International Affairs.

O'Connell, J. (2016a, May 11) Andreas Antonopoulos' folly on private blockchains. *Bitcoinist* <http://bitcoinist.com/antonopoulos-private-blockchains>.

O'Connell, J. (2016b, June 20) What are the use cases for private blockchains? The experts weigh in. *Bitcoin Magazine* <https://bitcoinmagazine.com/articles/what-are-the-use-cases-for-private-blockchains-the-experts-weigh-in-1466440884>.

O'Dwyer, R. (2014) Other values: considering digital currency as a commons. RGS-IBG Panel: From Co-production to Alternative futures (1): Creating Cracks: Value, Commons and Alternative Economy.

O'Dwyer, R. (2015a) Money talks: the enclosure of mobile payments. In Lovink, G., Tkacz, N., and de Vries, P. (2015) *MoneyLab Reader: An Intervention in Digital Economy.* Institute for Network Cultures.

O'Dwyer, R. (2015b, March 23) The revolution will (not) be decentralised: blockchains. P2P Foundation <https://blog.p2pfoundation.net/the-revolution-will-not-be-decentralised/2015/03/23>.

O'Hagan, A. (2016) The Satoshi Affair. *London Review of Books* 38 (13): 7–28.

Ohmae, K. (1990) *The Borderless World: Power and Strategy in the Interlinked Economy.* HarperCollins.

O'Kelly, M., and Grubesic, T. (2002) Backbone topology, access, and the commercial Internet, 1997–2000. *Environment and Planning B: Planning and Design* 29: 533–552.

O'Leary, R. (2017, November 10) Bitcoin Classic team to cease code support in wake of 2x suspension. *CoinDesk* <https://www.coindesk.com/bitcoin-classic-announces-closure-in-wake-of-segwit2x-suspension>.

Olma, S. (2014, October 16) Nevermind the sharing economy: here's platform capitalism. *Institute of Network Cultures Blog* <http://networkcultures.org/mycreativity/2014/10/16/never-mind-the-sharing-economy-heres-platform-capitalism>.

O'Mahony, S. (2006) Developing community software in a commodity world. In Downey, G., and Fisher, M. (eds) *Frontiers of Capital: Ethnographic Reflections on the New Economy.* Duke University Press.

O'Rian, S. (2004) Net-working for a living: Irish software developers in the global workplace. In Amin, A., and Thrift, N. (eds) *Cultural Economy Reader.* Blackwell.

Ormsby, E. (2012) Silk Road: the eBay of illegal drugs. *Kill Your Darlings* 11.

Ortega, M. (2013) The Bitcoin Transaction Graph Anonymity. Universitat Autònoma de Barcelona. Master's Thesis.

Ouellet, M. (2010) Cybernetic capitalism and the global information society: from the global panopticon to a 'brand' new world. In Best, J., and Paterson, M. (ed) *Cultural Political Economy.* Routledge.

Packer, G. (2011, November 28) No death, no taxes: the libertarian futurism of a Silicon Valley billionaire. *New Yorker* <http://www.newyorker.com/magazine/2011/11/28/no-death-no-taxes>.

Packer, J., and Wiley, S. (2011) *Communication Matters: Materialist Approaches to Media, Mobility and Networks.* Routledge.

Pal, R. (2013) Valuing Bitcoin using a macro framework. *Global Macro Investor* <https://www.zerohedge.com/sites/default/files/images/user5/imageroot/2013/11/Bitcoin.pdf>.

Paled, M. (2005) *China Blue*. Teddy Bear Films.

Parden, R. (1981) The manager's role and the high mobility of technical specialists in the Santa Clara Valley. *IEEE Transactions on Engineering Management* 28 (1): 2–8.

Parikka, J. (2015) *A Geology of Media*. University of Minnesota Press.

Parker, L. (2016, September 4) Bitcoin remittances '20 percent' of South Korea–Philippines corridor. *Brave New Coin* <https://bravenewcoin.com/news/bitcoin-remittances-20-percent-of-south-korea-philippines-corridor>.

Parr, H. (2003) Researching bodies in virtual space. In Blunt, A., Gruffudd, P., May, J., Ogborn, M., and Pinder, D. (eds) *Cultural Geography in Practice*. Arnold.

PBS (2015, April 18) The hack attack that takes your computer hostage until you pay. PBS News Hour <https://www.pbs.org/newshour/show/ransomware-hack-attacks-holding-data-ostage-avoid>.

Peel, J. (2000) *Religious Encounter and the Making of the Yoruba*. Indiana University Press.

Peetz, D., and Mall, G. (2018) Why Bitcoin is not a currency but a speculative real asset. SSRN.

Peikoff, L. (1993) *Objectivism: The Philosophy of Ayn Rand*. Meridian.

Pel, A. (2015) Money for nothing and bits for free: the geographies of Bitcoin. University of Toronto. Master's Thesis.

Pels, P. (1998) The spirit of matter: on fetish, rarity, fact, and fancy. In Spyer, P. (ed) *Border Fetishisms: Material Objects in Unstable Space*. Routledge.

Pels, P. (2010) Magical things: on fetishes, commodities, and computers. In Hicks, D., and Beaudry, M. (eds) *The Oxford Handbook of Material Culture Studies*. Oxford University Press.

Penenberg, A. (2011, October 11) The Bitcoin crypto-currency mystery reopened. The Fast Company <http://www.fastcompany.com/1785445/bitcoin-crypto-currency-mystery-reopened>.

Perez, Y. (2015, August 13) The real cost of applying for a New York BitLicense. *CoinDesk* <http://www.coindesk.com/real-cost-applying-new-york-bitlicense>.

Perrig, A., and Song, D. (1999) Hash visualization: a new technique to improve real-world security. International Workshop on Cryptographic Techniques and E-Commerce (CrypTEC '99): 439–458.

Peyton, A. (2017, February 24) R3 turns its back on blockchain? *FinTech Futures* <http://www.bankingtech.com/746692/r3-turns-its-back-on-blockchain>.

Pham, L. (2017, October 27) This company added the word 'Blockchain' to its name and saw its shares surge 394%. *Bloomberg Technology* <https://www.bloomberg.com/news/articles/2017-10-27/what-s-in-a-name-u-k-stock-surges-394-on-blockchain-rebrand>.

Philo, C. (1995) Where is poverty? The hidden geography of poverty in the United Kingdom. In Philo, C. (ed) *Off the Map: The Social Geography of Poverty in the UK*. Child Poverty Action Group.

Piepenbring, D. (2016, May 16) Tag archives: the adventure of a guinea. *Paris Review* <https://www.theparisreview.org/blog/tag/the-adventures-of-a-guinea>.

Pietz, W. (1985) The problem of the fetish, I. *Anthropology and Aesthetics* (9): 5–17.

Pike, A., Lagendijk, A., and Vale, M. (2000) Critical reflections on 'embeddedness' in economic geography: the case of labour market governance and training in the automotive industry in the north-east region of England. In Giunta, A., Lagendijk, A., and Pike, A. (eds) *Restructuring Industry and Territory: The Experience of Europe's Regions*. The Stationery Office.

Pike, A., Rodriquez-Pose, and A., Tomaney, J. (2006) *Local and Regional Development*. Routledge.

Pilkington, M. (2017) Bitcoin through the lenses of complexity theory: some non-orthodox implications for economic theorizing. In Martin, R., and Pollard, J. (eds) *Handbook on the Geographies of Money and Finance*. Edward Elgar.

Polanyi, K. (1944) *The Great Transformation*. Holt, Rinehart.

Popper, N. (2015a) *Digital Gold: Bitcoin and the Inside Story of the Misfits and Millionaires Trying to Reinvent Money*. Harper.

Popper, N. (2015b, May 18) How Silicon Valley joined the Bitcoin gold rush. *Fast Company* <https://www.fastcompany.com/3046417/when-bitcoin-went-to-silicon-valley>.

Popper, N. (2017, July 18) Some Bitcoin backers are defecting to create a rival currency. *New York Times* <https://www.nytimes.com/2017/07/25/business/dealbook/bitcoin-cash-split.html>.

Preukschat, A., Busquet, J., and Ares, J. (2014) *Bitcoin: The Hunt for Satoshi Nakamoto*. Europe Comics.

Price, R. (2016, June 13) We got a look inside a vast Icelandic Bitcoin mine. *Business Insider UK* <http://uk.businessinsider.com/photos-iceland-bitcoin-ethereum-mine-genesis-mining-cloud-2016-6?r=US&IR=T>.

Prisco, G. (2015a, April 3) UBS to open blockchain innovation lab in London. *Bitcoin Magazine* <https://bitcoinmagazine.com/articles/ubs-open-blockchain-innovation-lab-london-1428094554>.

Prisco, G. (2015b, December 11) SWIFT to launch global payments innovation initiative, develop blockchain roadmap. *Bitcoin Magazine* <https://bitcoinmagazine.com/articles/swift-to-launch-global-payments-innovation-initiative-develop-blockchain-roadmap-1449860661>.

R3 (2017) About R3. r3cev.com <http://www.r3cev.com/about>.

Rancière, J. (1998) *Disagreement*. University of Minnesota Press.

Rancière, J. (2005) *Chroniques des temps consensuels*. Seuil.

Rand, A. (1959) *The Mike Wallace Interview of Ayn Rand*. No Free Lunch Distributors.

Rand, A. (1984) *Philosophy: Who Needs It?* Signet.

Rand, A., Branden, N., Greenspan, A., and Hessen, R. (1967) *Capitalism: The Unknown Ideal*. Signet.

Raskin, M. (2013, April 12) Meet the Bitcoin millionaires: early adopters of the virtual currency are suddenly rich. *Bloomberg* <https://www.bloomberg.com/news/articles/2013-04-10/meet-the-bitcoin-millionaires>.

Ratcliff, J. (2014, January 11) Bring out your dead . . . Bitcoin that is. *Code Suppository* <https://codesuppository.blogspot.co.uk/2014/01/bring-out-your-dead-bitcoins-that-is.html>.

Raval, S. (2016) *Decentralized Applications: Harnessing Bitcoin's Blockchain Technology*. O'Reilly Media.

Raymond, E. (2001) *The Cathedral and the Bazaar: Musings on Linux and Open Source by an Accidental Revolutionary*. O'Reilly.

Raza, A. (2018, January 28) Coinbase warns VCs to back off after booking $1 billion in revenue. *CryptoSlate* <https://cryptoslate.com/coinbase-warn-vcs-back-off-booking-1-billion-revenue>.

Redmon, D. (2005) *Mardis Gras: Made in China*. Carnivalesque Films.

Reid, F., and Harrigan, M. (2012) An analysis of anonymity in the Bitcoin system. In Altshuler Y., Elovici Y., Cremers A., Aharony N., Pentland A. (eds) *Security and Privacy in Social Networks*. Springer.

Reijers, W., O'Brolcháin, F., and Haynes, P. (2016) Governance in blockchain technologies & social contract theories. *Ledger Journal* 1: 124–151.

Richards, B. (2014) Bitcoin is a Ponzi scheme. *The Forum* <http://tabbforum.com/videos/bitcoin-is-a-ponzi-scheme-marathons-richards>.

Richards, F. (2017, July 28) User activated soft fork explained [UASF/BIP148] (Litecoin/Bitcoin). Franklyn. YouTube. <https://www.youtube.com/watch?v=BY878HXxh-8&t=536s>.

Rizzo, P. (2014, February 5) CoinSummit San Francisco announces itinerary and speakers. *CoinDesk* <https://www.coindesk.com/coinsummit-san-francisco-announces-itinerary-speaker-list>.

Rizzo, P. (2015a, October 5) US Government to sell 44,000 BTC in final Silk Road auction. *CoinDesk* <http://www.coindesk.com/us-government-to-sell-44000-btc-in-final-silk-road-auction>.

Rizzo, P. (2015b, May 22) Internet security pioneer unveil project at Blockchain University. *CoinDesk* <https://www.coindesk.com/founding-ssl-developer-unveils-project-at-blockchain-university>.

Roberts, D. (2015, June 12) Bitcoin company ditches New York, blaming new regulations. *Fortune* <http://fortune.com/2015/06/11/bitcoin-shapeshift-new-york-bitlicense>.

Roberts, J. (2020) *Kings of Crypto: One Startup's Quest to Take Cryptocurrency Out of Silicon Valley and Onto Wall Street*. Harvard Business Review Press.

Roberts, S. (1994) Fictitious capital, fictitious spaces: the geography of Offshore Financial Flows. In Corbridge, S., Martin, R., Thrift, N. (eds) *Money, Power and Space*. Blackwell.

Rodden, J., Eskeland, G., and Litvack, J. (2003) *Fiscal Decentralisation and the Challenge of Hard Budget Constraints*. MIT Press.

Rodima-Taylor, D., and Grimes, W. (2018) Cryptocurrencies and digital payment rails in networked global governance: perspectives on inclusion and innovation. In Campbell-Verduyn, M. (ed) *Bitcoin and Beyond: Cryptocurrencies. Blockchains, and Global Governance*. Routledge.

Rogers, E., and Larsen, J. (1984) *Silicon Valley Fever*. Basic Books.

Ron, D., and Shamir, A. (2013) Quantitative analysis of the full Bitcoin transaction graph. In Sadeghi, A. (ed) *Financial Cryptography and Data Security* LNCS 7859: 6–24. Springer.

Rose, G. (2016) Rethinking the geographies of cultural 'objects' through digital technologies: interface, network and friction. *Progress in Human Geography* 40 (3): 334–351.

Ross, A. (2003) *No-collar: The Hidden Cost of the Humane Workplace*. Basic Books.

Rossiter, N. (2006) *Organized Networks: Media Theory, Creative Labour, New Institutions*. NAI.

Rossiter, N. (2016) *Software, Infrastructure, Labor: A Media Theory of Logistical Nightmares*. Routledge.

Rossiter, N. (2017) Automation, platform capitalism, and the state. Institute for Culture and Society—Digital Life Research Program (Western Sydney University). Technology's Limits: Automation, Invention, Labour, and the Exhausted Environment <https://www.westernsydney.edu.au/ics/events/technologys_limits>.

Russell, J. (2018, October 30) Coinbase is now valued at $8B after closing new $300M round. *TechCrunch* <https://techcrunch.com/2018/10/30/coinbase-is-now-valued-at-8b-after-closing-new-300m-round>.

Russell, J., and Tepper, F. (2017, December 19) Coinbase is investigating claims of insider trading from its Bitcoin Cash launch. *TechCrunch* https://techcrunch.com/2017/12/19/coinbase-inside-information-bitcoin-cash-launch>.

Rutter, D. (2017, February 14) When is a blockchain not a blockchain. *The R3 Report* <http://www.r3cev.com/blog/2017/2/24/when-is-a-blockchain-not-a-blockchain>.

Rutter, J., and Smith, G. (2005) Ethnographic presence in a nebulous setting. In Hine, C. (ed) *Virtual Methods: Issues in Social Research on the Internet*. Berg.

Ryle, G. (1949) *The Concept of Mind*. University of Chicago Press.

Samani, R. (2013) *Digital Laundry: An analysis of Online Currencies, and Their Use in Cybercrime*. McAfee.

Sample, M. (2011, January 14) Criminal code: the procedural logic of crime in videogames. *Sample Reality* <http://www.samplereality.com/2011/01/14/criminal-code-the-procedural-logic-of-crime-in-videogames>.

Sams, R. (2015, February 5) Which Fedcoin? *Cryptonomics* <https://cryptonomics.org/2015/02/05/which-fedcoin>.

Sassen, S. (1991) *The Global City*. Princeton University Press.

Sassen, S. (2004) The locational and institutional embeddedness of electronic markets: the case of the global capital markets. In Bevir, M., and Trentmann, F. (eds) *Markets in Historical Context: Ideas and Politics in the Modern World*. Cambridge University Press.

Sassen, S. (2005) The embeddedness of electronic markets: the case of global capital markets. In Knorr Centina, K., and Preda, A. (eds) *The Sociology of Financial Markets*. Oxford University Press.

Saxenian, A. (1981) Silicon chips and spatial structures: the industrial basis of urbanization in Santa Clara County, California. Institute of Urban and Regional Development, University of California.

Saxenian, A. (1983) The urban contradictions of Silicon Valley: regional growth and the restructuring of the semiconductor industry. *International Journal of Urban and Regional Research* 7 (2): 237–262.

Saxenian, A. (1989a) In search of power: the organization of business interests in Silicon Valley and Route 128. *Economy & Society* 18 (1): 25–70.

Saxenian, A. (1989b) The Cheshire Cat's grin: innovation and regional development in England. *Economy & Society* 18 (4): 448–477.

Saxenian, A. (2002) The Silicon Valley connection: transnational networks and regional development in Taiwan, China and India. *Science, Technology and Society* 7 (1): 117–149.

SBB (2016) Bitcoin on SBB ticket machines. SBB/CFF/FFS <https://company.sbb.ch/en/media/media-relations/press-releases/detail.html/2016/10/2810-3>.

Schaefer, S. (2013, March 14) A look back at Bear Stearns, five years after its shotgun wedding to JPMorgan. *Forbes* <http://www.forbes.com/sites/steveschaefer/2013/03/14/a-look-back-at-bear-stearns-five-years-after-its-shotgun-marriage-to-jpmorgan/#2a97bd917ddc>.

Scheper-Hughes, N. (2000) The global traffic in human organs. *Current Anthropology* 41 (2): 191–224.

Scheper-Hughes, N. (2004) Parts unknown: undercover ethnography of the organs-trafficking underworld. *Ethnography* 5 (1): 29–73.

Schmidt, V. (1990) *Democratizing France*. Cambridge University Press.

Schneider, N. (2014, April 7) Code your own utopia: meet Ethereum, Bitcoin's most ambitious successor. *Aljazeera America* <http://america.aljazeera.com/articles/2014/4/7/code-your-own-utopiameetethereumbitcoinasmostambitioussuccessor.html>.

Schneider, N. (2019) Decentralization: An incomplete ambition. *Journal of Cultural Economy* 12 (4): 265–285.

Scholz, T. (2017) *Uberworked and Underpaid: How Workers Are Disrupting the Digital Economy*. John Wiley and Sons.

Schonfield, E. (2011, May 25) The top 10 VC firms, according to InvestorRank. *TechCrunch* <https://techcrunch.com/2011/05/25/top-10-vc-firms-investorrank>.

Schuhmacher, S. (2014, December 18) Blockchain University: creating more blockchain developers. *Brave New Coin* <https://bravenewcoin.com/news/blockchain-university-creating-more-blockchain-developers>.

Scott, B. (2014a, December 30) Peer-to-peer review: the state of academic Bitcoin research 2014. Suitpossom: Anarchic Adventures in Arts, Activism, Anthropology and Alternative Economics.

Scott, B. (2014b, June 1) Visions of a Techno-Leviathan: the politics of the Bitcoin blockchain. *E-International Relations* <http://www.e-ir.info/2014/06/01/visions-of-a-techno-leviathan-the-politics-of-the-bitcoin-blockchain>.

Scott, B. (2016) How can cryptocurrency and blockchain technology play a role in building social and solidarity finance? UNRISD.

Scott, B. (2018) Cash in the era of the digital payments panopticon. In Gloerich, I., Lovink, G., and de Vries, P. (eds) *MoneyLab Reader 2: Overcoming the Hype*. Institute of Network Cultures.

Segal, H. (1985) *Technological Utopianism in American Culture*. University of Chicago Press.

Selgin, G. (2015) Synthetic commodity money. *Journal of Financial Stability* 17: 92–99.

Selwyn, N. (2004) Reconsidering political and popular understandings of the digital divide. *New Media & Society* 6 (3): 341–362.

Senate of Canada (2014, October 8) Proceedings of the Standing Senate Committee on banking, trade and commerce. Parliament of Canada 15 <https://sencanada.ca/en/Content/Sen/committee/412/banc/15ev-51627-e>.

Shah, A. (2008) *Macro Federalism and Local Finance, Public Sector Governance and Accountability Series*. The World Bank.

Shaiken, H., Herzenberg, S., and Kuhn, S. (1986) The work process under more flexible production. *Industrial Relations* 25 (2): 167–183.

Shieber, J. (2014, March 12) Goldman Sachs: Bitcoin is not a currency. *TechCrunch* <https://techcrunch.com/2014/03/12/goldman-sachs-bitcoin-is-not-a-currency>.

Shields, R. (2013) *Spatial Questions: Cultural Topologies and Social Spatialisation*. Sage.

Shin, L. (2017, February 7) The first government to secure land titles on the Bitcoin blockchain expands project. *Forbes*. <https://www.forbes.com/sites/laurashin/2017/02/07/

the-first-government-to-secure-land-titles-on-the-bitcoin-blockchain-expands-project/#351fbe944dcd>.

Shrestha, A., Zhu, Y., and Miller, B. (2013) Visualizing time and geography of open source software with storygraph. IEEE Working Conference on Software Visualization (VISSOFT).

Siegel, D. (2016, June 25) Understanding the DAO attack. *CoinDesk* <http://www.coindesk.com/understanding-dao-hack-journalists>.

Simmel, G. (1900) *The Philosophy of Money*. Verlag von Duncker & Humblot.

Simmonds, F. (2008) *Primark—on the Rack*. BBC.

Simpson, R. (2016) *Crypto Wars: 2000 Years of Cipher Evolution*. CreateSpace Independent Publishing Platform.

Sindreu, J. (2016, July 19) The central bankers' bold new idea: print Bitcoins. *Wall Street Journal* <https://www.wsj.com/articles/the-central-bankers-bold-new-idea-print-bitcoins-1468936751>.

Singh, S. (1999) *The Code Book: The Secret History of Codes and Code-Breaking*. Fourth Estate.

Slashdot (2016, May 29) Researchers criticize new DAO Ethereum VC fund <https://news.slashdot.org/story/16/05/30/003202/researchers-criticize-new-dao-ethereum-vc-fund>.

Smith, A. (1759) *The Theory of Moral Sentiments*. A. Millar.

Smith, A. (1776) *An Inquiry into the Nature and Causes of the Wealth of Nations*. William Strahan & Thomas Cadell.

Smith, B. (1985) *Decentralization: The Territorial Dimension of the State*. George Allen & Unwin Ltd.

Smith, P. (2015) Blockchain. *WIRED MONEY* <https://www.youtube.com/watch?v=3ehQY6M4X5M>.

Smith, T. (2004) Electricity theft—comparative analysis. *Energy Policy* 32 (18): 2067–2076.

Snyder, R. (2008) *Fugitive Denim: A Moving Story of People and Pants in the Borderless World of Global Trade*. Norton & Co.

Sokol, M. (2011) *Economic Geographies of Globalisation: A Short Introduction*. Edward Elgar.

Solnit, R. (2014a, February 20) Diary. *London Review of Books* 36 (4): 34–35 <http://www.lrb.co.uk/v36/n04/rebecca-solnit/diary>.

Solnit, R. (2014b, January 7) Rebecca Solnit: resisting monoculture. *Guernica* <https://www.guernicamag.com/rebecca-solnit-resisting-monoculture>.

Solnit, R. (2016, May 3) Gentrification's toll: 'It's you or the bottom line and sorry, it's not you'. *The Guardian* <https://www.theguardian.com/cities/2016/may/03/gentrification-climate-change-sierra-club-san-francisco>.

Song, J. (2017, July 31) A gentle introduction to Bitcoin Core development. Bitcoin Tech Talk. <https://bitcointechtalk.com/a-gentle-introduction-to-bitcoin-core-development-fdc95eaee6b8>.

Song, J. (2018, June 27) What is the Bitcoin Improvement Proposal process and how does that work? Off Chain. Youtube. <https://www.youtube.com/watch?v=NJqAuZGg1gU>.

Southurst, J. (2014, December 1) Bitcoin startup CoinJar cites tax as influence on UK relocation. *CoinDesk* <https://www.coindesk.com/bitcoin-startup-coinjar-cites-tax-influence-uk-relocation>.

Sparkes, M. (2015, March 5) US auctions 50,000 Bitcoins seized from Silk Road. *The Telegraph* <http://www.telegraph.co.uk/technology/news/11451379/US-auctions-50000-Bitcoins-seized-from-Silk-Road.html>.

Spaven, E. (2015, March 30) Bitcoin's 'first felon' Charlie Shrem begins 2-year sentence. *CoinDesk* <http://www.coindesk.com/bitcoins-first-felon-charlie-shrem-begins-2-year-sentence>.

Spencer, L. (2014, December 1) Australia's CoinJar moves HQ to UK for 'progressive' bitcoin scene. ZDNet <http://www.zdnet.com/article/australias-coinjar-moves-hq-to-uk-for-progressive-bitcoin-scene>.

Srnicek, N. (2017) *Platform Capitalism*. Polity Press.

Star, S. (1999) The ethnography of infrastructure. *American Behavioural Scientist* 43 (3): 377–391.

Star, S. (2002) Infrastructure and ethnographic practice: working on the fringes. *Scandinavian Journal of Information Systems* 14 (2): 107–122.

Starosielski, N. (2015) *The Undersea Network*. Duke University Press.

Steinmetz, G. (1999) *State/Culture: State-Formation after the Cultural Turn*. Cornell University Press.

Stinson, D. (2006) Some observations on the theory of cryptographic hash functions. *Designs, Codes and Cryptography* 38 (2): 259–277.

Storj (2018) Homepage. Storj Labs Inc. <https://storj.io>.

Strange, S. (1988) *States and Markets*. Pinter.

Stuckler, D., Meissner, C., and King, L. (2008) Can a bank crisis break your heart? *Globalization and Health—BioMed Central* 4 (1): 1–4.

Sturgeon, T. (2000) How Silicon Valley came to be. In Kenney, M. (2000) *Understanding Silicon Valley: The Anatomy of an Entrepreneurial Region*. Stanford University Press.

Sturgeon, T. (2003) What really goes on in Silicon Valley? Spatial clustering and dispersal in modular networks. MIT Working Paper.

Šurda, P. (2012) Economics of Bitcoin: is Bitcoin an alternative to fiat currencies and gold? *WU Vienna University of Economics and Business*. Master's Thesis.

Swan, D. (2014, December 2) Aussie Bitcon start-up CoinJar moves to the UK, *The Australian* <https://www.theaustralian.com.au/business/business-spectator/aussie-bitcoin-startup-coinjar-moves-to-the-uk/news-story/551f384bbeddf09ba7c001435624febe?nk=0 2413eae5c168d1d5a23f892fe64a232-1519912830>.

Swan, M. (2015) *Blockchain: Blueprint for a New Economy*. O'Reilly.

Swanson, T. (2014a) *The Anatomy of a Money-like Informational Commodity: A Study of Bitcoin*. Creative Commons.

Swanson, T. (2014b, November 22) Approximately 70% of all bitcoins have not moved in 6 or more months. *Great Wall of Numbers* <http://www.ofnumbers.com/2014/11/22/approximately-70-of-all-bitcoins-have-not-moved-in-6-or-more-months>.

Swanson, T. (2014c) Great chain of numbers: a guide to smart contracts, smart property, and trustless asset management. Creative Commons.

Swanson, T. (2017a, February 13) Chainwashing. Great Wall of Numbers <http://www.ofnumbers.com/2017/02/13/chainwashing>.

Swanson, T. (2017b, March 14) R3 report on Fedcoin. The R3 Report <http://www.r3cev.com/blog/2017/3/14/b772lwbuk4rkk429h1obxjqbxt3rdc>.

Swartz, L. (2017) Blockchain dreams: imagining techno-economic alternatives after Bitcoin. In Castells, M. (ed) *Another Economy is Possible: Culture and Economy in a Time of Crisis*. Polity Press.

SWIFT (2016) SWIFT on distributed ledger technologies. *Accenture* <http://www.ameda.org.eg/files/SWIFT_DLTs_position_paper_FINAL1804.pdf>

SWIFT (2017, January 12) SWIFT explores blockchain as part of its global payments innovation initiative. SWIFT <https://www.swift.com/news-events/press-releases/swift-explores-blockchain-as-part-of-its-global-payments-innovation-initiative>.

Swyngedouw, E. (2011) Interrogating post-democratization: reclaiming egalitarian political spaces. *Political Geography* 30 (7): 370–380.

Szabo, N. (1994) Smart contracts. <http://www.fon.hum.uva.nl/rob/Courses/Information-InSpeech/CDROM/Literature/LOTwinterschool2006/szabo.best.vwh.net/smart.con-tracts.html>.

Szabo, N. (2008, December 27) Bit gold. Unenumerated <https://unenumerated.blogspot.co.uk/2005/12/bit-gold.html>.

Taffel, S. (2012) Escaping attention: digital media hardware, materiality and ecological cost. *Culture Machine* 13: 1–28.

Taffel, S. (2015a) We have never been open: activism and cryptography in surveillance societies. *MediaNZ: Media Studies Journal of Aotearoa New Zealand* 14 (2): 52–72.

Taffel, S. (2015b) Archeologies of electronic waste. *Journal of Contemporary Archeology* 2 (1): 78–85.

Taffel, S. (2015c) Perspectives on the postdigital: beyond rhetorics of progress and novelty. *Convergence: The International Journal of Research into New Media Technologies* 22 (3): 324–338.

Taffel, S. (2016) Invisible bodies and forgotten spaces: materiality, toxicity, and labour in digital ecologies. In Randell-Moon, H., and Tippet, R. (eds) *Security, Race, Biopower: Essays on Technology and Corporeality*. Palgrave Macmillan.

Taibbi, M. (2010) The great American bubble machine. *Rolling Stone* <https://www.rollingstone.com/politics/news/the-great-american-bubble-machine-20100405>.

Takhteyev, Y. (2012) *Coding Places: Software Practice in a South American City*. MIT Press.

Takhteyev, Y., and Hills, A. (2010) Investigation the geography of open source software through GitHub. University of Toronto <http://takhteyev.org/papers/Takhteyev-Hilts-2010.pdf>.

Tally, R. (2011) *Geocritical Explorations: Space, Place, and Mapping in Literary and Cultural Studies*. Palgrave Macmillan.

Tapscott, D., and Tapscott, A. (2016) *Blockchain Revolution: How the Technology behind Bitcoin and Cryptocurrency Is Changing the Money, Business and the World*. Portfolio Penguin.

Taylor, E. (2014) Mobile money and the 'social good' of global financialization. MoneyLab Conference, Amsterdam <http://vimeo.com/90208804>.

Taylor, E. (2015) Mobile money: financial globalization, alternative, or both. In Lovink, G., Tkacz, N., and De Vries, P. (2015) *MoneyLab Reader: An Intervention in Digital Economy*. Institute for Network Cultures.

Taylor, M. (2013) Bitcoin and the age of bespoke silicon. International Conference on Compilers, Architecture and Synthesis for Embedded Systems.

Taylor, M. (2014) 'Being useful' after the Ivory Tower: combining research and activism with the Brixton Pound. *Area* 46 (3): 305–312.

Taylor, T. (2002) Living digitally: embodiment in virtual worlds. In Schroeder, R (ed) *The Social Life of Avatars: Presence and Interaction in Shared Virtual Environments*. Springer-Verlag.

Taylor, T. (1983) High-technology industry and the development of science parks. *Built Environment* 9 (1): 72–78.

Tepper, F. (2016, June 7) How a 30K-member Facebook group filled the void left by Uber and Lyft in Austin. *TechCrunch* <https://techcrunch.com/2016/06/07/how-a-30k-member-facebook-group-filled-the-void-left-by-uber-and-lyft-in-austin>.

Terlouw, K. (2001) Regions in geography and the regional geography of semiperipheral development. *Journal of Economic and Social Geography* 92 (1): 76–87.

Terranova, T. (2004) *Network Culture: Politics for the Information Age*. Pluto Press.

Terranova, T. (2006) Of sense and sensibility: immaterial labour in open systems. In Krysa, J. (ed) *Curating Immateriality: The Work of the Curator in the Age of Network Systems*. Autonomedia.

Terranova, T. (2014) Red stack attack! Algorithms, capital and the automation of the common. *Quarderni di San Precario* <http://effimera.org/red-stack-attack-algorithms-capital-and-the-automation-of-the-common-di-tiziana-terranova>.

Tett, G. (2018, February 9) When algorithms reinforce inequality. *Financial Times* <https://www.ft.com/content/fb583548-0b93-11e8-839d-41ca06376bf2>.

Thacker, E. (2004) Foreword: Protocol as protocol does. In Galloway, A. (2004) Protocol: How Control Exists after Decentralization. MIT Press.

thehighfiveghost (2016) Critical update RE: DAO vulnerability. Reddit <https://www.reddit.com/r/ethereum/comments/4oiqj7/critical_update_re_dao_vulnerability/>.

The Law Library of Congress (2018) Regulation of Cryptocurrency in Selected Jurisdictions <https://www.loc.gov/law/help/cryptocurrency/regulation-of-cryptocurrency.pdf>

Thiel, P. (2009, April 13) The education of a libertarian. *Cato Unbound: A Journal of Debate* <https://www.cato-unbound.org/2009/04/13/peter-thiel/education-libertarian>.

Thomas, K. (2010) Could the Wikileaks scandal lead to new virtual currency? *PC World* <https://www.pcworld.com/article/213230/could_wikileaks_scandal_lead_to_new_virtual_currency.html>.

Thornton, H. (1802) *An Enquiry into the Nature and Effects of the Paper Credit of Great Britain*. Hatchard.

Thrift, N. (1994) On the social and cultural determinants of international financial centres: the case of the City of London. In Corbridge, S., Thrift, N., and Martin, R. (eds) *Money, Power and Space*. Blackwell.

Thrift, N. (1996) *Spatial Formations*. Sage.

Thrift, N. (2000a) Performing cultures in the new economy. *Annals, Association of American Geographers* 90: 674–692.

Thrift, N. (2000b) Entanglements of power: shadows? In Sharp, J., Routledge, P., Philo, C., and Paddison, R. (eds) *Entanglements of Power: Geographies of Domination/Resistance*. Routledge.

Thrift, N. (2004) Movement-space: the changing domain of thinking resulting from the development of new kinds of spatial awareness. *Economy & Society* 33 (4): 582–604.

Thrift, N. (2008) *Non-Representational Theory: Space, Politics, Affect*. Routledge.

Thrift, N., and French, S. (2002) The automatic production of space. *Transactions of the British Institute of Geographers* 27 (3): 309–335.

Thung, F., Bissyande, T., Lo, D., and Jiang, L. (2013) Network structure of social coding in GitHub. European Conference on Software Maintenance and Reengineering 323–326.

Tkacz, N. (2015) *Wikipedia and the Politics of Openness*. University of Chicago Press.

Toffler, A. (1981) *The Third Wave*. Morrow.

Torpey, K. (2016, March 4) Four key disagreements between Bitcoin Classic and Bitcoin Core. *Bitcoin Magazine* <https://bitcoinmagazine.com/articles/four-key-disagreements-between-bitcoin-classic-and-bitcoin-core-four-key-disagreements-between-bitcoin-classic-and-bitcoin-core-four-key-disagreements-between-bitcoin-classic-and-bitcoin-core-1457106744>.

Townsend, A. (2001) The Internet and the rise of the new network cities, 1969–1999. *Environment and Planning B: Planning and Design* 28: 39–58.

Tschorsch, F., and Scheuermann, B. (2016) Bitcoin and beyond: a technical survey on decentralized digital currencies. *IEEE Communications & Tutorials* 18 (3): 2084–2123.

Tsing, A. (2004) Inside the economy of appearances. In Amin, A., and Thrift, N. (eds) *Cultural Economy Reader*. Blackwell.

Tsing, A. (2005) *Friction: An Ethnography of Global Connection*. Princeton University Press.

Turner, F. (2006) *From Counterculture to Cyberculture: Stewart Brand, the Whole Earth Network, and the Rise of Digital Utopianism*. University of Chicago Press.

Tuwiner, J. (2017, June 13) Bitcoin mining in China. Buy Bitcoin Worldwide <https://www.buybitcoinworldwide.com/mining/china>.

UASF Working Group (2017, August 1) BIP148 & UASF FAQ. *GitHub* <https://github.com/OPUASF/UASF>.

Underhill, G. (1991) Markets beyond politics? The state and the internationalization of financial markets. *European Journal of Political Research* 19: 197–225.

van Hout, M., and Bingham, T. (2014) Responsible vendors, intelligent consumers: Silk Road, the online revolution in drug trading. *International Journal of Drug Policy* 25 (2): 183–189.

van Houtum, H., Kramsch, O., and Zierhofer, W. (2005) *B/ordering Space*. Ashgate.

van Houtum, H., Van Naerssen, T. (2002) Bordering, ordering and othering. *Journal of Economic and Social Geography* 93 (2): 125–136.

van Valkenburgh, P. (2017) What is 'open source' and why is it important for cryptocurrency and open blockchain projects? Coin Center <https://coincenter.org/entry/what-is-open-source-and-why-is-it-important-for-cryptocurrency-and-open-blockchain-projects>.

van Wirdum, A. (2014, March 18) Why Bitcoin really does represent the democratization of money. *Bitcoin Magazine* <https://bitcoinmagazine.com/articles/bitcoin-really-represent-democratization-money-1395137137>.

van Wirdum, A. (2017a, August 23) The long road to SegWit: how Bitcoin's biggest protocol upgrade became a reality. *Bitcoin Magazine*. <https://bitcoinmagazine.com/articles/long-road-segwit-how-bitcoins-biggest-protocol-upgrade-became-reality>.

van Wirdum, A. (2017b, April 11) Breaking down Bitcoin's "AsicBoost Scandal". *Bitcoin Magazine* <https://bitcoinmagazine.com/articles/breaking-down-bitcoins-asicboost-scandal>.

van Wirdum, A. (2017c, July 27) The future of 'Bitcoin Cash': an interview with Bitcoin ABC lead developer Amaury Séchét. *Bitcoin Magazine* <https://bitcoinmagazine.com/articles/future-bitcoin-cash-interview-bitcoin-abc-lead-developer-amaury-séchet>.

Vannini, P. (2012) *Non-representational Theory and Ethnographic Research*. Routledge.

Velasco, P. (2016) Sketching Bitcoin: empirical research of digital affordances. In Kubitschko, S., and Kaun, A. (eds) *Innovative Methods in Media and Communication Research*. Springer.

Vermeulen, J. (2017, April 22) Bitcoin and Ethereum vs. Visa and Paypal—transactions per second. Mybroadband <https://mybroadband.co.za/news/banking/206742-bitcoin-and-ethereum-vs-visa-and-paypal-transactions-per-second.html>.

Vian, K., and Michalski, J. (2011) *Banking Deconstructed*. Institute for the Future.

Vigna, P. (2015, September 15) BitBeat: Wall Street, City banks join blockchain-focused consortium. *Wall Street Journal* <http://blogs.wsj.com/moneybeat/2015/09/15/bitbeat-wall-street-city-banks-join-blockchain-focused-consortium>.

Vigna, P., and Casey, M. (2015) *The Age of Cryptocurrency: How Bitcoin and Digital Money Are Challenging the Global Economic Order*. St. Martin's Press.

Vincent, D. (2016, May 4) We looked inside a secret Chinese bitcoin mine. *BBC* <http://www.bbc.com/future/story/20160504-we-looked-inside-a-secret-chinese-bitcoin-mine>.

VLAB (2015) Fintech: Silicon Valley takes on Wall Street. YouTube <https://www.youtube.com/watch?v=1XWdaHzKAgk>.

Volpicelli, G. (2017, October 6) This ICO for an AI blockchain is the most tech-hype idea of the year. *Wired* <http://www.wired.co.uk/article/singularitynet-is-an-ico-for-artificial-intelligence>.

von Schnitzler, A. (2008) Citizenship prepaid: water, calculability, and techno-politics in South Africa. *Journal of Southern African Studies* 34 (4): 899–917.

Voorhees, E. (2015, January 22) Is Bitcoin truly decentralized? Yes—and here is why it's important. *Bitcoin Magazine* <https://bitcoinmagazine.com/articles/bitcoin-truly-decentralized-yes-important-1421967133/.

Waldman, S. (2015, April 2) Soylent blockchains. Interfluidity <http://www.interfluidity.com/uploads/2015/04/soylent-blockchains-ethsv.pdf>.

Waldrip-Fruin, N. (2009) *Expressive Processing: Digital Fictions, Computer Games, and Software Studies*. MIT Press.

Walker, H., and Wile, R. (2014, April 1) What did this Swiss software developer have to do with the launch of Bitcoin? *Business Insider* <http://www.businessinsider.com/swiss-software-developer-bitcoin-2014-4?IR=T>.

Walker, R. (1993) *Inside/Outside. International Relations as Political Theory*. Cambridge University Press.

Wall Street Journal (2013) The Silicon Valley vs. Wall Street talent war. YouTube <https://www.youtube.com/watch?v=hVFKxHFmy5s>.

Walters, W. (2006) Rethinking borders beyond the state. *Comparative European Politics* 4 (2): 141–159.

Warschauer, M. (2004) *Technology and Social Inclusion: Rethinking the Digital Divide*. MIT Press.

Waters, R. (2016, May 17) Automated company raises equivalent of $120M in digital currency. *Financial Times* <https://www.ft.com/content/600e137a-1ba6-11e6-b286-cddde55ca122>.

Watson, S. (1995) *The Birth of the Beat Generation: Visionaries, Rebels and Hipsters 1944–1960*. Pantheon Books.

Weatherford, J. (1997) *The History of Money*. Crown Publications.

Weber, W. (2016) A Bitcoin standard: lessons from the gold standard. Bank of Canada <http://www.bankofcanada.ca/wp-content/uploads/2016/03/swp2016-14.pdf>.

Wellman B., Quan-Haase A., Boase J., Chen, W., Hampton, K., Díaz, I., and Miyata, K. (2003) The social affordances of the Internet for networked individualism. *Journal of Computer-Mediated Communication* 8 (3).

Wenger, E. (1998) *Communities of Practice: Learning, Meaning, and Identity*. Cambridge University Press.

Wenger, E., McDermott, R., and Snyder, W. (2002) *Cultivating Communities of Practice: A Guide to Managing Knowledge*. Harvard Business School Press.

Wenger, E., White, N., and Smith, J. (2009) *Digital Habitats: Stewarding Technology for Communities*. CPsquare.

Werbach, K. (2018) *The Blockchain and the New Architecture of Trust*. MIT Press.

Whatmore, S. (2002) *Hybrid Geographies: Natures Cultures Spaces*. Sage.

Wheeler, D., and O'Kelly, M. (1999) Network topology and city accessibility of the commercial Internet. *Professional Geographer* 51 (3): 327–339.

White, I. (2017) Blockchain and the material foundations for socialism. From here to there <https://ianwrightsite.wordpress.com/2017/01/02/blockchain-and-the-material-foundations-for-socialist-institutions>.

Whitley, R. (1999) *Divergent Capitalism: The Social Structuring and Change of Business Systems*. Oxford University Press.

Whittle, A., and Spicer, A. (2008) Is actor network theory critique? *Organization Studies* 29 (4): 611–629.

Wikipedia (2018) Bitcoin. <https://en.wikipedia.org/wiki/Bitcoin>.

Wilhelm, A. (2014, July 16) Popular Bitcoin mining pool promises to restrict its compute power to prevent feared '51%' fiasco. *TechCrunch* <https://techcrunch.com/2014/07/16/popular-bitcoin-mining-pool-promises-to-restrict-its-compute-power-to-prevent-feared-51-fiasco>.

Wilkinson, S., Boshevski, T., Prestwich, J., Hall, G., Gerbes, P., Hutchins, P., Pollard, C., and Buterin, V. (2016) Storj: a peer-to-peer cloud storage network <https://bravenewcoin.com/assets/Whitepapers/storj.pdf>.

Williams, R. (1989) *Resources of Hope*. Verso.

Williams-Grut, O. (2015, September 16) The CBA has joined eight other massive banks to take the technology behind bitcoin mainstream. *Business Insider: Australia* <https://www.businessinsider.com.au/jpmorgan-barclays-and-others-join-r3-on-blockchain-project-2015-9?r=UK&IR=T>.

Wilson, S. (2016, May 6) Blockchain: almost everything you hear is wrong. CIO <http://www.cio.co.nz/article/599399/blockchain-almost-everything-read-wrong>.

Winner, L. (1993) Upon opening the black box and finding it empty: social constructivism and the philosophy of technology. *Science, Technology and Human Values* 18: 362–378.

Winner, L. (1997) Cyberlibertarian myths and the prospects for community. *ACM SIGCAS Computers and Society* 27 (3): 14–19.

Wistrom, B. (2017, August 17) Scrutinized by governments, Austin's Arcade City expands Uber alternative ride-hailing model. *Austin Inno* <https://www.americaninno.com/austin/scrutinized-by-governments-austins-arcade-city-expands-uber-alternative-ride-hailing-model>.

Wolfe, C. (2009) *What Is Posthumanism?* University of Minnesota Press.

Wong, J. (2017a, December 17) Bitcoin's mysterious inventor is now one of the world's 50 richest people. *Quartz* <https://qz.com/1159188/bitcoin-price-approaches-20000-making-satoshi-nakamoto-worth-19-4-billion>.

Wong, J. (2017b, July 28) There's a strange new twist in bitcoin's 'civil war'—and a way to be on the outcome. *Quartz* <https://qz.com/1037971/bitcoin-cash-is-a-new-twist-in-the-hard-fork-debate-and-a-way-to-bet-on-the-outcome-of-the-cryptocurrencys-civil-war>.

Wood, P. (1997) *Maps of World Financial Law*. Allen and Overy.

Woodward, D., Figueiredo, O., and Guimarães, P. (2006) Beyond the Silicon Valley: university R&D and high-technology location. *Journal of Urban Economics* 60: 15–32.

Woolf, N. (2016, June 9) With no Uber or Lyft, a Texas city is crowdsourcing rides on Facebook. *The Guardian* <https://www.theguardian.com/technology/2016/jun/09/uber-lyft-austin-texas-facebook-rideshare-program>.

World Bank (2004) *Decentralization in Madagascar*. World Bank Publications.

World Bank (2009) *Decentralization, Democracy, and Development: Recent Experience from Sierra Leone*. World Bank Publications.

World Bank (2013) What is decentralization? *Earth Institute: Columbia University* <http://www.ciesin.org/decentralization/English/General/Different_forms.html>.

Worner, D., von Bomhard, T., Schreier, Y., and Bilgeri, D. (2016) The Bitcoin ecosystem: disruption beyond financial services? Twenty-Fourth European Conference on Information Systems (ECIS), Istanbul, Turkey.

Wray, L. (2004) *Credit and State Theories of Money: The Contributions of A. Mitchell Innes.* Edward Elgar.

Wriston, W. (1992) *The Twilight of Sovereignty: How the Information Revolution Is Transforming Our World.* Charles Scribner's Sons.

Wylie, J. (2007) *Landscape.* Routledge.

Xingzhe, L. (2017, June 21) Inside the world of Chinese bitcoin 'mining'. *ChinaFile* <http://www.chinafile.com/multimedia/photo-gallery/inside-world-of-chinese-bitcoin-mining>.

Yates, T. (2017, June 7) The consequences of allowing a cryptocurrency takeover, or trying to head one off. *Financial Times* <https://ftalphaville.ft.com/2017/06/07/2189849/guest-post-the-consequences-of-allowing-a-cryptocurrency-takeover-or-trying-to-head-one-off>.

Yermack, D. (2013) Is Bitcoin a real currency? National Bureau of Economic Research.

Young, J. (2015a, August 30) BitPay: 'Silicon Valley is becoming a Bitcoin hub'. *The CoinTelegraph* <https://cointelegraph.com/news/bitpay-silicon-valley-is-becoming-a-bitcoin-hub>.

Young, J. (2015b, August 10) Kraken joins exchanges refusing to apply for a BitLicense, suspends service in New York. *Bitcoin Magazine* <https://bitcoinmagazine.com/articles/kraken-joins-exchanges-refusing-apply-bitlicense-suspends-service-new-york-1439245937>.

Young, J. (2015c, August 9) BitFinex exits New York due to BitLicense. *The CoinTelegraph* <https://cointelegraph.com/news/bitfinex-exits-new-york-due-to-bitlicense>.

Zaloom, C. (2006) *Out of the Pits: Traders and Technology from Chicago to London.* University of Chicago Press.

Zeilinger, M. (2018) Contemporary art between algomysticism and fintech activism. In Gloerich, I., Lovink, G., and de Vries, P. (eds) *MoneyLab Reader 2: Overcoming the Hype.* Institute of Network Cultures.

Zelizer, V. (1989) The social meaning of money: 'special monies'. *American Journal of Sociology* 95 (2): 342–377.

Zelizer, V. (1997) *The Social Meaning of Money: Pin Money, Paychecks, Poor Relief, and Other Currencies.* Princeton University Press.

Zerlan, J. (2014) Bitcoin as the ultimate democratic tool. *WIRED* <https://www.wired.com/insights/2014/04/bitcoin-ultimate-democratic-tool>.

Zhang, J. (2003) *High-Tech Start-Ups and and Industry Dynamics in Silicon Valley.* Public Policy Institute of California.

Zhang, L. (2006) Behind the 'Great Firewall': decoding China's Internet media policies from the inside. *Convergence: The International Journal of Research into New Media Technologies* 12 (3): 271–291.

Zimmermann, P. (1995) *The Official PGP User's Guide.* MIT Press.

Žižek, S. (1999) *The Ticklish Subject: The Absent Centre of Political Ontology.* Verso.

Zook, M. (2002) Grounded capital: venture financing and the geography of the Internet industry, 1994–2000. *Journal of Economic Geography* 2: 151–177.

Zook, M. (2005) *The Geography of the Internet Industry: Venture Capital, Dot-Coms, and Local Knowledge.* Blackwell.

Zook, M. (2006) The geographies of the Internet. *Annual Review of Information Science and Technology* 40 (1): 53–78.

Zook, M. (2012) Code/Space: Software and Everyday Life. *Regional Studies* 46 (8): 1105–1106.

Zook, M., Dodge, M., Aoyama, Y., and Townsend, A. (2004) New digital geographies: information, communication, and place. In Brunn, D., Cutter, S., and Harrington, J. (eds) *Geography and Technology.* Kluwer Academic Publishers.

Index